IN THE PRESENCE OF POWER

In the Presence of Power

Court and Performance in the Pre-Modern Middle East

Edited by
Maurice A. Pomerantz *and* Evelyn Birge Vitz

NEW YORK UNIVERSITY PRESS
New York

NEW YORK UNIVERSITY PRESS

New York

www.nyupress.org

Library of Congress Cataloging-in-Publication Data
Names: Pomerantz, Maurice A. editor. | Vitz, Evelyn Birge editor.
Title: In the presence of power : court and performance in the pre-modern Middle East / edited by Maurice A. Pomerantz and Evelyn Birge Vitz.
Description: New York : New York University Press, 2017. |
Includes bibliographical references and index.
Identifiers: LCCN 2017010735 | ISBN 9781479879366 (cl : alk. paper) |
ISBN 9781479883004 (pb : alk. paper)
Subjects: LCSH: Islamic Empire—Courts and courtiers. | Performing arts—Islamic Empire. |
Rites and ceremonies—Islamic Empire. | Oral tradition—Islamic Empire.
Classification: LCC DS36.855 I45 2017 | DDC 306.4/8409560902—dc23
LC record available at https://lccn.loc.gov/2017010735

New York University Press books are printed on acid-free paper, and their binding materials are chosen for strength and durability. We strive to use environmentally responsible suppliers and materials to the greatest extent possible in publishing our books.

Manufactured in the United States of America

10 9 8 7 6 5 4 3 2 1

Also available as an ebook

We dedicate this book to our wonderful families.

CONTENTS

ACKNOWLEDGMENTS

This publication is supported by a grant from the NYU Abu Dhabi Institute, a major hub of intellectual and creative activity and advanced research. The institute hosts academic conferences, workshops, cultural events, and other public programs and is a center of scholarly life in Abu Dhabi, bringing together faculty and researchers from institutions of higher education throughout the region and the world.

We wish to thank the outside readers of this volume for their valuable suggestions; our editor, Chip Rossetti; Managing Editor Dorothea Stillman Halliday; the Center for the Humanities at New York University; Pierke Bosschieter for compiling the index; and special thanks to Tara Zend for her help with all aspects of this manuscript.

Introduction

EVELYN BIRGE VITZ AND MAURICE A. POMERANTZ

The 102nd night of *The Arabian Nights* begins a tale (which goes on for a great many pages) featuring a hunchback who is the favorite minstrel of the king of China. A tailor and his wife, out for a stroll, meet this cheerful and elegantly dressed hunchback. They take him home, where he performs on his tambourine, sings, and tells them funny stories with many gestures. But during dinner, the hunchback chokes on a fish bone, which the tailor had pushed down his throat as a joke, and he suffocates. The rest of this tale and numerous subsequent ones focus on attempts to dispose of the body of the hunchback—no one wants to be found with a dead body in his home! The tailor deposits the body on the staircase of a Jewish physician, who then dumps it at the door of a Christian broker, and so on. Eventually the hunchback's lifeless body is discovered—and when the king of China hears that his favorite clown is dead, he threatens to hang the guilty party. (We are indeed in the presence of power.) A barber notices that the unconscious hunchback is in fact alive, bursts out laughing, and pulls out the offending fish bone with tweezers. The hunchback wakes up, stands up, and sneezes. All ends well. The king commands that the story be written down and gives robes and honors to everyone involved. He keeps the barber with him (along with the hunchback), and they enjoy "each other's company until they [are] overtaken by death, the destroyer of all delights."[1]

In the story of this hunchback, we see a talented entertainer who tells stories, sings, and plays a musical instrument: he has many performance skills. Richly rewarded by his master, he is elegantly and colorfully dressed—with fancy scarf, Egyptian-style inner and outer robes, a tall green hat with knots of yellow silk filled with ambergris—all clearly the gifts of the king of China. That king—like some other rulers we will see—is to a substantial degree a fantasy figure, not a "real" monarch. His kingdom is peopled by a wide range of characters of varying religions—Jews, Christians, Muslims, and others—and of various stations of life: tailors, physicians, brokers, barbers, and so on. (Similarly, this volume will show us a multiplicity of figures of varied origins and status, drawn, in different ways, to the presence of power.) This king, like some others we will meet, is both a positive and a negative figure, characterized both by the brutality of his power (whoever is responsible for the death of the hunchback must die, even if the death occurred by accident) and also by his generosity to people with luck. Life in the presence of the king is both full of risks—the danger of dishonor or death—and rich in opportunities for increased wealth and status for those who are fortunate enough to succeed in pleasing him. The king is a patron both of clowns and of written literature: it is at his command that this story is recorded for posterity.

We hope this volume can give us an echo of some of the delights—snatched in part from oblivion—that are spoken of in the last sentence of the tale. We hope as well that it can provide a sense of the many types of performance and performativity found in spectacles and literature associated with courts in the pre-modern Middle East.

Courts in the Pre-Modern Middle East

The "Hunchback's Tale" is first attested in the famed Galland manuscript, the oldest known collection of the *Arabian Nights*. Representing the first 282 nights, the manuscript has been dated by scholars to mid-fourteenth- or early-fifteenth-century Syria. For the first audiences of this tale, China would have been a region at the far eastern edge of the world. This marvelous land beyond the seas served as the proper setting for this wondrous tale.

Rulers and performing hunchbacks, too, would not have been unfamiliar to audiences in fourteenth-century Syria. The Mamlūk sultans who reigned over Egypt and Syria from 1250 to 1517 CE supported lively court culture in their main cities of Cairo and Damascus. Storytelling of the kind found in the *Arabian Nights* seems to have been a much-sought-after form of entertainment. Popular performers of Cairo, such as the hunchback, would have likely also been a common sight both within the rulers' courts and sometimes roaming the streets.

This volume's title suggests that we will be examining courts in the pre-modern Middle East. Like much modern terminology applied to distant times and remote locations, these three complex terms warrant further explanation.

The pre-modern period in this volume extends roughly seven centuries. The period opens with the first dynasty of Islam, the Umayyads, whose reign marked an important watershed for Late Antique culture in the eighth century, and closes with the rule of the so-called gunpowder empires of the Ottomans and Safavids over much of the Near East in the sixteenth century. Although treating such a long span has some inherent liabilities, the editors of the volume believe that the potential for seeing commonalities across time outweighs the drive for a comprehensive coverage of performance practices.

We have likewise chosen to treat the geographical and cultural limits implied in the term "Middle East" with a similar degree of latitude. Our selections in this regard were informed by the desire not only to show commonalities within the Islamicate literary cultures of Persian, Turkish, and Arabic (which are regrettably all too often still siloed within modern nationalist narratives) but also to demonstrate the important cross-pollinations that occurred between Islamicate, Byzantine, and Carolingian courts. And rather than viewing distinct physical boundaries to the Middle East (an activity that is surely still problematic in the postcolonial twenty-first century), we aimed to consider imaginary voyages and travels to the region as important for our volume as "real" events. After all, is not the imagination of performance as important as its memory?

The ruler's court, although it might seem to be the most immediately tangible of the terms in our title, is perhaps the most elusive. Our use of the term "court" in this volume most directly derives from scholars of the medieval West. The modern English term "court" derives from the medieval Latin term *cohors, cohortis*, meaning "enclosure." It eventually came to denote the ruler's country residence.[2] As Malcolm Vale writes in his study *The Princely Court: Medieval Courts and Culture in North-West Europe, 1270–1380*,

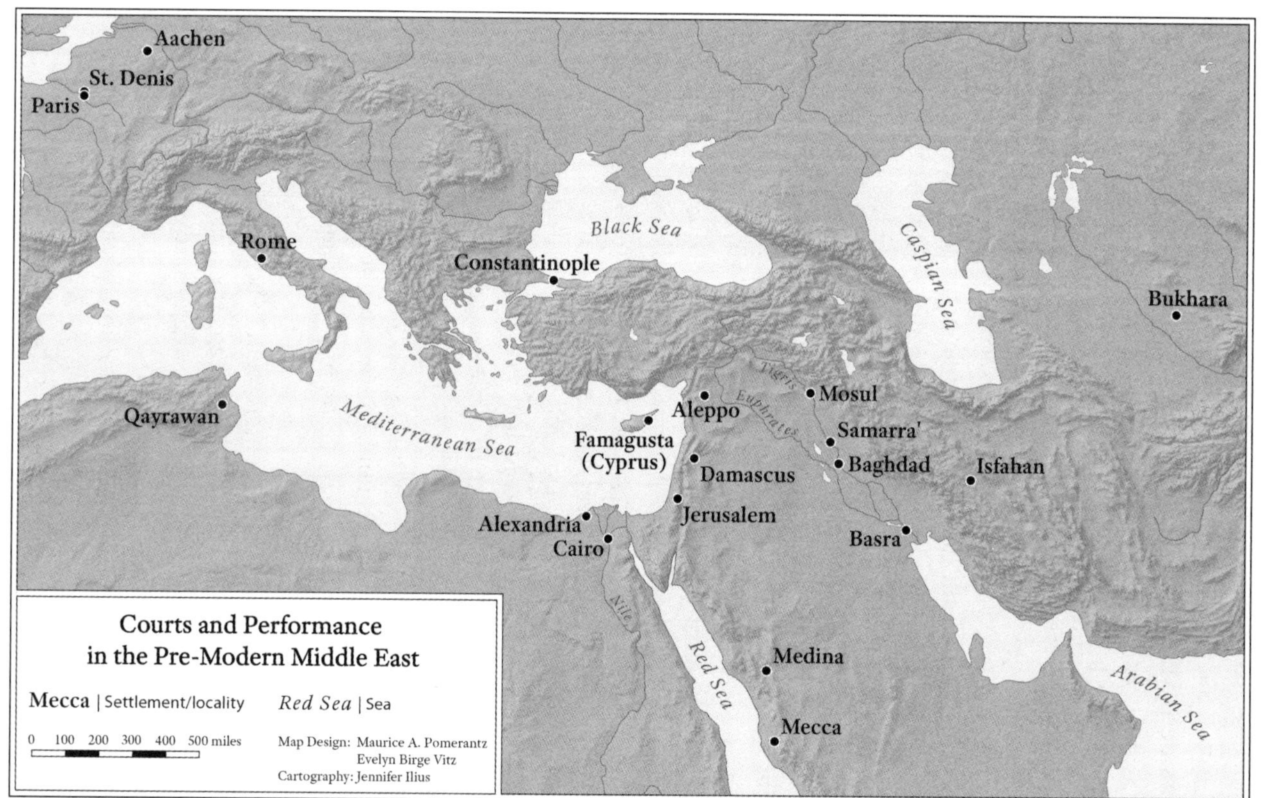

Courts and cities in the pre-modern Middle East and Europe (Credit: Jennifer Ilius)

> What was "the court" in the later Middle Ages? What did contemporaries mean by the term? Satisfactory answers to these questions are notoriously difficult to arrive at, partly because the term could carry different meanings according to the context in which it was used. There is, however, a broad measure of agreement that a ruler's household (domus, hospitium, hôtel) played a fundamental part in giving substance to the idea of "the court." The material infrastructure, or underpinning, of all princely courts—in both the medieval and modern periods—was provided by the household. Court and household were never entirely synonymous, yet courts could not have existed without household organizations behind and within them.[3]

In this formulation, the court is an institution—a place that is related to the ruler's home but more expansive. From it came a multitude of terms such as "courtier," "courteousness," and "courtliness" that all have particular meanings today. This definition should prompt us to consider that the court, as an interpretative category, demands further precision.

Among Byzantinists, the court has also been a central term in their studies of ritual and performance, political and material culture, literature, and theology.[4] Yet as Alexander P. Kazhdan and Michael McCormick note, there is no single term that "exactly corresponds" to the modern term "court." They state that the Greek *to palation*, "palace," best "circumscribes the specific reality of the court."[5] Indeed, as Paul Magdalino suggests for Byzantines, the notions of court culture that are so important in Western studies were unnecessary to articulate, and thus they did not have as well developed a terminology of words surrounding the institution of the court.[6]

For courts of Muslim rulers, the situation mirrors that found in Byzantine sources. Nadia Maria El Cheikh, a contributor to this volume, has carefully considered the terminology associated with courts and courtiers for tenth-century Abbasid Baghdad. El Cheikh's conclusion is that the multiplicity of terms suggests something about the court's complex social reality. El Cheikh states, "Navigating between *Ḥashiya/Ḥawāshī*, *Ḥasham*, *Khaṣṣa/khawāṣṣ*, to mean, in a variety of contexts, attendant, court attendant, courtier, servants, the terminology does not translate adequately into any clear definition of court and courtier. The ambiguity of our sources is, of course, telling: The court was not an institution in any formal sense but rather a gathering of people, often fluid in composition and constantly changing."[7] As El Cheikh contends, it is the very terminological instability that evinces the multiplicity of meanings. Hers is a salutary reminder that close examination of the local particularities and specifics of courtly life are the necessary foundation for any comparative study.

This volume aims at locating similarities across the Western medieval, Byzantine, and Islamicate courtly cultures. Such a study does not presume the presence of one shared courtly institution across time and space but rather seeks to understand the different ways in which contemporaries experienced and spoke about these places of power.

We turn now to the relationship between court and performance: some recent studies (several referred to earlier) have provided valuable new knowledge of and approaches to court and court life that have relevance to our volume. For example, *Court Cultures in the Muslim World, Seventh to Nineteenth Centuries*, edited by Albrecht Fuess and Jan-Peter Hartung,[8] takes up many important matters relating to Muslim courts. Among relevant issues discussed are social elites at the Fatimid court, outdoor and indoor royal representations at the Mamluk court in Egypt, and patronage in various courts. While this book refers briefly to dancers and to singers, speaks sporadically of music, discusses at various points the role of poets, and refers to cooking at several points in passing, at no point does any contributor focus attention on performance as such. In *A Global History of Power, 1300–1800*,[9] Jeroen Duindam also takes up a wide diversity of courts, as well as numerous aspects of court life and organization. Perhaps especially interesting from our perspective are his discussions of inner versus outer courts, court culture and society, hospitality, pageantry, and patronage. But Duindam does not at any point explicitly discuss performance or performers. Yet other recent studies present valuable information about courts and power—but with only a minor (if any) focus on performance. For example, *The Byzantine Court: Source of Power and Culture: Papers from the Second International Sevgi Gönül Byzantine Studies Symposium, Istanbul 21–23 June 2010*, edited by Ayda Ödekan, Nevra Necipoğlu, and Engin Akyürek,[10] takes up such issues as court architecture and court ceremonies but does not explicitly address performance. We hope that our volume will fill gaps relating to performance in this recent scholarship.

Performance

What is performance?[11] Our basic definition comes from the ethnographer and folklorist Richard Bauman: performance is a "special, artful mode of communication"; of particular importance is "the accountability to an audience for a display of communicative competence, which is subject to evaluation for the skill and effectiveness with which the act of expression has been accomplished."[12] Another useful definition of performance is Erving Goffman's: "all the activity of an individual which occurs during a period marked by his continuous presence before a particular set of observers and which has some influence on the observers."[13]

As to what kinds of performances to include, this volume adopts a latitudinarian approach, casting its nets widely to look at all manner of pre-modern Middle Eastern communicative and performative displays and practices. We naturally invited in such clear performance phenomena as exuberant expressions of love in Arabic stories, shadow plays in Mamluk Cairo, and Byzantine storytelling. Many types of performance in the region and period consist largely of the verbal arts; therefore, along with storytelling, we explore oratory, conversation, and advice: courtiers throughout the region—in Persia, the Umayyad and Abbasid courts, and beyond—attempt to win the favor of the ruler and to shine before other courtiers.

We also include, within the ambit of performance, a variety of less clearly articulated court-related phenomena: political and ethnographic performances. For instance, there is that of kingship itself: courts are centrally concerned with the performance of the power of the ruler, in relation to members of the court and to other rulers and courts. Public punishments and executions, such as those in Byzantium, are performances: rulers are represented as forcefully displaying their power (and sometimes their mercy) over their defeated adversaries. Similarly, the official exchange of prisoners generally has a performance component.[14] Moving to another end of the spectrum—to a more purely cultural, even a "micro" level—we delve into the little-known (and highly entertaining) culinary performance of strongly symbolic red and white foods in medieval Christian Cyprus.

In many genres and works, performance is unquestionably present, whereas in others, it is necessary to look for performance indicators.

But wherever we see—or sense—the presence of communicative public display and audience, performance abounds.

The range of performances and of court settings included here opens the door to a variety of theoretical frameworks. Richard Schechner is one of the foremost scholars and theoreticians of performance working today. In his classic volume *Performance Studies: An Introduction*, Schechner, often drawing on the work of other performance theorists, makes a number of important and useful distinctions regarding performance. We focus here on three major points. First is the distinction between "is" and "as" performance:

> What is the difference between "is" performance and "as" performance? Certain events are performances and other events less so. There are limits to what "is" performance. But just about anything can be studied "as" performance. Something "is" a performance when historical and social context, convention, usage, and tradition say it is. Rituals, play and games, and the roles of everyday life are performances because convention, context, usage and tradition say so. One cannot determine what "is" a performance without referring to specific cultural circumstances. . . . From the vantage of the kind of performance theory I am propounding, every action is a performance. But from the vantage of cultural practice, some actions will be deemed performances and other not; and this will vary from culture to culture, historical period to historical period.[15]

Some of the performances discussed in this volume clearly belong to the "is" category, while others belong to the "as" category.

Schechner also discusses what he sees as seven functions of performance: to entertain; to make something that is beautiful; to mark or change identity; to make or foster community; to heal; to teach, persuade, or convince; to deal with the sacred and/or the demonic. This is a conceptual framework of particular use to us: we have, for example, a number of performances and works whose purpose is clearly to entertain; the purpose of others is to persuade (see, for example, the "advice to princes" literature in the next section); yet others (e.g., Orfali's) are centrally concerned with the sacred.

Finally, the concept of "performativity" is of substantial relevance to this volume. Performativity is a complex (and somewhat controversial) topic, but we will focus here on just one aspect of the concept: the basic idea that words can be performative in the sense that they can make things happen; they *change* things. This concept comes in large part from the work of J. L. Austin, in particular, *How to Do Things with Words*. Austin provides the classic example: "I take this woman to be my lawful wedded wife."[16] Performances can be performative—can change things. This will be clear in various chapters in this volume, for example, that of Vitz.

The Contents and Shape of This Volume

Power Performed

Kingship and court life involve performance in fundamental—and sometimes surprising—ways, as rulers demonstrate their power toward the courtiers and their inferiors. Sometimes these demonstrations of power are grounded in the realities of court life, while in other cases they may have a strong fantasy component, as Evelyn Birge Vitz demonstrates in chapter 1. She shows how, in the twelfth-century French epic *The Voyage of Charlemagne to Jerusalem and Constantinople*, courts of the Middle East—Jerusalem and Constantinople—were fantasized and even joked about; the geography itself is largely imaginary. This work also reflects (occasionally tongue-in-cheek) a warrior and Crusader mentality: what matters for a monarch and a court is not wealth or learning or high culture. Rather, this epic focuses, to a remarkable degree, on people and things—kings, knights, women, palaces, God, and relics—as *performing* their power, which is indeed *performative*.

In chapter 2, Stavroula Constantinou focuses on the theatrical character of the imperial punishments imposed on male iconophile saints, as seen in Byzantine hagiographical works of the middle Byzantine period. The descriptions of the performance of these punishments are lurid and violent—though the accounts may reflect a literary tradition more than a historical reality.

Spectacles, games, and processions were another important feature of court performance. In these ritual displays, participants and observers could witness and experience the power of the state. In chapter 3, Babak Rahimi points to the ways that Safavid rulers in the sixteenth and seventeenth centuries created public "gaming" spectacles in their public square, called the "Image of the World" (*Maydān-i Naqsh-i Jahān*).

Rahimi argues that this urban space was used as a ritual site wherein the king, his court, aristocrats, diplomats, travelers, and the population of the city of Isfahan could engage in communal play. Rahimi argues that this square in both joyful celebrations and solemn moments (such as the commemorations of *al-Muḥarram*) served as a vital performative space for the Safavid state.

Persuasion

A well-known Arabic expression tells us that "for every situation, there is something appropriate to say" (*li-kull maqām maqāl*). This something is often good advice to the ruler. Courtiers attempted to persuade their patrons about a great many things, including the virtue of generosity (often to courtiers) and friendship (its importance and perils), the importance of justice and mercy, and their behavior (especially at night).

Advice was a pervasive presence in the courtly and larger political and ethical cultures of the early centuries of the Islamic era. Focusing on Iran in the tenth century, Louise Marlow in chapter 4 discusses the Arabic "Advice to Kings" (*Naṣīḥat al-mulūk*) attributed to al-Māwardī. She shows how rulers not only solicited and received advice (the education of princes being a prominent function of mirrors for princes) but also dispensed and performed it themselves. Marlow argues that what made advice compelling was its grounding in established authorities, including the sacred sources, the examples of venerated figures of the early Islamic era, and the conduct and sayings of caliphs, kings, and sages of the past. The roles of the monarch as wise dispenser or humble recipient of advice exposed him to potential challenges, and advisory literature prescribes the spatial and temporal boundaries within which caliphs and kings received advice but also attests to their transgression.

Conversation is often thought of as a spontaneous and playful art. But consulting manuals on how to serve kings (*khidmat al-mulūk*), Nadia Maria El Cheikh explores in chapter 5 how Abbasid courtiers during the ninth to eleventh centuries regulated their speech and gestures in order to impress and to be persuasive. Her chapter demonstrates how courtiers conformed to prescriptive codes of literary cultivation known as *adab* and reveals how courtiers sometimes managed to subvert or elude them.

Eloquent rhymed oratory has long held a great value among speakers of the Arabic language for its ability to persuade. Famously, upon listening to two orators speak, the Prophet Muhammad reportedly said, "Indeed there is magic in clear expression," pointing to the power of rhymed and rhythmic prose. Despite the esteem in which the oratorical tradition in Arabic has been held, its history has been difficult to study because of a lack of reliable source material from the first century of Islam. Jaakko Hämeen-Anttila in chapter 6 discusses the survival of the oral performances of one famous orator's preaching (*khuṭbas*) and asks what the literary preservation of his preaching might have to do with its performance.

Entertainment

It was essential for rulers and members of their courts to be entertained. Entertainment has of course taken an immense variety of forms and has also existed in many venues. In chapter 7, Margaret Mullett argues that, outside of Constantinople, court literature was dominated by storytelling and that most of this form of entertainment took place in tents: "tent poems" survive; some major tales also seem to be associated with tents; and letters also apparently were received and performed in tents. There are clear connections between the emperor and these stories.

In chapter 8, Maurice A. Pomerantz focuses on the literary collection *al-Hafawāt al-Nādira* (The rare slips), composed by the fifth-/eleventh-century Baghdadī scholar Ghars al-Niʿma b. Hilāl al-Ṣābiʾ. Pomerantz shows how these verbal errors—slips of the tongue—became part of the entertainment record of the Abbasid court. He argues that Ṣābiʾ's attention to the verbal errors at court can be productively compared to Freud's famed inquiries into the question of *lapsus linguae* in his *Psychopathology of Everyday Life*.

In chapter 9, Li Guo focuses on episodes from "The Phantom," by Ibn Dāniyāl (d. 1310), showing how they contain a substantial amount of cross-gender acting. Guo also argues that such gender-bending is to a certain degree a literary device for characterization. It was also an element of the art of a one-man-band type of performer, who was able not only to play both sexes but also to sing and dance—and was thus a highly versatile entertainer.

Delight

Courtiers often describe the court as a location that stood outside ordinary experience. At the ruler's court, men and women wore elaborate costumes, sang enchanting melodies, told compelling and elaborate tales, gave and admired ornate gifts, and ate sumptuous foods. Court spectacles, banquets, songs, and tales could inspire delight and wonder and even foster intense emotions.

Feasting and drinking were of course modes of entertainment and delight at court, but they also could have other functions. A fascinating example of "as performance" is chapter 10, by William Woys Weaver. He explores a system of dietetics, possibly particular to Cyprus, in which foods are divided into two classes, red or white, according to whether they contain blood. Blood foods were carnal, while white foods were vegan and thus appropriate for religious fasting. This system then synchronized red and white foods according to their Galenic humors and thus led to a decorative play on colors in Cypriot court cuisine, whereby fasting dishes were colored to resemble meat and meat dishes were made to look white—in short, visual puzzles and puns intended to amuse. The Frankish nobility thus transformed cuisine into entertainment: religious fasting without suffering and inconvenience. Weaver's chapter also explores the possible ideas underlying this dietary system, in early Christian, Jewish, and Near Eastern religious ideas. This chapter reminds us just how true it is, as Barbara Kirschenblatt-Gimblett has famously pointed out, that "food is performance."[17]

Singers and musicians at the Abbasid court created a long-lasting tradition of sung poetic texts for the delight of rulers. Compendia such as Abū l-Faraj al-Iṣfahānī's *Book of Songs* (*Kitāb al-Aghānī*) catalogue the most famous song texts and singers of the Abbasid court. In chapter 11, Bilal Orfali demonstrates how Sufi mystics adopted the poetic themes of Abbasid poetry and refashioned them for a part of Sufi ritual known as "beatific audition" (*samāʿ*), in which believers were supposed to find rapture through the recollection (*dhikr*) of God. Orfali's chapter shows how Sufis adapted themes of court poetry, such as standing at the ruins of the beloved's campsite, recalling the journey of a poet through the desert, and love poetry (*ghazal*), demonstrating the ways that court performance profoundly influenced modes of religious experience.

In chapter 12, Jocelyn Sharlet focuses on a set of Arabic stories from the Umayyad period (661–750) that were further elaborated in the literature of the Abbasid period (750–1258). These tales about chaste lovers typically feature a pastoral setting, a male point of view, a melancholy mood, and lovers who live, suffer, and die for love—providing delight for the court audiences for whom they were performed. Not all stories about chaste love, however, fit the dominant paradigm, and unusual cases can shed light on ways in which the Umayyads were viewed in the Abbasid imagination, point to intersections between love story and political life, and show how stories of chaste love live on in courtly and Sufi discourse.

The culture of performance throughout the pre-modern Middle East is a vast and in some ways still-uncharted territory. We hope that these studies, which combine rigorous textual scholarship and new approaches, will serve as signposts for further explorations. In the epilogue to this volume, we pull out some of the many important threads of the various chapters, drawing out major points, and with a comparative focus.

NOTES

1. Haddawy, *Arabian Nights*, 249–356.
2. Kazhdan and McCormick, "Social World," 175.
3. Vale, *Princely Court*, 12.
4. See Maguire, *Byzantine Court Culture*; Beihammer, Constantinou, and Parani, *Court Ceremonies and Rituals of Power*; Ödekan, Necipoğlu, and Akyürek, *Byzantine Court.*
5. Kazhdan and McCormick, "Social World," 173.
6. See Magdalino, "In Search of the Byzantine Courtier," 141.
7. El Cheikh, "Court of al-Muqtadir," 336.
8. Fuess and Hartung, *Court Cultures.*
9. Duindam, *Global History of Power.*
10. Ödekan, Necipoğlu, and Akyürek, *Byzantine Court.*
11. The contributors to this volume draw on a wide variety of definitions and approaches to performance. We refer readers to the discussions of performance in Öztürkmen and Vitz, *Medieval and Early Modern Performance in the Eastern Mediterranean*, which can serve as a companion volume to this one.

12. Bauman, "American Folklore Studies," 177.
13. Goffman, "Social Life as Drama," 97.
14. See Durak, "Performance and Ideology."
15. Schechner, *Performance Studies*, 30.
16. Austin, *How to Do Things with Words*, 5.
17. Kirschenblatt-Gimblett, "Playing to the Senses," 1–2, quoted in Schechner, *Performance Studies*, 33.

PART I

Power Performed

1

Performance and Competition of Kingship and Court in *Le Voyage de Charlemagne à Jerusalem et à Constantinople*

Real and Imaginary Encounters between the Medieval West and the Middle East

EVELYN BIRGE VITZ

This chapter focuses on the ways in which both kingship and court were understood as performed—indeed as performative—in a very curious and entertaining medieval work. This is an epic recounting of a journey/pilgrimage that Charlemagne was said to have made to Jerusalem and Constantinople. The epic also shows how the Middle East, and in particular its courts and kingship, were understood—known, fantasized, envied, and sometimes joked about—in the West: this is in some respects quite a funny work.

This epic is, in important ways, about the competition between two rulers and their courts—or, more precisely, about Charlemagne's desire to outshine the Byzantine ruler and his court. My focus is on the following issues: What makes a king great—one superior to others? How does he show, perform, and create his greatness? And how is a court understood in this work—that is, as constituted by whom or what? What matters most in demonstrating superiority: the greatness of the ruler himself—and as measured how? the wealth and culture of the court? the impressiveness and manliness of its knights? their relationship to God? When kings complete, how do they produce their power performatively? Can they achieve a harmonious resolution—and, if so, how?

This epic, composed sometime during the twelfth century, survived in a single manuscript, which is now lost; it had however been transcribed.[1] It is a short epic song, to which the title *Le Voyage de Charlemagne à Jerusalem et à Constantinople* is probably most accurately ascribed.[2] Since this work is not widely known outside of French medievalist circles, it will be useful to walk through the plot rather closely: many details will turn out to be important. Then we will draw out the basic underlying issues—the types and levels of competition—and show how and why Charlemagne manages to come out ahead in this epic.[3]

The Story

One day at Saint Denis (Charlemagne is French in this work), King Charles puts the crown on his head and crosses himself. He asks his wife if she has ever seen a man under heaven who wears his crown and sword as well as he. Foolishly, she replies that, yes, she does in fact know of a man who has greater presence than Charles when he wears his crown among his knights:

> Cele ne fud pas sage, folement respondeit:
> "Emperere," dist ele, "trop vus poez preiser.
> Uncore en sa jo un ki plus se fait leger,
> Quant il porte corune entre ses chevalers.
> Kaunt il la met sur sa teste, plus belement lui set." (ll. 12–16, p. 30)[4]
> (The queen lacked sense and made a foolish reply. "Emperor," she said, "you think too highly of yourself. I know someone even more dashing than you when he wears his crown in the company of his knights. When he puts it on his head, it suits him better than yours. [p. 31])

Charles, enraged, threatens to behead her if she does not tell him who and where this king is. He declares that the two kings will wear their crowns side by side, and the French will judge who wears his crown better. If the queen has lied, he will cut off her head. The queen is (not surprisingly) sorry that she spoke and throws herself at the king's feet, saying that she was just joking and did not want to disgrace him; she offers to undergo an ordeal to prove the innocence of her intentions. But she is compelled to say that she has heard much about the handsome and noble King Hugo the Strong who rules Greece, Constantinople, and Persia: this is then a competing royal/imperial court.[5] The king doubts that his queen's head will long remain on her shoulders: she should not have had so poor a view of his "vertu"—his power. He will not rest until he has seen this other king.

Charlemagne decides to make a trip to Jerusalem, after which he will go look for this other king of whom he has heard. He takes with him on his pilgrimage *cum* trip all his great men; this is, then, essentially a traveling court.

> Rolland e Oliver en ad ot sei amenez,
> E Willeme de Orenge e Naimon l'adurez,
> Oger de Denemarche, Gerin et Berenger,
> Le arceveske Turpin e Ernalz e Haimer,
> E Bernard de Brusban e Bertram l'adurez,
> E tel .m. chevalier ki sunt de France nez. (ll. 61–66, p. 32)
> ([He took] with him Roland and Oliver, William of Orange and doughty Naimes, Ogier of Denmark, Gerin and Berenger, Archbishop Turpin, Ernaut, Aimer, Bernard of Brusban and the doughty Bertrand, and a thousand knights from France. [p. 33])

The men leave as pilgrims, carrying pilgrim scrip but no swords, lances, or shields; they ride mules. Charles does, however, take many chests filled with treasure: these are, then, wealthy but unarmed pilgrims. After crossing numerous lands, they arrive in Jerusalem, that "ancient city." They go into the beautifully painted marble church, where God himself celebrated Mass, and the apostles did as well. There are twelve seats, with a thirteenth in the center, on which Charles sits down, with his twelve peers in the others. No one had done that before, and no one has since. Charles looks so proud and his head is held so high that a Jew who comes in the door trembles, thinking that this is God himself.[6]

> Karles out fer le vis, si out le chef levez.
> Uns Judeus i entrat ki ben l'out esgardét.
> Cum il vit Karleun, cumençat a trembler:
> Tant out fer le visage, ne l'osat esgarder:
> A poi que il ne chet, fuant s'en est turnét,
> Et si muntet d'elais tuz les marbrins degrez,
> Vint al patriarche, prist l'en a parler:
> "Alez, sire, al muster, pur les funz aprester.

Orendreit me frai baptizer e lever.
Duze cuntes vi ore en cel muster entrer:
Ovoec eulzs le trezime, unc ne vi si formét.
Par le men escientre, ço est meimes Deus:
Il e li duze apostle vus venent visiter." (ll. 128–40, p. 36)

(Charles's countenance was fierce and he held his head high. A Jew entered and stared at him. When he saw Charles he began to tremble: so fierce was Charles's countenance that he dared not look upon him and almost fell to the ground. He turned and fled, rushing up the marble steps and coming to the patriarch with the words: "Come to the church, Lord, to prepare the fonts. I wish to be baptized forthwith, for I have just seen twelve counts enter the church and with them a thirteenth. I have never seen anyone so striking in appearance and, if I am not mistaken, it is God himself. He and the twelve apostles have come to visit you." [p. 37])

The patriarch summons his priests and clerks, and fully vested, they come to the church in a grand procession. Charles takes off his hat and bows to the patriarch—clearly, as God's representative on earth. Charles tells him of the twelve kings he has conquered, saying that he is going soon to look for a thirteenth king of whom he has heard. He has come to Jerusalem to adore the Cross and the Sepulcher. The patriarch declares that since Charles has sat in the seat where God himself sat, from now on he should bear the name Charlemagne and be considered the greatest of kings:

Et dist li patriarches: "Sire, mult estes beer!
Sis as en la chaere u sist mames Deus:
Aies nun Charles Maines sur tuz reis curunez." (ll. 156–58, p. 36)

("My Lord," replied the patriarch, "you are a man of great worth and have sat in the chair in which God himself sat. May your name be Charlemagne, crowned above all kings." [p. 37])

Charles asks for holy relics to take back to France, and the patriarch offers him many splendid, valuable relics. In Charlemagne's hands, the relics start working immediately; many people are healed, to great rejoicing. Charles and his men remain for four months in Jerusalem, living well (the patriarch is very wealthy). He then asks for permission to leave; the patriarch accepts and insists that they take his vast treasure, provided that they undertake to destroy the Saracens, who hate holy Christendom—"sainte Cristïentez" (l. 225). Charlemagne promises he will go to Spain to do this. (Roland and the Twelve Peers will later die in Spain.) The French ride off, accompanied for part of the way by the patriarch; on separating, he and Charlemagne embrace each other.

On the way to Constantinople, many miracles occur through the relics in French hands: through God's "granz vertuz" (great power), the blind see, the lame walk, the dumb speak; when the Frenchmen come to rivers, the waters part to make fords for their crossing.

The French can finally see Constantinople, with its bell towers, eagle-topped roofs, and shining domes; there are flowers everywhere. They see twenty thousand knights sitting there, lavishly dressed; many beautiful and elegantly dressed maidens are there too; lovers are embracing. This is a beautiful, wealthy, and sophisticated court.

> Vint mile chevalers i troverent seant,
> E sunt vestut de pailes e de heremins blans
> Et de granz peus de martre jokes a pez trainanz.
> As echés e as tables se vunt esbaneant,
> E portent lur falcuns et lur osturs asquanz;
> E treis mile puceles a orfreis relusant,
> Vestues sunt de pailes e ount les cors avenanz,
> E tenent lur amis, si se vunt deportant. (ll. 267–74, p. 42)
> (They found twenty thousand knights seated there, dressed in silk and white ermine with great marten skins reaching down to their feet, playing games of chess and backgammon. Some had with them their falcons and their hawks. Three thousand comely maidens were there, clad in shimmering silks and clinging to their lovers in great delight. [p. 43])

The French look for King Hugo, whom they find working the earth himself, with a plow made of gold and a silken canopy over him. King Hugo sees Charles's proud face and powerful body. They exchange introductions and greetings, Hugo saying that he had heard that no king on earth has as much power as Charles. He invites Charles to stay for a year, offering him great treasures. As they prepare to go to the palace, Hugo leaves his golden plow behind. The French express concern that it will be stolen, but Hugo replies that there are no thieves in Byzantium; it is in no danger (Guillaume d'Orange says if he and his fellow peer Bertrand had it in France, they would destroy it with stakes and hammers). The French are welcomed into the palace, filled with men and women dressed in furs and silks from Persia. The palace itself is highly impressive—elaborately constructed, with tables and chairs of fine gold, hung with silk, and with walls beautifully painted. Moreover, the entire palace rotates when the wind blows, and statues of children playing horns resound loudly as it turns. Charles admires and envies this rich palace and now considers his own possessions "worth less than a glove"; he remembers how he had threatened his wife! The palace begins to turn so fast that Charles and all the Frenchmen have to sit on the floor, apparently from dizziness; they cover their heads. Hugo reassures them that when the wind falls, the turning will cease. The French sit down to an ample and luxurious dinner with Hugo, his wife, and his beautiful daughter, with whom Oliver falls in love: he mutters to himself that he would like to have his will—"tutes mes voluntez" (l. 407)—with her.

The French are led to an elegant vaulted and painted bedroom, with huge heavy beds—the thirteenth of which, for Charles, has a coverlet made by a famous fairy. The room is lit by a shining carbuncle, through which a spy starts to listen in on the conversations of the French. As the Frenchmen talk, drinking wine and claret, they get quite drunk and begin to boast.[7] Some of the boasts clearly articulate the envy and resentment, even some hostility, that the French feel toward their wealthy and powerful host. Charles and each of the Twelve Peers call out their boasts. Each boast is punctuated at the end by the frequently horrified reaction of the spy: he cannot wait to report all he has heard to Hugo, who will be outraged and insulted. Charlemagne boasts first—that, if Hugo lends him a sword, he will cleave the helmet, the hauberk, and the saddle of the horse of any knight of Hugo's, and moreover, if he lets the sword go, it will strike the ground so hard that it cannot be pulled out. Oliver boasts that if he can get the princess into bed, he will make love to her a hundred times in a single night. Guillaume d'Orange boasts that he will roll the gigantic ball in the corner of the room so hard that it will knock down forty lengths of the palace wall. Bernard will make the river leave its bed, rise, and flood the palace. And so on. Not all are as outrageous or hostile as these; some are merely amazing feats of strength or agility that the men claim they can perform.

The spy reports all he has heard to Hugo, who is indeed furious and saddened by the news. In the morning, he confronts Charlemagne and threatens to cut off the Frenchmen's heads if they cannot carry out their boasts. Charlemagne explains that before Frenchmen go to bed at night, they joke and "gabent," engaging in talk that is sometimes wise, sometimes foolish. The French go off to talk among themselves; Charles admits that they had all drunk too much wine and had said things they should not have said, but it is clear that they will now have to deliver on their boasts. He has the relics brought, before which they pray and beat their breasts in guilt. They beg God for help, and an angel comes down who tells them that their boasts were indeed "grande folie" (l. 675), but this one time, God will help them: none of their boasts will fail; they will indeed be able to perform them. But they must never do this sort of boasting again!

Meeting again with Hugo, Charles complains that having a spy listen in on their conversation was a great "outrage," but he asserts that the French will indeed perform all their boasts. Charlemagne is not asked to perform his gab. Rather, Hugo chooses to begin with Oliver, who, with the princess's permission, does make love to her—though only (!) thirty, not a hundred, times. But because she is now his "drue"—and they have exchanged vows of loyalty—the princess tells her father that it was indeed a hundred times. The powerful Guillaume d'Orange succeeds in knocking down a large part of the palace walls. Bernard makes the river rise and flood the palace. Hugo now tells the Frenchmen to stop all this destruction, and he says he will give Charles his treasure and become his "homme," holding his kingdom from him henceforth. Charles prays to make the water recede: God performs this miracle, and the water returns to its bed. Hugo wants no more boasts fulfilled—he would suffer too much damage if the Frenchmen were allowed to continue making good their boasts.

The two kings make peace and hold a celebration. They wear their crowns side by side, and it is obvious that King Hugo wears his lower—fifteen inches, to be exact—than Charlemagne.[8] The French all agree that the queen spoke "folie" and "tord": she was in the wrong in what she said. There is a great feast—food, minstrels, and other delights. Hugo offers Charles his treasure, but Charles refuses, saying that the French already have so much that they cannot carry it all. The two kings embrace, commending each other to God. The French depart. Charles is happy: he has conquered another great king, and without a single battle. The French ride back home to Paris; at Saint Denis, they prostrate themselves and pray to God, putting some of the great relics on the altar (others are distributed throughout the kingdom). The queen falls at the king's feet and is forgiven; his "mautalent" ("ill will") is ended, for the sake of the Holy Sepulcher, where he has worshiped.

* * *

Such is the basic plotline, with the key details that concern us. Let us now look more closely at the fundamental issues: how is competition between kings and courts constructed and performed, and why is Charlemagne the victor in the rivalry? I have a twofold focus: one on kings, the other on their court and the persons who compose it. My basic argument here is that, while Charlemagne shows himself to be the greatest king—and, specifically, greater (and literally taller) than his Byzantine rival—without the manliness of his great warriors (the Twelve Peers) and the support of God and his representative on earth, the patriarch, Charlemagne would have failed to perform his superiority. (Moreover, he and his men might all have died.) A harmonious ending is made possible by King Hugo's recognition of Charlemagne's superiority and his feudal submission to the French emperor.

Kings and Their Greatness: The Majesty of the King

Charlemagne's greatness—and that of Hugo—are in flux through much of the epic, rising and falling over the course of various episodes, which we should examine.

The wearing of the crown—we begin and end with the issue: who wears his crown better, and what does "better" mean? At the start, it is not clear exactly what the queen is referring to when she says that King Hugo may wear his crown "better." But at the end, when the two kings ride side by side, it is clear that Charlemagne is literally bigger—taller—than Hugo. It is hard to know whether this is a joke—a pun on the meanings of Charles's being "magne" (this is a very playful epic). But it is true that, by this time, Charles's greatness has already been established—settled, at least for the French, if not for the Byzantines. He is the victor.

Charles's greatness—which is put into doubt at the start of the epic, thanks to his uppity wife—clearly receives major upward thrust in Jerusalem (this, in advance of his actual competition with Hugo). This occurs in four related scenes when the French get to Jerusalem. First, in the Church of the Holy Sepulcher, Charles is able to sit down in the seat, or throne, of Christ (never had anyone done so since the time of Christ). Second, because he is so impressive and majestic looking, the Jew thinks he is God, does not even dare to look at him, and asks to be baptized. Third, the patriarch is very impressed with him and grants him the name of Charles the Great: Charlemagne. And fourth, the patriarch gives him powerful relics, which immediately begin to work miracles—they have performative power, showing the greatness and power both of God and of Charles. Charlemagne promises to fight the pagans in Spain. Charlemagne is, then, shown to be a majestic, impressive, and (perhaps incomparably) great Christian ruler.

Charlemagne's reputation for greatness takes serious hits, however, when he gets to Constantinople. King Hugo is very rich indeed. (The scene where he is plowing is ambiguous: is Hugo to be seen as a very rich "peasant"?—damaging, surely, to his status—or does this scene show that Hugo is putting in a useful day's work? Or perhaps a bit of both?) Moreover, in Hugo's realm, people are honest (no one would steal that golden plow if it were left in the field). His wealthy and powerful stature becomes clearer still when the French arrive at his court. Hugo's palace is not only beautiful and rich—making Charlemagne envious and think regretfully of his threats to his wife—but the palace spins so that it makes Charles and the French fall literally to their knees. The French have to be reassured by Hugo that everything will soon be okay. This is all clearly a set of humiliating scenes for Charles.

Moreover, after Hugo hears about their insulting and threatening gabs, the French are in danger of being killed by Hugo: they are in his power. Hugo is, at this point in the epic, thus superior to Charlemagne on various dimensions: he is rich and sophisticated, he has impressive "technology"—automata—and he is the man in power in this court. The French are his guests but also his prisoners: he can have them executed if he so chooses.

Charles's greatness now takes yet further hits—but it also begins to rise. First, he has to explain (and more or less apologize) to Hugo for his and his men's gabs. Then the French must confess their sin to God—beat their breasts—and ask for his help. But their confession, though humbling them before God, also has the effect of raising them up: God promises to help the French carry out all their ridiculous boasts. He will help them perform these boasts—and Charlemagne's greatness.

By the time the various Peers have performed their gabs—Oliver having repeated intercourse with the princess, whose love he has won, and the others either showing their incredible power and agility or practically tearing down Hugo's palace—Charlemagne's greatness is established: Hugo does not want to compete further: he recognizes the greater power of the French ruler; he submits and becomes Charlemagne's vassal. And we go to the scene of the wearing of the crowns.

But before that final scene, let us turn briefly to the members of the two courts.

At Charlemagne's court at Saint Denis, there is no emphasis whatever on Charles's palace: we do not see one at all. All emphasis falls on his men—and they are indeed heavily accentuated. The Twelve Peers—fully listed—accompany the king on his pilgrimage/journey, as pilgrims but also as warriors-in-waiting, so to speak. These men are big names in the French epic, for example, in the great *Chanson de Roland*; they are names well-known to all audiences. It is worth noting that the audience for this epic may well have been the numerous and varied French people who attended an important twelfth-century fair, known as Lendit, held at Saint Denis.[9]

When the traveling party arrives in Jerusalem, while Charles sits in the seat of Christ, his Twelve Peers sit down on the seats of the Twelve Apostles. These very actions show that they are impressive men. These knights do not wear beautiful clothing, and there is no emphasis on their charm or sophistication. Indeed all that is accentuated about them is their virile aggressiveness, in particular, their readiness to make violent jokes—to *gaber*. And all these jokes and threats are about either making remarkably repeated love to a beautiful young woman or attacking Hugo or damaging his palace. (One could well see them as expressions of envy and powerlessness; talk is cheap.) Not a single one of the gabs directly involves competition with the men at Hugo's court—the French display virtually no interest in their fellow knights. (It is to be noted, however, that the French have not brought their weapons or warhorses, as they are traveling as pilgrims; Charles would have to borrow a sword from Hugo to carry out his boast.) Their aggressive energy is focused on Hugo's person, his palace, and his daughter.

It is Charlemagne's men and the help of God that in fact enable him to subjugate Hugo: when the French are required to make good on their extreme boasts, they are able to do so, and they do it in a destructive fashion that (as we have seen) strikes terror into Hugo's heart; he calls quits to the fulfillment of the gabs, and he submits to Charlemagne. Now some of the Peers do perfectly well on their own; they can do what they said they could do: Oliver (more or less), Guillaume d'Orange, and others. But some of the boasts do require the help of God—that is, miracles. Thus, it is Charles's men, plus God, who bring the competition to a satisfactory close.

Let us draw out the contrasts between Charles's court and that of Hugo. As we have seen, the Byzantine ruler's court is beautiful and wealthy: he has many well-dressed men and women sitting around; there are lovers everywhere.

King Hugo's palace is grand, with beautiful architecture, a rotating tower, great food, and other impressive features. It all makes Charlemagne envious. But one thing that is striking is that these beautifully dressed men apparently do nothing—they just look good. Thus, implicitly, there is a competition between the snazzy Byzantines and the French, who may not be elegant charmers but who can deliver, both in bed and on the field—they can perform!

Another important difference between the two courts (and their rulers) in this epic is that while, theoretically of course, the Byzantines are also Christians, it is the religious identity and commitment of the French that enable them to carry the day. God loves them, and he helps them—and they will help him, and indeed die for him, later in Spain.

* * *

Despite some genuine but clearly spotty knowledge of the Middle East, this epic represents for the most part a fantasy about the relationship between France and the French monarchy, on the one hand, and the Holy Land and Byzantium, on the other. It can be understood as an imaginary victory over the Byzantine court by the French, thanks to Charlemagne's almost-divine greatness—and his literal size—to the greatness of his barons and to God's love for the French.

But in closing, let me return to the performance: this work focuses, to perhaps a remarkable degree, on people as performing or things being performed.[10] There are minstrels who perform in court (I have barely mentioned them, though they are present). But of course this goes much further: How does a king perform his kingship—both "act" it and create it performatively? By how he wears his crown and also by plowing a field. What do relics do? They work powerful miracles. What does an impressive palace do? It rotates and makes Frenchmen fall down. What do French knights do? They boast and then do amazing feats of strength (their Byzantine counterparts just lounge around with ladies). What does God do? Forgive, give advice (through an angel), and then work miracles: make Charles shine. None of this is, then, about a king's or court's greatness in any ontological, or even strictly material, sense; nor is it about any sort of static identity. Impressive people and things *perform*.[11]

Thus, in this epic, a monarch's greatness arises not from the wealth and sophistication (however great) of the material culture that characterize his court but rather from how well he wears his crown, from how his men perform their deeds of manliness, and from how dramatically God demonstrates his support for this king and his court.

This work reflects, though occasionally tongue-in-cheek, a warrior and Crusader mentality: what matters, for a monarch and a court, is not wealth or learning or high culture. What counts is what strong men (and God and a woman or two) do: how they perform.

In closing, let us reflect briefly on one of the functions of ritual performance: to "enhance group cohesion."[12] James C. McKinley, Jr., writing about the psychological and physiological importance of "rooting" for a team, discusses a study that shows that "testosterone levels in male fans rise markedly after a victory and drop just as sharply after a defeat."[13] The performance of *Charlemagne's* victorious *Voyage*—however cheerfully and even humorously it may have been told—is likely to have given a boost to the testosterone of French audiences, nine hundred years ago.

NOTES

1. The manuscript in question was Royal 16 E VIII of the British Library, dating apparently from the thirteenth century; its disappearance was noted on June 7, 1879. See, e.g., Burgess, *Pilgrimage of Charlemagne.*
2. Medieval French works rarely bear titles and have typically been given titles by their modern editors. This work is often called the "pilgrimage" of Charlemagne, but as we will see, this title is problematic: is this a pilgrimage or rather a trip?
3. This epic, however, is very well-known and appreciated among French medievalists. Numerous controversies surround it, most of which need not concern us. The edition I am using is that of Burgess and Cobby (*Pilgrimage of Charlemagne*). This edition also contains a useful introduction and extensive bibliography. Another useful modern edition with translation (and in my view a more sensible title) is Picherit, *Journey of Charlemagne to Jerusalem and Constantinople*; it, too, has a useful bibliography.
4. As noted, quotations and translations are taken from Burgess and Cobby, *Pilgrimage of Charlemagne*; hereafter cited in the text.
5. The terms "king" and "emperor" are not reliably distinguished here, but it is surely not trivial that Charles is commonly referred to as "emperor," Hugo as "king." The latter is called "Hugun," but I refer to him by the Anglicized "Hugo."
6. Among the various controversies concerning this often-entertaining epic is the question: is this Jew's reaction on seeing Charlemagne intended to be comic or not?
7. These aggressive boasts, called "gabs," are a standard feature in French—and many other—epics.
8. On the importance of physical size in medieval narrative, see, e.g., Vitz, "Type et individu dans l'autobiographie médiévale."
9. See Picherit, *Journey of Charlemagne to Jerusalem and Constantinople*, 73n1.
10. Numerous articles in Öztürkmen and Vitz, *Medieval and Early Modern Performance*, address the importance of performance in medieval and early-modern courts in the Mediterranean and Middle East. Nor was it just entertainers of all kinds who showed their wares or displays such as fireworks that demonstrated the ruler's wealth and status; the exchange of prisoners (for example) also consisted of a highly performative set of gestures.
11. Malcolm Vale, in his valuable *The Princely Court*, focuses on a very different region and period. His emphasis is on material culture in all its richness, but he places little or no emphasis on performance issues.
12. Schechner, *Performance Studies*, 54–57.
13. McKinley, "It Isn't Just a Game." Other recent studies confirm the power of victory in sports to boost the testosterone level of spectators. See, for example, Bernhardt et al., "Testosterone Changes"; and Nicholson, "Science Shows Dominant Behavior and Posture Increase Testosterone." One must assume that the effect is even greater for the vicarious spectators of war and other kinds of serious conflicts.

2

Bloodthirsty Emperors

Performances of Imperial Punishment in Byzantine Hagiography

STAVROULA CONSTANTINOU

In a ninth-century anonymous Byzantine hagiographical text about Michael the Synkellos, an iconophile saint who was born in Jerusalem in 761 and died in Constantinople in 846, we read the following:

> Καὶ κελεύει ἐκδυθῆναι τοὺς ἁγίους τὰς αὐτῶν ἐσθῆτας καὶ γυμνοὺς στῆναι ἔμπροσθεν αὐτοῦ. Ὡς δὲ ἐξεδύθησαν οἱ ἅγιοι τοῦ Χριστοῦ μάρτυρες, ἐκέλευσεν ὁ βασιλεὺς ἄνδρας δυνατοὺς τῇ ἰσχύϊ ἱμᾶσι λεπτοῖς δήσαντες αὐτῶν τὰς χεῖρας τεῖναι ἐπὶ πολὺ ἀνὰ ἓξ ἑκάστῳ αὐτῶν, ὅπως μὴ ἰσχύωσι τυπτόμενοι κλονεῖσθαι ὧδε κἀκεῖσε. Ταθέντων δὲ τῶν ἁγίων σφοδρῶς, ἐκέλευσεν ἕνα ἔμπροσθεν καὶ ἕνα ὄπισθεν σταθέντας βουνεύροις τύπτειν αὐτοὺς ἀφειδῶς. Ἐπὶ τοσοῦτον δὲ αὐτοὺς ἔτυψαν, ὥστε ἀλλαγῆναι ἑνὶ ἑκάστῳ αὐτῶν ἀνὰ τεσσάρων στρατιωτῶν. Τυπτομένων δὲ τῶν ἁγίων τά τε νῶτα αὐτῶν καὶ στήθη, οὐδὲν ἄλλο παρ' αὐτῶν ἠκούετο ἢ τὸ "Κύριε ἐλέησον" καὶ τὸ "Ἁγία Θεοτόκε, ἐλθὲ εἰς βοήθειαν ἡμῶν." Ὁ δὲ βασιλεὺς ταῦτα ἀκούσας εὐχομένων τῶν ἁγίων, θυμομαχῶν καὶ ἀπαύστως βοῶν καὶ καθ' ἑαυτὸν ἐνορκῶν, τοὺς τύπτοντας ἐπέτρεπεν οὑτωσὶ λέγων "Ὡς ἔχεις ἐμέ, δὸς καλά."
>
> Ὡς δὲ κατέτεμον τοὺς ἁγίους ἐπὶ πολὺ, ὥστε μὴ ἰσχύειν ἀνταποκρίνεσθαι, καὶ τοῦ αἵματος αὐτῶν οἱονεὶ ποταμίου ῥεύματος τὸ ἔδαφος ἅπαν καταχρώσαντος, συρῆναι ἐκέλευσε τούτους καὶ οὕτως ἀπαχθῆναι ἐν τῇ φυλακῇ. Ἐξελθόντων δὲ τῶν ἁγίων, μόλις ἴσχυον βαδίζειν ἐκ τῶν ἀφορήτων πληγῶν.[1]

> He then [emperor Theophilos] commanded that the saints be stripped of their clothing and made to stand naked before him. When the holy martyrs of Christ had been stripped, the emperor ordered very strong men

> to bind their hands with fine thongs and then to stretch six thongs tightly over each of them, so that it would not be possible for them to sway back and forth as they were beaten. When the saints had been firmly stretched out, he commanded one man to stand in front and another behind each of them and he commanded them to strike the saints mercilessly with ox-hide whips. They struck them with so many blows that it was necessary to alternate four soldiers for each one of them. As the saints were being struck both on their backs and on their chests, nothing was heard from them except, "Lord, have mercy," and "Holy Mother of God, come to our aid!" When the emperor heard the saints praying thus he was angry and shouting ceaselessly and swearing to himself, he urged on those striking them, saying, "As you love me, thrash them well!"
>
> When they had lacerated the saints to the extent that they were powerless to offer a reply and their blood like the stream of a river had stained the whole floor, he commanded that they be dragged and thus taken back to prison. As the saints departed they were scarcely able to walk after the unendurable blows. (*Life of Michael the Synkellos*, p. 91)

This is a very disturbing and an extremely spectacular scene that provokes horror, outrage, nausea, and disgust. Yet it exercises a fascination on the text's reader or listener, who is invited through the dramatic infliction of corporal punishment to contemplate the splendor and explosive glory of torture that in this case acquires a pornographic dimension.[2] This is a kind of pornography of murderous pleasures enjoyed by the hagiographer and his audiences,[3] as well as by the torturers and the spectators situated within the text: the emperor, the people at his court, and the senators whom he invites to the Golden Triclinium (the imperial reception and dining room), to attend this horrific, yet fascinating, spectacle of punishment.

The scene in question, placed in the very middle of the narrative, stages bodily punishments that the Byzantine emperor Theophilos (813–42) imposes on the holy protagonist's most important disciples, the saintly brothers Theodore and Theophanes Graptoi, for their iconophile stance.[4] Such dramatic scenes of violent punishments taking place in an iconoclast emperor's court or in the city center lie at the heart of a number of hagiographical narratives that commemorate the Byzantine martyrs who undergo horrendous tortures for venerating icons representing saints, Christ, and the Virgin.[5] The iconoclast emperors, who are five in number—Leo III (717–41), his son Constantine V (741–75), Leo V (813–20), Michael II (820–29), and finally Michael's son Theophilos (829–42)—are represented in these narratives as bloodthirsty and monstrous punishers of innumerable iconophile clerics, ascetics, and monks.

The performance of imperial punishments on male iconophile saints is this chapter's theme.[6] Following Michel Foucault's argument in his seminal book *Discipline and Punish* that punishment is an art that rests on a technology of representation, I treat the tortures of iconophile holy men as spectacles carefully designed to have an impact on their audiences, both fictional and actual. In fact, Foucault's punishment theory is extremely useful here since the hagiographers in question and their heroes treat torture and punishment as spectacles. As Theophanes of Caesaria, another hagiographer of the ninth century, writes in his encomium of the aforementioned Theodore and Theophanes, their tortures constitute a "wonderful" and "radiant" theater ("τὸ θαυμάσιον ἐκεῖνο πάλιν θέατρον," "οὕτω λαμπροῦ διατεθέντος ἐκείνου τοῦ θεάτρου"; *Encomium of Theodore Graptos*, § 26, § 37).[7] Theophanes even goes so far as to openly acknowledge that his graphic descriptions of the two brothers' bodily punishments function as a device that is an essential element of his aesthetics. At one point, he turns to his audience to say the following words:

> Τί οὖν; μέχρι τούτου ἡμῖν ἡ Θεοδώρου ἀρετὴ καὶ τὰ κατορθώματα; οὐ μὲν οὖν. ἔχω γάρ τι τούτου σεμνότερον εἰπεῖν, ὃ μᾶλλον κἀμοῦ κοσμήσει τὸν λόγον καὶ τοὺς ἀκροατὰς εὐφρανεῖ. (*Encomium of Theodore Graptos*, § 23)

> And now what? Are Theodore's virtue and exploits exhausted here? Of course not. I have something to say that is more pious than this, which will beautify my account even further, and will please the listeners.[8]

The aim of this chapter is twofold. First is to show how in iconophile hagiography of the middle Byzantine period the iconoclast emperors' courts function as stages on which theaters of violence and atrocity are enacted. In so doing, I would like to point out the strong theatrical character of the texts in question, which in turn proves their literariness.

This very fact leads to the chapter's second goal, which is to demonstrate through a literary analysis that iconophile hagiography should not be used as a mine of historical information. Treating these texts as historical documents, some contemporary historians have concluded that the iconoclastic controversy led to acts of extreme violence.[9] The lurid spectacles of violence that are depicted in iconophile hagiography, as the following analysis demonstrates, reflect a literary tradition rather than a historical reality. This tradition goes back to the Hellenistic novel and the Apocryphal Acts of the Apostles and is continued with the martyr legends, the medieval violence literature par excellence that our iconophile hagiographers use as models for their own works.

The punishment scene from the *Life of Michael the Synkellos* quoted at the beginning of this chapter is one of a series of punishments of increasing harshness that the two brothers undergo at the directives of all the emperors (Leo V, Michael II, and Theophilos) of the second phase of the iconoclastic controversy (813–42). In fact, this is the third time that Theodore and Theophanes are brought to the emperor's Golden dining hall. The first time they are forced to enter the imperial palace is when emperor Leo V summons them with Michael, their spiritual father, and another iconophile named Job (*Life of Michael the Synkellos*, § 10). During this first audience and before the presence of all the members of the senate and a number of the emperor's entourage, the holy men's iconophile standpoint is revealed. This very fact provokes Leo's extremely strong and violent reaction (*Life of Michael the Synkellos*, §§ 10–12), which does not differ from those of the pagan emperors and prefects in martyr legends.[10]

Our hagiographer, following his predecessors, describes Leo's behavior in a theatrical way. The emperor is likened to a wild beast, an enraged lion that is about to attack and destroy its victims. He immediately orders that the holy men be beaten harshly, and while the beating takes place, he issues many accusations against the iconophiles (*Life of Michael the Synkellos*, 12.1–7). Here, the text's reader or listener is invited to focus on Leo's spectacular overreaction. His great and absurd anger is fueled even further when the three men resist and courageously express their lack of fear before his threats. They tell the emperor's servant, "beat, banish, slaughter, carry out whatever you wish and desire" (τύπτε, ἐξόριζε, σφάττε, ποίει ὅ τι ἂν θέλῃς καὶ βούλῃ; *Life of Michael the Synkellos*, 13.13–14, p. 70).

The holy men's words recall those said by the protagonists of earlier literature when they are threatened with torture. Leucippe, for example, the female protagonist of the Hellenistic novel *Leucippe and Clitophon* (second century AD), a text that was widely read and appreciated in Byzantium,[11] says to Thersandros, the man who threatens to use torture to enforce his will on her,

> τὰς βασάνους παράστησον, φερέτω τροχόν ἰδοὺ χεῖρες, τεινέτω. φερέτω καὶ μάστιγας ἰδοὺ νῶτον, τυπτέτω. κομιζέτω πῦρ ἰδοὺ σῶμα, καιέτω, φερέτω καὶ σίδηρον ἰδοὺ δέρη, σφαζέτω. (*Leucippe and Clitophon*, book 6.21)[12]

> Prepare the tortures! Someone bring in the wheel and stretch my hands: here they are! Someone bring in the whips, too, and beat my back: here it is! Someone bring in fire and burn my body: here it is! Someone bring in a blade and slice up my skin: here it is![13]

In a similar vein, the legendary martyr Irene, for example, says to one of her torturers, the emperor Sedekias, who advises her to sacrifice to the Roman gods and in so doing to avoid further torments, "I am not afraid of you emperor; I disregard your threats. Prepare your tortures; they will not affect me" (Οὐ δέδοικά σε, βασιλεῦ, οὐ φροντίζω τῆς ἀπειλῆς σου. ἑτοίμαζε βασάνους τὰς οὐκ ἐνεργούσας μοι; *Passion of Irene*, ll. 472–75).[14] Thus, Michael's and his disciples' reaction to their torturers' threats is not a historical fact but a literary rewriting of the behavior of earlier fictional personas with which Byzantine listening and reading audiences were familiar.

Theodore and Theophanes are taken to the imperial dining room for a second time when Theophilos, the last iconoclast emperor, ascends the throne and commands his servants to bring before him the two brothers, whom his predecessor has exiled. The two men's first audience with Theophilos is much more ceremonial and spectacular than the one with Leo V. In this case, the hagiographer does not fail to present in vivid detail how their entrance to the palace is prepared, how everybody expects their appearance and punishment, how they enter the Golden Triclinium, how they are brought before the emperor, how he reacts upon seeing them, how their punishment is enacted, how they endure their bodily sufferings, and how one of the spectators reacts to a statement made by the punishing emperor:

> Τῆς δὲ ἀφίξεως αὐτῶν ἐν ταῖς διανοίαις πάντων προεγνωσμένης ἤδη καὶ προσδοκωμένης, ὡς τῷ βασιλεῖ παραστησομένους καὶ δίκας ὑφέξοντας, οὐδὲν ἦν ἄλλο ἰδεῖν καὶ ἀκοῦσαι ἀλλ' ἢ φόβους καὶ ἀπειλάς, ἃς οἱ ὑπηρέται τοῦ παμπόνηρου βασιλέως προσῆγον αὐτοῖς. . . . Εἰσελθόντες δὲ καὶ τῆς πύλης ἐπιβάντες, προαγόντος αὐτῶν τοῦ ἐπάρχου, ὤφθη αὐτοῖς ὁ βασιλεὺς πολλοῦ θυμοῦ καὶ ὀργῆς πνέων, ἱκανῶν αὐτῷ τῶν τῆς συγκλήτου βουλῆς τῶν ἀρχόντων παρισταμένων. . . . Εἰσῆλθον δὲ οἱ ἅγιοι μετὰ πολλοῦ τοῦ θάρσους μηδὲν δειλιῶντες . . . ὥστε ἐκ τῆς ὄψεως αὐτῶν ἔκθαμβον γενέσθαι τὸν βασιλέα.
>
> . . . Ῥαπιζομένων δὲ τῶν ἁγίων ἀνηλεῶς ἐπὶ πολλὴν ὥραν καὶ μὴ δυναμένων αὐτῶν ἵστασθαι ἐκ τῶν ἀφορήτων πληγῶν (ἐσκοτίζοντο γὰρ τῇ φορᾷ τῶν μαστίγων, ὥστε πίπτειν αὐτοὺς καὶ ἀνίστασθαι . . .) ἐκράτησεν ἕκαστος αὐτῶν τοῦ στήθους τοῦ παίοντος αὐτόν. . . .
>
> . . . Παυσαμένων δὲ τῶν παιόντων, λέγει πρὸς αὐτοὺς ὁ βασιλεύς "Τίνος χάριν ἐληλύθατε ἐνταῦθα, ἀνόσιοι"; . . . Τῶν δὲ ἁγίων σιωπησάντων καὶ μηδ' ὅλως αὐτῷ ἀποκριναμένων καὶ εἰς γῆν νενευκότων, ἔφη πρὸς τὸν ὕπαρχον ὁ βασιλεύς "Ἆρον τοὺς ἀνοσίους τούτους καὶ γράψον τὰ πρόσωπα αὐτῶν, ἐγκολάψας τούσδε τοὺς ἰάμβους. . . ." Ἵστατο δὲ πλησίον τοῦ βασιλέως ὁ ἔχων τοὺς ἰάμβους . . . , ᾧ καὶ ἐπαναγινώσκειν εἰς ἐπήκοον πάντων προσέταξεν, προσθεὶς καὶ τοῦτο "Κἂν οὔκ εἰσι καλοί κατὰ σύνταξιν, μή σοι μελέτω." . . . Καί τις παρὼν χαριζόμενος τῷ βασιλεῖ ἔφη "Οὐδὲ εἴσιν ἄξιοι, ὦ δέσποτα, οὗτοι, ἵνα κάλλιον ὦσιν οἱ ἴαμβοι." (*Life of Michael the Synkellos*, 18.5–17, 19.18–30)

When their arrival was known in advance and expected in the minds of all and it was understood that they were to be brought before the emperor and to undergo punishment, all that was to be seen or heard were the terrors and threats to which the servants of the wholly depraved emperor subjected them. . . . With the prefect preceding them they entered and crossed the threshold and beheld the emperor breathing forth

> great anger and fury, while a fair number of officials of the senate were in attendance. . . . But the saints entered courageously, fearing nothing. . . . The emperor was struck with amazement at their appearance.
>
> . . . After the saints had been harshly beaten for a long time and were unable to stand on account of the unendurable blows (for they were made dizzy by the force of the whips so that they fell and were made to stand again . . .), each of the saints held on to the chest of the man who was beating him. . . .
>
> . . . When the men beating them had stopped, the emperor said to them, "For what reason have you come here, impious ones?" . . . But when the saints remained silent, returned no answer and bent their heads towards the ground, the emperor said to his prefect, "Raise up these impious men and inscribe their foreheads, incising these iambics." . . . Near the emperor there stood a man . . . with the iambics which he had composed. The emperor commanded him to read them aloud in everyone's hearing and he added, "Even if they are badly composed, never mind." . . . One of those present, wishing to please the emperor, said, "But they are not worthy, O lord, of better iambics." (*Life of Michael the Synkellos*, 83, 85)

After the spectator's provocative comment that the two tortured brothers are not "worthy of better iambics," Theophilos orders his servants to take them to the imperial prisons for the inscribing of their faces. While they are on their way to the prisons, Theophilos changes his mind and asks for the holy men to be fetched back to the dining hall. As he emphatically points out, he wants them to be further mocked and to be more cruelly tortured before having their faces inscribed. What follows is the scene quoted at the opening of this chapter.

As has been obvious so far, all these punishment and torture scenes, as well as those included in other iconophile hagiographical narratives of the same period, are great spectacles demanding the closest attention. Most of all, however, are the protagonists' tortured bodies and their unbearable pain, which function as powerful means that compel fascination. In the case of Theodore and Theophanes, the audiences' gazes are fixed on the two young men's striking and noble appearance and on how their naked bodies react under the most brutal tortures: when they fall and are made to stand by holding to the chest of their tormentors, their firm stretching out, their agony, their cries, their resistance, their silence, and their ejaculation of blood. They are caught in a painful convulsion. The signs of their distress are etched in their short prayers, the excess of their blood that stains the floor of the imperial dining room, and their subsequent silence. Of course, the behavior of the two brothers' bodies functions as a powerful sign of their strong resistance and their extremely difficult fight for their religious beliefs, which the text's audiences are invited to espouse.

Theophilos's attraction to the violation of young male flesh is marked not only through the way in which he treats the two brothers but also by the fact that he avoids torturing Michael the Synkellos. As pointed out at some point in the narrative, Theophilos spares Michael the tortures because he is "old, worn down by many afflictions and illnesses, overpowered by dim-sightedness and stooping" (ὡς ἅτε γηραι[ὸν] καὶ ἐκ τῶν πολλῶν θλίψεών τε καὶ ἀσθενειῶν τετρυχώμεν[ος] καὶ ἀμβλυωπίᾳ καὶ κυφότητι κεκρατημέν[ος]; *Life of Michael the Synkellos*, 18.27–29, p. 79). Obviously, the real reason behind the two brothers' tortures is not their iconophile stand. If this were the case, the emperor would not have failed to make an example of their teacher, Michael, who is a powerful iconophile leader and constitutes a serious threat to his imperial authority.

The paradigmatic and spectacular punishment of the young disciple(s) while the religious teacher is spared can be found also in martyr legends. A case in point is the popular *Life and Passion of Febronia* (sixth or seventh century), in which the soldiers of the Roman emperor Diocletian (284–305), an infamous persecutor of Christians, enter the nunnery of Bryene in Nisibis (Mesopotamia), and instead of arresting the three Christian women they find there, as would have been expected, they seize one nun only. The two women left behind, the abbess Bryene and her assistant Thomaïs, are old women. The arrested nun, on the other hand, who is Febronia herself, is a young woman (twenty years old) of extreme beauty.

The fact that it is due to Febronia's youth and beauty that the Roman political authorities treat her differently from Bryene and Thomaïs is very well acknowledged by the two old nuns. Thomaïs, for instance, says to the protagonist, "My child, Febronia, this is the time of battle. If the army arrests us, the tyrants will soon execute us as old women. They will, however, spare you because you are young and very beautiful" (Τέκνον μου Φεβρωνία, ἰδοὺ καιρὸς ἀγῶνός ἐστιν ἐὰν οὖν συλληφθῶμεν ὑπὸ τῶν στρατιωτῶν, ἡμεῖς μὲν ὡς προβεβηκυῖαι συντόμως ἀναιρεθησώμεθα ὑπὸ τῶν τυράννων, σὲ δὲ περιποιήσονται ὡς νεάνιδα καὶ περικαλλῆ; *Life and Passion of Febronia*, § 14).[15] Eventually, Febronia is made to undergo horrendous tortures whose aim is the disfigurement of her loveliness, while Bryene and Thomaïs are never made to undergo any sufferings despite their Christian identities.[16]

Theophilos thus stages the two brothers' horrendous tortures because he wants to provide himself and the people of his court with an appealing spectacle. Such a spectacle could not be offered through the punishment of Michael's ugly, old, and ill body that is unable to resist. The two brothers' series of escalating tortures, on the contrary, through which the male body is eroticized, offer a feast for the spectators' eyes. In fact, the violation of beautiful young, mainly female, bodies is a recurrent theme in the Hellenistic novel, the Apostles' Acts, and the martyr's Passion.[17] Consequently, our hagiographer, apart from providing his audiences with a captivating narrative, rewrites a literary tradition.

The beauty and the erotic dimension of the two brothers' tortured flesh is also implied in the consoling letter that Michael sends to his young disciples as soon as they are taken unconscious to prison. He writes to them,

> Καὶ μακαρίζω ὑμῶν τὰ μέλη, τὰ καταξανθέντα μάστιξιν. . . . Ὑπερεπαινῶ δὲ καὶ περιπτύσομαι τὰ στήθη καὶ νῶτα τοῖς αἵμασι καταρραντισθέντα. . . . Ἀσπάζομαι τὰ τίμιά μοι καὶ φίλτατα πρόσωπα ἐκεῖνα. . . . Καταφιλῶ τὰς ἐμψύχους εἰκόνας καὶ μορφάς, τὰς ὑπὲρ τῆς ἀναστηλουμένης καὶ γραφομένης εἰκόνος καὶ μορφῆς τοῦ Λυτρωτοῦ μου καὶ Σωτῆρος σιδήρῳ κατακεντηθείσας καὶ μελανθείσας. (*Life of Michael the Synkellos*, 24.17–26)

> I bless your limbs, which have been lacerated by whips. . . . I praise above measure and embrace the breasts and backs, which were spattered with blood. . . . I salute those honorable and most beloved countenances, which were marked by letters. . . . I caress the living icons and forms which were pricked with iron and blackened on behalf of the erected and painted icon and form of my Redeemer and Saviour. (*Life of Michael the Synkellos*, p. 97)

This letter in which Michael re-creates through his words his disciples' tortures, which he has not seen, reveals that the iconophile Christian's approach to the two brothers' bodily punishments does not differ from that of their tormentors. Their tortures are seen as powerful spectacles providing aesthetic pleasure, which we are invited to share through the narrator's graphic narration.

Byzantine iconophile hagiographers, as is the case with the large majority of medieval hagiographers, were more interested in providing their audiences with fascinating narratives than in reporting historical events.[18] For this reason, they placed at the very center of their texts spectacular torture scenes in which young, naked, male bodies in great pain play a protagonistic role. Their aesthetics of punishment was to a large degree inspired by martyr legends, whose spectacular and often sexualized violence rendered them extremely popular throughout the whole Byzantine period.[19] Of course, it has to be pointed out that some iconophile hagiographers, in their own rewriting of martyr legends' theatrical violence, made three important changes related to gender, space, and pain.

While martyr legends eroticize mostly the female body, iconophile hagiography focuses on the beauty of men's lacerated bodies. It thus substitutes the rape plot of virgin martyr with that of male pornography.[20] Concerning the space of the punishment theater, the public square and the arena in martyr legends, which are populated by diverse audiences numbering in the thousands, are in many cases substituted by the emperor's palace, where torture becomes a private spectacle for a small, homosocial, invitation-only audience of elites. In other words, the new male martyrs' pornographic torture is often turned into an elite event centered on class and gender exclusion.

As for pain, whereas martyr legends, both male and female, focus on the martyr's release from pain, iconophile hagiography depicts its protagonists in the most extreme pain. Through the dramatic display of the iconophile saints' suffering in relentlessly graphic fashion, iconophile hagiography acquires a realism that further strengthens its male pornographic dimension, as the audiences' attention is drawn to the agony of the violated body, which excites fascination.

These three differences between martyr legends and iconophile hagiography, as is the case with their obvious similarities, further support this chapter's argument that the latter cannot provide any historical information on the actual acts of iconoclastic emperors,[21] just as Byzantine martyr legends cannot be treated as trustworthy sources for Christians' persecutions in the Roman empire. However, a more detailed research into such and possibly other variations between martyrs and iconophile saints that are not related to the theatrical aspect of violence, which has been examined here, might lead to some interesting and revealing conclusions about the history of Byzantine mentalities.

NOTES

1. Cunningham, *Life of Michael the Synkellos*, 21.8–25. Subsequent citations of this source refer to this version and appear parenthetically in the text.
2. On hagiography and pornography, see Burgwinkle and Howie, *Sanctity and Pornography*.
3. Even though the identity of the discussed hagiographer is unknown to us, we are almost certain about his male gender identity. The editor of the text, Mary Cunningham, argues convincingly that he was a monk of the Chora monastery in Constantinople (*Life of Michael the Synkellos*, § 5–7). In general, Byzantine hagiographers are in the vast majority men. The only known women hagiographers are Sergia (seventh century) and Theodora Raoulaina Kantekouzena Palaiologina (thirteenth century).
4. In fact, the hagiographical work that the aforementioned Theodora wrote is a life of the Graptoi brothers. It has been suggested that her interest in the two brothers' lives is autobiographical: Theodora identifies the Graptoi brothers' stance and punishment with those of her own brothers, who were forcibly blinded for their opposition to the Union of Lyons. Nicol, "Greeks and the Union of the Churches." Interestingly, Theodora's version of the Graptoi brothers' tortures does not have the pornographic dimension that is found in the *Life of Michael the Synkellos* or in other iconophile literature of the middle Byzantine period. One wonders whether this dissimilarity is related to the hagiographers' gender difference or to Theodora's own personal and political agenda.
5. See, for example, the *Life of Andrew in Tribunal*, the *Life of Stephen the Younger* by Stephen the Deacon, and the *Encomium of Theodore Graptos* by Theophanes of Caesarea.
6. The hagiographical texts devoted to iconophile women are very few and do not include the violent scenes found in the hagiographies of their male counterparts.
7. Featherstone, "Praise of Theodore Graptos." Subsequent citations of the encomium are to this version and appear parenthetically in the text.
8. My translation.
9. See, for example, Alexander, "Religion Persecution and Resistance"; Hatlie, *Monks and Monasteries*, 389–90; Morris, *Monks and Laymen*, 12. It has to be pointed out,

however, that the most recent work on Byzantine iconoclasm, which treats iconophile hagiography with skepticism, has come to the conclusion that the persecution during the iconoclast era was "moderate" and "limited in scope"; Brubaker and Haldon, *Byzantium in the Iconoclast Era*, 382.

10. See Constantinou, "Satirical Elements."
11. See Burton, "Byzantine Readers"; and Roilos, *Amphoteroglossia*, 40–50.
12. From the following edition: Garnaud, *Achille Tatius d'Alexandrie*.
13. Whitmarsh, *Achilles Tatius*, 110.
14. See this edition: Wirth, *Danae in christlichen Legenden*, 116–48; my translation.
15. The text is edited in Chiesa, *Le versioni latine della Passio Sanctae Febroniae*, 368–95; my translation.
16. See Constantinou, "Rewriting Beauty and Youth."
17. See Constantinou, *Female Corporeal Performances*, 19–58; Frankfurter, "Martyrology"; Haynes, *Fashioning the Feminine*; Morales, *Vision and Narrative*; and Shaw, "Body/Power/Identity."
18. See Coon, *Sacred Fictions*; Elliott, *Roads to Paradise*; Robertson, *Medieval Saints' Lives*.
19. See Constantinou, *Female Corporeal Performances*, 19.
20. See Gravdal, *Ravishing Maidens*.
21. For example, iconophile hagiography, which mostly celebrates the deeds of men, does not represent the historical reality concerning Byzantine women's involvement in iconoclasm. Contemporary research has shown that women played an instrumental role in the development of image veneration and the defense of icons during the iconoclastic period. Herrin, "Women and the Faith in Icons," 68–75; Kazhdan and Talbot, "Women and Iconoclasm."

3

Maydān-i Naqsh-i Jahān

The Safavid Isfahan Public Square as "A Playing Field"

BABAK RAHIMI

As the most recognizable landmark in Isfahan, the Maydān-i Naqsh-i Jahān has served as a pivotal public site in the city's history since the early seventeenth century. Built under the reign of Shāh 'Abbās I (1587–1629), the square is one of the most admired architectural sites in a country famous for its mosques, markets, paradisiacal gardens, and aesthetic ambience. The Madyān, along with numerous other building sites such as Chahār Bāgh Avenue in the southwest of the city, also represents the civic life of the Safavid Empire, which ruled Iran between 1501 and 1722. Under the Safavids, the Maydān, as an open space, was where many people congregated and enjoyed the prosperity that the monarchy claimed to provide.

But the Maydān also displayed royal power. In a seminal study of Safavid Isfahan, Sussan Babaie has shown how the construction of the Maydān, during the most intense centralization phase of Safavid rule under Shāh 'Abbās in the early seventeenth century, enunciated a distinct state ideology. This ideology fused the ancient Persian ethos of royal sovereignty and Shi'i Islamic conceptions of cosmic authority associated with the holy Imāms and the family of the Prophet Muḥammad to create a form of political rule that relied on multiple cultural and spiritual sources for legitimacy.[1] The merging of the Persian and Shi'i Islamic notions of politics also helped solidify Safavid authority in a land where most inhabitants were Sunni Muslims. The imperial Maydāns functioned as a performative stage of kingship that enunciated a new imperial ideology through the medium of a public architectural site. It took decades after Shāh 'Abbās's rule for Shi'ism to fully become consolidated in Iran, and in striking ways, architectural projects and other public cultural practices, promoted by the state, bolstered the spread of Shiʿi Islam and ultimately helped the Safavids maintain power.

The new urban scheme, with the design of the Maydān and Chahār Bāgh Avenue along with new bridges, suburbs, and parks, brought about a creative symbiosis between civic, religious, and royal spaces. The scheme also pronounced a holistic conception of the Safavid domains with an integrated relationship between urban denizens and royal authority. The design of the new Isfahan, with its various civic and courtly spaces of conviviality and hospitality, signified a conception of state power that, in the words of Babaie, "communicate[s] a charismatic practice of absolutism where access to the king and his personal engagement, even if illusory, were paramount."[2] The Maydān in this spirit of accessibility animated an urban experience of sociability in which all, even the king, could feel a sense of belonging as a member of an imperial order.

In the Isfahan urban scheme, however, visibility was designed primarily to promote state power. The specific process in the construction of the Maydān signifies a distinct Shiʿi Islamic-Persianate project that staged royal power with its claim to divine hierarchy, visible and accessible to the public. Such openness of urban space has been the unique hallmark of the Maydān, along with numerous other public sites such as bridges and palaces. The square dramatizes the open field of public interaction and state power, where elites and citizenry intermingle through architectural design. In this regard, the publicity of the square, mostly evident in its imperial design, underscore a dramatic significance in strategically foregrounding the interplay between civic and royal power, as mundane and spiritual authority intermingle in integrated spaces of conviviality and sociability. Viewed from this vantage, the buildings in the Maydān, as Babaie explains, were "cast into a theatrical perspective, forming a visible climax for those about to traverse its length." She adds, "The *maydan* indeed became the theater for staging imperial drama."[3]

While the theatrical aspect of power plays an important role in the Maydān architectural scheme, in this chapter, I also want to underscore the central role of gaming performances, in the form of various ceremonial rituals and sporting practices that also defined the square, as imperial assemblies of public significance.[4] By "gaming performances," I refer to a set of rule-abiding playful practices primarily undertaken for social leisure, with the defining trait of collective interaction in a public arena.[5]

These playful practices included ceremonies, rituals, dramatic and gaming performances, athletic events (in particular equestrian sports), and other official or popular spectacles marked by mundane or sacral significance. Gaming performances are not always organized in a confined space, but when they are, as in the case of games, they achieve a focused visibility on a public stage for a large crowd of spectators. The gaming arenas become spaces of spectacle, similar to stadiums, where the audiences also become vicarious participants, experiencing the play and its rules in shared time and space.

The characteristics of such gaming performances under the Safavids define the Maydān as a central landmark of the newly formed urban structure. The displays of games, through a range of formal processions to violent rituals, dramatized the life of denizens within the Maydān's arena. These dramatizations convey powerful meanings and experiences for a multitude of people, who participate in the spirit of the imperial community through game performances. Thus, the Maydān generates a distinct authority of public importance, a stage of social drama for view and consumption of those who partake as participants and audiences, sharing an imperial ensemble in the production of an architecturally confined public space and yet revolving around symbolic themes of universal ideals. The piazza in its Safavid manifestation serves as the staging site wherein everyone, including the king, his court, aristocrats, diplomats, travelers, and the ordinary people of Isfahan, could engage with playful yet meaningful action and feel incorporated into an imperial order.

In this short study, I refer to Maydān-i Naqsh-i Jahān as a public arena with a significant performative dimension. The idea of a public arena should evoke the image of a field designed to showcase ritualized actions ranging from ceremonies to sports and games. The staging of game practices, in particular, identifies a performance of play with Maydān as a symbolic spatial structure where public culture and state power intermingle. The public dimension is critical in this study since it allows us to understand the building of the new Isfahan, with the Maydān as a central urban structure, designed to heighten the collective experience of an imperial character. In an important sense, the public gathering in the Maydān identifies both audiences and participants with a collective experience of performances that conveyed Safavid state-political ideology. This communal dimension also underscores how the Maydān enhanced a shared consciousness and feelings of a Shiʿi Persianate identity that the Safavids promoted when they established their empire in 1501.

Distinct Shiʿi Islamic and Persianate cultures are characterized by a public platform where all—the court, clerics, administrators, merchants, military, civilians, and even foreign dignitaries—could network and forge an imperial community of feeling that audiences have of belonging in the temporary event of assembly. Equally important are Central Asian practices of equestrian sport games, martial performances, and polo games, appropriated as key social practices in defining the Maydān as a unique fusion of Perso-Shiʿi and Turko-Mongol architectural sites. These games, some of which resemble warlike performances, I argue, facilitated a shared sense of belonging through spectacles of gaming competition and conflict.

What follows is a discussion that primarily focuses on the performative practices that define a major transcultural urban space in late-sixteenth- and early-seventeenth-century Iran. This is done by focusing on the interlacing of space and games that the square came to represent as a distinct Safavid civilizing process. Such a process is intimately linked with Safavid state building as a unique political project in the post-Timurid era.

The Centralization of Safavid Rule

The famous English traveler Sir Thomas Herbert, who visited Safavid Iran between 1626 and 1629, described the imperial capital city, Isfahan, as "the metropolis of the Persian monarchy; yea, the greatest and best built City throughout the Orient."[6] The "metropolis" that Herbert encountered in the early seventeenth century had already seen a major phase of construction that was commenced by Shāh ʿAbbās in 1590/91. Known as the beginnings of the Isfāhānī stage of Safavid rule (1590–1722), this critical historical juncture signaled a transformative period in the early-modern history of Iran. The Isfāhānī stage was marked with the construction of new urban spaces that emphasized articulating state power in an architecturally centralized form made spatially visible and symbolically significant to everyday life.[7] Such an emphasis on refashioning urban life around the absolutist notion of imperial power was concurrent with the centralization of the military and the increasing institutionalization of the *ghulām* elite forces, composed of imported Georgian and Circassian slaves and the most important elite unit of the Safavid military apparatus.[8] In order to marginalize the Qizilbāsh, whose loyalty to the Shāh was tarnished with the revolts of Afshar and Zūl Qadar tribal forces, which led to the second civil war (1576–90), the slave-soldiers (*ghulāmān*) achieved high governmental positions at key official posts. The *ghulāmān* initiated and oversaw the construction of new urban and cultural sites, from which they extended their influence throughout the capital city and the empire at large.[9]

The centralization project marked a crucial phase in the Safavid state's major transformation from its tribal origins to a sedentary, imperial power, a transformation that largely began under Shāh ʿAbbās and reached its peak under ʿAbbās II (1642–66).[10] Part and parcel of this centralization was the regaining of lost territories from the Ottomans and the building of emerging elite networks to govern newly converted crown lands, most prominently those in Isfahan, Qazvīn, Yazd, Gīlān, and Māzandarān. This territorial expansion developed concurrent with Iran's growing silk industry and the state's promotion of transregional trade. Commerce played a key role in expanding the Safavid state's ability to govern and regulate its imperial domain through taxation. With increased security over roads and construction of caravanserais, where traders could rest before pressing on with their long-distance journeys, the commercial activities of key economic players—such as the Armenian merchants, who were resettled by the Shāh in the suburb of Isfahan, known as the New Julfā—became a major source of royal revenue.[11]

Equally important was the centralization of the religious institutions under the authority of the clerical class. The origins of the Safavids can be traced to a fourteenth-century Sufi (mystical) brotherhood movement, with a strong tradition of "heterodoxy," based in eastern Anatolia. The Safavid order was founded by Shaykh Ṣāfi al-Dīn (1252–1334) and fashioned into a militant revolutionary current that was constituted by Qizilbāsh tribal forces in the mid-fifteenth century and that further expanded under the leadership of Junayd (r. 1447–60) and later Ḥaydar (r. 1460–88). In 1501, Ḥaydar's son Ismāʿīl (r. 1501–24) captured Tabriz and declared Shiʿi Islam the official religion of the newly founded Safavid state. With the central creed in the rightful succession of ʿAlī ibn Abī

Tālīb (601–61), the son-in-law and the cousin of the Prophet, Shiʿism saw, for the first time since the Fatimid Caliphate (909–1171), a revival under the Safavids. However, the type of Shiʿism that the formative years of Safavid rule practiced, known as Qizilbāsh Shiʿism, combined belief in the celestial power of the Imams, as inheritors to the Prophet; devotional love for Ismāʿīl as a messianic figure; and complex shamanistic practices with Central Asiatic origins.[12] Critical to the consolidation of the Safavid monarchy as it vied with neighboring Sunni powers was the policy of downplaying the heterodox origins of the Safavid household and institutionalizing "orthodoxy" or "Imāmi Shiʿism," with its emphasis on religious law and clerics as its interpreters.[13]

The reign of Tahmāsb (1514–76) marked a crucial phase in the ascendancy of "orthodoxy." Babaie describes this period as the "Shiʿification project," a period when diverse aesthetic and symbolic strategies were introduced in order to convert the Sunni population of Iran to Shiʿism.[14] The period also saw the migration of Shiʿi Arab clerics, who were invited from Lebanon and the Persian Gulf sheikdoms to assume religious authority, propagate orthodoxy, and legitimize the political rule of the Safavids as representatives of the Hidden Imam, whose reappearance at the end of time would bring divine justice back to earth.[15] The ascendency of Shāh ʿAbbās assured the continuation of clerical influence within state apparatus, as a powerful elite class whose administrative and spiritual authority would play a significant role in converting Iran to Shiʿism. The reign of Shāh ʿAbbās also embodied a new age of economic prosperity and urban construction throughout parts of the empire. More importantly was ʿAbbās's focus on building a new Safavid capital that would serve as the administrative, commercial, and cosmopolitan center of the Shiʿi Iranian empire.

The New Isfahan, the New Maydān

In this historical context, the design of a new urban scheme was closely tied to the centralization of economic, military, and especially religious cultures and institutions in building state power. Although historically Isfahan had seen a significant Shiʿi presence, the majority of the population was most likely Sunni Muslim prior to Shāh ʿAbbās's ascent to power in 1587.[16] The construction of the new Maydān would facilitate a new congregational space for practicing, sharing, and performing Shiʿi cultural and ritual motifs. The most significant was the promotion of Muḥarram, annual commemorations of the martyrdom of the Prophet's grandson Ḥusayn in the battlefields of Karbala in 680 CE, within the newly built piazza that served as a way for the Isfāhānī population to participate in the narrative and reenactments of the Karbala drama.[17] But the new Maydān was not just a place for religious commemoration. It was also the heart of a new city of a revived Safavid power.

Isfahan, which had also been a major urban center under the Buyids (932–1062) and Seljuk Ṭughril (1051–63), became the new imperial capital city (*dār al-mulk shāhanshāhi*) in 1597/98. In line with Shāh ʿAbbās's other ambitious urban projects such as the construction of Faraḥābād and the expansion of Kirmān, he officially transferred the capital from Qazvin to Isfahan and inaugurated a period of radical urban change that lasted for more than a century. With the end of the second civil war in 1587, when the young Safavid king emerged victorious after internal military challenges to his authority, ʿAbbās's claim to the throne was supported by a host of provincial rulers and several Qizilbash tribes, who had originally brought the Safavid household to power under the leadership of Shāh Ismāʿīl in 1501. The decision to move the capital from Qazvīn to Isfahan was therefore a strategic decision to transfer the seat of government away from enemy territories and, more importantly, a reflection of a sense of royal confidence in rebuilding the imperial realm as a way to compete with the Sunni Ottomans (in the west) and the Mughuls and the Uzbeks (in the east).

The constructions began in 1590–91 when Shāh ʿAbbās issued a decree to build a new city, neighboring the older parts of the city and linked to it.[18] Although the older urban center of the city, Maydān-i Hārūn Vilāyat, was also refurnished as a place of commerce and social congregation (a project that lasted until 1595), the construction of the planned city began with the building of a Maydān cluster on the old Maydān-i Asb and Bāgh-i Naqsh-i Jahān, southwest of the older sectors of the city.[19] As the Italian archaeologist Eugenio Galdieri has shown, the Maydān was built in two stages, beginning with the flattening of the square, the construction of the Qayṣariyya Bāzār or the Imperial Market, and the erection of the walls of a single-story walkway, as Babaie describes, "before a row of shops that could be whitewashed and decorated with murals, as they were in 1595."[20] The building of the rectangular boundary walls, marked with colorful tiles and stones, played a critical role in the way the Maydān was demarcated as a central stage for the new city. It was within this walled complex that buildings of political and religious significance were also built.

As Robert McChesney has shown, the first building stage of the Maydān began in 1590, and the second phase took place from 1602–3 to 1611, ending with the initial construction of the Royal Mosque at the southern end of the square.[21] The construction of the two-story ʿĀlī Qāpū palace, at the western side of the Maydān, and the Qayṣariyya Bāzār (begun in 1590–91), at the northern side, represented the significance of political and commercial life within the newly built square. Eight years after the construction of Chahār Bāgh began (1596), the Maydān underwent another phase of expansion with the building of the second line of shops and a second-story façade complex, looking outward onto the square.

Galdieri explains the difference between these two stages as the following: "The initial project did not foresee a row of privileged shops open towards the Square, as opposed to the inner ones placed on the other side of the internal street of the Bazaar, but only the concentric ring represented by the internal street, with an uninterrupted series of arcades on the side of the square."[22] The twofold feature of the rectangular wall perimeter was most likely included in the initial design to transform the square into a multifunctional public space. Babaie argues that the building of the second row should not be seen as a frivolous addition to the Maydān but rather part of a grand urban design that, on a massive scale, was foreseen to involve different stages of urban construction.[23] In an important way, I suggest, the building of the second row introduced a dimension of spectatorship to the square, opened toward the square and designed similar to an amphitheater perspective, with the middle of the square as a vast focal stage.

The two monumental mosques of Shaykh Lūṭf-Allāh, also known as the chapel-mosque (begun in 1602), and the Masjid-i Shāh, known as the "pinnacles of Safavid architecture," enhanced the visual connection between the bazaar, marked with the victory archway of the Qayṣariyya Gateway (completed in 1617–18), and religious "orthodoxy," represented by the two mosques.[24] The Royal Mosque, the final monumental building constructed, took more than thirty-five years to complete. It underscored the role of Friday prayers in the new public life of imperial Isfahan as the most important religious event under the supervision of the clerics, who represented the official Shiʿism of the newly centralized Safavid state.

The royal authority was further reinforced by the massive two-story palace erected on the western side, ʿĀlī Qāpū. The palace served as a ceremonial site for the monarchy that combined the functions of a royal lodge and the official government. In the initial phase of the Maydān construction, ʿĀlī Qāpū also acted as one of the principal gateways to the royal gardens. In the second stage, the palace was "reimagined in 1602 on a magnified scale of usage and ceremony and the ʿĀlī Qāpū thereby assumed an entirely new significance in the ceremonies of the Safavid household."[25] The result of this second building stage was the formation of two upper levels as a platform for ceremonial performances that overlooked the square. The addition of the fifth floor around 1615 and the Tālār, or terrace, in 1644 only enhanced the performative significance of the palace as a staging device, as its massive height reminded those who viewed it from the square of the palace's hierarchical importance within the Maydān complex while symbolically projecting royal power.

With the completion of the new Maydān in 1611, it became the focal point of the new city. Just years after the final phases of construction, Iskandar Bek Munshi, ʿAbbās's biographer, described the design of the completed new city by the Shāh in the following words:

> In the spring of 1598, he approved plans for the construction of magnificent buildings in the Naqš-e Jahān district, and architects and engineers strove to complete them. From the Darb-e Dowlat, which is the name for the city gate located within the Naqš-e Jahān precincts, he constructed an avenue to the Zāyand-rūd. Four Parks [Chahār Bāgh] were laid out on each side of the avenue, and fine buildings adorned each. The avenue was continued across the river as far as the mountains bounding Isfahan to the south. The emirs and officers of state were charged with the creation of parks and the construction of lodges on a royal scale within the parks, each to consist of reception rooms, covered ways, porticos, balconies, finely adorned belvederes, and murals in gold and lapis lazuli.[26]

This is a depiction of the sumptuous new city and the Maydān, their links with other newly built sites, and the grandeur that their scale evinced in the urban landscape. The attempt to complete the Maydān district appears in the beginning of the description, where Munshi is keen to show its priority in the overall urban-planning scheme. It also bespeaks the significance that the open piazza had for the imperial urban project, tempered by the millenarian belief that the new Maydān would serve as the "pivot of the universe from where the expected Mahdi would emerge."[27] The leveling of a new field symbolically alluded to the realization of cosmic time in the expectation of an apocalyptic sense of beginning, setting a fresh world to come. The Maydān marked the space of beginnings with an anticipated end of time, in which the king claimed full legitimacy as the shadow of God on earth.

The Civic-Imperial Amphitheater

But was the new Maydān of Isfahan merely a symbolic site for the return of the promised Mahdī? And, accordingly, was the Maydān an architectural site to affirm royal authority? Historians have long debated the functions of the Maydān. Turning to the first construction phase in 1590–91, McChesney, for instance, argues that Shāh ʿAbbās originally wanted the Maydān to serve as a place of ceremony and entertainment, but in reaction to resistance from the affluent class based in the older Maydān, he then merged the commercial projects of his urbanization plan into the new public square.[28] According to Robert Hillenbrand, the Maydān represents a massive court based on designs in ancient Iranian courtyards that can still be found in mosques or private houses.[29] In a highly symbolist-spiritualist approach, the Swiss scholar Henri Stierlin identifies the Maydān and the new Isfahan as symbolic representations of paradisiac imagery based on Qur'anic verses.[30]

My suggestion is that the Maydān includes a pivotal performative theme that did not in fact revolve around the building complex but was interwoven within its walled structures, encompassing the mosques, the bazaar, and the palace. These buildings certainly played a role, but in both phases of the Maydān's construction, the central leveled field, congruent with the wall demarcating the inside arena from the outside urban landscape, served as the theatrical focus of the open square, an open field for viewing and being seen by all. It is not what particular buildings in the Maydān complex represent that is the key to the public square—and one could obviously single out royal authority as a key feature—but rather the vast, open space within the rectangular arena that defines the square as a performative site of public assembly. The key symbolic feature here is the performance of civic culture manifested within the square in the form of varied activities, many of which revolve around games and ceremonies. These activities define the square as a living arena where interactions, expressions of meaning, and experiences of public performance become enacted and embodied in spectacle.

I base my argument on a seminal paragraph in the account of Mīrzā Ḥasan, a Safavid historian, in his writings about the Maydān:

> At that moment, since the *dār al-mulk*, Isfahan, on account of its abundant supply of water and the talents and numbers of its people, had come to bear the stamp of a paradisiacal place and [to be] the place for a sovereign of heavenly authority, the full attention of the *padshāh* was directed towards the design and construction of this Paradise-like city. First, he decreed the expansion of a square which stood in front of the shrine of the one worthy of exaltation, Harun Wilāyat. In a short time, in accordance with the command of the Darius of the time, the Isfahanis had laid out a spacious rectangular maydān measuring 300 *jarībs* in area, by the *jarīb* in use in Isfahan. Any observer casting his glance on it would be filled with delight. In the very center of the maydān was [erected] a sublimely lofty pole for the game of the spearing the ring [but] much of the time the "shah of time and space" had the maydan's playing field set up for polo and looking as good as the fourth celestial sphere.[31]

The reference to "playing field," an open area for gaming activities marked by a fusion of entertainment and military practices, is key in this paragraph. With the order of the "Darius of the time," a clear reference to the Persianate tradition of royal authority, the spacious rectangular building was built in relation to two important equestrian sports: first is the pole for the game of spearing the ring, but more importantly was the game of polo. The reference to the fourth celestial sphere is to cosmology, but one that sees the games as interplaying with the symbolic sacred features of the Maydān. The Maydān's "playing field" also included bull- and cockfighting, wrestling, and fireworks, a common spectacle during major festivals, all enhancing the centrality of gaming in shaping the square as a civic staging of the empire.

Why did polo play a central role? Originally played by nomadic people of Central Asia and introduced to Iran most likely by the Parthian dynasty (247 BCE–224 CE), polo was a game that brought rulers and ruled together in encounters in a festive and yet competitive way.[32] But polo was a kind of equestrian sport that facilitated military skills and training for cavalry units in a competitive spirit. More importantly, I suggest, was polo's most likely historical Central Asiatic origin as a hunting game. In games known as *būzkashī* that are still played in Central Asia, horse-riding players compete to place a headless domestic animal, usually a goat, in a goal. Though evidence to link these two games would require a separate study, my assumption is that polo is a civilizing game version of *būzkashī* that replaced the animal with a ball. This was most likely developed as the game moved from a tribal to an imperial game under Parthians. But the key point here is that polo is not just for "entertainment" but a military training practice that affirmed the militaristic character of the Safavids. What the Maydān provided was a confined and visible site for the staging of military prowess, as the games came to represent.

Royal spectacles play an important role. The Safavid *shāh*s extended patronage and even played in these games along with their male family members during public festivals.[33] When Shāh ʿAbbās, the king, played polo, his performance was accompanied by drums and trumpets, as at the Maydān in the first capital in Qazvīn and later in Isfahan.[34] The open field of the Maydān, in its vast rectangular structure, incorporated a massive polo arena with goal posts on the north and south sides of the new square, still visible to this day. The presence of goal posts underlines that the games were not meant for temporary display but served as an intrinsic feature of the Maydān. In fact, I argue, the goal posts were as permanent as the Shāh's palace and the Royal Mosque, a material site that cannot be ignored today, as the posts still stand erect as the only architectural material remaining in the square from the Safavid period.

Along with other equestrian sports, such as *qoboq-andāzī* (horseback archery games), polo displayed masculine power. First, on a collective level, polo served as a way to cross communal boundaries. While the king played a significant role as ultimate observer of the games, it was with the civic actors—horsemen, gamers, watchers, consumers, and travelers—that games such as polo were able to produce a new collectivity. But a second point to note here is that such collectivity was based on gender and status. The sporting drama heightened shared emotions as male performances displayed triumph, defeat, surprise, and tragedy that brought gaming evocations of the interlacing of civic, entertainment, and consumption practices. The square marked a playing field primarily because of the games that shaped Safavid identity into a male-dominated imperial military order.

Numerous accounts, in both Persian and European languages, testify to the relationship between militant masculinity and the playing-field aspect of the square. In an important way, war-like parades and ritual combats were closely linked with polo games as well. War-like exercises including army processions and also camel-sacrifice rituals, promoted under Shāh ʿAbbās—in which different factions in the city would fight over the sacrificed camel—foreground a violent side of the festive life of the Maydān.[35] Festivals were a way not just to celebrate imperial power but also to reinforce emotions of belonging. On a central gaming platform, both the general populace—at times segregated according to class and gender—and the elites could participate in an imagined collective identity through military gaming competition and ritualized conflict. It is interesting to observe here that an often-ignored key architectural motif of the square was the ceremonial Tower of Skulls, a tall structure decorated with skulls of domesticated animals sacrificed most likely in religious rituals.[36] The tower is representative of a Turko-Mongol tradition of hunting games that ultimately served a military practice. In the post-ʿAbbās Safavid period, even Muḥarram rituals, known for their (male-led) mournful public displays, had become a major male spectacle that dramatized mourning into an event of public staging of masculine sacrifice held in the middle of the square.[37] Games and rituals such as Muharram aimed to communicate the imperial solidarity of masculinity.

Equally important to note is that the king and others as audience also participated in various gaming and ritual practices.[38] The royals and their entourage watched and at times were engaged in games or ceremonies as performers, especially during religious ceremonies. Polo matches were particularly a favorite of the king, who was very fond of the Maydān.[39] The presence of the king, his ministers, and foreign ambassadors during major public ceremonies, in particular the Muḥarram performances, bespeaks the symbolic and physical way royal masculinity was projected onto the square during ritual events. Yet projection also involved royal visibility. ʿĀlī Qāpū and its balcony, which overlooks the Maydān, represented a kind of luxury box where the elites—partaking in the ceremonies in the square from above—could see and be seen by all. The spectatorship of the elite over gaming practices heightened the role of imperial authority across class, tribal, and neighborhood lines in a shared experience made visible to all in the public square.

The role of spectatorship is significant to what I describe as a civic-imperial amphitheater. As a vast rectangular piazza, the Maydān was most visible because of its two-story walls that surrounded the square. The German traveler Engelbert Kaempfer (1651–1716), who visited Isfahan in 1684, described the Maydān in his travelogue:

> The Great Square was laid out by Shah Abbas I at the same time as the adjoining royal palace and the district of Abbasabad. It far exceeds the Old Square in size and magnificence and, forming as it were a forecourt to the palace itself, I shall describe it here in more detail. The shape of the square is a rectangle of 660 paces in length (in a north-south direction) and 212 paces in width. It is surrounded by two-storeyed vaulted buildings with recesses. The upper floors are divided into small rooms that are rented out as dormitories to all sorts of foreigners as well as to the prostitutes. The ground floor of this arcade serves partly as a covered walk for pedestrians but in the main to accommodate spacious bazaar stalls for shopkeepers and craftsmen, who produce and sell a variety of goods there. There is no disorder, however, but all are lodged systematically according to their professions. These neat rows of uniformly high bazaar apartments, screened by ornamental lattices, give the Shah's Square its specific attractive style.[40]

Here, Kaempfer depicts the Maydān's complex as foremost a public space of communal vitality. The most interesting details are the upper floors, enclosed within the walls surrounding the square. In the late seventeenth century, they appear to characterize liminal spaces that could be used for temporary residents such as prostitutes. Such residential features also underscore how the second floor, in distinction from other monumental buildings in the square, could accommodate those (mostly men) who traversed or visited the square for leisure and conviviality. On the first floor, the spaces of commerce and leisure intermingled with various shops (e.g., butcher, artisans, rope makers, cotton beaters), kitchen caravanserai, and coffee shops, reinforcing the spectacles of social interaction within the public square as a major cosmopolitan site.[41] The upper residences around the Maydān, with their balconies facing the square, could in this sense also be thought of as a form of staging, with an open perspective visible to all those who visited, shopped, resided, and watched the games and rituals at the Maydān.[42]

The open-air venue on the field is primarily evident in the spaces of intertwining palace, bazaar, coffeehouses, travel lodges, and second-story balconies overlooking the Maydān. One exception is the Shaykh Luṭf Allāh Mosque, which served as a private chapel for the royal family and hence was closed off, without windows or balconies, from public view. The Royal Mosque, tilted toward Kaaba, also receded onto the Maydān, perhaps signifying the internalized life of ascetic devotion in contrast to the aesthetics of leisure, as displayed in the public square. While interaction between the Maydān's buildings characterizes the multifunctionality of this urban space, the overlapping spheres of life within the square highlight a major social performative site, especially given the focus on the center of the square as the ceremonial heartbeat of the new urban lifestyle. Despite varying architectural purposes, incorporating Persianate, Islamic, and Turko-Mongol motifs, such overlapping spheres of life highlighted the centrality of spectatorship, with the dramatic design of the square facing the open playing field where multiple perspectives merge to form an imperial community.

Scholarship has mostly focused on explaining the architecture of the Maydān-i Naqsh-i Jahān based on royal power and its symbolic relations with commerce, religion, and popular culture. In this study, I have suggested that the new Maydān, built under Shāh ʿAbbās, represented a huge arena in which an imperial identity was performed through the gaming performances, many of which had militaristic features, that took place at the center stage of the open square. I make this suggestion in line with McChesney's argument that ʿAbbās's original plan for the Maydān was to serve as a ceremonial and gaming space for the empire. While horse-riding games such as polo hint at the Central Asiatic cultural origins of the Safavids, the rituals and games performed at the Maydān primarily identify complex social practices that testified to the military strength of the empire and its confidence in appearing on a playing field to heighten the impact of the spectacle and royal visibility, which all were meant to experience and feel.

NOTES

I wish to thank Afshin Marashi, Rosemary Stanfield-Johnson, and Maurice Pomerantz for their helpful comments on an earlier version of this chapter.

1. See Babaie, *Isfahan and Its Palaces*; and Babaie, "Sacred Sites of Kingship."
2. Babaie, *Isfahan and Its Palaces*, 12.
3. Babaie et al., *Slaves of the Shah*, 85.
4. By this claim, I do not intent to disagree with Babaie but in fact aim to expand her original argument that the Maydān and other newly built major urban arenas served as institutional settings for the staging of performances aimed at making visible royal power legitimate and sacred. What I would like to add, however, is that the ritual culture that revolved around the Maydān was not just a way for the Shāh, his court, and government officials to communicate legitimacy but constructed a "theater state" in which all actors participated and made state power a theatrical event, with the square as an architectural and public forum part and parcel of the performative practices. See also Rahimi, *Theater State*.
5. Jane McGonigal, in her famous study on games, explains the defining traits of games as goal, rules, a feedback system, and voluntary participation. While goal and rules set specific outcomes and limitations in what players need to achieve, the feedback system informs players about their progress in achieving the goals and, accordingly, provide incentive for the players to continue to play the game according to the rules. Voluntary participation is the underlying need for all the players to knowingly and willingly accept the goal, rules, and feedback. See McGonigal, *Reality Is Broken*, esp. 20–34. In this study, voluntary participations are performed in a complex set of bodily, symbolic, and imaginary institutional processes that enable the mobilization of crowds into a public square and enact solidarity toward a new sense of collectivity.
6. Herbert, *Some Yeares of Travels*, 153.
7. For a broad account of the Isfāhāni phase of Safavid rule, see Babayan, *Mystics, Monarchs, and Messiahs*, 348–402.
8. The policy of importing *ghulāms*, or slave soldiers, began with Shāh Ismāʿīl in the early sixteenth century when imported Christian slaves were included as part of the Safavid army. While the process of institutionalizing the *ghulāms* increased

under Shāh Tahmāsb, it was under Shāh Abbās that the process was intensified as a way to marginalize Qizilbash tribal forces. See Babaie et al., *Slaves of the Shah*.

9. See ibid., 110–13. A major incorporation of slave-soldiers, however, took place after the Georgian campaign (1614–15), when numerous captured slaves were incorporated into the state apparatus as both bureaucrats and army officers.
10. For a detailed account of the sedentarization process, see Babayan, *Mystics, Monarchs, and Messiahs*, 295–402.
11. For a study of Safavid commerce under Shāh ʿAbbās, see Matthee, *Politics of Trade*.
12. Babayan, *Mystics, Monarchs, and Messiahs*, xxxii.
13. The other name for Imāmi Shiʿism is "Twelver Shiʿism," known for the dogma of twelve (male) descendants of the Prophet, with Mahdi as the twelfth Imam who is in occultation and will return at the end of time. Today, Twelver Shiʿism is the largest branch of Shiʿi Islam and has more adherents in Iran than other branches of Shiʿism do.
14. Babaie, *Isfahan and Its Palaces*, 95; see also Abisaab, *Converting Persia*.
15. For the institutionalization of the clerical class in Safavid Iran, see Arjomand, *Shadow of God*, 112–59.
16. For a study of Shiʿism in the pre-Safavid period, see Jaʿfariyān, "Pishīni-yi tashayyuʿ dar Isfahan."
17. See Calmard, "Shiʿi Rituals and Power II."
18. Munajjim, *Tārīkh-i ʿAbbāsī ya ruznāma-yi Mullā Jalāl*, 113.
19. See McChesney, "Four Sources." The date of construction was marked prior to the official transfer date of the capital city to Isfāhān, which shows that ʿAbbās most likely had plans to relocate the Safavid capital earlier than the official date suggests.
20. Babaie, *Isfahan and Its Palaces*, 84; for the account of the two-building stages, see Galdieri, "Two Building Phases." See also Haneda, "Character of the Urbanization of Isfahan." It is worth noting that Stephen Blake, relying on Persian sources, disagrees with Galdieri's claim that the Maydān was built in two stages. See Blake, *Half of the World*, 105.
21. See McChesney, "Four Sources."
22. Galdieri, "Two Building Phases," 66.
23. Babaie, *Isfahan and Its Palaces*, 84.
24. For an architectural description of the two mosques as "pinnacles of Safavid architecture," see Canby, *Golden Age of Persian Art*, 98–100.
25. Babaie, *Isfahan and Its Palaces*, 144.
26. Munshī, *History of Shah ʿAbbās the Great*, 2:724.
27. Babayan, *Mystics, Monarchs, and Messiahs*, 230. It is interesting to note that the twelve horses, symbolic of the Twelve Imams of Twelver Shiʿism, stood at each side of the portal of Ali Qāpu.
28. See McChesney, "Four Sources."
29. Hillenbrand, "Safavid Architecture."

30. Stierlin, *Isfahan.*
31. Junabadi, *Rawzat al-Safaviyya*, quoted in McChesney, "Postscript." I have simplified McChesney's translation, deleting Persian terms in parentheses, unless they have been mentioned in the main text.
32. For a history of polo in Iran, see Chehabi and Guttmann, "From Iran to All of Asia."
33. It is important to note that the Venetian traveler Michele Membrè described Shāh Tahmāsb playing games with his brothers in the Maydān of Tabriz. But the polo grounds at the Tabriz Maydān was a makeshift field, as the goal posts in the form of two pillars could be removed after the games. See Membrè, *Mission to the Lord Sophy*, 32.
34. *Three Brothers*, 70–71; see also *Journeys of Pietro della Valle*, 173–75.
35. For rituals of camel sacrifice, see Rahimi, "Rebound Theater State."
36. It is unclear what kinds of animal skulls were included in the tower. After the camel-sacrifice rituals, the skull of the dead animal, after being beheaded and fought for among competing groups, would be placed on the tower. This example again highlights the hunting-ritual feature associated with the tower.
37. Rahimi, *Theater State*, 273–320.
38. An in-depth analysis of the Maydān gaming practices that involve the royalty would require a separate study with references to available sources.
39. Munshī, *History of Shah ʿAbbās the Great*, .2:838
40. Haberland, *Engelbert Kaempfer*, 32.
41. For an account of coffee-consumption culture at the Maydān, see Matthee, *Pursuit of Pleasure*, 144–74.
42. The role of gender is significant in this social space, where women frequented the Maydān as shoppers, though primarily as audiences for major religious, sporting, or royal ceremonial events.

PART II

Persuasion

4

Performances of Advice and Admonition in the Courts of Muslim Rulers of the Ninth to Eleventh Centuries

LOUISE MARLOW

Mirrors for princes, in the courts of medieval Islam, Byzantium, and the Latin West, belonged to the trappings of kingship. Like the arrangement of parades and festivals; the provision of feasts and receptions; the orchestration of hunts, games, and contests; the donning of distinctive clothing, insignia, and weaponry; and the distribution of royal largess, the king's delivery and reception of advice displayed his exceptional status. As written documents, mirrors for princes were durable physical artifacts: their presentation in courtly settings bound participants and observers, addressees, and authors within a system of mutual obligations and expectations. The wise maxims that recurred in mirrors for princes were also inscribed into the architecture of palaces and administrative buildings and adorned royal vestments, thrones, seals, and vessels. These material manifestations of an advice-centered mentality, some of them portable, complemented the oral dissemination of moral aphorisms and edifying narratives well beyond the confines of the royal court.

With reference to mirrors of the early Islamic period and especially the ninth-century Arabic *Akhlāq al-mulūk* (better known as the *Kitāb al-Tāj*), the tenth-century Arabic *Naṣīḥat al-mulūk*, and the eleventh-century Persian *Siyar al-mulūk*,[1] this chapter explores the roles and representations of kings as central figures in a public culture of advice. The individuals who dispensed counsel and moral exhortation were diverse in their backgrounds and interests; they included kings, princes, and provincial governors; viziers, secretaries, and accountants; scholars of the religious sciences and the "ancient" or "foreign" sciences; courtiers and boon companions; and littérateurs. Authors of "mirrors for princes," as the term implies, characteristically addressed their advice to rulers or to their royal children; indeed, moral instruction constituted an essential element in the education of princes. Rulers were not only the recipients of advice, however; they also figure prominently among the dispensers of counsel, and their delivery of edifying and cautionary instruction accrued to their posthumous reputations. The historian al-Ṭabarī (c. 224–310/838–923) relates several incidents (in the form of *akhbār*, narrative accounts; sing. *khabar*) in which the caliph al-Manṣūr (r. 136–58/754–75), having designated his son the future al-Mahdī (r. 158–69/775–85) as heir apparent, counseled him in matters pertaining to his moral disposition and the principles of governance; these pronouncements, moreover, contributed to the fashioning of al-Manṣūr's lasting image in Arabic historiography.[2] The model is recapitulated in Persian materials, such as the *Andarznāmeh* or *Qābūsnāmeh* (475/1082–83), addressed by the Ziyarid ruler ʿUnṣur al-Maʿālī Kaykāʾūs b. Iskandar (r. from 441/1049) to his son and heir Gīlānshāh. It appears that many caliphs and kings, concerned for their posterity, delivered such advice; at the same time, the aging ruler who, having acquired experience and wisdom, counsels his young son and successor constitutes a topos that recurs in the Arabic and Persian literature of the early centuries with which this chapter is principally concerned. Indebted to the work of Tayeb El-Hibri and Michael Cooperson, whose studies of such *akhbār* have illuminated the complicated interplay of recalled events and their shifting, meaningfully adapted narrative forms, this chapter addresses, in part, the selection and deployment of similar materials in advisory texts, where they contribute to the determining of the audience's response to the author's composition.[3]

Rulers exhorted not only the members of their families and households but also groups outside the courtly milieu; in certain settings, the delivery of edificatory orations was among the duties of the ruler. Early Arabic works of historiography and *adab*, including mirrors for princes, record numerous accounts in which caliphs and their governors address their fellow Muslims in mosques, especially in Mecca during the pilgrimage.[4] In order for the king's oration to meet with a positive reception, it was necessary for his perceived conduct to reflect the moral standards that he urged his listening subjects to uphold. Such accounts (*akhbār*) again combine memories of historical occurrences and the shaping forces of literary topoi. A recurrent element in these representations is the figure of the anonymous common man, sometimes transformed into a "caliph-denouncing zealot," who challenges the caliph or king during his address to the crowd.[5] These *akhbār* sometimes conclude with the caliph's effective response to the heckler, but it is often the heckler who is given the last word.[6] Such *akhbār* sometimes include the further topos of the caliphal adviser, who advocates severe punishment for the zealot; the caliph rejects the suggestion and demonstrates his forbearance and generosity.[7]

These incidents and related topoi attest to a pervasive advisory culture, a mentality of wisdom and ethics, in which the central position belonged to the ruler, who both dispensed and received advice in instances of public display. The literary genres that provided vehicles for the conveyance of advice frequently assumed highly personalized forms. For instance, the *waṣiyya* or *ʿahd* characteristically took the form of a "testament" delivered at a particular moment in the context of a specific relationship, such as the advice of a dying father, often a king, to his son and heir. Despite such appearances of intimacy, the king or prince was never alone. His delivery and reception of advice were public events, staged in the presence of members of the king's *khāṣṣa*, persons of privilege and varying degrees of authority; on occasion, these events involved members of the *ʿāmma*, or common people, as well. The presence of witnesses to the king's participation in this advisory culture was essential to its effectiveness. To a significant degree, the counsels purveyed in mirrors for princes coincided with the values of local and urban populations. Public display of the king's centrality in this system of values promoted his reputation and his legitimacy and strengthened the ties between the royal court and the subject communities. For example, the celebrated *waṣiyya* of Ṭāhir b. al-Ḥusayn (r. 205–7/821–22), governor of Khurasan and founder of the Tahirid dynasty, takes the form of an intimate communication from a father, a seasoned holder of high office, to his son, as the latter prepared to assume a governorship; yet this ostensibly personal communication from an experienced father to his cherished son became, according to the report of al-Ṭabarī, the object of competition among ordinary people, who vied with one another to obtain copies of it, wrote it out, and studied it together, so that it became widely disseminated. In the course of this general circulation, news of Ṭāhir's composition reached the caliph al-Maʾmūn (r. 198–218/813–33), who asked for it to be read aloud to him, pronounced it complete in its stipulations regarding all matters of importance, and ordered it to be copied and distributed among his officials in every province.[8]

This pervasive advisory culture embraced worldly and otherworldly (*dunyawī* and *dīnī*) perspectives. Many mirrors for princes included not only pragmatic recommendations related to specific issues but also moral exhortation related to the cultivation of virtues and the pursuit of praiseworthy conduct. Kings were not the only persons involved in the exercise of power. Their assistants and their assistants' assistants also held positions of responsibility, and many of these individuals sought to exercise their authority in ways that would enhance, rather than compromise, their moral well-being. Achieving a balance between the requirements of *dunyā* and *dīn* was a matter of widespread concern; for this reason, secretaries and accountants, merchants, master craftsmen, and artisans, despite the vast differences in their power and status, might draw inspiration from the examples of kings and viziers reputed for their just, honest, and compassionate treatment of persons who depended on them.

Authors of mirrors distinguished between advice that benefited the entire courtly assembly, even when ostensibly addressed to the king, and advice necessary for the management of matters of immediate concern. As the authors of mirrors invariably pointed out, matters of the latter kind frequently required the confidential disclosure of certain kinds of information and the keeping of secrets (*kitmān al-sirr*). The formulation of strategic and practical advice, often in response to such confidential communications, could only take place in (at least relative) privacy. It was counsel in such practical matters—"in everything to do with the country and its cultivation, the military and the peasantry, warfare, raids, punishments, stores, matrimonial alliances and travels"—that Niẓām al-Mulk had in mind when he stipulated that boon companions should not participate in advising the king.[9] This kind of interaction, more likely to be considered under the rubric of "consultation" (*mashwara, mushāwara*) than "advice" (*naṣīḥa*), lies beyond the scope of this chapter.

As the studies of Julie Scott Meisami and Beatrice Gruendler, in particular, have established, the public communication of advice in courtly settings complemented, and to some extent coincided with, the performance of courtly and panaegyric poetry (*madīḥ*), which provided a subtle means to instruct, negotiate with, and even coerce the patron-recipient.[10] According to Meisami, "panegyric preoccupations were never far removed from didactic ones" in court poetry, and the panaegyric ode allowed the poet to reaffirm, for the benefit of the ruler and the community, the accepted model of ideal monarchy.[11] The close relationship between panaegyric and didactic poetry found formal acknowledgment in the literary analysis of Ibn Rashīq (d. 463/1070–71), who included among the subdivisions of panaegyric the improvement of moral character (*taḥsīn al-akhlāq*), a category that contained maxims (*ḥikam*), exhortations (*mawāʿiẓ*), abstinence from material things (*al-zuhd fī l-dunyā*), and contentment (*qināʿa*).[12] Several poets who kept the company of rulers, notably al-ʿAbbās b. al-Aḥnaf (d. 188/803, or after 193/808),[13] Abū Nuwās (c. 140–c. 198 / c. 755–c. 813),[14] and Abū l-ʿAtāhiya (131–211/748–826),[15] addressed edifying themes in their compositions. Abū l-ʿAtāhiya was particularly noted, if not uniformly acclaimed, for his large corpus of *zuhdiyyāt*, poems on the theme of *zuhd*, "austerity" or "renunciation." These poems emphasized the transience of worldly concerns and the proximity of death.[16] The association of panaegyric and didactic interests is evident in depictions of the caliph Hārūn al-Rashīd (r. 170–93/786–809), who is reported to have loved poetry and poets (*kāna yuḥibbu al-shuʿarāʾ wa-l-shiʿr wa-yamīlu ilā ahl al-adab wa-l-fiqh*; "he loved poets and poetry, and was favorably inclined towards specialists in literary culture and religious understanding"), especially panaegyric poetry (*kāna yuḥibbu l-madīḥ*), and to have solicited and responded with marked emotion, usually copious weeping, to moral exhortation.[17] The polymath al-Masʿūdī (d. 345/956) reports the *khabar* in which the philologist al-Aṣmaʿī (d. 213/828) encountered the caliph, shortly before he died, in floods of tears occasioned by his stumbling upon some inscribed verses of Abū l-ʿAtāhiya.[18]

Some descriptions of the expected functions of the *nadīm*, or boon companion, include the provision of moral instruction on suitable occasions, and the corpus of advisory literature is replete with *akhbār* in which a boon companion avails himself of an opportunity to instruct and edify his ruler-patron.[19] In a celebrated example, the caliph al-Maʾmūn is reported to have eaten too much of a certain food, and the doctors were at a loss to relieve him of its ill effects. Observing the situation, the boon companion Thumāma b. al-Ashras (d. 213/828–29) reminded the caliph of the virtue of royal resolve: "*Yā amīr al-muʾminīn, fa-ayna ʿazma min ʿazamāt al-khilāfa!*" (O Commander of the Faithful, show some of the resolve proper to the office of the caliphate!). Upon this call to moral virtue, the caliph dismissed the physicians, duly "cured" by Thumāma's reminder of appropriate royal behavior. According to the author of the Arabic *Naṣīḥat al-mulūk*, the caliph had been "overcome by the desire for" this food (*kāna ghalaba ʿalā al-Maʾmūn amīr al-muʾminīn shahwat al-ṭ.w.y.n*), and Thumāma's intervention facilitated the restoration of his self-control.[20] Three centuries later, in a discussion of the seven qualities that rulers should seek to unite in themselves, the scientist, philosopher, and polymath Naṣīr al-Dīn Ṭūsī (597–672/1201–74) relates the same anecdote in his discussion of the virtue of perfect resolve.[21] Elsewhere, however, authors of advisory literature invoke the more austere example of the caliph al-Manṣūr, reputed to have shunned not only musical instruments and entertainment but also the company of boon companions.[22] As will be seen in what follows, the author of the *Naṣīḥat al-mulūk* expressed in explicit terms his suspicion of the king's boon companions.

Implicit in the *khabar* concerning al-Maʿmūn is the important point that, as Andras Hamori has demonstrated with reference to the works of Ibn al-Muqaffaʿ (d. c. 139/756), unethical conduct on the part of the ruler resulted not only in injury to his practical interests but also in personal shame.[23] This idea accompanies and underlines the emphasis on the courtier-secretary's role as an ethical educator to the ruler. Authors of mirrors (and other works of *adab*) draw extensively on *Kalīla wa-Dimna* and, like Ibn al-Muqaffaʿ, assume a code of behavior proper to the "men of excellence," a code on which the reputation and the self-respect of the idealized courtier-secretary depends.[24]

While the king occupied the central position in an advisory culture that embraced and linked large sections of the population, the offering of advice to the sovereign inevitably involved considerable risk. An individual who took it upon himself to counsel the ruler placed the latter, at least symbolically, in a (morally) subordinate position and threatened his dignity; as Meisami has written of the court poet, "if he presumes to preach to his prince, [he] is surely destined for a short career, if not for a swift journey to the next world."[25] Furthermore, several of the literary figures whose criticism of governmental practices or of aspects of courtly culture was most overt, such as Ibn al-Muqaffaʿ, Abū l-ʿAtāhiya, and Ṣāliḥ Ibn ʿAbd al-Quddūs (d. c. 167/783),[26] were accused of *zandaqa* and subjected to imprisonment and in some cases execution. (It is possible, however, that Abū l-ʿAtāhiya and Ibn ʿAbd al-Quddūs wrote their *zuhdiyyāt* in response to accusations of *zandaqa*.)[27] In an explicit acknowledgment of the constraints under which members of the royal retinue operated, the author of the *Naṣīḥat al-mulūk* pronounces the king's boon companions (*nudamāʾ*), as well as his assistants and viziers, unfit and unwilling to offer advice; fearful for their lives and mindful of their advancement, none of them would risk giving voice to critical observations and recommendations for improvement.[28]

To impart moral guidance without incurring the ruler's anger, authors of mirrors for princes, like poets, developed techniques that allowed them to "conceal and reveal" their advice and to avoid the direct criticism that would risk or even necessitate a punitive response.[29] The exemption of the addressee from the need for advice—the conceit that the recipient already exemplified the ideals that were rehearsed in the gift presented to him—was a common strategy, especially in later works of counsel.[30] But authors also created an environment conducive to the appreciative reception of their counsels by a variety of literary techniques: the presentation of arguments, supported by carefully selected authorities; the logical movement from generally accepted statements to their specific application; the depiction of praiseworthy examples of rulers who accepted and heeded advice; and the demonstration of the enhancement to the reputation of such monarchs. Authors cited encounters that took the form of *akhbār* associated with historical figures, including recent caliphs and rulers, and of narratives associated with exemplary rulers of the past, including the distant past, whose names had become bywords for royal virtue and sagacity.

The culture of advice, then, imposed restrictions on counselors, who in most cases eschewed direct criticism of their royal addressees. Authors could, however, imply criticism through their use of exemplary narratives, especially narratives set in the distant and legendary past, and of narratives that, in an acknowledged and established trope, depicted harsh criticism, even insult, of power. Authors could also tailor their presentations of advice to the interests and dispositions of their recipients, appealing, for example, to the compelling obligation to maintain and enhance the fine reputation of their royal predecessors or to their associations with individuals reputed for their moral qualities. Despite the constraints of the genre, many mirrors are strikingly individual, and each composition addressed a particular historical moment. The administrator and littérateur al-Ḥusayn b. ʿAlī al-Wazīr al-Maghribī (370–418/981–1027) in his *Kitāb fī l-Siyāsa* offered specific advice in accordance with his royal recipient's characteristics and disposition.[31] In another example, Kaykāʾūs perceived the political instability likely to face his son and advised him to pursue the most beneficial conduct possible in a variety of possible circumstances, including numerous professions that, in lieu of kingship, Gīlānshāh might find himself obliged to adopt.

The Arabic *Naṣīḥat al-mulūk* provides an interesting example of an author's efforts to anticipate and control his audience's response to an apparently unsolicited offering of advice. The unknown author of this mirror devotes his preface to establishing the duty of the rationally intelligent (*ʿuqalāʾ*), whom God has urged to seek recompense, and the properly educated and virtuous (*fuḍalāʾ*), in whose natures the desire for (literally, "love of") an enduring memory has been instilled, to instruct and not to conceal the elucidation that they are equipped to impart. The author asserts further that kings are particularly appropriate recipients of counsels, for in their well-being or corruption lies the well-being or corruption of the subjects.[32] After this preface, the author devotes his first chapter (of ten) to "urging (kings) to accept counsels" (*al-ḥathth ʿalā qubūl al-naṣāʾiḥ*). He enumerates six reasons for rulers being the most appropriate of persons to accept advice and listen to admonition (*qubūl al-naṣīḥa wa-samāʿ al-mawʿiẓa*):

> Firstly: that thereby they may raise themselves above any similarity to the foolish and ignorant, the badly brought up and poorly behaved, the incapable of distinguishing between that which brings them benefit [*manāfiʿ*] and that which brings them harm [*maḍārr*] or of differentiating between that which wins them praise [*maḥāmid*] and that which earns them censure [*madhāmm*]; and above the level of the person whose passions [*shahawāt*] have taken possession of him and whose desire [*hawan*] overwhelms him to the point that it seizes his heart, and he finds himself

among those whose hearts do not comprehend, whose eyes do not see, and whose ears do not hear [cf. Q 7:179]. It is incumbent on those possessed of high aspirations and lofty souls that by means of their aspiration they should rise above and transcend this state.

Secondly: that they should become desirous of the results of counsels [*an yugharribū fī natā'ij al-naṣā'iḥ*], for advice constitutes guidance toward the paths of righteousness [*subul al-rashād*] and a conveyance toward the attainment of correctness [*sadād*]. These results will earn him praise in this life and in the life to come, in his beginnings (in this world) and in the hereafter.

Thirdly: they are the people occupied with the greatest number of affairs and encumbered with the greatest burdens, yet they are the least likely of people to conduct their affairs themselves or to witness conditions in the most distant of their provinces with their own eyes. Not every one whose assistance is sought offers help, and not every governor assumes responsibility for that which is entrusted to his control.

Fourthly: they are the least likely of people to associate with scholars in their assemblies or to attend the sessions of renunciants, preachers, and jurists [*annahum ab'ad al-nās min mujālasat al-'ulamā' wa-ḥuḍūr majālis al-zuhhād wa-l-wā'iẓīna wa-l-fuqahā'*], those by whom minds are sharpened and eyes made to see and by whom persons are made mindful of deceit; for kings are secluded from these individuals and prevented and preoccupied from conferring with them [*fa-hum 'anhu maḥjūbūna wa-'an mufāwaḍatihim mamnū'ūna mashghūlūna*].

Fifthly: They are the least likely of people to heed admonition, to follow reminders (regarding the consequences of their actions), or to accept advice when it runs counter to their desires, for in their case, or the generality of them, might, wealth, security, power, recklessness, enjoyment, pleasure, and delight have got the better of them. All of these are qualities that lead to the hardening of hearts and a refusal to learn the sciences, even though it is in them that their success [*najāḥ*] lies; and to an aversion against receiving admonition, even though it is in it that their well-being [*ṣalāḥ*] resides.

Sixthly: they among all the people have the smallest portion of sincere counselors and sympathetic well-wishers, for most of the people who surround them, namely, their viziers, assistants, and boon companions, speak to them only in accordance with their desires. They do not bring

> up anything contrary to the king's opinions out of fear for their lives and in order to protect their persons, in an effort to further their ambitions and maintain their ranks. This situation arises from the fact that most of those who attach themselves to the courts of kings, frequent their palaces, and exert themselves in service to them are seekers of this world and dealers in its vanities. They incline with it where it inclines, and they subside with it as it subsides. Yet true advice does not involve the pursuit of passion, nor is it in the nature of the truth to correspond to desires.[33]

The author's first and second reasons suggest a cautious posture: advice should enable the king to distinguish between the beneficial and the harmful, that which enhances his reputation and that which diminishes it. The notion that the counselor should guide the ruler toward such discrimination is apparent, as Hamori has indicated, in *Kalīla wa-Dimna* and the works of Ibn al-Muqaffaʿ;[34] it is also evident in the *Kitāb al-Tāj*.[35] This gentle approach corresponds perhaps to what Samer Ali has described as "engaged resistance."[36] The author's remaining reasons are expressed in increasingly frank and critical terms. Rulers are unlikely to attend the assemblies of scholars and men of piety. The author's use of the passive voice (*maḥjūbūna, mamnūʿūna, mashghūlūna*) implies that the ruler's exclusion from such sessions arises from the practice of royal seclusion (*ḥijāb*) and the efforts of self-interested parties to impede his access to sources of knowledge and wisdom. The author's sixth point involves explicit criticism of the king's officials and entourage. The proper relationship between men of religion and rulers was contentious, and it is likely that the author sought to persuade not only rulers of their need to solicit advice from disinterested persons but also men of religion of their duty to offer counsel to monarchs.

The first chapter of *Naṣīḥat al-mulūk* continues with Qurʾanic quotations, Prophetic hadith, and unattributed sayings, as well as pointed observations and warnings of the deceit of viziers and assistants. The author then remarks that many resolute kings, caliphs, and leaders have loved best those persons who were most honest with them regarding their faults.[37] After adducing a series of unattributed sayings, Prophetic hadith, and quotations from the Sasanian monarchs Ardashir and Shapur, Aristotle, and the caliph ʿUmar, the author turns to a set of *akhbār* concerning idealized Abbasid caliphs:

Many of the caliphs, when they sensed in themselves vanity, boorishness, pride, or cruelty, asked the scholars to counsel them and admonish them. Concerning Abū Jaʿfar al-Manṣūr (r. 13–58/754–75), we have heard that he said to Sufyān al-Thawrī (97–161/716–78),[38] "Admonish me—but be brief!" Sufyān said, "O Commander of the Faithful, imagine that your urine were obstructed and would not flow unless you ransomed your entire dominion for it." The caliph said, "I would sacrifice my entire dominion for it." Sufyān said, "And of what use is a dominion of such worth as this?"[39]

ʿAmr b. ʿUbayd (80–144/699–761)[40] entered the presence of Abū Jaʿfar (al-Manṣūr). The latter said to him, "Admonish me." He admonished him with a lengthy discourse, and opened it by saying, "Had this authority [*amr*] endured for those who preceded you, then it would not have reached you. God has given you this world in its entirety, so purchase your soul from Him (for the price of) a portion of the world. Know that He is your observer and your questioner as to the atom's weight's worth of good and bad and that the community of Muhammad will be your prosecutors on the Day of Resurrection. God will not be content with you except in that with which you would be content for yourself; you would never be content with regard to yourself unless you were treated with justice, and He will not be content with you unless you exercise justice toward the subjects. Behind your gate are fires kindled by injustice." This passage belongs to a long speech that he composed, and it was part of the extensive practice of censure [*ʿitāb*] that passed between them.[41]

Hārūn al-Rashīd (r. 170–93/786–809) said to Ibn al-Sammāk (d. 183/799),[42] "Admonish me." He replied, "Know that that you are not the first caliph to die." The caliph said, "Tell me more." Ibn al-Sammāk said, "Had those who came before you not died, then that which you now enjoy would not have passed to you." He said, "Tell me more." The renunciant then recited in verse,

> Miserable wretch, do you aspire to live forever?
> Are you troubled lest the hand of fate should seize you?
> By God, fate has a messenger who, once
> He reaches you, will not release you

> It is as if the earth were already piling up over you
> And the mourners were dividing up your wealth
> Depart, then, from the world in salutary and sound condition
> And shrug off the earthly things that now compel you
> For you will leave nothing behind among the people
> And will be accompanied by nothing but your deeds.[43]

> Such were the early kings. Alexander frequently asked the philosophers to supply him on his journeys with (wisdom) to which he could have recourse in his sovereignty, and he constantly wrote to his teacher Aristotle, who replied to him with admonitions and conveyed counsels to him. We shall mention some of his admonitions to him and counsels for him at their proper places in our book. . . .[44]

> Were we to pursue this subject among the accounts of the kings and leaders [*akhbār al-mulūk wa-l-a'imma*], the book would grow long. We have selected only examples that illustrate our purpose in this book of ours, namely, to manifest sincere advice and truth in admonition. There is no surety that it will not contain some elements that will prove contrary to the opinion of certain possessors of kingdoms and provinces, who incline toward the passions and amuse themselves with pleasures; their ears will reject our advice, and their hearts will recoil from it. But it is not permissible for the person who wishes for advice to measure it against his desire; rather, it is necessary that he measure both the advice and his desire against that which is right and that which rational intelligence requires. Where these two things are in conformity with the advice, he should accept it; and where they conflict with it, he should oppose it. Sometimes that which weighs heavily on one's nature and is odious to the heart is more praiseworthy in terms of the ultimate outcome, more salutary in terms of the final end, more abundant in the reward that it brings, and better in terms of the enduring remembrance that it creates. God, great is His mention, said, "It may be that you hate a thing in which God has placed much good" (Q 4:19), and He said, "It may be that you hate a thing that is good for you, and it may be that you love a thing that is bad for you" (Q 2:216).[45]

These passages display this author's efforts to establish his grounds for offering advice and to ensure a positive reception for his work. He supports his appeal with quotations from numerous authorities of varied provenances and associations: the sacred sources of the Qur'an and Prophetic example, revered figures of the early Islamic era, Sasanian kings, Aristotle and Alexander, and *akhbār* involving Abbasid caliphs and ascetics (*zuhhād*). The varied and eclectic character of the author's examples support his assertion of the universality and timeless relevance of his advice, applied in this instance in a specific context. By devoting his preface to the duty of men of intellect and virtue to offer their advice to rulers and his first chapter to the merit of rulers' heeding such advice, the author seeks to predispose his audience to attend to the counsel and criticism that follow. His selection of interlocutors highlights the role of the ascetic, who offers exhortation only at the request of the caliph. As El-Hibri and Cooperson have demonstrated, the forms, wording, and meanings of these narratives vary from one source to another. In the *Naṣīḥat al-mulūk*, the narratives appear as abbreviated, allusive indicators of royal magnanimity in the face of criticism; by their invocation, the author holds up models of praiseworthy behavior and by implication limits the scope of the recipient's response to his work. Pointedly adducing examples that demonstrate inclusivity, the author offers a sequence of passages that follow one another in an associative pattern linked by the theme of *memento mori*. This theme and its many articulations in prose and verse offered an invitation to the text's audience, created a climate in which the royal recipient was constrained to exercise forbearance, and afforded an opportunity for the public display of pious humility.

It was not only the language of the text but also the circumstances of its presentation that affected its reception. As has already been established, the ruler's *majlis* provided a suitable environment for the delivery of edifying poetry and conversation. Poetry and prose that, like the examples cited by Pseudo-Māwardī, emphasized the transience of the ruler's power and the mortality of kings and commoners alike were particularly suited for contemplative occasions, such as Fridays, the month of Ramadan, and the hajj. The greater the emphasis in advisory materials on personal morality, responsibility, and the fleeting nature of life, the more likely they were to have accompanied times set aside for personal and religious reflection, prayer, and meditation, including certain periods of the day.[46] The division of the king's time according to annual, weekly, and daily cycles provided a protective framework for the apparent inversion of relations between superior and inferior, patron and dependent, enacted in the delivery of advice. The establishment of conventions to govern interactions between the king and those who were in his presence preserved the royal dignity, on the one hand, and the personal safety of those who were admitted to his presence, on the other. Like other exemplary *akhbār*, accounts of the caliphs' divisions of their daily time fuse historical elements with the dictates of evolving topoi and provided authors of mirrors with models to support their portrayals of the daily routines appropriate to royal office.[47]

The evidence for the hearing of advisory texts of the early period is sparse, but parts of the Arabic *Naṣīḥat al-mulūk* suggest a context in occasions designated for *wa'ẓ* and *tadhkīr*. The author noted the exclusion of rulers from the gatherings of individuals devoted to moral edification and sought to introduce the theme into the ruler's *majlis*. Some two centuries later, the preacher Ibn al-Jawzī (d. 597/1200), who addressed caliphs as well as urban communities, described sessions dedicated to exhortation in which the exercise of political authority occupied a central position. In his *al-Miṣbāḥ al-muḍī' fī khilāfat al-Mustaḍī'*, Ibn al-Jawzī, like Pseudo-Māwardī, describes the ruler (*al-sulṭān*) as the most needy of persons for reminding (*al-tadhkīr*), "because the kingdom affords might, power, arrogance, and merriment, and that occasions the self's delight in the things that it seeks and renews a state that resembles drunkenness."[48] He pronounces the hearing of exhortations and counsels (*samā' al-mawā'iẓ wa-l-naṣā'iḥ*) a component of thankfulness to God for His bounties, noting that elevation of rank (*rif'at al-qadr*) and abundance of knowledge (*kathrat al-'ilm*) do not remove the need for the repetition of remembrance, as the examples of the Prophet, the caliph 'Umar, and numerous others attest. Furthermore, he who hears exhortation and does not act on it incurs a proof against himself (*man sami'a maw'iẓa fa-lam ya'mal bihā kānat 'alayhi ḥujja*).[49] As Ella Almagor has noted, Ibn al-Jawzī's attention to the *majlis al-tadhkīr* and his particular interest in themes concerning the relationship between piety and political power characterize several parts of his oeuvre.[50]

Such exhortative counsel, which affirmed ethical principles and reminded ruler and subjects alike of their moral responsibilities to God and to each other, enjoyed a wide audience and passed readily between oral and written media. In an example of the interplay of oral and written materials, the authors of the Arabic *Naṣiḥat al-mulūk*, the Persian *Naṣīḥat al-mulūk*, and the Persian *Siyar al-mulūk* relate versions of the story of a king who was hard of hearing and devised the stratagem of having his petitioners dress in red, so that he could identify them and invite them to voice their grievances in a quiet place. Erika Glassen has documented the use of this story in a sermon (*khuṭba*) delivered in Baghdad shortly before Niẓām al-Mulk related it in his *Siyar al-mulūk*.[51] The example illustrates the diffusion of advisory literature beyond the circles of the court into the lives of urban communities, as well as the living quality of the material, transformed in transmission and performance.

Advisory texts address the requirements of courtly etiquette for persons in the royal presence. For example, the *Kitāb al-Tāj* stipulates that customarily kings should not be exposed to intercourse with common persons. In the event that such a person was required to impart certain information in the king's presence, however, the encounter required proper management:

> If the king needs to communicate orally [*mushāfahatan*] with an undistinguished [*khāmil*] or base [*waḍīʿ*] person and is obliged to do so, either for purposes of a counsel [*naṣīḥa*] that should be conveyed to him in secret or for a matter about which he has enquired from him, it is the king's right that no one who comes close to him should be left alone unless he has been investigated first; then two persons should take him under the arm, one on his right and the other on his left. When the visitor has disclosed the information that he had to impart and the king has received it, then it is part of his rightful claim that he should be treated well, receive compensation, and have his petition—if he has one—addressed, so that persons who have counsel to bring to the king's attention will be encouraged to approach him with their advice [*li-yuraghghaba dhawū l-naṣā'iḥ fī rafʿihā ilā mulūkihim*].[52]

The passage indicates that in cases of necessity, even obscure persons might enter the king's presence and speak in confidence. But it was essential that the social distance between the king and his interlocutor remain clearly marked.

Authors of mirrors, in another topos, recount numerous stories in which rulers, sometimes in disguise, encounter persons of low status and are subjected to vociferous complaints against their injustice. Pseudo-Māwardī's previously mentioned examples involving al-Manṣūr and Hārūn belong to the large set of narratives in which an ascetic challenges the caliph.[53] The same author adduces a lengthier *khabar* in which an incognito al-Manṣūr, at large during the night, hears the complaints of an anonymous stranger in a mosque.[54] These *akhbār* invariably portray the subject's complaints as the stimulus for positive transformation on the part of the patient and magnanimous ruler. In the same topos, Niẓām al-Mulk narrates cases in which the least of the king's subjects offers advice or delivers a robust complaint directly to the king's person: the elderly woman, the solitary dervish, the aggrieved peasant—persons on the margins of society, persons with little or nothing left to lose but who still place confidence in the justice of the ruler. The stories emphasize the contrast between the vulnerability of the aggrieved, invariably single figures, and the vast power and wealth of the king. In some narratives, the protagonist is unaware of the king's identity, but in several cases, he or she is perfectly aware of the royal status of the addressee.[55] In every case, the narratives in the *Siyar al-mulūk* depict the ruler's magnanimous response; moved by the subject's plight, filled with anxiety regarding the consequences in the next life of his failure to prevent the injustice, and immediately attentive to rectifying the wrong and compensating the aggrieved party, the ruler in these stories demonstrates the proper reception of advice, however inconvenient or disruptive its delivery. The differential in power and the risk of displeasure and punishment are acknowledged everywhere, and in such acknowledgment lies a potential allaying of the danger; kings insist on hearing the truth from persons who agree to speak only on condition that the ruler assure them of their lives and property.[56]

These strategies, elements of the larger advisory culture, appear to have evoked positive responses in some recipients. Hārūn al-Rashīd is reported to have emulated the conduct of al-Manṣūr (*kāna yaqtafī āthār al-Manṣūr*), with the exception of al-Manṣūr's notorious reluctance to spend money.[57] ʿAbdallāh b. Ṭāhir is reported to have strived to follow his father's prescriptions in his conduct and his actions.[58] The historian Bayhaqī (385–470/995–1077) noted that Sultan Maḥmūd

(r. 388–421/998–1030), when hunting, consciously imitated the Sasanian monarch Bahrām-i Gūr.[59] These reports reinforced the positive expectation that kings should emulate and seek to perpetuate the illustrious examples of their predecessors.

No less than panaegyric poetry, mirrors for princes required the maintenance of a delicate equilibrium among the personae involved in the enactment of kingship. Accordingly, just as the performance of praise unfolded according to established rules of protocol, which, when breached, opened opportunities for the unpredictable, the performance of advice similarly took place in prescribed temporal and spatial settings and subject to controlled forms. Various conditions, times, and occasions mitigated the disturbance of hierarchy and enabled the figure in power to submit to advice without losing dignity.

Yet, in another divergence from prescribed protocol, authors of mirrors not infrequently make use of the second-person-imperative form in their writings. According to the *Kitāb al-Tāj* and the *Siyar al-mulūk*, interlocutors should not use the imperative form in speaking to the king.[60] For the protection of both parties, the gulf between ruler and subject had to be maintained and the manner and enactment of contact strictly regulated.[61] Despite these prescriptions, authors of advisory texts not infrequently adopted a directly personal mode of address and readily employed the second-person singular. The use of direct address and imperative forms was especially characteristic of the *waṣiyya*.[62]

The ruler's receptivity to advice, perhaps to a greater extent than other elements of royal ceremonial, held the potential to demonstrate the ruler's legitimacy. It indicated to an audience of the king's *khāṣṣa* and, occasionally, the *'āmma* his adherence to and upholding of a set of values rooted in religious and cultural authorities: the sacred sources of the Qur'an and the Prophetic example, the actions and sayings of venerated figures from the early Islamic period, the conduct and utterances of exemplary kings and sages from earlier communities, the pronouncements of philosophers and purveyors of wisdom, the apt formulations of poets and men of letters. The importance of the monarch's public affirmation of these values and its beneficial effects on his reputation are evident in the reports of rulers' conscious emulation of their praiseworthy predecessors. It is equally apparent in the material artifacts that demonstrate in a visual medium the king's centrality in a diffuse advisory culture;

among these objects, mirrors for princes, presented at the court and often preserved in royal libraries, provided direct testimony to a ruler's legitimacy and moral stature.

NOTES

I am deeply grateful to the Institute for Advanced Study in Princeton, New Jersey, where during my term as Willis F. Doney Member at the School of Historical Studies, I was able to conduct the research involved in the preparation of this chapter.

1. Some uncertainty surrounds the authorship of each of these texts, which for purposes of the current discussion are taken as the works of al-Taghlibī (or al-Thaʿlabī), Pseudo-Māwardī, and the vizier Niẓām al-Mulk, respectively. See Schoeler, "Verfasser und Titel"; Aḥmad, *Naṣīḥat al-mulūk al-mansūb ilā Abī l-Ḥasan al-Māwardī*; Marlow, "Samanid Work"; Khismatulin, "To Forge a Book."
2. Al-Ṭabarī, *Ta'rīkh*, 8:71; H. Kennedy, *Al-Manṣūr and al-Mahdī*, 106; Ibn al-Athīr, *al-Kāmil fī l-ta'rīkh*, 6:18–21, 27–28.
3. El-Hibri, *Reinterpreting Islamic Historiography*, esp. 2, 11–16; Cooperson, *Classical Arabic Biography*, esp. 1–23. On uses of the *khabar*, see also Leder, "Literary Use of the *Khabar*."
4. E.g., al-Ṭurṭūshī, *Sirāj al-mulūk*, 1:17–116.
5. Cooperson, *Classical Arabic Biography*, 40–64; the phrase is Cooperson's (45).
6. The caliph al-Manṣūr is again the subject of several examples; see al-Ṭabarī, *Ta'rīkh*, 8:89–90; al-Ṭurṭūshī, *Sirāj al-mulūk*, 1:127–28; El-Hibri, *Reinterpreting Islamic Historiography*, 27.
7. For an example involving Hārūn al-Rashīd, see al-Ṭabarī, *Ta'rīkh*, 8:358–59; Bosworth, *ʿAbbāsid Caliphate in Equilibrium*, 324–25.
8. Al-Ṭabarī, *Ta'rīkh*, 8:591. On the limits of the appearances of intimacy in royal gatherings, see Brookshaw, "Palaces, Pavilions and Pleasure-Gardens," 200.
9. For these matters, the king should consult his ministers, nobles of the state, and experienced elders; see Niẓām al-Mulk, *Siyar al-mulūk*, 120–22; Darke, *Book of Government*, 90, cf. 91–92.
10. Meisami, *Medieval Persian Court Poetry*; Gruendler, *Medieval Arabic Praise Poetry*.
11. Meisami, *Medieval Persian Court Poetry*, 11, 44, cf. 46.
12. Ibn Rashīq al-Qayrawānī, *al-ʿUmda*, 1:99–103, esp. 101. The tenth-century specialist Ibn Wahb al-Kātib had subdivided the category of gnomic poetry (*ḥikma*) into proverbs (*amthāl*), exhortations to austerity (*tazhīd*), and admonitions (*mawāʿiẓ*). Ibn Wahb al-Kātib, *al-Burhān fī wujūh al-bayān*, 170–71. See Schoeler, "Die Einteilung der Dichtung," 9–55, 16–21, 24–55.
13. Jacobi, "Al-ʿAbbās b. al-Aḥnaf."
14. Schoeler, "Abū Nuwās"; P. Kennedy, *Wine Song*, esp. 194–240.
15. P. Kennedy, "Abū al-ʿAtāhiya." According to al-Masʿūdī, the poet affected an ascetic manner and dressed in wool (*mutanassikan lābisan lil-ṣūf*); he accompanied

Hārūn on some of his pilgrimages (*Murūj al-dhahab*, 3:450). Cf. al-Iṣfahānī, *Kitāb al-Aghānī* (2002/1422), 4:1–112.

16. Abū l-ʿAtāhiya's *zuhdiyyāt* cover 443 pages in the collection *Abū l-ʿAtāhiya*. See further Sperl, *Mannerism in Arabic Poetry*, 71–96. On the *zuhdiyya*, see Hamori, "Ascetic Poetry"; Schoeler, "Bashshār b. Burd, Abū 'l-ʿAtāhiyah and Abū Nuwās"; P. Kennedy, "Zuhdiyya"; P. Kennedy, *Wine Song*, 86–148.

17. Al-Ṭabarī, *Ta'rīkh*, 8: 347; 347–59; Bosworth, *ʿAbbāsid Caliphate in Equilibrium*, 306, 305–25; Ibn al-Athīr, *al-Kāmil fī l-ta'rīkh*, 6:217–21. Abū l-Faraj al-Iṣfahānī describes Hārūn as exceptionally responsive to exhortation: *wa-kāna al-Rashīd min aghzar al-nās dumūʿan fī waqt al-mawʿiẓa* (*Kitāb al-Aghānī* [2002/1422], 4:104). See also Rosenthal, *Ibn Khaldûn*, 1:33; El-Hibri, *Reinterpreting Islamic Historiography*, 25–31.

18. Al-Masʿūdī, *Murūj al-dhahab wa-maʿādin al-jawhar*, 3:366–67.

19. For instance, Pacha, *Kitāb al-Tāj fī akhlāq al-mulūk*, 71–72 (cf. Schoeler, "Verfasser und Titel," 217–25); cf. Meisami, *Medieval Persian Court Poetry*, 7–8.

20. Aḥmad, *Naṣīḥat al-mulūk*, 71. The name of the foodstuff should perhaps be read *ṭīn*, "clay" or "chalk," in consistency with the Persian *gil* that appears in the *Akhlāq-i Nāṣirī* (see the following note). On Thumāma, see van Ess, "Thumāma b. Ashras." Cooperson recounts another of the several anecdotes involving Thumāma (*Classical Arabic Biography*, 47).

21. Naṣīr al-Dīn Ṭūsī, *Akhlāq-i Nāṣirī*, 301; the text reads "one of the *nudamā*" (cf. ibid., 398); Wickens, *Nasirean Ethics by Naṣīr ad-Dīn Ṭūsī*, 227–28.

22. Sadan, "Division of the Day," 261 and n19.

23. Hamori, "Shameful and Injurious."

24. Cf. Hamori, "Prudence, Virtue, and Self-Respect."

25. Meisami, *Medieval Persian Court Poetry*, 14.

26. Van Gelder, "Ṣāliḥ ibn ʿAbd al-Quddūs."

27. Cf. P. Kennedy, "Abū al-ʿAtāhiya," 1:27; Zakeri, "Ṣāliḥ b. ʿAbd al-Ḳuddūs."

28. Ahmad, *Naṣīḥat al-mulūk*, 50–51.

29. Cf. Meisami, *Medieval Persian Court Poetry*, 14.

30. See Marlow, "Way of Viziers." The same conceit appears in Erasmus (c. 1469–1536); see *Education of a Christian Prince*.

31. Al-Wazīr Abū l-Qāsim al-Ḥusayn b. ʿAlī al-Maghribī, *Kitāb fī l-Siyāsa*; Leder, "Aspekte arabischer und persischer Fürstenspiegel."

32. Aḥmad, *Naṣīḥat al-mulūk*, 43–46.

33. Aḥmad, *Naṣīḥat al-mulūk*, 49–51.

34. Hamori, "Shameful and Injurious," 198–200.

35. Pacha, *Kitāb al-Tāj*, 71.

36. Ali, *Arabic Literary Salons*, 156.

37. Aḥmad, *Naṣīḥat al-mulūk*, 53.

38. Raddatz, "Sufyān al-Thawrī."

39. Pseudo-Māwardī's version of this *khabar* omits a preceding exchange, concerning a drink of water, between the caliph and the ascetic. In most versions, the

protagonists are the caliph Hārūn al-Rashīd and the ascetic Ibn al-Sammāk (al-Ṭabarī, *Ta'rīkh al-Ṭabarī*, 8:357–58; Bosworth, *'Abbāsid Caliphate in Equilibrium*, 323; Ibn al-Athīr, *al-Kāmil fī l-ta'rīkh*, 6:219–20). In the version of al-Ṭurṭūshī, Hārūn is about to drink some water. Ibn al-Sammāk asks what, if the water were withheld from him, he would give to receive it, and the caliph responds that he would give up his kingdom for it. Ibn al-Sammāk then asks whether, if the water were prevented from leaving his body, the king would ransom it with his kingdom, and the caliph answers that he would. The ascetic responded, "There is no good in a dominion that is not even equal (in value) to a drink or a urination" (al-Ṭurṭūshī, *Sirāj al-mulūk*, 1:27–28). See further El-Hibri, *Reinterpreting Islamic Historiography*, 26–27, 92. The anecdote is somewhat similar to one recounted in the *Siyar al-mulūk* (Niẓām al-Mulk, *Siyar al-mulūk*, 64; Darke, *Book of Government*, 48).

40. van Ess, "'Amr b. 'Obayd." Many authors record how al-Manṣūr solicited admonition from 'Amr b. 'Ubayd, who was well known for his closeness to al-Ḥasan al-Baṣrī (d. 110/729), both before and after his accession. See al-Mas'ūdī, *Murūj al-dhahab*, 3:302–3.
41. Aḥmad, *Naṣīḥat al-mulūk*, 56–57. For variants, see Ibrāhīm b. 'Alī al-Ḥuṣrī, *Zahr al-ādāb wa-thamar al-albāb* (1953), 1:102–3; El-Hibri, *Reinterpreting Islamic Historiography*, 41n59.
42. The Kufan traditionist and frequent preacher (*wā'iẓ*) at Hārūn's court appears in many such anecdotes with the caliph; see al-Ṭabarī, *Ta'rīkh al-Ṭabarī*, 8:357; Bosworth, *'Abbāsid Caliphate in Equilibrium*, 322; al-Baghdādī, *Ta'rīkh Baghdād*, 5:368–73; al-Ṭurṭūshī, *Sirāj al-mulūk*, 1:120.
43. Aḥmad, *Naṣīḥat al-mulūk*, 58. The poem, by Abū l-'Atāhiya (see *Abū l-'Atāhiya*, 273, no. 290), appears in various versions; the version recorded in al-Rāghib al-Iṣfahānī, *Muḥāḍarāt al-udabā' wa-muḥāwarāt al-shu'arā' wa-l-bulaghā'*, 3:242, is similar to the text produced in the *Naṣīḥat al-mulūk*. The translation follows the version that appears in *Naṣīḥat al-mulūk*.
44. Aḥmad, *Naṣīḥat al-mulūk*, 58.
45. Ibid., 59–60.
46. For example, Pacha, *Kitāb al-Tāj*, 151.
47. See Sadan, "Division of the Day."
48. Ibn al-Jawzī, *al-Miṣbāḥ al-muḍī' fī khilāfat al-Mustaḍī'*, 160.
49. Ibid., 180, 197.
50. Almagor, "Pious Man and the Ruler," 179–92, 180–81.
51. Aḥmad, *Naṣīḥat al-mulūk*, 397–99; Niẓām al-Mulk, *Siyar al-mulūk*, 19; Darke, *Book of Government*, 14; Ghazālī, *Naṣīḥat al-mulūk*, 31–32 (cf. 310–11); Bagley, *Ghazālī's Book of Counsel for Kings*, 21. See also Glassen, *Der mittlere Weg*, 91–92.
52. Pacha, *Kitāb al-Tāj*, 53.
53. The ascetic sometimes takes the place of the commoner in such accounts; see Cooperson, *Classical Arabic Biography*, 44–45.
54. Aḥmad, *Naṣīḥat al-mulūk*, 397–400.

55. See, for example, Niẓām al-Mulk, *Siyar al-mulūk*, 86–87; Darke, *Book of Government*, 65.
56. Niẓām al-Mulk, *Siyar al-mulūk*, 226–27; Darke, *Book of Government*, 167–68.
57. Al-Ṭabarī, *Ta'rīkh al-Ṭabarī*, 8:347; Bosworth, *'Abbāsid Caliphate in Equilibrium*, 305–6; Ibn al-Athīr, *al-Kāmil fī l-ta'rīkh*, 6:217.
58. Gruendler, *Medieval Arabic Praise Poetry*, 263–64.
59. Omidsalar, "Storytellers in Classical Persian Texts."
60. Pacha, *Kitāb al-Tāj*, 112–13; Niẓām al-Mulk, *Siyar al-mulūk*, 121; Darke, *Book of Government*, 90. Ibn Qutayba likewise insists on the use of appropriate language with peers and superiors; in the case of the latter, language that "implies an imperative, or command," should not be employed (Günther, "Praise to the Book!," 136).
61. See Pacha, *Kitāb al-Tāj*, 83.
62. Harmsen, *Die Wasiya als literarisches Genre*, 50–58.

5

Conversation as Performance

Adab al-Muḥādatha at the Abbasid Court

NADIA MARIA EL CHEIKH

Political power needs not only an executive apparatus to endure. It also needs to be conveyed through visual symbolic representations and ceremonial arrangements. Court cultures express their inner constitution through the creation of "spatial structures, the semiotics of dress and body postures, as well as the semantics of formulaic speech."[1] Scholars analyzing the European medieval courts have proposed that "to view the court as a stage is to emphasize the essentially performative quality of court life."[2] Norbert Elias, in his work on early modern Europe, illustrated how political power can be projected through the "performance" of authority, specifically, that the court existed as a theater for the performance of power.[3] Historians of the early-modern court, in general, have tended to think about the court in terms of theater: spaces prepared like theater sets, bodies moving in choreographed motions, scripted speech and gesture, and formal structures including the arrangement of spectators.[4] John Adamson states, in the same vein, that the early-modern court spoke primarily in the language of gesture as "the courtier lived a 'semiotic existence,' dealing daily with coded and symbolic meanings " including rules governing courtly politesse, mostly concerned with the deportment of the individual courtier.[5]

The court of the Abbasid caliphs shared some of these theatrical and performative qualities. Forms of visual and aural display, including colors of dress, a particular etiquette, and precise spatial and temporal disposition of the bodies, were deployed in the enunciation of royal power. They served to dramatize the locus of power and to amplify absolutism.[6] Social intercourse at the caliphal court presupposed certain codes of phrases, gestures, and manners. In the words of Aziz al-Azmeh, "it is as if the entire art of ruling, and of playing court, consists of prophylactic speech, observation and behavior in a situation where individuals find themselves entrapped by a precariousness stemming from a power whose arbitrariness . . . is a manifestation of its boundlessness."[7] More particularly, etiquette at the Abbasid court served two primary purposes: for the majority, it provided a safe distance from the throne; for a select few, "it modulated an intimate rapport with the king." Visitors allowed into the proximity of the ruler had to display gratitude in the form of deference, the more so the closer they got. Etiquette, in this context, was not a constraint on intimacy but rather a means of managing it.[8]

This chapter discusses the subject of performance at the Abbasid court by looking at *adab al-muḥādatha* (etiquette of conversation) in texts belonging to the genre of mirrors for princes. These are treatises on monarchical government with the aim of advising kings and rulers about the most appropriate comportment to follow on both the ethical and practical levels. A subgenre on the subject of serving the ruler (*khidmat al-mulūk*) was destined not for the sovereign but for those who serve him, in other words, for the human grouping that surrounded the ruler through acquiring a position or political or religious employment and indirectly through attending his *majlis*.[9] Counsel, in such instances, relates to how to serve the ruler well.[10] The material for this chapter relies on this subgenre and addresses the art of conversation associated primarily with the boon companion.

Majlis and Boon Companions

Dominic Brookshaw states that the term *majlis* denotes both an assembly hosted by a caliph or another high official and the audience hall where such a session was held.[11] The *majlis* was a versatile social and cultural institution that could house activities ranging from serious religious and intellectual debate to lightweight poetic recitation or composition, singing, wine drinking, and a general enjoyment of leisure in the company of witty and elegant people.[12] G. E. Von Grunebaum notes that what ensured success in such social gatherings was primarily esprit: "An epigrammatic turn of mind would . . . go far in making a visitor to the *majlis* an effective contributor."[13]

Texts that discuss these activities draw a distinction between the intimate world of the *majlis al-uns* and displays such as those organized for the benefit of ambassadors. Not very much is known about the actual procedures of a private audience at court. Cynthia Robinson has described the *majlis al-uns*—as it obtained in al-Andalus in the fifth/eleventh century—as "a gathering of a small number of carefully chosen courtiers possessing the physical and intellectual refinements requisite for such an honor in the presence of the host, the caliph."[14] This description seems to fit quite well the informal *majlis* in the Abbasid context. These were occasions when few participants were involved and when equality in the comportment and treatment of all present was observed within an atmosphere of leisure and relaxation.

Nadīm (pl. *nudamā'*) is the term most consistently used to refer to those who were present at an intimate *majlis*. Drinking companions, friends, or confidants, the *nudama'* were individuals of learning, wit, and graceful manners who were sought for their company. The *Nudama'* as boon companions were selected for their talents to befriend the caliph, to keep him company in his times of solitude, and to partake with him in hunting parties, chess games, and drinking and literary sessions.[15] The *nadīm*'s task was to maintain the good humor of the ruler. Anecdotes and fables provided him with an appropriate repertoire with which to divert and amuse his audience. The *nadīm* was also expected to function as a source of counsel and moral guidance so long as his words were couched in elegant, courtly terms.[16] The position of the *nadīm* eventually became a quasi-official post, the most important qualification of which was wit, with the ability to listen and drink and dress in ways that would please the caliph.[17]

The institution of boon companionship was justified on the premise that rulers should have suitable companions with whom they could enjoy freedom and intimacy in their times of leisure.[18] The *Siyāsatnāma* of the Seljuk chief minister Niẓām al-Mulk (408/1018–485/1092), written in Persian in 484/1091, states that a king needs boon companions "with whom he can enjoy complete freedom and intimacy." In addition to providing the king with company in a familiar and relaxing atmosphere, boon companions could also function as his bodyguards, listen to the king's serious and frivolous chatter, and report to him about all kinds of matters.[19] This intimate court was not an extension of the circle of servants. The criteria for recruitment emanated directly from the personal choice of the caliphs. The boon companions constituted, thus, an important group at the court of the ruler and were part of a well-organized institution with a set of rigorous requirements and protocol. Its very existence allowed the meeting of two axes of organization and sociability, a horizontal egalitarian axis, that of fraternity; and, a vertical hierarchical axis, that of "distinction."

One source mentions the qualities expected of an Abbasid court poet for the benefit of such gatherings, stating that he had to be "pleasant-looking, a good-converser, jester, graced with permanent good luck, blessed with moderate piety, neither ascetic nor libertine, and above all eager to serve."[20] Most importantly, a *nadīm* was expected to converse about all sorts of subjects: he would be well versed in music, literature, poetry, prosody, grammar, history, Qur'ān, prophetic traditions, horse breeding, backgammon, chess, buffoonery, and magic. The *nadīm* would have been a companion like the author of the famous *Kitāb al-Aghānī*, Abū al-Faraj al-Iṣfahānī, who had achieved an impressive array of knowledge:

> [He had] committed to memory a quantity of poetry songs, anecdotes, historical reports, authenticated *ḥadīths* and genealogies. . . . Besides that he was knowledgeable in lexicography, grammar, fantastic stories, life histories, and accounts of conquests and he was widely versed in the subjects courtiers are required to be conversant with such as birds and animals of the hunt, veterinary science, medicine, astrology and drinks.[21]

Moreover, boon companions had to possess the qualities of the *ẓarīf*—that is, "gentlemen of good behavior (*adab*), of virtue (*murū'a*) and refined and elegant manners (*ẓarf*)."[22] The Arabic root *ẓ-r-f* means "to be charming, chic, nice, elegant, neat" or "to be witty and full of *esprit*." A *ẓarīf*, according to Cynthia Robinson, is a refined, an elegant, but above all, an eloquent person.[23] Boon companions had to be agreeable conversationalists with a lively mind and quick at repartee. The *majlis* was an arena for the display of skill: association with it certified one's social and verbal abilities.[24] A protocol was developed for the conduct of the *majlis*, notably, guidelines detailing rules of conversation that should obtain between the ruler and those who attended the *majlis*.

Adab al-muḥādatha

Material for the rules of conversation at court are included in *Akhlāq al-mulūk* by Muḥammad b. al-Ḥārith al-Thaʿlabī (d. 250/864) (formerly attributed to al-Jāḥiẓ), a work of advice literature that entered Arabic literary culture through a translation from Pahlavi in the third/ninth century and enjoyed long popularity. It includes topics such as the conduct of rulers, organization of the court, and the interaction between rulers and their *nudamāʾ*.[25] It broaches specific subjects such as the etiquette of drinking, the use of the curtain, the ways to address the ruler, how to behave when the ruler stands up and when he speaks, and rules to follow when the ruler falls asleep. Through its style, its classifications, and its anecdotes, it came to constitute an authority for later similar texts.[26]

The information on *adab al-muḥādatha* in *Akhlāq al-mulūk* can be classified under two main categories: comportment when the ruler is speaking and comportment when the one in attendance is speaking. Behavior, in both speech and body language, is carefully regulated: the person who attends the *majlis* of the king should be most careful in "his words, his gestures, his immobility, the language he chooses and his *adab*, even his breathing."[27] The boon companion ought not address the king before the king himself starts.[28] Once the ruler starts speaking, a series of injunctions are listed, notably concentrating both attention and thinking in the direction of the king. A statement by the Umayyad caliph Muʿāwiya is inserted in affirmation of this behavior: "Caliph Muʿāwiya stated that the king can be dominated by . . . the attention given to his conversation."[29] In addition to displaying clear attention, the listeners have to react in a prescribed way: "If someone knows the subject that the king is conversing about, he should listen to it as if he has never before heard of it. . . . He should express his joy for receiving from the king useful information. This attitude presents two advantages: on the one hand, he shows his good education [*ḥusn adabih*], and on the other hand, he fulfills his duty toward the king by being a good listener."[30] Emphasis on being a good listener is highlighted by alluding to a conversation that supposedly took place between Saʿīd b. Salm and the Abbasid caliph al-Maʾmūn. Saʿīd b. Salm thanked God for the favor that the caliph was showing him by conversing with him, and the caliph replied, "The Prince of the faithful finds in you a clarity of exposition when you talk, and a level of comprehension when you listen, that he has never encountered before."[31] The king's companions should neither interrupt nor contradict him as their sole aim ought to be to listen well and accord him their full attention. It is only once the king has finished and has looked at one of them that they should understand this to be an authorization on his part to speak on the same subject.[32]

When it is the turn of those who are attendance to speak, they have to be vigilant about both the manner and content of their speech. Indeed, the art of comportment, which is carefully elaborated, manifests itself, particularly, in conversation. Those in attendance should not speak loudly, for it is respectful and deferential to lower one's voice in the presence of the king. In support of this constraint, *Akhlāq al-mulūk* cites the Qur'ānic verse (49:2) that prescribed such behavior to the Companions of the Prophet: "Raise not your voice above the Prophet's voice, and be not loud in your speech to him, as you are loud to one another, lest your works fail while you are not aware."[33]

The form and style of the conversation are, moreover, regulated: the one who converses with the king should be cautious about his choice of words. He should not say, for example, "listen to me," "understand me well," "Oh you," "don't you see." Usage of such expressions "reveals the inability of the one who uses them and stuffing in his language, a lack of ease in the elocution, a proof of clumsiness in speech and mediocrity."[34] The language should be easy, the discourse agreeable and well connected, and the vulgarities rare.[35]

The famous *adab* anthology by Ibn 'Abd Rabbih, *Al-'Iqd al-Farīd*, provides some clarification as to what is meant in the preceding passage. It defines eloquence as "the choice of words and making others understand well" or "fewness of words and conciseness of right ideas." The eloquent man is thus described as someone "whose words are few and who hits decisive ideas and meanings"[36] and elsewhere as he "who can transmit his need to you and make you understand his meaning without repeating, without having a speech defect, and without seeking help." The last injunction, namely, "seeking help," is explained in the following way: "If the man interrupts his speech by saying, 'Listen to me,' or Understand me,' or if he rubs his beard or twiddles his fingers or unnecessarily keeps turning around or pretending to clear his throat without having a cough or if he becomes breathless in his speech."[37]

These directives place constraints on the linguistic form and encourage speaking with a certain naturalness and ease, with a sort of a studied nonchalance. One can only imagine the tension that underlay this seemingly effortless performance.

In addition to form and style, the content needs to be controlled: the speaker should not move on to another subject, no matter how similar or connected to the topic just broached, before making sure that the king is interested in it.[38] Repetition is, moreover, condemned: "The same account should not be repeated twice to the king." *Akhlāq al-mulūk* cites, in support of this regulation, a statement by Rawḥ b. Zinbāʿa, who is said to have stayed with the Umayyad caliph ʿAbd al-Malik for seventeen years without ever once repeating an account to him. Al-Shaʿbī is also made to say, "I have never related twice the same prophetic tradition to the same person."[39] The boon companion was, thus, expected to judiciously put to use gracious wit, making sure not to belabor any point for fear of causing boredom.

Adab al-muḥādatha also includes instructions on body language. Laughter is, for instance, prohibited when the king is relating his account because it is "insolent to laugh in his presence."[40] And when those who are familiar with the king are laughing with him, they should stop laughing when a visitor steps in; instead, they should lower their eyes, keep silent, and stay still.[41] The general directives pertaining to behavior and physical performance state, "The one who is conversing with the king should not speak quickly but should twist tightly his words, without making gestures with his hands, not moving his head, nor slide from his seat, nor change his position, nor elevate his voice, nor turn his face to the right and left, nor turn toward anybody else."[42] Details of posture and gesture, how the *nadīm* should sit, how he should move in that space, how and when he should punctuate his speech and his silence, are the markers of larger social and political meanings, and the spectators understood the momentous significance of the details that underlay this most sensitive of performances.

Great value is, thus, attached in *Akhlāq al-mulūk* to the act of addressing the monarch, as the work devotes much attention to the practical details pertaining to such performances. This is also the case with the work of Kushājim (d. ca. 350/961), the fourth/tenth-century courtier of the Ḥamdānid court (first in Mosul and then in Aleppo). Kushājim includes in his *Adab al-nadīm* a section on the characteristics of boon companions, including the required character, the types of knowledge that they ought to have, physical attire, and a special section on *adab al-muḥādatha*. As a matter of fact, Kushājim asserts that the raison d'être of the *nadīm* and his capital is conversation (*muḥādatha*).[43] The etiquette of conversation (*adab al-ḥadīth*) requires that it be abridged and "not to start it and then to interrupt it and promise that you will finish it later." Kushājim also instructs not to vie with the ruler over a conversation "merely because you know the substance of it. On the contrary you have to show him . . . that it did not even occur to you." As important, if not more so, it is essential to be a good listener. Good listening entails granting time to the speaker until his communication is over and "to pay attention to it and not distract yourself either by glancing away or busying your limbs with action or occupying your mind with a thought."[44] *Adab al-muḥādatha* also entails, according to Kushājim, that the speaker not smile or laugh excessively.[45]

In the chapter on the service of the ruler (*fī al-khidma*) of *Adāb al-mulūk* of the anthologist Abū Manṣūr al-Thaʿālibī (d. 429/1038), the *nadīm* is instructed to focus all his attention and all his manners for the sake of the service of the ruler. The prescriptions concerning the rules of conversations state, "He [the *nadīm*] should lower his eyes and his voice in his [the king's] presence and never start the conversation until the king starts it first. He should listen well to his [the king's] words and direct toward him the totality of his thought and mind. If he happens to know the substance of the conversation that the king is communicating, let him listen in the way of someone who never heard it before."[46]

A later work, *Rusūm dār al-Khilāfa* of Hilāl al-Ṣābiʾ (d. 448/1056), relates the rules and regulations of the Abbasid court and includes a myriad of material ranging from advice to viziers, secretaries, boon companions, and others on how to dress, how to sit, and how to address the caliph to descriptions of caliphal audiences. *Rusūm dār al-khilāfa* includes an important chapter focusing on the rules of attendance (*adāb al-khidma*), which does not address the *nudamāʾ* specifically but rather anyone who is in the presence of the caliph. The regulations listed bear many resemblances to the rules outlined earlier, with regard to the prescribed style and content of the speech as well as in the required body language. *Rusūm dār al-khilāfa* reiterates that it is not appropriate for people in attendance to "mention anything without having been asked about it or to relate information or make any report without permission." They must avoid asking the caliph to clarify his utterances, to confirm an order, or to repeat what he has said. And even if the ruler utters faulty speech, whether an unsound *ḥadīth* (prophetic tradition) or a broken line of poetry, the people in his presence, be they close relations or companions, should not correct him directly but should do it, if at all, by insinuation and by citing analogies. Furthermore, those in attendance must avoid relating a story that might appear to be unbelievable or a speech that might be considered vulgar.[47]

Guidelines about body language are echoed in this later text. The speaker's voice must be low, and he should minimize turning to his sides or his back as well as the movements of his hands. His attention, once again, should be focused on the caliph alone. He must not laugh and should avoid blowing his nose or spitting, coughing, or sneezing.[48]

Rusūm dār al-khilāfa warns the people keeping company with kings that they should be circumspect and should neither contradict a king nor feel safe with him. The ultimate goal being that of pleasing the ruler, those who were almost constantly in attendance had to be wary of his disposition, keeping a constant vigilance for any signs of satisfaction and dissatisfaction. Caprice was a correlate of absolute power, as reflected in the work of Ibn Qutayba, who devotes a section to the topic of royal caprice and inconstancy.[49] *Rusūm dār al-khilāfa* highlights this matter in a council to the caliph's entourage:

> Beware of arguing with the sultan when he is angry or of urging him to leniency when he is obstinate. Try to avoid him when you detect his wrath mounting. Wait to present your excuse . . . until his anger is calmed. . . . Guard against the temptation of speech. Let your answer about matters with risky consequences be more of a hint than a direct expression, more of the probable than of the definite. It is easier for you to say what you have not said than to retract what you have already uttered.[50]

Self-control and composure were prerequisites for survival, and caution in matters pertaining to speech could be a matter of life and death, since through an unconsidered word or gesture, the courtier could incur the disfavor of his master.

Speech also occupies a special status in the *Kitāb waṣāya Aflāṭūn al-Ḥakīm fī khidmat al-mulūk*, where its concrete power is highlighted: to speak is considered a way of acting, and therefore, imprudent speech can be a source of worry: "Pay attention to the words that you utter when you are addressing the monarch; be careful that your words do not go beyond what is strictly indispensable."[51] Advice is given not to speak without being asked, and when allowed to, not to go beyond the bounds of the necessary: "If the enemy is outwardly hostile in the presence of the monarch, do not address him before having obtained authorization from the monarch. Remind him also that . . . you do not take the liberty to say all that comes to your mind concerning the enemy, due to the respect that his majesty has in your eyes."[52] The precariousness linked to the ruler's whims clearly fostered an ethics of dissimulation.

Performing Conversation at the Abbasid Court

In all of these texts, importance is given to the act of speaking, which should remain moderate, responsible, and discreet. The operational power of speech is stressed. Ways of speaking, including the pitch and the tone of the voice as well as the specific words that are spoken, define social roles.[53] Linguistic anthropology sees performance as a marked way of speaking that sets up "a special interpretive frame within which the act of speaking is to be understood" and that amplifies "awareness of the act of speaking and licenses the audience to evaluate the skill and effectiveness of the performer's accomplishment."[54] Erving Goffman used the term "performance" to refer "to all the activity of an individual which occurs during a period marked by his continuous presence before a particular set of observers and which has some influence on the observers."[55]

In a world in which the court was central and where prudent accommodation and even deception were seen as virtues, self-fashioning was necessary in order to survive or advance in the high-stakes world of court society.[56] Speaking about the French court in early-modern times, Bernard Hours stated that "la cour s'apprend" and that the courtesan needed to master a savoir-faire. The foundation of this culture of appearances, which rested on language and conversation, meant that the courtier's art was to distill enough of his knowledge to please the ruler without incurring his ire either by the content or by the form of conversation and comportment. It also implied enormous constraints on the words, which were subjected to a vigilant self-censure.[57] The courtier was a creature of language, whose action is constructed in words and whose language is a discourse of action.[58] *Adab* was a concept central to Abbasid cultural practice that in addition to denoting "a corpus of varied literary knowledge," referred to "a constellation of courtly manners and tastes to be conditioned and exhibited."[59] *Adab* was speech and conduct as echoed in *Al-ʿIqd al-Farīd*: "He who is associated with the ruler should not withhold advice from him even if the ruler finds it annoying. However, his speech to him should be kind, not stupidly unthoughtful, so that he may inform him of his fault without saying it to his face. He should rather speak proverbially and tell him of the fault of others so that he may know his own fault."[60] While this passage is included in "The Book of the Pearl: On the Ruler," Ibn ʿAbd Rabbih introduces "The Book of Coral: On Addressing Kings" with a paragraph in praise of eloquence: "We will now speak about addressing kings, currying favor with them through the magic of eloquent speech that affects the soul with its subtlety and agrees with it in finesse. Fine speech captivates hearts, for it can sometimes win over someone burning with rage."[61] The type of material in this particular section of this voluminous *adab* anthology is somewhat different from that in the *adab al-khidma* subgenre. The project in "The Book of Coral" is to mention "those who escaped from the noose of ruin and the snare of death by their good wits, genial pleas, smooth answers, and pleasant excuses."[62] They are thus anecdotes often similar to the relief-after-adversity (*al-faraj baʿda al-shidda*) type and include no clearly prescriptive statements of the sort that are found in the smaller monographs of *al-adāb al-ṣulṭāniyya*. Some general prescriptive injunctions are found in "The Book of the Ruby on Learning and Good Manners," in a section titled "Courtesy in Speaking and Listening." These injunctions are not directed specifically to the boon companions or those who sat in the presence of a ruler: "Wise men have said: The main elements of all courtesy is to understand well and try to comprehend, and to listen intently to one's interlocutor." And it also contains the statement by the wise man who told his son, "My son, learn to listen well just as you learn to speak well." Listening is as important as, if not more than, speaking; but one also needs to be mindful not to interrupt or dispute one's interlocutor: "It is courteous not to try to confute someone in his speech. . . . If he speaks on any subject, don't dispute him, don't interrupt him, and don't show him that you are teaching him. . . . Learn to listen well just as you learn to speak well."[63]

What all these texts have in common is *adab*, which was a performance that based itself on a scrupulous sense of propriety, the elegant, decorous, and urbane being merely the outer signs of inner virtue and harmony; *adab* showed itself in the courtly context of manners and gesture, especially in conversation. The performers could gain influence by virtue of their skill and their ability to elicit validation.[64] Speaking about the court of early-modern Europe, Norbert Elias stated, "A man who knows the court is master of his gestures, of his eyes and of his face; he is profound, impenetrable. . . . He dissimulates, . . . smiles, controls his irritation, disguises his passions, . . . speaks and acts against his feelings."[65] These people, that is, the courtiers, had to meticulously weigh their gestures and expressions as well as each of their utterances. Indeed, since the courtier expressed himself primarily in speech, he had to become a master of the tactics of conversation, proceeding "with an extreme control and deliberation that are not apparent to his interlocutor."[66]

But the Abbasid boon companions were engaged in a double performance since their essential role was to produce the relaxing atmosphere expected of such sessions. To talk in an informal, spontaneous, and relaxed way, they had to design the script with painstaking care and exert attention in order to maintain the impression that is fostered, adjusting their performance in the minutest detail. One can imagine these boon companions navigating a complicated mood of ambition, ironic amusement, curiosity, and at times even revulsion, while participating in and watching the enactment of this performance. The real and the fictive are merged in the life of the individual who performed these histrionic improvisations, living life "as a character thrust into a play, constantly renewing oneself extemporaneously and forever aware of one's own unreality."[67] It was a difficult balance to keep, as is revealed clearly in the performance that the fourth/tenth-century man of letters and philosopher Abū Ḥayyān al-Tawḥīdī had to put on for his patron, the vizier: he had to appear as the educated and self-confident scholar, impressing the vizier with his knowledge and rhetoric, while making sure that he neither bored him nor lectured him, remaining forever mindful of their different positions in the hierarchy.[68]

The composition of the *majlis*, including the number of those who attended, their professions, and their social status, as well as the location of the *majlis*, were factors that affected "the structure, content, creativity, and quality of a performance."[69] While dissimulation and feigning were important components of the performance, the precarious position in which these performers found themselves meant that at any moment in their performance something could have happened to catch them out.[70] This concern is reflected in the texts discussed earlier, in which we find a constant exhortation to exercise prudence, in speech and act.

The prescriptive texts mentioned in this chapter include verbal and behavioral strategies on which depended a successful conversational performance. I have focused on a few monographs belonging to the genre of *khidmat al-mulūk*, stretching from the third/ninth to the fifth/eleventh centuries. This chapter has excluded from the discussion poetic performances at court, which had their own etiquette and structure. Beatrice Gruendler has mentioned that poetic recitations required an audience for whose exclusive audition they were being performed, an audience that adopted, as if in a theater, "the double role of participating in the unreal world of the emotions the poet enacts, as well as in the real world of the poet's skill, in his . . . delivery of the poem, and in the poem's claim to reward."[71] The poet's performance, clearly, differed from that of the boon companions, and this has mostly to do with the fact that the poet's performance at the court of the ruler functioned as "a public act of allegiance" and was part and parcel of the "iconography of power."[72] By contrast, the boon companions tended to be found in the intimate assembly of the ruler, the character of which was mostly private. However, what the poet and the boon companion had in common is that in both cases, "action occurs through the exchange of words, speech being the sole vehicle for interaction."[73]

The boon companion had two audiences: the other boon companions, who appreciated him because they understood his performance, and the ruler, who could reward him. Talking about the ideal courtier of the Renaissance, Baldassare Castiglione placed the boon companion at the "center of a game played by the 'real' courtiers of Urbino: he is their work of art, the reflection of their skills, behavioral and verbal."[74] The grace of the courtier depended on a difficult performance that gave the impression of facility. While there were no rules or recipes to guarantee that the performance would be a success, prudence, discretion, good judgment, adjustment in style, and conversational skills were all necessary.

The texts discussed in this chapter define fundamental elements in mastering the tactics of conversation as they singled out how conversation was to be performed at the Abbasid court. With regard to purely formal features, these prescriptions contain some of the trappings of performance at work, putting the act of speaking on display and paying attention to delivery style, voice volume, and facial and bodily gesture. The directives place great constraints on the linguistic form and the content of speech. The rhetorical strategy, including turn taking and performer-audience, is central in shaping the structure and dynamics of the performance and, in turn, the social relations at court.[75] Indeed, a lot depended on the outcome of such a conversation/performance, since to lead one's higher-ranking interlocutor deliberately but imperceptibly where one wishes was the chief requirement of this courtly manner of dealing with people.[76] By succeeding in such performances, boon companions would demonstrate their membership to this courtly elite.

NOTES

1. Leder, "Royal Dishes," 360.
2. Gunn and Janse, *Court as a Stage*, 2.
3. Elias portrayed Louis XIV as tightening his control over his aristocratic subjects through a public distribution of signs of authority and favor at court and through court ceremonies (*Court Society*).
4. Dillon, *Language of Space*, 10, 13.
5. J. Adamson, "Making of the Ancien-Regime Court."
6. Al-Azmeh, *Muslim Kingship*, 131.
7. Ibid., 126.
8. Ali, *Arabic Literary Salons*, 82–83.
9. Al-ʿAllam, *Al-Ṣulṭa wa al-siyāsa fī al-adab al-ṣulṭānī* , 95.
10. Bauden and Ghersetti, "L'art de servir son monarque: À propos"; Bauden and Ghersetti, "L'art de servir son monarque: Le *Kitāb*."
11. Brookshaw, "Palaces, Pavilions and Pleasure-Gardens."
12. Robinson, *In Praise of Song*, 75.
13. Grunebaum, "Aspects of Arabic Urban Literature."
14. Robinson, *In Praise of Song*, 50.

15. Gutas, *Greek Thought, Arabic Culture*, 127–28; Chejne, "Boon-Companion in Early ʿAbbāsid Times."
16. Allen, *Arabic Literary Heritage*, 238. See also Meisami, *Medieval Persian Court Poetry*, 7; and Robinson, *In Praise of Song*, 67.
17. Al-Heitty, *Role of the Poetess*, 50.
18. Chejne, "Boon-Companion in Early ʿAbbāsid Times."
19. Niẓām al-Mulk, *Book of Government or Rules for Kings*, 92–93.
20. Gruendler, "Meeting the Patron."
21. Kilpatrick, *Making the Great Book of Songs*, 17.
22. Sawa, *Music Performance Practice*, 119.
23. Robinson, *In Praise of Song*, 70.
24. Ali, *Arabic Literary Salons*, 49.
25. Marlow, "Advice and Advice Literature."
26. Al-ʿAllām, *Al- ulṭaswa-l-siyāsa*, 65–66.
27. Al-Thaʿlabī, *Akhlāq al-mulūk*, 91.
28. Ibid., 74.
29. Ibid., 77–78, 83.
30. Ibid., 77–78.
31. Ibid., 78–79.
32. Ibid., 128.
33. Ibid., 90. Translation of the Qurʾānic verse in Arberry, *Koran Interpreted*, 536.
34. Al-Thaʿlabī, *Akhlāq al-mulūk*, 128.
35. Ibid., 129.
36. Ibn ʿAbd Rabbih, *Al-ʿIqd al-Farīd* (ed. Amīn et al., 1940–49), 2:261–62. Translation in *Unique Necklace*, 2:102. These references occur in the chapter titled "Kitāb al-yāqūta fī al-ʿilm wa al-adab" and more specifically in the subsection on "al-Balāgha wa ṣifātuha."
37. Ibn ʿAbd Rabbih, *Al-ʿIqd al-Farīd*, 2:265; Ibn ʿAbd Rabbih, *Unique Necklace*, 2:105.
38. Al-Thaʿlabī, *Akhlāq al-mulūk*, 129.
39. Ibid., 129–30.
40. Ibid., 129
41. Ibid., 90.
42. Ibid., 131.
43. Kushājim, *Adab al-nadīm*, 58.
44. Ibid., 59.
45. Ibid., 61.
46. Al-Thaʿālibī, *Adāb al-mulūk*, 241.
47. Al-Ṣābiʾ, *Rusūm dār al-khilāfa*, 1964), 33–35. Translated by Salem as *Rusūm dār al-khilāfa: The Rules and Regulations of the ʿAbbāsid Court*, 31–32, 46.
48. Al-Ṣābiʾ, *Rusūm dār al-khilāfa*, 34–35; Salem, *Rusūm dār al-khilāfa*, 31–32.
49. Al-Azmeh, *Muslim Kingship*, 125; Ibn Qutayba, *ʿUyūn al-akhbār*, 1:73–82.
50. Al-Ṣābiʾ, *Rusūm dār al-khilāfa*, 87–88; Salem, *Rusūm dār al-khilāfa*, 70–71.

51. "Kitāb waṣāya Aflāṭūn," no. 69. The compilation, which dates from the sixth/twelfth century, is based on fourth/tenth- and fifth/eleventh-century materials.
52. "Kitāb waṣāya Aflāṭūn," no. 38.
53. Morales, "Gender and Identity."
54. Bauman and Briggs, "Poetics and Performance."
55. Goffman, "Social Life as Drama," 97.
56. Martin, "Inventing Sincerity."
57. Hours, *Louis XV et sa cour*, 38, 40.
58. Revel, "Court," 102.
59. Ali, *Arabic Literary Salons*, 33–35.
60. Ibn ʿAbd Rabbih, *Al-ʿIqd al-Farīd*, 1:20; Ibn ʿAbd Rabbih, *Unique Necklace*, 1:12.
61. Ibn ʿAbd Rabbih, *Al-ʿIqd al-Farīd*, 2:122; Ibn ʿAbd Rabbih, *Unique Necklace*, 2:1. This reference is found in "Kitab al-murjāna fī mukhāṭabāt al-mulūk."
62. Ibn ʿAbd Rabbih, *Al-ʿIqd al-Farīd*, 2:122; Ibn ʿAbd Rabbih, *Unique Necklace*, 2:1.
63. Ibn ʿAbd Rabbih, *Al-ʿIqd al-Farīd*, 2:427–28; Ibn ʿAbd Rabbih, *Unique Necklace*, 2:226–27.
64. Bauman, *Verbal Art as Performance* (1978), 45. For a recent discussion of *adab*, see Orfali, "Art of Anthology."
65. Elias, *Court Society*, 105.
66. Ibid., 108.
67. Greenblatt, *Renaissance Self-Fashioning*, 31.
68. Behzadi, "Art of Entertainment." Another instance occurs with the poet Abū al-Ibar, who decided, for instance, to turn to poetry of joking (*hazl*) and stupidity (*ḥumq*) in order to make a fortune. He reveals in one anecdote that he was not stupid but that he simply pretended stupidity to attain different goods. In Ostafin, "Abū al-Ibar al-Hāshimī."
69. Sawa, *Music Performance Practice*, 120.
70. Goffman, "Social Life as Drama," 100–104.
71. Gruendler, "*Qaṣīda*."
72. Ali, *Arabic Literary Salons*, 86.
73. Gruendler, *Medieval Arabic Praise Poetry*, 79.
74. Hanning, "Castiglione's Verbal Portrait."
75. Bauman and Briggs, "Poetics and Performance."
76. Elias, *Court Society*, 108.

6

Khālid Ibn Ṣafwān

An Orator at the Umayyad and Abbasid Courts

JAAKKO HÄMEEN-ANTTILA

The formative period of Arabic prose literature coincided with a change of dynasties from Umayyads to Abbasids in the mid-eighth century. During the Umayyad Caliphate (661–750), literary prose was virtually nonexistent, and even scholarly literature was largely underdeveloped. The Qur'ān has aesthetic qualities, but it is sui generis. From the late seventh century forward, when pre-Islamic poems started to be recorded, collectors occasionally jotted remarks on their background stories, the *sālifas*, but before the mid-eighth century, these were rarely more than notes to the poems themselves. The first *rasā'il*, or tractates, and didactic mirrors for princes were written just before the dynastic change to the Abbasids. The translation of Middle Persian literature into Arabic with its myths, fables, and historical stories commenced at about the same time.[1]

Most sources are unanimous, though, in claiming that the early Arabs were great orators. The *khuṭba*, or speech, was seen as *the* mode of Bedouin eloquence, and famous speeches attributed both to pre-Islamic Bedouins and to early Islamic preachers are known from later sources. The meandering monograph of al-Jāḥiẓ, *Kitāb al-Bayān wa-l-tabyīn*, is a monument to the oratorical talents of the early Arabs.

The role of this oral prose in the development of written prose has been little studied.[2] An obvious reason for this is that problems of authenticity and transmission can be acute and, at times, create seemingly insurmountable obstacles. It is too early to discuss the question in general terms, as there are few detailed studies of the materials. For this reason, I shall restrict myself to discussing one specific character, Khālid ibn Ṣafwān, and four speeches or sayings attributed to him.

In most modern histories of classical Arabic literature, Régis Blachère's *Histoire de la littérature arabe* (731–32) forming a delightful exception, one vainly searches for any mention of Khālid, but in medieval *adab* collections, he was a well-known figure.[3] Khālid lived in Basra and inherited the position of the tribal leader of Tamīm from his father, although the late Umayyad period saw a decrease in importance of these tribal leaders with the growth of a central administration. His family had been famous for their oratorical talent since the time of the Prophet, and the succeeding generation retained some of this fame. The oratorical talents of Khālid's great-grandfather ʿAmr ibn al-Ahtam's invited the often-cited comment from the Prophet himself, "There is magic in some eloquence and there is wisdom in some poetry" (*inna min al-bayāni la-siḥran wa-inna min al-shiʿri la-ḥukman*).[4]

Khālid was an admired orator, and his speeches as well as stories about him were collected by both al-Madāʾinī (d. 250/850 or earlier) and al-Julūdī (d. after 330/941–42), possibly from local Basran tradition.[5] Later, their monographs were lost, but scattered fragments live on in *adab* works and historical literature, with a substantial collection of 115 items, mainly based on al-Madāʾinī, in al-Balādhurī's *Ansāb al-ashrāf* (7.1:55–88).[6] Khālid did not leave a written heritage, and among all the extant materials, there is no indication that he was literate, although the possibility cannot be ruled out.[7] Yāqūt, *Irshād* (ed. Shamsaddīn), 3:280 (= ed. Margoliouth, 4:165), is the only source that provides an exact date for his death, namely, 135/752–53.[8]

Khālid is often cited as one of the great orators. Al-Murtaḍā (*Amālī*, 2:262), considers him famous for his oratorical talents, Makkī ibn Sawād praises his talents in a poem, and even al-Jāḥiẓ joins in the praise (*Bayān* 1:339).[9] Later, Khālid's name became proverbial for oratorical talent.[10] Abū Tammām's use of his name as a proverb is perhaps one of the highest praises Khālid has ever received, though the list could easily be extended to several pages.[11]

The sources link Khālid reliably to the courts of Governor Khālid ibn ʿAbdallāh al-Qasrī and Caliph Hishām ibn ʿAbdalmalik.[12] Khalid is also often described as performing in the presence of the first Abbasid caliph, al-Saffāḥ, implying that he survived the dynastic change and managed to keep his position. Al-Jāḥiẓ (*Bayān* 1:339) and al-Masʿūdī (*Murūj*, § 2350) even tell us that Khālid was one of the nightly companions of the Abbasid caliph.[13] His relations with this caliph will be discussed shortly.

Obviously, Khālid was an important figure who well deserves a place in the histories of Arabic literature. Likewise, one can a priori assume that his and other orators' craft influenced later literature. The earliest preserved literary prose from around 750 onward retains features of the purported Umayyad oral prose, such as parallelism and a moderate use of rhymed prose, which we know not only from the—in itself spurious—pre-Islamic *saj'* but also from other Semitic literary traditions (e.g., biblical Hebrew), and this links the Arabic tradition to the Common Semitic tradition. The oral prose of the Umayyad period fits this lineal development from Common Semitic to pre-Islamic to Abbasid prose.[14]

However, there are at least three features that make the study of this early oratorical craft difficult: attribution of the stories, upgrading of the interlocutors, and manipulation of the text. First of all, unlike poetry and, perhaps, religious texts, the attribution of oral prose was rather fluid, and stories about, as well as the speeches of, lesser authorities have easily been attached to other, usually more famous, names. In anecdotal literature, this is commonplace, and one finds characters becoming standardized for certain roles. An anecdote about any infamous, wine-imbibing poet will be attached to the name of Abū Nuwās, whoever the original protagonist was, and a story about a miser may well become affixed to the name of Khālid. This is especially common in the case of a family or a circle of characters with similar roles.

In Khālid's case, we find *khuṭbas* attributed both to him and to his less famous relatives. His grandfather 'Abdallāh is credited with an admonition to 'Umar II ibn 'Abdal'azīz, transmitted by Khālid (in al-Jāḥiẓ, *Bayān*, 2:117–20), but already in Ibn 'Abdalḥakam (*Al-Khalīfa al-'ādil*, 111–14), this has become a sermon delivered by Khālid. Chronological facts support the attribution of this story to a senior member of the family, and it seems, in general, that anecdotes rarely flow from a major figure to a minor one. Hence, prima facie, we should doubt all anecdotes that link Khālid to 'Umar ibn 'Abdal'azīz and consider the possibility that the original protagonist was Khālid's elder relative.[15]

The second general problem is what I refer to as upgrading, which is very common in anecdotal literature. Upgrading refers to changing the protagonist's interlocutor. We often find versions of an anecdote with the same protagonist but with a different interlocutor. In some, usually earlier versions, the interlocutor may be anonymous or little known, while in other, usually later versions, he has become the caliph or an official on the uppermost steps of the social ladder and the administrative hierarchy.

In several previous articles, I discussed the famous anecdote of Khālid and Umm Salama, the wife of al-Saffāḥ.[16] The story is among the finest and structurally most elaborate prose narratives of classical Arabic literature. It includes two ornate and witty speeches by Khālid, delivered in front of al-Saffāḥ, the first Abbasid caliph, urging him not to restrain himself from having more than one wife, and the second, delivered when Khālid realizes that Umm Salama is listening to their discussion, quickly turning the tables and admonishing against polygamy.

At first, this story might be thought to shed light on courtly life in the critical period during the change from the Umayyads to the Abbasids. It might also induce one to speculate on the role of Umayyad courtiers in their new situation under the Abbasids. It is obvious that the Abbasids could have but chose not to dismiss the earlier aristocracy in its entirety. The Abbasids may have done their best to exterminate the Umayyads, but the intricate network of mighty Arab families could not be eradicated without destroying the whole empire. Hence, well-connected men of many talents, like Khālid, could have retained their place in the caliphal court.

But had Khālid retained his? Stories linking him to al-Saffāḥ are not lacking in later literature, though few early sources settle him in the Abbasid court, and some that do so may well be instances of upgrading. The story of Khālid and Umm Salama can be shown to have been compiled, perhaps not before the early tenth century, from two separate anecdotes, only one of which places Khālid in the caliphal court, the second instead naming as his interlocutor the little-known (Durust) ibn Ribāṭ al-Fuqaymī. Only the core elements of the witty speeches of the anecdote are present in these early sources, and thus the elaboration must have occurred later, when the two stories were joined and Khālid's interlocutor in the second story was upgraded.[17] Hence, the story of Khālid and Umm Salama does not tell us anything about the courtly life as it was in al-Saffāḥ's time but rather as it was later imagined to have been.

There are also other stories that seem to link Khālid to al-Saffāḥ. One worth quoting appears in al-Balādhurī, *Ansāb*, § 37:

> One day Abū l-ʿAbbās al-Saffāḥ ordered Khālid to be brought to him. Entering, Khālid said to Abū l-ʿAbbās, "You have been commissioned to the caliphate, and you are the man for it and its rightful place. You tend the right in its pastures and bring it to its watering places. You have given everybody his due of your attention, justice, politeness [*adab*], and company [*majlis*] so that it is as if you belonged to everyone [i.e., to every tribe] or to none." This pleased Abū l-ʿAbbās, who ordered money to be given to him.

Virtually the same story is related in many sources: al-Balādhurī, *Ansāb*, 3:167 (= ed. ʿAẓm, 3:187) (< Abū Masʿūd al-Kūfī < ʿAbdaljabbār al-Kātib); al-Qālī, *Amālī*, 1:213; Ibn Qutayba, *ʿUyūn*, 1:172; Ibn ʿAbdrabbih, *ʿIqd*, 2:135; al-Bakrī, *Simṭ*, 1:502 (from al-Qālī); al-Ḥuṣrī, *Zahr*, 916, 1079; al-Rāghib al-Iṣfahānī, *Muḥāḍarāt* (1961), 1:195. In some versions, like that of al-Qālī, Khālid's interlocutor is an anonymous *wālī*.

Al-Qālī's *isnād* deserves special attention. He narrates this on the following authority: Abū ʿAbdallāh Nifṭawayh < Abū l-ʿAbbās Aḥmad ibn Yaḥyā (i.e., Thaʿlab) < Ḥammād ibn Isḥāq < his father < his paternal uncle Ṣabbāḥ ibn Khāqān, whose great-grandfather was the brother of Khālid's great-grandfather ʿAmr ibn al-Ahtam.[18]

There are several noteworthy implications in the *isnād*, but the one that concerns us here is that there seems to have been a family tradition of Khālid's sayings, at least three generations long. Ṣabbāḥ was of Khālid's generation and a probable witness at the event or a person to whom Khālid himself may have told about it.

The version of al-Qālī is, thus, based on a close family tradition. It gives as Khālid's interlocutor merely an anonymous *wālī*, not the mighty caliph.[19] The family tradition seems strong enough to validate this version. The family hardly had reason to eliminate a famous interlocutor from the story and to replace him with an anonymous one, and the last links in the *isnād* consist of famous grammarians whom one might not easily credit with omitting the name of the first Abbasid caliph from the story. Hence, it seems that the development must have been the other way around. Subsequent sources upgraded the interlocutor, replacing an anonymous *wālī* with the immensely famous al-Saffāḥ. This sort of upgrading of stories is very common in both tales about Khālid and other anecdotes.[20]

However, I am not claiming that Khālid could not have visited the Abbasid court. Even in al-Balādhurī, there are half a dozen cases (*Ansāb*, §§ 24, 37, 67, 82/86/101, 102) that place Khalid in al-Saffāḥ's court, and we may glean from various works further examples, some more credible than others. It is logical that when Khālid's stories were upgraded, they were set in the courts that he was known to have visited, but we must realize that this upgrading creates an illusion of intimacy because a handful of perhaps genuine stories are supplemented by scores of suspect ones. A similar phenomenon is to be seen in the case of the *rajaz* poet Dukayn, who seems to have visited the court of ʿUmar ibn ʿAbdalʿazīz perhaps only once when ʿUmar was the governor of Medina. In later versions, he is cast as an intimate friend of the caliph.[21]

The third problem may also be clarified with a story linking Khālid to al-Saffāḥ. In al-Balādhurī's *Ansāb*, there is a set of four stories (§§ 52, 82, 86, 101) that basically duplicate each other.[22] The longest (§ 82) of these reads,

> They say: The Commander of the Believers Abū l-ʿAbbās summoned Ibrāhīm ibn Makhrama al-Kindī, some people from Banū l-Ḥārith ibn Kaʿb, who were maternal uncles to Abū l-ʿAbbās, and Khālid ibn Ṣafwān. They started boasting.
>
> Ibn Makhrama said: "The people of Yemen are the kings of the Arabs. In the age of the Jāhiliyya, to them belonged the Bedouinship and the kingship, and they passed it on as an inheritance, one mighty man inheriting from another, the latter from the former and the bygone from his ancestors. To them belonged the Nuʿmāns, the Mundhirs, and the Qābūses, to them belonged ʿIyāḍ, the lord of the sea, as well as the one whose flesh was protected by bees. To them belonged the one whose body the angels washed and the one on whose death the Throne shook. To them belonged the one spoken to by the wolf and the one who used to take every ship by force.[23] There is nothing important that is not attributed to them, neither a fine horse nor a cutting sword, neither strong armor nor a valuable garment. When they were asked, they gave, and when a guest alighted by them, they received him hospitably. No one can vie with them nor boast to them. They are the real Arabs, while others just want to pass as Arabs!"

Abū l-ʿAbbās said: "I do not think the Tamīmī will agree on this." Khālid said: "The rash fellow has erred without knowledge and spoken amiss when he boasted to Muḍar, to whom belonged the Messenger of God (may God bless him and salute him) as well as the caliphs and the members of his family. How can he boast to Muḍar of people who ride asses, weave clothes, train monkeys, and tan hides?[24] A hoopoe led (Solomon) to them, and a rat drowned them."

Then he turned to al-Kindī and said: "Are you boasting of fine horses and sharp swords and strong armor? What glory is there more glorious than Muḥammad, the best of mankind and the most noble of the nobles? God has bestowed him graciously on both us and you. They were his followers, and they were known and respected because of him.[25] To us belong the Chosen Prophet and the Accepted Caliph, the lordship and the nobility. To us belong the founded Temple, the raised roof, and the *minbar* where he preached. To us belong the Zamzam, with its lowlands and the office of giving water (to pilgrims).[26] Can anyone be equal to us? Do anyone's words reach our glory? To us belonged Ibn ʿAbbās, the learned among people, whose stories are sweet and whose sayings are being followed. To us belongs the Lion of God and His Sword, to us belongs the Veracious One and the Distinguisher and ʿAlī ibn Abī Ṭālib (may God, He is exalted, be pleased with him). He never disbelieved in God, and he never swerved from truth to vanity. To us belongs the man of Two Lights, the martyred ʿUthmān."

Then the son of al-Ahtam continued: "How about your knowledge of your people's language? What do they call fingers among you?" He replied: "*Shanātir*." Khālid asked: "What about the ear?" He replied: "*Ṣinnāra*." Khālid asked: "And the beard?" He replied: "*Zubb*." Khālid said: "But God, be He praised and exalted, has spoken 'in clear Arabic tongue.' Yet have you heard Him say: 'Put your *shanātir* into your *ṣinnārāt*'? Or: 'Do not take me by the *zubb*'?"[27]

Abū l-ʿAbbās (may God be pleased with him) said: "What have you, Yemeni, to do with the men of Muḍar?" Then he ordered Khālid to be rewarded, giving him money and property in Basra.

The story is found more or less in the same form in al-Zubayr ibn Bakkār, *Muwaffaqiyyāt*, 112–17; Ibn al-Faqīh, *Mukhtaṣar*, 39–41; al-Masʿūdī, *Murūj*, § 1257; Ibn Ḥamdūn, *Tadhkira*, 3:411–13 (no. 1102); Ibn

Manẓūr, *Mukhtaṣar Ta'rīkh Dimashq*, 7:359–62; al-Itlīdī, *I'lām*, 114–17; and al-Bayhaqī, *Maḥāsin*, 94–96.[28]

A pithy version of Khālid's reply is found in al-Balādhurī, *Ansāb*, § 52: "A Yemeni man boasted to Khālid at the door of al-Ḥajjāj [d. 95/714]. Khālid replied: 'From among us come the sent prophet and the hoped-for caliph. Among us is the revealed (*munzal*) Book and the House toward which one prays.'" Here one might draw attention to the brevity of the reply, in contrast to the long list in § 82, and to the lower rank of the person in whose presence the incident takes place, as well as to the anonymity of his Yemeni opponent. Compared with § 52, § 82 would seem to have been both enormously lengthened (by addition of originally independent anecdotes?) and upgraded.

Al-Balādhurī, *Ansāb*, § 86, seems related to § 82:

> They say: Khālid came to Abū l-'Abbās, may God, He is exalted, have mercy on him. Abū l-'Abbās said to him: "O Khālid, how well do you know my maternal relatives?" Khālid asked: "Which of them, O Commander of the Believers? I know all of them." Abū l-'Abbās said: "Those who are closest to me and have the strongest claim on me, the offspring of al-Ḥārith ibn Ka'b." Khālid said: "O Commander of the Believers, there (among them) is the summit of nobility and the trunk of generosity. They have features that have never combined in any other of their people. Among their people, they have the best condition and the noblest disposition. They keep their covenant best, and they have the furthest aspirations. In war, they are a firebrand, and under duress, a support. They are the heads, while others are but tails." Abū l-'Abbās said: "How excellent you are, O son of Ṣafwān. You have well described them!"

This story is paralleled by al-Balādhurī, *Ansāb*, 3:166–167 (= ed. al-'Aẓm, 3:188); al-Washshā', *Fāḍil*, 80–81 (with variants); al-Ḥuṣrī, *Zahr*, 872, 1079; al-Ābī, *Nathr*, 6:37–38; and al-Sharīshī, *Sharḥ*, 4:135.[29]

The fourth anecdote (al-Balādhurī, *Ansāb*, § 101) reads,

> Abū l-Ḥasan al-Madā'inī has said: Khālid spent an evening at the court of the Commander of the Believers, Abū l-'Abbās. Some people of Banū l-Ḥārith boasted, but Khālid remained silent. The Commander of the Believers said to him: "O son of Ṣafwān, what is the matter? Why do you

> not say anything?" Khālid replied: "But these are the maternal relatives of the Commander of the Believers!" The caliph said: "You are my paternal relative. Paternal relatives are not below maternal relatives." Khālid said: "But what should I say to people who weave clothes, train monkeys, and tan hides? A hoopoe led the way to them, and a rat drowned them." Abū l-ʿAbbās laughed at this.

Compare al-Balādhurī, *Ansāb* (ed. al-ʿAẓm), 3:187 (< al-Madāʾinī); al-Jāḥiẓ, *Bighāl*, 2:273 (= ed. Pellat, 59); al-Jāḥiẓ, *Ḥayawān*, 6:152; al-Jāḥiẓ, *Bayān*, 1:339; Ibn Qutayba, *ʿUyūn*, 1:317; al-Zamakhsharī, *Rabīʿ*, 2:185; al-Thaʿālibī, *Thimār*, 412; al-Tawḥīdī, *Baṣāʾir*, 6:169 (no. 508); al-Waṭwāṭ, *Ghurar*, 260; Ibn ʿAbdrabbih, *ʿIqd*, 3:330, 4:46; al-Maqqarī, *Mukhtār*, 204; al-Azdī, *Ḥikāya*, 120, 140; Yāqūt, *Muʿjam* (ed. Wüstenfeld), 4:387, 1036; and al-ʿAskarī, *Dīwān al-maʿānī* (ed. Dār al-Jīl), 1:150–51.[30]

In the third anecdote, § 86, Khālid surprisingly takes the opposite, southern Arab side. It is true that there was a genre of *al-maḥāsin wa-l-masāwī* in Arabic literature, corresponding to the Latin *pro et contra*, but one hardly expects to find traces of it in the historical court of the caliph, where tribal politics retained some of its former importance and an acrimonious attack on a tribe was not merely a verbal exercise but a political move.[31]

Stories §§ 82 and 101 centered on one memorable expression that is found almost unchanged in dozens of Khālid's stories: the reference to "people who ride asses, weave clothes, train monkeys, and tan hides. A hoopoe led (Solomon) to them, and a rat drowned them." This devastating criticism is brief and could well have been memorized. The other parts of the stories are more elaborate and much longer than this specific and widespread witticism. It taxes one's imagination that such long and elaborate speeches could first have been extemporized and then retained in the memory.

What is more probable is that we have a concise historical core, a witty saying by Khālid that has been freely elaborated on by various anonymous authors, to produce a more artistic and longer version as represented by § 82, which better suited late-ninth-century taste. This may have been done by joining together originally separate anecdotes (Ibn Makhrama's speech; Khālid's religious boast about the northern Arabs; a philological joke at the expense of the southern Arabs). Khālid's counterboast praising the southern Arabs was not included in the longest versions.

Such freedoms were taken by authors who did not consider themselves forgers. It may be a different matter with religious material and pre-Islamic poetry, in which the prestige of the material necessitated a certain fidelity to the text, but in "mere" anecdotes, such loyalty was not expected. If there were good ingredients in an anecdote for a witty story, these could be added to another to create a partly fictitious longer story, with no qualms of conscience. This could then be used by authors of historical or semihistorical works, such as al-Masʿūdī's *Murūj*, with the fictitious material, thus, finding its way into historical works. The real authors of these long versions remain anonymous.[32]

Partly the changes may be due to early oral transmission, which may have changed the story unknowingly. However, it is clear that even when the textual transmission was literary, similar freedoms were taken without hesitation. Let us take an example from a completely different genre. The Persian Book of Kings tradition is highly complicated but clearly literary, at least from the late ninth century onward. The historian al-Ṭabarī (d. 314/923) received passages of this history of Persia and inserted them into his grand historical work.[33] In *Taʾrīkh*, 1:208, al-Ṭabarī begins to narrate the story of the insurrection led by the smith Kāve against the tyrant Zahhak (al-Ḍaḥḥāk). The passage is quoted on al-Ṭabarī's authority by al-Thaʿālibī (d. 429/1038), *Ghurar*, 26–27.[34] In the following excerpt from al-Ṭabarī, passages exactly quoted by al-Thaʿālibī are marked in small caps and slightly modified passages in italics:[35]

> wa-zaʿamū annahū lam yusmaʿ min umūri l-Ḍaḥḥāk shayʾun yustaḥsanu ghayru shayʾin wāḥidin wa-huwa anna *baliyyatahū lammā shtaddat* wa-dāma *jawruhū* wa-ṭālat ayyāmuhū ʿaẓuma ʿalā l-nāsi mā laqū minhu fa-tarāsala l-wujūhu fī amrihī fa-ajmaʿū ʿalā l-maṣīri ilā bābihī fa-wāfā bābahū l-wujūhu wa-l-ʿuẓamāʾu min al-kuwari wa-l-nawāḥī fa-tanāẓarū fī l-dukhūli ʿalayhi wa-l-*taẓallumi* ilayhi wa-l-taʿattī li-stiʿṭāfihī fa-ttafaqū ʿalā an yuqaddimū li-l-khiṭābi ʿanhum *Kābī al-Iṣbahāniyya* fa-lammā *ṣārū ilā bābihī* uʿlima bi-makānihim fa-ADHINA LAHUM fa-dakhalū wa-Kābī mutaqaddimun lahum fa-mathula bayna yadayhi wa-amsaka ʿan-i l-salāmi thumma qāla: AYYUHĀ L-MALIKU AYYA L-SALĀMI USALLIMU ʿALAYKA? A-SALĀMA MAN YAMLIKU

hādhihī L-AQĀLĪMA KULLAHĀ AM SALĀMA MAN YAMLIKU HĀDHĀ L-IQLĪMA L-WĀḤIDA—YAʿNĪ BĀBILA. FA-QĀLA lahū L-ḌAḤḤĀKU: BAL SALĀMA MAN YAMLIKU hādhihī l-AQĀLĪMA kullahā LI-INNĪ MALIKU L-ARḌI FA-QĀLA lahū *l-Iṣbahāniyyu*: FA-IDHĀ KUNTA TAMLIKU L-AQĀLĪMA KULLAHĀ wa-kānat yaduka tanāluhā ajmaʿa FA-MĀ BĀLUNĀ QAD KHUṢIṢNĀ BI-maʿūnatika wa-taḥāmulika wa-isāʾatika MIN BAYNI AHLI L-AQĀLĪMI WA-KAYFA lam TAQSIM amra kadhā-wa-kadhā BAYNANĀ WA-BAYNA l-aqālīmi. wa-ʿaddada ʿalayhi ashyāʾa kāna yumkinuhū takhfīfuhā ʿanhum.

They assert that only one thing that could be considered good was ever said of al-Ḍaḥḥāk. When his affliction became great, his tyranny prolonged, and his days lengthened, the people felt that they were suffering so badly under his rule that their notables discussed the situation and agreed to travel to al-Ḍaḥḥāk's gate. When the notables and powerful men from various districts and regions reached his gate, they argued among themselves about coming into his presence and complaining to him and achieving reconciliation with him. They agreed that Kābī al-Iṣbahānī would approach him to speak on their behalf. When they were traveling toward al-Ḍaḥḥāk's gate, al-Ḍaḥḥāk was told that they were coming and permitted them to enter, which they did, with Kābī leading them. The latter appeared before al-Ḍaḥḥāk but refrained from greeting him. He said, "O king! What greeting should one give you? The greeting for one who rules all the climes or the greeting for one who rules only this clime—meaning Babylon?" Al-Ḍaḥḥāk replied, "Nay, but the greeting for one who rules all these climes, for I am king of the earth." Then al-Iṣbahānī said to him, "If you rule all the climes and your sway extends to all of them, why then have we in particular been assigned the burden of you, your intolerance, and your misdeeds out of all the peoples of the climes? Why then do you not divide such-and-such a matter between us and the other regions?" Speaking the truth boldly, he addressed the issue and enumerated to al-Ḍaḥḥāk the ways in which the latter would be able to lighten their burdens.[36]

Al-Thaʿālibī claims to be quoting al-Ṭabarī (*wa-dhakara l-Ṭabarī ʿan baʿḍ shuyūkhihi*), but a close comparison of the texts shows that, in fact, he quotes only the punch line from al-Ṭabarī. As can be seen, al-Thaʿālibī, after claiming to be quoting from al-Ṭabarī, freely rewrites the passage instead of merely copying what al-Ṭabarī had written. The only passage he quotes exactly is the short witticism, of the same length as Khālid's note on the weavers of cloth and trainers of monkeys. This quotation he is able to reproduce with only negligible differences, which shows that the freedoms he takes in other parts of this passage are intentional modifications. For al-Thaʿālibī, saying that a passage comes from "*al-Ṭabarī ʿan baʿḍ shuyūkhihi*" does not necessitate an exact quotation.

This suggests that there was no attempt to transmit even literary material verbatim. Oral lore must have been transmitted with even less fidelity. The punch lines in Khālid's speeches are the basis for his oeuvre, whereas all else is to be considered suspect of having been freely modified by later authors, even when they received their material in written form.

What does this reveal about the relations between the caliphs and their courtiers in late Umayyad and early Abbasid times? Unfortunately, we have to be very circumspect before claiming to know anything about the court etiquette of the time and, perhaps, of later caliphs as well. I leave it to others to assess how extensively the same problems apply to later periods, but when it comes to the mid-eighth century, one has to admit that without a detailed study of a particular story, we cannot claim to learn anything about its context, which may be centuries later than its characters suggest and, thus, largely fictitious and subject to the imagination of later generations.

The same applies to the study of nascent Arabic prose. Poems seem to have been transmitted rather faithfully during Islamic times, abbreviations and loss of material notwithstanding, but prose was freely rewritten, as the case of Ibn al-Muqaffaʿ's *Kalīla wa-Dimna* shows.[37] This does not mean that the texts of early books would necessarily have been in a fluid state.[38] The case of the preceding al-Ṭabarī quotation shows unequivocally that al-Thaʿālibī did not seek to reproduce his source exactly. The differences do not mean that al-Ṭabarī's historical work would still have been in a fluid state around AD 1000 but that authors quoting from him did not feel themselves compelled to do so verbatim.

A cursory look at the longer orations by Khālid shows that they exhibit great variation in different sources, whereas many shorter and pithy sayings have been transmitted almost exactly as is in scores of sources.

Thus, we cannot avoid the verdict given by Régis Blachère in his *Histoire* that Khālid's discourses are perfect specimens of literary prose and, because of this, clearly composed at a later date than Khālid himself.[39] It seems that these longer speeches are often built around a core saying that found a fixed form very early, at least in the case of those sayings that are found widely distributed as early as the ninth century. If not by Khālid, these sayings are at least specimens of mid- to late-eighth-century prose. However, the context of these sayings could easily be changed by reattributing and upgrading the characters, which makes it a precarious business, for example, to write a cultural history of the Umayyad or early Abbasid court. The stories do not so much tell us what happened in the courts but what was later thought to have happened there.

The longer speeches and more elaborate anecdotes can and should, however, be taken into account when writing a history of Arabic literature. Scholars, save for folklorists, tend to become uneasy with anonymous material. Still, we cannot just ignore Khālid's elaborate speeches. Though perhaps not examples of Umayyad prose, they are illustrative of early Abbasid prose, and in most cases, they seem to have received their form prior to al-Jāḥiẓ's generation. Likewise, the courtly scenes should be read as ninth-century fictions about the Umayyad or early Abbasid court. Khālid died in 752–53, but his prose continued to thrive until the tenth century, when it found its final form and was henceforth transmitted with only occasional changes.

NOTES

1. Works translated from Greek and Syriac were mainly scholarly, not literary. For further insight on how this translation movement developed in general, see Gutas, *Greek Thought, Arabic Culture*.
2. For *khuṭbas* in general, see Dähne, *Reden der Araber*.
3. Blachère, *Histoire de la littérature arabe*. See also Brockelmann, *Geschichte der arabischen Literatur: Supplementbände*, 1:105.
4. E.g., al-Balādhurī, *Ansāb* (ed. Baʿlabakkī), 7.1:50–52; al-Jāḥiẓ, *Bayān*, 1:349; Pseudo-Jāḥiẓ, *Maḥāsin*, 22–23; al-Ḥuṣrī, *Zahr* (4th ed.), 38–39. The latter also contains a short biography of ʿAmr ibn al-Ahtam. In al-Balādhurī, *Ansāb*, 7.1:89, the story is told about "Ibn al-Ahtam"—probably meaning "a descendant of al-Ahtam" but not specifically ʿAmr ibn al-Ahtam—and ʿUmar ibn ʿAbdalʿazīz, which would have been a more credible pair than the Prophet and ʿAmr ibn al-Ahtam. For Khālid's family, see, besides al-Balādhurī, *Ansāb*, 7.1:49–94, Abū

ʿUbayd al-Qāsim ibn Sallām, *Kitāb al-Nasab*, 39; Ibn Khallikān, *Wafayāt al-aʿyān*, 6:182; Ibn Qutayba, *Al-Maʿārif*, 403–404; Ibn Rustah, *Kitāb Aʿlāq al-nafīsa*, 206. For the family's place in the wider setting of Arab tribes, see Ibn al-Kalbī, *Jamharat al-nasab*, table 76. For the orators of Banū Minqar, see al-Jāḥiẓ, *Bayān*, 1:355–56.

5. For al-Madāʾinī, see Ibn an-Nadīm, *Fihrist* (ed. Tajaddud), 116; Dodge, *Fihrist of al-Nadīm*, 1:226 (*Kitāb Khālid ibn Ṣafwān*); Yāqūt, *Irshād al-arīb ilā maʿrifat al-adīb* (ed. Margoliouth), 5:317; al-Ṣafadī, *al-Wāfī bi-l-wafayāt*, 22:46. For al-Julūdī, see Ibn al-Nadīm, *Fihrist* (ed. Tajaddud), 128; Ibn al-Nadīm, *Fihrist* (ed. Flügel), 115; Dodge, *Fihrist of al-Nadīm*, 1:252 (*Kitāb Akhbār Khālid ibn Ṣafwān*). Abū Aḥmad ʿAbdalʿazīz ibn Yaḥyā ibn Aḥmad ibn ʿĪsā al-Julūdī is little known. In ʿAbdalqādir al-Baghdādī, *Khizānat al-adab*, his *Kitāb Akhbār al-Farazdaq*, not known to Ibn al-Nadīm, is quoted through ʿAlī ibn Ḥamza al-Baṣrī's (d. 375/985) *Al-Tanbīh ʿalā aghlāṭ al-ruwāh* from the section on the mistakes made by Abū Ziyād al-Kilābī (cf. Brockelmann, *Geschichte der arabischen Literatur: Supplementbände*, 1:85). Al-Jāḥiẓ (*Bayān*, 1:340) mentions "a book on the sayings [*kalām*] of Khālid which circulates in the hands of booksellers [*al-warrāqīn*]," and Ibn Qutayba (*ʿUyūn al-akhbār*, 1:78), mentioned an *Akhbār Khālid ibn Ṣafwān* as his source, although it is not clear whether we should take this as a book title or not. As the *isnāds* attached to some Khālid stories show, the family of Khālid also carried on his memory.
6. These are not numbered in the edition, but I have numbered them in my forthcoming translation of the Khālid stories. In the following, I am referring to the stories by the number they will have in this translation. The four items discussed in detail in this article (§§ 52, 82, 86, 101) are found on pp. 71, 77–79, 80, and 85 of the edition. The material in al-Balādhurī may be supplemented by more than one hundred other stories found scattered elsewhere in Arabic literature, not to mention the variant versions of the stories found in al-Balādhurī.
7. His younger cousin Shabīb ibn Shayba is, however, occasionally implied to have been literate; cf., e.g., an anecdote in al-Balādhurī, *Ansāb*, 7.1:90, in which his servant girl brings him a dish of paper for food, saying that it is the sole commodity in the house.
8. But note that Yāqūt is perhaps not always reliable with his dates; cf. the case of Dukayn al-Rājiz, discussed in Hämeen-Anttila, "Dukayn."
9. Al-Sharīf al-Murtaḍā, *Amālī*; al-Jāḥiẓ, *Bayān* 1:339–40. The same verses are quoted by al-Ḥuṣrī, *Zahr*, 954; al-Marzubānī, *Muʿjam al-shuʿarāʾ*, 1:543; Ibn al-Sarrāj, *Jawāhir al-adab wa-dhakhāʾir al-shuʿarāʾ wa-l-kuttāb*, 1:618 (vols. 1 and 3 attributed to Bakr ibn Sawāda).
10. Cf., e.g., al-Kāmil al-Khwārizmī (see Hämeen-Anttila, "Al-Kāmil al-Khwārizmī," 144); Ibn al-Shajarī, *Amālī*, 1:121; al-Khwārizmī, *Rasāʾil*, 403.
11. Al-Ḥuṣrī, *Zahr*, 953 (= Abū Tammām, *Dīwān*, 86). One might add in passing, though, that Khālid was equally famous for being one of the four Arab misers,

together with al-Ḥuṭay'a, Ḥumayd al-Arqaṭ, and Abū l-Aswad al-Du'alī; cf. Yāqūt, *Irshād* (ed. Shamsaddīn), 3:267 (an article on Ḥumayd al-Arqaṭ, on the authority of Abū 'Ubayda; note that the same Abū 'Ubayda labels half of Khālid's family as makers of solecisms, *laḥn*, in Ibn 'Abd Rabbih, *'Iqd* [3rd ed.], 2:478); al-Salawī ('Abdalqādir ibn 'Abdarraḥmān), *Al-Kawkab al-thāqib fī akhbār al-shu'arā' wa-ghayrihim min dhawī l-manāqib*, 1:39; Ibn Ḥamdūn, *Tadhkira*, 2:318 (no. 819); al-Marzubānī, *Kitāb Nūr al-qabas al-Mukhtaṣar min al-Muqtabas*, 146; al-Nuwayrī, *Nihāyat al-arab*, 3:297; and al-Ibshīhī, *Al-Mustaṭraf fī kull fann mustaẓraf*, 1:171. Cf. also Pellat, *Le milieu Baṣrien*, 148. Khālid was also famous for his "blunders" (*hafawāt*) and found a place in al-Ṣābi', *Al-Hafawāt al-nādira*.

12. Cf. Yāqūt, *Irshād* (ed. Shamsaddīn), 3:274.
13. Al-Mas'ūdī, *Murūj al-dhahab* (ed. Meynard and Courteille; rev. Pellat).
14. For the use of *saj'* in Khālid's speeches, see Hämeen-Anttila, "Khālid ibn Ṣafwān," 73–75.
15. Pace van Ess, *Theologie*, 2:243. In al-Jāḥiẓ, *Bayān*, 1:24, Khālid is linked to a son of 'Umar ibn 'Abdal'azīz, 'Abdallāh, the governor of Iraq. See in general van Ess, *Theologie*, 2:241–44, which dates this encounter between 'Abdallāh and the orators between 126/744 and 129/746–47. Khālid was also often confused with his father, Ṣafwān (e.g., al-Jāḥiẓ, *Kitāb al-Bighāl*, 2:218 = *Kitāb al-Qawl fī l-bighāl*, 13; cf. al-Jāḥiẓ, *Kitāb al-Qawl fī l-bighāl*, 2:220 = *Kitāb al-Qawl fī l-bighāl*, 15), and his cousin Shabīb ibn Shayba. Bashshār ibn Burd, *Dīwān*, 4:79, from *Bayān*; al-Jāḥiẓ, *Bayān*, 1:24; Yāqūt, *Irshād* (ed. Shamsaddīn), 5:567. Ibn al-Murtaḍā (*Bāb dhikr al-Mu'tazila*, 18–19) calls Khālid and Shabīb "the two Khālids." A nicely symmetric case is a story in which either Khālid defines what kind of a man Shabīb is or the other way round: as a saying by Khālid about Shabīb; see al-Balādhurī, *Ansāb*, § 49; al-Jāḥiẓ, *Bayān*, 1:47, 340; al-Jāḥiẓ, *Kitāb al-Ḥayawān*, 5:592; Ibn Qutayba, *'Uyūn*, 3:84; Ibn abī l-Ḥadīd, *Sharḥ Nahj al-balāgha*, 5:500; al-Zamakhsharī, *Rabī' al-abrār wa-nuṣūṣ al-akhbār*, 1:439–40; al-Ḥuṣrī, *Zahr*, 953; Ibn Jinnī, *Al-Fasr*, 3:692–93; Ibn Shuhayd, *Rasā'il*, 182 = Ibn Bassām, *Al-Dhakhīra fī maḥāsin ahl al-Jazīra*, 1:237 (quoting Ibn Shuhayd); al-Jāḥiẓ, *Kitāb Faṣl mā bayna l-'adāwa wa-l-ḥasad*, 357; al-'Askarī Abū Hilāl, *Ṣinā'atayn*, 310; al-Tawḥīdī, *Risālat al-Ṣadāqa wa-l-ṣadīq*, 193 (Khālid about "some man"). As a saying by Shabīb about Khālid: Ibn 'Abd Rabbih, *'Iqd*, 2:270, 2:337, 3:105; Ibn Ḥamdūn, *Tadhkira*, 4:370 (no. 963). For a similar situation between Ru'ba and his son 'Uqba, see, e.g., al-Jāḥiẓ, *Bayān*, 1:68. For an appreciative evaluation of Shabīb by Khālid, see al-Balādhurī, *Ansāb*, § 63; *Shurūḥ Saqṭ al-zand*, 3:1348 (al-Khwārizmī); Ibn Ḥamdūn, *Tadhkira*, 8:25–26 (no. 32); Ibn Manẓūr, *Muhktaṣar Ta'rīkh Dimashq li-Ibn 'Asākir*, 26:326; Ibn Khallikān, *Wafayāt*, 6:24; al-Ṣūlī, *Akhbār al-Buḥturī*, 69–70; Ibn Qutayba, *'Uyūn*, 3:135); Ibn 'Abdrabbih, *'Iqd*, 1:242, 2:251. For an appreciative evaluation of Khālid by Shabīb, see al-'Askarī, *Ṣinā'atayn*, 2:442.
16. Hämeen-Anttila, "Unity and Variation"; Hämeen-Anttila, "Khālid ibn Ṣafwān," 77–79, 116–18; Hämeen-Anttila, "Short Stories."
17. See Hämeen-Anttila, "Short Stories."

18. Ḥammād was also an authority for Wakīʿ; see Werkmeister, *Quellenuntersuchungen*, 219. For Ṣabbāḥ, see al-Balādhurī, *Ansāb*, 7.1:93. He is mentioned with much respect by al-Jāḥiẓ in *Bayān*, 1:355–56, and by Abū Nuwās, *Dīwān*, 2:92–93.
19. Besides al-Qālī, Ibn Qutayba, Ibn ʿAbd Rabbih, al-Bakrī, and al-Ḥuṣrī (both versions) also give an anonymous *wālī* as Khālid's interlocutor.
20. See Hämeen-Anttila, "Short Stories," 36–40.
21. See Hämeen-Anttila, "Dukayn." Al-Raqīq al-Qayrawānī (*Quṭb al-surūr*, 325) explicitly claims Khālid to have been on intimate terms with al-Saffāḥ, but the author probably had little historical information to back his claim, merely deducing this from the story he was telling, namely, Khālid's and Umm Salama's story. Cf. also al-Jāḥiẓ, *Bayān*, 1:339; and al-Masʿūdī, *Murūj*, § 2350.
22. Khālid is also connected with many other *mufākharas* between northern and southern Arabs and between Basrans and Kufans; see, e.g., al-Balādhurī, *Ansāb*, § 54 (al-Jāḥiẓ, *Bayān*, 1:336; Pseudo-Jāḥiẓ, *Maḥāsin*, 23–24; Ibn ʿAbdrabbih, *ʿIqd*, 4:39; al-Murtaḍā, *Amālī*, 1:295; Abū Ṭāhir al-Baghdādī, *Qānūn al-balāgha fī naqd al-nathr wa-l-shiʿr*, 31; al-Khafājī, *Sirr al-faṣāḥa*, 188–89; Ibn al-Sarrāj, *Jawāhir*, 767; Jirābaddawla, *Min Kitāb Tarwīḥ al-arwāḥ wa-miftāḥ al-surūr wa-l-afrāḥ*, 96; al-Waṭwāṭ, *Ghurar al-khaṣāʾiṣ al-wāḍiḥa wa-ʿurar al-naqāʾiṣ al-fāḍiḥa*, 259; al-ʿAskarī, *Ṣināʿatayn*, 323); al-Balādhurī, *Ansāb* § 70 (al-Akhfash al-Aṣghar, *Kitāb al-Ikhtiyārayn*, 66; al-Jāḥiẓ, *Bayān*, 2:297; Ibn Qutayba, *ʿUyūn*, 1:322; Yāqūt, *Muʿjam al-buldān*, 1:77); al-Balādhurī, *Ansāb* § 81 (Ibn al-Faqīh, *Mukhataṣar K. al-Buldān*, 121–22, 192; Ibn Manẓūr, *Mukhtaṣar Taʾrīkh Dimashq*, 7:357–59 < al-Haytham ibn ʿAdī; al-Jāḥiẓ, *Bayān*, 2:93–94; al-Jāḥiẓ, *Ḥayawān*, 7:232; al-Tawḥīdī, *Baṣāʾir*, 3:37 [no. 82], major differences; Ibn Qutayba, *ʿUyūn*, 1:317; al-Rāghib al-Iṣfahānī, *Muḥāḍarāt*, 4:587, 592; Yāqūt, *Muʿjam al-buldān*, 1:438–439; al-Masʿūdī, *Murūj*, § 2102); al-Masʿūdī, *Murūj*, § 2350; Ibn Qutayba, *ʿUyūn*, 1:321; Ibn al-Faqīh, *Buldān*, 175–76; al-Jāḥiẓ, *Bayān*, 2:297; Ibn Qutayba, *ʿUyūn*, 1:322; Yāqūt, *Muʿjam al-Buldān*, 1:77. For the theme in general, see Wagner, *Die arabische Rangstreitdichtung*, 448.
23. Baʿlabakkī vocalizes *mukallim*, the one who spoke to wolves.
24. The passage is not as innocent as it might at first seem, as there is an obscene connotation in the word *ʿard*, "ass," which also means "erect penis." For cases of this word used in the latter meaning, see, e.g., Pseudo-Jāḥiẓ, *Maḥāsin*, 352; al-Qālī, *Amālī*, 2:106 (a verse by a daughter of Humām ibn Murra). For the association of Yemenis with monkeys, see, e.g., al-Damīrī, *Ḥayāt al-ḥayawān al-kubrā*, 2:201 ("The Yemenis teach their monkeys to serve them so that a butcher or a greengrocer may teach his monkey to take care of the shop until its master has returned from his errands"); al-Thaʿālibī, *al-Kināya wa-l-taʿrīḍ*, 32 ("If a man is ugly and repulsive, one may allude to this by saying that he has relatives in Yemen—for there are many monkeys there").
25. I.e., the northern Arabs.
26. For the *baṭḥāʾ* of Mecca, see Yāqūt, *Muʿjam*, 1:446.
27. Cf. al-Khalīl ibn Aḥmad, *Kitāb al-ʿAyn*, 7:353; and al-Iskāfī, *Kitāb al-ʿAyn*, 2:1056, where *al-zubb* is explained as *al-ḥayya* (read: *al-liḥya*) in the language of Yemen

(Wild, *Das Kitāb al-ʿAin und die arabische Lexikographie*, 54, vocalizes this as *zibb*). The last example has a deliberately obscene connotation (Arabic *zubb*, "penis"). The version of Ibn al-Faqīh and those following him continues with the word for wolf (*kutaʿ*), which flattens the obscene climax. The obscenity is further underlined in al-Zubayr's version, where, besides *zubb*, Khālid asks the last but one question about *faqḥa* (North Arabic "anus") and receives the answer that it means *al-rāḥa* in South Arabic. Khālid's reference to Q 20:94, though, shows that one should read *al-ra's* instead. The final question concerns the word *kutaʿ* (wolf), which falls apart even for semantic reasons, as all the other questions concern body parts. For the Yemeni words, see Piamenta, *Dictionary of Post-Classical Yemeni Arabic*, 1:195, 288; al-Selwi, *Jemenitische Wörter*, 57, 125–26. For the Qurʾānic allusions, see Q 2:19, 20:94.

28. Al-Zubayr ibn Bakkār's version (*Al-Akhbār al-muwaffaqiyyāt*) essentially differs from those of both al-Balādhurī and Ibn al-Faqīh and his followers. Al-Zubayr transmits the story on the authority of his uncle Muṣʿab ibn ʿAbdallāh < his grandfather ʿAbdallāh ibn Muṣʿab < "*jalīs li-Abī l-ʿAbbās*." The final, anonymous transmitter sounds fictitious, and the whole story seems a later elaboration. There is a change of focus in the discussion of the words and their South Arabic equivalences. In al-Zubayr's version, Khālid asks about the South Arabic words (starting with *fa-akhbirnī ʿan al-shanātir*), and Ibrāhīm answers by giving the North Arabic equivalent. Ibn al-Faqīh gives a somewhat more elaborate version, also on the authority of al-Madāʾinī. The allusions are identified in the notes to Ibn al-Faqīh, q.v., and in Hämeen-Anttila, "Khālid ibn Ṣafwān," 110–11. Ibn al-Faqīh and his followers end their versions by letting Khālid ask Ibrahim about four things, and he either has to admit his point or commit the crime of unbelief: to which of them belongs the Prophet, the Qurʾān, the House (of God), and the *minbar* (i.e., the office of Friday preaching or, in other words, the caliphate). Ibrāhīm has to admit that all these belong to northern Arabs, after hearing which, Khālid concludes, "So begone, and let everything else freely belong to you!" Khālid's famous, or even notorious, sentence about the Yemenis being trainers of monkeys and tanners of hides is here reserved as the parting shot by Khālid after his final victory and its approval by al-Saffāḥ. Al-Zubayr's version also ends with four questions, but these are slightly different (To whom does the Prophet belong? To whom does the caliph belong? To whom was the Qurʾān revealed? And, finally, to whom does the house [the edition has wrongly *kitāb*] of God belong?). Here the parting shot of Khālid is "*fa-ayyu shayʾin taʿdilu hādhihi l-khiṣāl?*" after which the caliph gives his final verdict and rewards Khālid—in Ibn al-Faqīh's version both receive a reward, though Khālid is given a more generous one. The version of al-Masʿūdī is much abbreviated. He says that after Khālid's famous sentence about tanners and weavers, he went on to expostulate on the blame of the southern Arabs, finishing with the story of how the Ethiopians conquered their country and how the Persians enslaved them. Though this end to al-Masʿūdī's version may well have been freely

invented, it would fit Khālid's reputation as an important transmitter of historical stories, a claim that is often made but seldom substantiated. See al-Balādhurī, *Ansāb*, 3:169 (= ed. al-ʿAẓm, 3:180–81); al-Ḥuṣrī, *Zahr*, 954. Cf. also Lecker, "Tribes in Pre- and Early Islamic Arabia," 72–73; al-Itlīdī, *Iʿlām an-nās*. Ibn Ḥamdūn, Ibn Manẓūr, and al-Itlīdī mainly follow Ibn al-Faqīh's version, Ibn Manẓūr and al-Itlīdī transmitting it on the authority of al-Haytham ibn ʿAdī. The apparent length of the versions of al-Zubayr ibn Bakkār and al-Itlīdī is due to the layout of the respective editions. Al-Bayhaqī, *Al-Maḥāsin wa-l-masāwī*.

29. The version of al-Balādhurī, *Ansāb*, 3:166–167, is given on the authority of al-Madāʾinī, with slight variation and some abbreviation. Al-Washshāʾ, *Kitāb al-Fāḍil fī ṣifat al-adab al-kāmil*; al-Ābī, *Nathr al-durr*; al-Sharīshī, *Sharḥ maqāmāt al-Ḥarīrī*; al-Ḥuṣrī, *Zahr*, 872. Al-Ābī and al-Sharīshī link this story to § 101. Al-Ḥuṣrī, *Zahr*, 1079, gives an abbreviated version of § 86 only.

30. Al-Jāḥiẓ, *Ḥayawān*, 6:152, relates this anecdote in a story about the rat gnawing a hole in the al-ʿArim dam. Here the interlocutor is presented as "the Yemeni," and the caliph in whose presence this takes place is al-Mahdī, whose rule began only in 158/775. The version, though, does not claim that the discussion took place during his caliphate, which, technically, saves it from being openly anachronistic. Al-Thaʿālibī's version follows that of al-Jāḥiẓ, *Ḥayawān*, 6:152. Al-Maqqarī sets the scene in the court of Hishām ibn ʿAbdalmalik.

31. For the genre of *al-maḥāsin wa-l-masāwī*, see, in general, Geries, *Un genre littéraire arabe*. The genre has often been misunderstood. Perusing, e.g., al-Bayhaqī's or Pseudo-Jāḥiẓ's *Maḥāsin*, one soon notes that very often the case is not a matter of praising and blaming the same thing but of praising one thing and blaming its opposite. In § 82, there are details that arouse suspicion, such as the positive role given to ʿUthmān at the end of the anecdote. Al-Ḥuṣrī, *Zahr*, 872–73, adds a laudatory comment by al-Jāḥiẓ on Khālid's ability in the *pro et contra*: "Yamūt ibn al-Muzarriʿ has said: I heard my maternal uncle al-Jāḥiẓ mention this speech of Khālid and say: 'By God, even if he had thought for a year of all their blames and how to put their defects concisely after this refined praise, that would have been a short time. Yet he extemporized this without any exertion of thought!' "

32. Cf. Leder's "unauthored literature" ("Authorship and Transmission in Unauthored Literature"). As the situation in historical literature and the anecdotes are very similar and the genres freely borrow from each other, their development should always be studied in tandem.

33. It need not detain us here whether he had at his disposal Ibn al-Muqaffaʿ's translation. For the translations of the Middle Persian *Khwadāy-nāmag*(s) and the question of the Arabic Book of Kings tradition, see Hämeen-Anttila, "Al-Kisrawī."

34. Al-Thaʿālibī, *Ghurar*. The attribution of the *Ghurar* to al-Thaʿālibī is slightly problematic but probably correct. The question of attribution does not, however, affect the relation of the text to al-Ṭabarī, and in any case, we know that the *Ghurar* was written around 410/1019. See Zotenberg's preface to the *Ghurar*, vii–viii.

35. A similar passage is also found in *Taʾrīkh*, 1:204–205, but 1:208 is clearly the source for al-Thaʿālibī.
36. Brinner, *Prophets and Patriarchs*, 8.
37. Cf. de Blois, *Burzōy's Voyage to India*.
38. Cf. Schoeler, *Oral and the Written*.
39. Blachère, *Histoire de la littérature arabe*, 3:732.

PART III

Entertainment

7

Performing Court Literature in Medieval Byzantium

Tales Told in Tents

MARGARET MULLETT

In a recent article, I decided that it is possible to agree that Byzantium had a court society, at least in the sense that other medieval societies had one, and that it also had a court culture, though one that was deeply imbued with a sense of city values, or *asteiotes* or *urbanitas*.[1] What I am not absolutely certain about is whether Byzantium had a court literature. It certainly had the prescriptive texts of the ninth, tenth, and fourteenth centuries like the well-known *De Cerimoniis* but also the less well-known *Typikon of the Great Church* and Pseudo-Kodinos.[2] And it had, particularly in the twelfth century, a great richness of rhetorical texts, which in that article I claimed were the true court literature of the Byzantines. But court literature in the sense of other societies considered in this volume, I am not so sure.

For a start, we are very short of the texts. We have no wine poetry after the Greek Anthology and no love poetry (except a few included pieces); we have one heroic poem and four romances from the twelfth century and more from the thirteenth to fifteenth centuries.[3] And they have distinctly uncourtly settings: the wild frontier, the classical household of a Greek city-state in the Mediterranean world.[4] What I want to make a case for here is that much of the literature we do have from the mid-eleventh to the twelfth centuries, and most of the performance practice, has its basis not in the grand plots of epic or romance but in storytelling.[5] And I would further suggest that what we have learned to call the culture of *sylloge* puts together discrete stories and binds them into a monastic florilegium or a work of advice to a prince or a synoptic or autoptic history or a saint's life.[6] I would like to suggest that the training for telling stories was achieved with the basic rhetorical education open to any courtier and its *progymnasmata* of mythos and diegesis.[7]

I also want to suggest a setting that has not been normally considered as synonymous with the Byzantine court: the setting of the tent.[8]

The hardest thing to document is in fact "performance," and I have been increasingly worried by a youthful pronouncement that has come back to haunt me in the works of younger scholars: "The most uncompromisingly literary works, it is now accepted, were written for performance in the *theatra* of Constantinople. This viewpoint has been greatly facilitated by the work of social anthropologists and psychologists (as well as oral historians and the students of folk poetry); using this theoretical perspective it begins to look as if Byzantinists should identify as exceptional those texts which were not written for performance."[9]

In fact, we are still at the stage of spotting "performance indicators," and the best progress has been in rhetoric.[10] I cannot adduce good evidence for most of the specific texts I shall discuss, but I think that storytelling is in itself a performance, even if it is a performance of one to one.[11] The best image of narrating in Byzantium is that of a dream narrative, told by Basil I's mother to a dream interpreter and depicted in the Madrid Skylitzes.[12] But let me lead you into one of the mobile palaces of the Byzantines, their ephemeral architecture.

On Her Tent Which Had Different Animals Depicted on It

My lady, Muse of Muses, akropolis of beauty,
The porch of your tent is filled with delights.
Cupids are plucking strings and quietly strumming the kithara,
Satyrs seem to play, centaurs gambol,
The Muses join in the dance, the Nereids are leaping,
Birds fly above, while others hunt
the golden birds of India which fly together.
The gold-feathered parrot, jewel of beauty,
vies with the golden emerald of the peacocks,
And with those proud birds and the circle of their feathers
contrasts and makes comparisons together
with the freshness of the gold upon their backs.
Cunning foxes, abandoning their wiles,
devote themselves to the lyre, dance to the kithara.
Who then could look at this porch and curtain

and not be amazed, in fact dumbfounded?
For if the delights in the entrance are so great,
How great must be the marvel of delight inside the tent,
She who is absolutely unique and first of the Graces?
Cupids play outside while inside there are other cupids
submitting with bent necks on bended knee to their mistress,
taking on a more servile aspect.
And thanks be to your brilliance and the virtues that adorn you.
You were born Cupid of Cupids and Grace of Graces,
you have become Siren of Sirens, you have proved Muse of Muses.
You cannot be compared with mortal women.
I revere you with the Muses, I honour you with the Sirens,
I do reverence to you with the Graces, I link you with the Hours,
with Hera, with Thetis, with the immortals.
Greetings, Grace and Siren and Muse Kalliope![13]

The poem does just that, pausing on the decoration of the porch before entering to see past the *aulaia* (a curtain with theatrical connotations)[14] to the Lady with her entourage, a Lady who is eventually compared with the Queen of Heaven, the mother of Achilles, and the muse of epic poetry. This tent may never have existed, any more than her fanciful retinue did, but we know that the *Sebastokratorissa* Eirene did spend time on campaign with the emperor Manuel I in the 1140s, and both tent and retinue were what her poet Manganeios Prodromos thought she deserved (and could safely be said).[15] Nor is this the only tent poem we have: this poem to Eirene has a shorter counterpart that compares a tent to the transience of human life, possibly designed for embroidery onto a tent,[16] and we have another pair of tent poems from two generations earlier, written by the archbishop of Ochrid for a cousin of the emperor Alexios I around 1100, again a longer poem perhaps for delivery in the tent and a shorter moralizing one perhaps for embroidery on the tent, thanking the aristocrat for his entertainment in the tent.[17] And we have a riddle, recorded in the many riddle collections of the eleventh and twelfth centuries, starting with Christopher of Mytilene:

I am a house with no stone and I move about.
I go on the earth, but I'm not attached to it.

> Neither mud nor plaster raised me.
> Neither saw nor axe cut me—
> Unless you're speaking of my head or my base.
> I draw light in though I am fenced all about.
> The columns I bear stand together obliquely.
> Though on every side my columns are disturbed
> I remain, keeping my shape and standing undamaged.
> Here's what's new about me: if you use force to cast me down,
> You wouldn't shatter me; I am safe for you
> For I stand up and again remain a house.[18]

But apart from these tent poems, we know that other texts were received and performed in tents: in the ninth century, the emperor Theophilos received a letter from the caliph in Baghdad.[19] We do not have his reaction to the letter—except that he thought it inappropriate to give knowledge to the enemy—but here is another letter, not very far in time from the text that tells us about it:

> I thought that the season was already autumn and not spring. Where then did this nightingale of spring come from? Listening to the liquid notes I stand spellbound. Yet though the voice of this most beautiful bird is that of a nightingale, its form is of a swallow: its song is clear and melodious like the nightingale's, but on its body two contrasting colors are wonderfully blended together like the swallow's. Whether a nightingale or a swallow, this marvelous letter filled me with complete joy.[20]

Campaigning emperors spent more time away from Constantinople than in it, and some of that time was spent under canvas. As the emperor John II says in Niketas Choniates, "I remained but little in the palace. Nearly my whole life was lived out of a tent, and I have always diligently sought the open air."[21] Tents in the period were regarded as having advantages over built structures, particularly built structures away from the palace: they offered security and control; they could be pitched to best effect; they could allow special light effects; they were intimate, versatile, elegant; and their rich materials offered the chance of display. They were used for reception, for acclamation, for negotiations, for love, for family quarrels, for liturgy, and for feasting.[22] What we might forget is that with the emperor went his household; he traveled *panoiki*.[23] The baggage train of Constantine Porphyrogennetos provides for rich silver tableware to be carried with the baggage of the vestiarion and separately four solid gold plates, two gold vases, and two solid gold jugs for use when foreign guests eat with the emperor.[24] And it is perhaps at these feasts that we can envisage the performance of some of the poems, letters, riddles and stories which reached the imperial court on campaign.

Stories—and the Period

I should like to focus on the reign of Alexios I Komnenos (1081–1118) rather than the inventive 1140s, when so many genres were reborn and new ways of stitching together the stories were arrived at and something like Bakhtin's process of novelization happened to Byzantine literature.[25] And the storytelling I want to look at will concentrate on the individual unit rather than the stitched-together narrative,[26] so on the Mini going on its rounds rather than the Porsche in front of the door, as Nancy Ševčenko calls the eleventh-century ten-volume illustrated metaphrastic menologia.[27] I shall include stories about Alexios even if we know them from a stitched-together composition of a later period.

We should start with the text known as *Stephanites kai Ichnilates*,[28] which is the only direct evidence we have for the literary patronage of Alexios, apart from his commissioning of an encyclopedia of heresies by Zygabenos[29] to assist in (we assume) the set-piece debates he organized with the archbishop of Milan and his entourage in 1112 and the Paulicians in Philippoupolis in 1114.[30] It is not of course in origin a Byzantine work.[31]

Stephanites kai Ichnilates has much in common with another imported composite narrative text of the late eleventh century, *The Book of the Philosopher Syntipas*, attributed to Mousos the Persian and translated from the Syriac by Michael Andreopoulos for Gabriel *doux* of Melitene. But there are also differences: though the latter text's thematic concentration on the role of philosophers in princely education and as advisers to rulers makes it immediately relevant to our concerns, it does not have the metropolitan cachet of *Stephanites* or its explicitly courtly origin,[32] and the frame story is much more tightly plotted than in *Stephanites*,[33] looking forward to twelfth-century novelization rather than to *sylloge*.

Stephanites and Ichnilates is described by its translator Symeon Seth, philosopher, botanist, and occult scientist, as "a story about matters concerning life; for each topic has been set out by one of the philosophers of India through mythical examples fitting to it; on the exhortation of the one who was king there written in the ancestral language and script; and it was translated into Greek in Constantinople on the order of the famous emperor Lord Alexios Komnenos."[34] *Stephanites* is not—as Alexander Kazhdan said—a story for courtesans, but there is plenty of material in it for courtiers, including the "dictator's dilemma": how do you know that courtiers actually love you? What is true friendship?[35] Its eight chapters deal with seven questions put by a king to a philosopher (the seventh, the last, is, "so tell me what happened next"), and animal fables are nested within animal fables.[36] The jackals who give the collection its title survive only to the end of chapter 2, though their conversations about how to deal with a prince are the third level of nest until Stephanites commits suicide and Ichnelates is executed to deter others. After that, the structure is simpler, and the philosopher answers the questions with one or two animal fables: how can friendship turn to hatred?[37] What examples are there of people who are friends and always act in conformity with friendship?[38] How does one keep a close eye on one's enemy even when he makes a display of loyalty?[39] How does someone who often partakes of what he desires, in desiring more, lose what he has already? (There is a sense that the questioner already knows the answers.)[40] Tell me about someone who strives to do a deal but lacks the patience to learn about it before he attempts it.[41] How can a king keep his household safe from harm?[42] How can one beware of enmities and keep a close eye on wrongs?[43] The text belongs to the category of advice literature,[44] and it has in common with that genre the long lists it offers:[45] the three desirable things, the four things that must be done to ensure them, the six things that will lose you power, the three things that no prudent person dares, the three things that no mean-spirited person can attempt, the five unnatural deeds, and so on.[46] It is written from the point of view of the ruler (When should I go to war? Is so-and-so really plotting against me? When is it right to give gifts?), but the concerns of the courtier are addressed also (Don't give unwelcome advice if you want to live. Is it better to be content with one's lot or risk all on action?).[47]

> And Stephanites asked: "And now suppose that you have approached the lion, how then will you be able to find favour with him?" "When I approach him," replied Ichnelates, "and discern the inclination of his character and his mind, I will follow those; and if he wishes to make an attack on one who will be profitable I will rouse him to action and will prepare him to delight in an accomplished purpose. But if he pursues some useless thing I will reveal to him the harm ensuing from such a deed, and the advantage in leaving it alone. I will do this cunningly and flatteringly, and I think that in such a way the lion will notice me and prefer me above the others. For an intelligent man is able to cancel out what is true and to introduce what is false, just as the finest painter also has the power to falsify the truth, sketching in the exits and entrances of some people at ground level." Stephanites said, "If you wish for these things, you should watch the intimacy of the king closely, for it is said that no prudent person dares these three things: proximity to kings, testing poison, and entrusting secrets to women. For the king is to be compared to a precipitous and inaccessible mountain, completely covered with all sort of fruit and grasses and full of wild beasts on which the ascent is difficult and the stay is treacherous."[48]

In this world, ambition is ambivalent, wise counsel beyond jewels, prudence superior to strength, jealousy the motive for courtly dispute, and an excessively greedy mind the reason for all ills in life. For everything there is a *mythos*, as taught at the beginning of the graded school exercises, and each could be detached from the whole and circulate independently.[49]

Stephanites ends like this: "The sensible man considers his parents to be his friends, his brothers his companions, women his acquaintances, his sons his memorial, young girls as troublemakers, his family as moneylenders and himself as a solitary."[50] This cautious and suspicious attitude brings us to another storytelling tradition, more closely attached to advice literature and a little earlier than the Greek *Stephanites* but associated with Byzantine frontier warfare, the *Strategikon* of Kekaumenos.[51]

Here the courtly jealousy and envy, greed and rage we have seen in *Stephanites* give way to fear.[52] The lapidary pieces of advice—do not visit doctors, do not eat mushrooms, do not go to drinking parties, do not have people to stay in your house because they will seduce your womenfolk, or if they do not, they will pretend they have and hurl it in your face in battle![53]—are sometimes illustrated by little stories, which are clearly differentiated from the memoir-like sections on the Vlach wars:[54]

> Akrites, guard the kastra and countryside you trust; and don't trust toparchs near you even if they say they are your friends. An example: there is in a region of Great Armenia a kastron in a high place overlooking a countryside rich in arable land, pasture for beasts and all the population's needs. Defended by cliffs and gorges, it offers no place from which to attack. The only way up is by one narrow track, and then one would have to pass first through the gate and this with great difficulty. There was nothing safer than this strongpoint. The toparch of Tibion (and my grandfather) wanted to gain control of it. So what ploy did he devise? With the help of many gifts he made the commander of the kastron his friend telling him that he would gladly send him anything he needed and vice versa. It happened that the commander who was enchanted by this, was in need of corn and told him so. He answered with joy, "All you ask." He sent off a thousand animals loaded with corn, and a man followed with two donkeys in order (would you believe it?) to look after them. For the commander reckoned "if my kastron is provisioned by this enemy of mine from the empire how great am I?" When the corn arrived, he joyfully opened the gates for the animals and those escorting them to enter. When they got in with their weapons concealed, they flung open the gates of the kastron, killed the guards and gained control of the kastron. In this case friendship was a memorable proxenos of disaster. So you should be more on your guard against friends than enemies. For if the commander had not trusted those he thought were his friends and had ordered the corn to be unloaded outside the gate, he would have gained possession of it, and their trickery would have been in vain and the commander would have had no worries.[55]

These stories may be more comfortably set and told in a frontier castle than in a tent, but they are the kind of story that might well circulate on campaign, again independently of the frame text. The books mentioned in the *De Cerimoniis* include liturgical texts, military manuals, siege craft, histories, a dream book, books of chances and occurrences, weather lore, a treatise on thunder, a treatise on earthquakes.[56] Anna describes her father, Alexios, as taking military lessons from Old Testament battles and her mother, Eirene, ever the intellectual snob, reading Maximos Confessor.[57]

Byzantine histories have a similar kind of construction whether, in Catherine Holmes's distinction, they are autoptic or synoptic.[58] Synoptic texts like chronicles we expect to be composed of little stories, strung together by their annual chronology, stories such as Roger Scott has traced, like Andrew and his dog in Justinian's reign or, definitely more aulic, the story of Theodosios and the apple.[59] These stories pass easily down the tradition of synoptic text and in Alexios's reign can be found in the history of Skylitzes. This is where we go to see Stephanites put into Byzantine action: the fraudulent ousting of a bishop,[60] the jackal-like splitting of father from son,[61] the commission of a terrifying painting,[62] spies behind curtains.[63] But the more ambitious autoptic texts like those of Michael Psellos, Anna Komnene, and Niketas Choniates are also studded with these little gems.[64] Michael Psellos's *Chronographia* has a thoroughly aulic feel to it, hardly leaving the palace for anything except Manzikiert and a spectacular tented embassy;[65] the Bulgarian wars of Basil II are notoriously absent. Niketas is able to take the court out on campaign and include particularly good stories of the hated future emperor Andronikos Komnenos, like the one of him caught in his tent flagrante delicto with the daughter of the *sebastokratorissa*:

> Once when he was lying in the woman's embraces in his tent at Pelagonia, Eudokia's blood relations, on being so informed, surrounded the tent with a large number of armed troops and stood guard over the exit, intending to cut him down on the spot. Eudokia was well aware of the plot, even though her mind was occupied with other matters for she had either been alerted by one of her kinsmen or warned in some other way of the ambush planned against her corrupter. Contrary to the nature of women, she was quick-witted and gifted with sagacity. While in the embraces of Andronikos, she informed him of the plot. Shaken by what he heard, he leaped out of bed and girding on his long sword, deliberated on what

> he should do. Eudokia proposed to her lover that he don female attire and that she should order aloud and by name one of her maidservants to bring a lantern to the tent, and that as soon as the ambushers heard her voice he should exit and make his escape. However he was not convinced by her persuasive argument, afraid that he might lose his way, be taken captive, and be led before the emperor, ignobly dragged by the hair, and worse, made to suffer a womanish and inglorious death. Hence, unsheathing his sword and taking it in his right hand, he cut slantwise through the tent, leaped forth and in one mighty bound, like a Thessalian, hurdled the barrier that chanced to be standing in front of the tent and the space occupied by the stakes and ropes; the ambushers were left agape: by escaping both obstacles the prey transformed defeat into a marvel.[66]

Anna Komnene tells her own stories from the palace and polo ground, the hunting grounds of the environs of Constantinople, stories of gift-giving and reception, the crusader who sat on her father's imperial throne, punishments, and rebellions.[67] But she also retells stories told to her by her military uncles, especially George Palaiologos, not just the big battle set pieces but character pieces also: the vision of Leo of Chalcedon seen by George in battle[68] and the details about courtiers of the day. What we know about Rodomir Aaron, a cousin and descendant of the last Bulgarian tsar, comes from three little episodes in Anna's account. He first appears before the battle of Lebounion in 1091, when he went off to spy on and was able to identify an approaching army as belonging to the Caesar Melissenos rather than a band of Pechenegs.[69] He next appears threatening Alexios's subterfuge at the capture of Nicaea in 1097, when with Monastras he was conducting a group of Turks to the emperor but was taken prisoner by them and only by offering them freedom with gifts in his excellent Turkish was he able to complete the assignment—to Alexios's extreme annoyance.

> These arguments convinced the Turks. Pledges were exchanged and both parties set out on their way to the emperor. On their arrival at Pelekanos, all were received by the emperor with a cheerful smile, although inwardly he was very angry with Rodomir and Monastras. For the present they were sent off to rest. The next day all those Turks who were eager to serve him received numerous benefits; those who desired to go home were permitted

> to follow their own inclination—and they too departed with not a few gifts. It was only after this that the emperor severely rebuked Rodomir and Monastras for their folly, but seeing that they were too ashamed to look him in the face he altered his attitude and with words of forgiveness strove to conciliate them. We will leave Rodomir and Monastras there.[70]

Rodomir's final appearance is in November 1107 after the landing of Bohemond, when the imperial army en route to Thessalonike was troubled at Psyllos by an assassination attempt by Rodomir and his brother, which failed, and they were reduced to having a slave throw pamphlets into Alexios's tent. Both brothers and their mother were exiled, though Rodomir's place of exile is a lacuna.[71] Stephanites or Jeremy Patterson would have identified this as the counterproductive effect of royal anger.[72]

So far, these are the most obvious of sources for storytelling on campaign: courtly vicissitudes, especially on campaign, moral tales about courtly behavior in animals or humans, *racontes* of frontier rivalries. Here a word might be said about another body of frontier material that might be expected to figure here but that raises various difficulties. This is the "matter of Digenes," the macho exploits of a cross-cultural hero who defeated wild beasts, bandits, and an amazon, while establishing a country house and its Byzantine household on the frontier.[73] While offering a mid-twelfth-century imperial connection (Alexios's grandson Manuel I is seen as a second Digenes) and also a set of texts that may have functioned as individual adventures as well as complex narrative,[74] the stories that have come down to us in six manuscripts of a heroic poem and a group of related folk songs from Crete, Cyprus, and Asia Minor are unlikely to represent the kind of storytelling we have posited for courts on the move, in that they appear to have circulated in verse (only one Greek prose version has survived) and so require a specialist (though not necessarily professional) jongleur/rhapsode.[75] This is a different kind of storytelling performance from what we have envisaged so far, though it equally deserves its place on Wilson's "performance continuum" and may also have been represented in Alexios's mobile court.

But there is a different tradition of storytelling that I would suggest should be considered. This is tales found in manuscripts from a monastic milieu. Monasteries were not as far apart from the court in middle Byzantium as their founders would have liked,[76] and holy men were part of that court on the move (Alexios I's mother made sure he always had a spiritual father in his tent). Prime among this tradition are the "edifying tales" that appear in collections from the sayings of the Desert Fathers onward, in collections of sayings about holy men, *gerontika*, and in ascetic anthologies.[77] These offer both the best evidence for performance of storytelling and the best-sellers of Byzantium. The seventh-century *Pratum spirituale* of John Moschos has for frame story a journey by the author and his spiritual brother, the patriarch Sophronios, and stories begin with "then we went to the monastery of . . . ," and the brothers greet them and tell them a story of father so-and-so. They are a mixture of urban, rural, and ascetic stories from the eastern Mediterranean with a stunning group of surreal tales from Sinai and some very worldly accounts as well.[78]

In the eleventh century, the founder Paul of the suburban monastery of the Theotokos Evergetis put together a large progressive anthology, the *Synagoge*, which combined theological with narrative passages on a "ladder" of the spiritual life. This collection has manuscripts that are addressed to the faithful rather than to monks, so it appears by the end of the eleventh century to have a double audience/readership (we are so much better informed about monastic settings for its reception).[79] We also know that the Komnenoi had adopted the texts of that monastery by the time of the foundation of Alexios and Eirene's double monastery, so this could well be court reading material.[80] There are two hundred "hypotheses" in four books, and we are led from the beginning of the monastic life to the heights of abbatial leadership. One story will suffice. Very popular in the eleventh century was the story of the *Forty Martyrs of Sebasteia*, which takes us from the imprisonment and trial to the ordeal on the lake, the guard's sacrifice, and eventually the phosphorescence and invention of the bones.[81] From this wonderful story, the only passage adopted by the *Synagoge* is the story of the mother of the youngest martyr, modeled on the mother of the Maccabees, who throws her son back on the cart to allow him to die with his companions and receive his crown.[82] It is excerpted under the hypothesis of *apotage* to emphasize the importance for a monk of cutting oneself off from all human ties: it could also be read as an example of *storge*, motherly love, on the model of the wise and heroic mothers like the lion's in *Stephanites*[83] or Alexios's, who took on the administration of the empire so that he could go to war.[84]

Another text that falls between monastic and courtly milieus is the *Diegesis merike*, a text that tells of the interactions of the Holy Mountain and Alexios's court, including monastic embassies to Constantinople and a set piece at the deathbed of the patriarch Nicholas III Grammatikos.[85] It is an epistolary narrative including vivid first-person stories:

> The patriarch, having written this, sent it to our powerful and holy emperor, and, having blessed us and given beside us a pound of coins, dismissed us in peace. The emperor, having read it, gave us the same amount and 100 coins, and, turning to right and left, he said to those standing by, "as you have seen me do, do ye likewise." And many of the sebastoi contributed to our travelling costs with many contributions, and we proceeded on our way. Saying only this, the emperor sent us off: "Say to the *protos* and the whole *gerousia* as from me: 'Pray for the power of my empire.' "[86]

Occasionally the satire of the court turns nasty, as here:

> At that time the emperor dispatched the eunuch Mosynopolites, saying, "Bring me here the *epitropos* of my in-law caesar Melissenos," and I was then found in the palace. And if I had not intervened they would have slit the noses of the seven monks. Why? Because of the opposition which the monks mounted to the emperor, saying, "Master, the prophets and all the Fathers were relaxed about boys and beardless youths." On account of this retort he wished to slit the noses of the seven monks and have them conducted and dispatched to the Mountain for not being pleased with his words when he said, "*they have Moses and the prophets*." At any rate, the most humane emperor was angry with them but he did not harm them; instead he dispatched them to the patriarch to hear his divinely inspired words. And so they withdrew.[87]

Diegesis merike is overwhelmingly monastic in its sympathies, but its vignettes of court life—Alexios threatening to cut off the noses of the monks if they did not return to their monasteries, Alexios encouraging courtiers to have a whip round for the monks on another occasion, Alexios's son hanging behind at the deathbed to try to get the patriarch's support for his own succession[88]—made fascinating tales for courtiers who were daily facing the anger and stinginess of the emperor and positioning themselves all the time between the ambitions of Komnenian children in the succession crisis. That there might well be a connection from Athos to the court is suggested by one of the authors of the text who was related to the Komnenoi through Alexios's in-law the Caesar Melissenos.[89]

Finally, another text that spans court and monastery is the mid-twelfth-century life of Cyril Phileotes, which argues to the emperor that an alliance with monks is advisable and urges monks to lose less desirable aspects of their way of life.[90] The points where court and monastery meet are carefully crafted works, allowing both saint and emperor (Alexios, of course) their moments in the sun. When the family of the emperor, after a visit *panoiki* to the monastery, take off their silken clothes and give them to the monks is one of these points where a court audience might have been enthralled.

> As the emperor with his most pious *augousta* and his children had said farewell to the geron, their hearts were so happy from the sight and the sweet conversation of the holy man, that they took off their *himatia* and gave them to the brothers in Christ, not only their children but also those who accompanied them did the same; the brothers in Christ received them; later they sold them in the city. Who could buy them, they were so valuable? And there was joy in that land through the grace of Christ and the holy prayers of the *geron*, such as there had never been before.[91]

Another is the pair of parallel accounts of how two courtiers measure up when they meet the holy man: one, Constantine Choirosphaktes, tries to give him a property he owns near the monastery, and the saint refuses, quoting scripture, which the good courtier thinks is inaccurate—but (unfairly) the saint had had a vision that morning in which the text was quoted as he had reported it. Over their conversation about riches, Constantine learns, as he says at the end, that "in truth you do not need my property. He who is rich with real riches is opposed to apparent riches. No one according the word of the lord can serve two masters."[92] The contrast with the visit of Eumathios Philokales could not be greater. He immediately attacks the *doux*: "Why have you come here, thirsty man? Why have you come here, lone wolf, who has no fear of the shepherd, does not fear the dogs and tears the flocks pitilessly?" He traces a devastating picture of the eternal punishment that awaits him, and the other falls to his feet. He then proceeds to display a complete lack of understanding of the picture painted or the failings that are being discussed: wickedness, cruelty, greed, lack of self-control, avarice, love of pleasure. He fails to learn over the course of their long conversation, and when he asked for the saint's blessing, he is still firmly cleaving to his former deeds. In the end, he is not the one who is "*eumathios*," a good learner, and the saint says that evil men, even when they promise reform, are not to be believed.[93] Here the contrast between the two as told in a court setting would play off the competitiveness of aulic reputations.

So we have looked at examples of composite narrative/paraenetic import, paraenetic memoir, synoptic and autoptic history, ascetic collection, epistolary narrative, and experimental saint's life and have identified in each detachable tales that could have circulated in an aulic context; these cry out for analysis of genre, plot, and performance indicators that must, however, wait for another occasion. In this chapter, I have hardly managed to do more than sketch possible sources for the oral storytelling of a Komnenian court before the revival of fiction in the twelfth century. I have tried to look for stories for which the audience and narrators were interchangeable, rather than looking for professional or specialized storytellers.[94] I have tried in each case to make the connection between the stories and the emperor and between the different genres into which the stories are sooner or later incorporated. Of course, this may be to put the cart before the horse, but I would be surprised if such good stories had not circulated independently of the frames into which they were written down. There is a great deal still to do in terms of this compositional history, the performativity of storytelling, and the rooting of the tales in any aulic setting, let alone in the tents of the Komnenoi. But for me, the aulic passions[95] of fear, anger, lust, greed, ambition, rage, and above all *phthonos*, envy, shine through all these stories and suggest a performance at once advisory, affirmative, and ludic.[96]

NOTES

1. Mullett, "Did Byzantium Have a Court Literature?"; Grünbart and Beyer, "Urbanitas und ἀστειότης."
2. For the *Kleterologion* of Philotheos, see Oikonomides, *Les listes de préséance byzantines*, 65–235; for *De Cerimoniis*, see also *Travaux et mémoires* 13 (2000) for the French project; for the *Typikon of the Great Church*, see *Le Typicon de la Grande*

Église: ms. Sainte-Croix no. 40, Xe siècle: Introduction, texte critique, traduction et notes, ed. Juan Mateos, S.J. (OCA, 165–66, Rome, 1962–63); for Pseudo-Kodinos, see *Pseudo-Kodinos*.

3. For wine poetry, see Beta, *Vino e Poesia*, 16, on wine epigrams, but note his qualification on wine as a subject of literature; on love poetry, see Lauxtermann, "Ninth-Century Classicism"; for the love poetry of Niketas Eugeneianos included in *Drosilla and Charikles*, see 2.326–85, 3.263–88, 3.297–322, 4.156–219 (pp. 38–41, 54–57, 56–59, 70–75); for the heroic poem, see Jeffreys, *Digenis Akritis*; for romances/novels, see Beaton, *Medieval Greek Romance*; for the twelfth-century novels, see Conca, *Il romanzo bizantino*; and the translation by Jeffreys, *Four Byzantine Novels*.
4. On Digenes as frontier literature, see Hook, "Digenes Akrites." Bryer, "Historian's *Digenes Akritas*," looks for the realia of frontier life and, like Oikonomides, "L'épopée de Digénis," does not find it. Beaton, "Cappadocians at Court," makes the case for the poem as metropolitan exile literature. Jeffreys, "Grottaferrata Version of Digenes Akrites," suggests the frontier context of southern Italy in the thirteenth century. For the setting of the twelfth-century novels, especially their classical elements, see for example Burton, "Reemergence of Theocritean Poetry"; Jouanno, "Byzantine Novelist."
5. By this, I mean more than the current use of "storytelling" for all narrative in all media, in, e.g., the persuasive Gottschall, *Storytelling Animal*; I am thinking specifically of the social sharing of story in oral performance and of the individual stories, not unlike those analyzed in Bauman, *Story, Performance, and Event*. The difference between romance on the one hand and this kind of storytelling on the other is a matter of scale and sophistication of plotting, rather than alternate or successive modes of narrative; the case of heroic poetry is more complex; see later in the chapter.
6. Odorico, "La cultura della συλλογή."
7. For the progymnasmata, see Spengel, *Rhetores Graeci*; Webb, "Progymnasmata as Practice."
8. See Mullett, "Reading the Tent"; Mullett, "Tented Ceremony"; Mullett, "Experiencing the Byzantine Text."
9. Mullett, "Writing in Early Mediaeval Byzantium," 159–60.
10. See for example Stone, "Aurality."
11. For a helpful definition, see Bauman, *Verbal Art*, 11: "Fundamentally, performance as a mode of spoken verbal communication consists in the assumption of responsibility to an audience for a display of communicative competence"; and for indicative characteristics and "the performance continuum," see Wilson, *Storytelling and Theatre*, 9–11. But note with Bauman, *Verbal Art*, 13, the culture-specific nature of storytelling as performance: among the Ilongot of the Philippines, storytelling is not a form of performance.
12. Madrid Codex vitr. 26–2, fol. 84r; see Tsamakda, *Illustrated Chronicle*, fig. 203.

13. *Manganeios Prodromos*, ed. and trans. Michael Jeffreys, in Anderson and Jeffreys, "Decoration of the Sebastokratorissa's Tent," 11–13.
14. H. G. Liddell and R. Scott, eds., *A Greek English Lexicon*, rev. ed., ed. H. S. Jones, 2 vols. (Oxford: Oxford University Press, 1940), 1:276.
15. Jeffreys and Jeffreys, "Who Was Eirene the Sevastokratorissa?"; M. Jeffreys, "Manuel Komnenos' Macedonian Military Camps."
16. Anderson and Jeffreys, "Decoration of the Sebastokratorissa's Tent," 12–13.
17. Theophylact of Ochrid, poems 11 and 12, in Gautier, *Théophylacte d'Achrida*, 366–67.
18. Mitylenaios, Poem 71, "On a Tent."
19. The letter is quoted in John Skylitzes, *Synopsis Chronike*, 104.55–68; translated in Wortley, *Synopsis of Byzantine History*, 104–5, and illustrated as Madrid cod. vitr. 26–2, fol. 75v; see Tsamakda, *Illustrated Chronicle*, fig. 184.
20. John Mauropous, ep. 1, in *Ioannis Mauropodis*, 43.
21. Niketas Choniates, *Synopsis historion*, 43 (trans. Magoulias, *O City of Byzantium*, 25).
22. See Mullett, "Experiencing the Byzantine Text."
23. The word is used to describe the arrival of the emperor with his household on a visit to a local holy man, Cyril Phileotes; see Nicholas Kataskepenos, chap. 47.1 of *Bios kai politeia*, 225.
24. *Osa dei ginesthai tou megalou kai ypsilou basileos ton Romaion mellontos phossateusai* (Text C), 275–80, in Haldon, *Constantine Porphyrogenitus*, 112.
25. Mullett and Smythe, *Alexios I Komnenos*; on the 1140s, see Mullett, "Novelisation in Byzantium."
26. Literature as stitching together is implied in the description of the performance of Greek epic poetry in the fifth and fourth centuries BC as rhapsodia and its performer as a rhapsode; for the incorporation of oral tradition into historiography, see Beaton, "Byzantine Historiography," without comment on the subject of the tale.
27. Ševčenko, *Illustrated Manuscripts.*
28. Symeon Seth, *Stephanites kai Ichnilates*, in Sjöberg, *Stephanites und Ichnilates* (trans. Noble, "Cultural Interchange"); Condylis-Bassoukos, *Stephanites kai Ichnelates*.
29. Anna Komnene, *Alexiad*, 15.9.1, in Reinsch and Kambylis, *Annae Comnenae Alexias*, 1:489 (trans. Sewter, *Alexiad of Anna Comnena*, 500).
30. Darrouzès, "Les conférances de 1112"; Anna Komnene, *Alexiad*, 14.8.1–14.9.5, in Reinsch and Kambylis, *Annae Comnenae Alexias*, 1:454–60 (Sewter, *Alexiad of Anna Comnena*, 426–30).
31. Symeon Seth, *Stephanites and Ichnelates*, in Sjöberg, *Stephanites und Ichnilates*, 151 (Noble, "Cultural Interchange," 1:54; study in vol. 1; translation in vol. 2).
32. *Istorikon Syntipa tou philosophou oraiotaton panu*, in Eberhard, *Fabulae romanenses graece conscriptae*, 1–135; see Toth, "Authorship and Authority."

33. A wicked wife of king Kyros plots to have his only son killed, and over seven days when the boy is unable to speak, her seven stories are contested by fourteen stories from seven philosophers. On the eighth day, the boy is able to speak in his own defense, and then the court reflects on the culpability of the actors (Syntipas the tutor, the emperor, the woman, the boy) should the boy have been killed. In the end, the wicked wife gets her deserts, the king and his son are reconciled, and the tutor Syntipas is honored. The frame plot is more developed than in *Stephanites*, there is a regular pattern of introducing the elements of the plot, the structure is tighter, and the stories are longer than those in *Stephanites*, creating an impression of coherence and unity.
34. Symeon Seth, *Stephanites kai Ichnelates*, in Sjöberg, *Stephanites und Ichnilates*, 151 (Noble, "Cultural Interchange," 1:54).
35. Kazhdan and Epstein, *Change in Byzantine Culture*, 182; on the dictator's dilemma, see Patterson, "Friends in High Places," 134–40.
36. The twenty-four stories of *Syntipas* divide between those told on each of seven days, when each of seven philosophers tells two stories in his support and the wicked wife responds with one urging the king to execute him, and those told after the eighth day, when the boy is free to speak again and tells two stories, the wife tells another, and Syntipas tells the last. The stories of *Syntipas* are about kings and merchants, wives and parrots, rather than the animal protagonists of *Stephanites*.
37. Symeon Seth, *Stephanites kai Ichnilates*, 1.54, in Sjöberg, *Stephanites und Ichnilates*, 190 (Noble, "Cultural Interchange," 1:81).
38. Symeon Seth, *Stephanites kai Ichnilates*, 3.74, in Sjöberg, *Stephanites und Ichnilates*, 199–200 (Noble, "Cultural Interchange," 1:91).
39. Symeon Seth, *Stephanites kai Ichnilates*, 4.89, in Sjöberg, *Stephanites und Ichnilates*, 215 (Noble, "Cultural Interchange," 1:102).
40. Symeon Seth, *Stephanites kai Ichnilates*, 5.115, in Sjöberg, *Stephanites und Ichnilates*, 228 (Noble, "Cultural Interchange," 1:111).
41. Symeon Seth, *Stephanites kai Ichnilates*, 6.119, in Sjöberg, *Stephanites und Ichnilates*, 233 (Noble, "Cultural Interchange," 1:114).
42. Symeon Seth, *Stephanites kai Ichnilates*, 7.124, in Sjöberg, *Stephanites und Ichnilates*, 235 (Noble, "Cultural Interchange," 1:116).
43. Symeon Seth, *Stephanites kai Ichnilates*, 8.132 (= Puntoni IX), in Sjöberg, *Stephanites und Ichnilates*, 243 (Noble, "Cultural Interchange," 1:120).
44. The prologue of *Syntipas* underlines its function as beneficial narrative; Eberhard, *Fabulae romanenses graece conscriptae*, 1.
45. Joel Kalvesmaki kindly refers me to an *Arithmologia ethike* in the Athens Parliament library, ms. 65, fols. 193r–210v, which does just this.
46. Symeon Seth, *Stephanites kai Ichnilates*, 1.2, 1.2, 1.24c, 1.9, 1.9, 2.60, in Sjöberg, *Stephanites und Ichnilates*, 151–52, 152, 165–66, 158, 159, 195 (Noble, "Cultural Interchange," 1:54, 54, 64, 59, 59, 85).
47. For the ruler's viewpoint, see Symeon Seth, *Stephanites kai Ichnilates*, 1.37, 1.44, 1.31–42b, 4.91, in Sjöberg, *Stephanites und Ichnilates*, 183–84, 185, 171–85 (Noble,

"Cultural Interchange," 1:76, 77, 68–77, 102–3). For the courtier's angle, see Symeon Seth, *Stephanites kai Ichnilates*, 1.31, 1.9, in Sjöberg, *Stephanites und Ichnilates*, 171–72, 155–56 (Noble, "Cultural Interchange," 1:68, 56–57).

48. Symeon Seth, *Stephanites kai Ichnilates*, 1.9, in Sjöberg, *Stephanites und Ichnilates*, 158–59 (Noble, "Cultural Interchange," 1:58–59).
49. On mythos, see Aphthonios, in Spengel, *Rhetores Graeci*, 2:21 (example: mythos of ants and cicadas) (trans. Kennedy, *Progymnasmata*, 96); Hermogenes, in Spengel, *Rhetores Graeci*, 2:3–4 (Kennedy, *Progymnasmata*, 74–75); Theon, in Spengel, *Rhetores Graeci*, 2:72–78 (Kennedy, *Progymnasmata*, 23–28); Nikolaos, in Spengel, *Rhetores Graeci*, 3:451–55 (Kennedy, *Progymnasmata*, 133–36). The stories in *Syntipas* are described as *diegeseis*, another of the progymnasmata.
50. Symeon Seth, *Stephanites kai Ichnilates*, in Sjöberg, *Stephanites und Ichnilates*, 243–44 (Noble, "Cultural Interchange," 2:121–22).
51. Kekaumenos, in Wassiliewsky and Jernstedt, *Cecaumeni Strategicon*; Lemerle, *Prolégomènes*; and many recent articles by Charlotte Roueché, including "Literary Background," "Rhetoric of Kekaumenos," "Place of Kekaumenos," which place the first reception of Kekaumenos among the toparchs. Roueché is preparing a comprehensive web edition with multiple modern-language translations including the English version of her grandmother Georgina Buckler and herself.
52. As in the reading of Kazhdan, in Kazhdan and Constable, *People and Power*, 26.
53. Kekaumenos, 125, 9, 101, in Wassiliewsky and Jernstedt, *Cecaumeni Strategicon*, 53, 4, 42–43.
54. On the Vlach wars, see Roueché, "Defining the Foreign."
55. Kekaumenos, 73, in Wassiliewsky and Jernstedt, *Cecaumeni Strategicon*, 26–27.
56. *Osa dei ginesthai tou megalou kai ypsilou basileos ton Romaion mellontos phossateusai (Text C)*, 196–204, in Haldon, *Constantine Porphyrogenitus*, 106–7.
57. Anna Komnene, *Alexiad*, 5.9.3, in Reinsch and Kambylis, *Annae Comnenae Alexias*, 165 (Sewter, *Alexiad of Anna Comnena*, 150).
58. Holmes, *Basil II*. The discussion of chronicle versus history is still live; see Scott, "Byzantine Chronicles."
59. For Andrew's dog, see Scott, "Narrating Justinian," 45–46; for Theodosios's apple, see Scott, "Text and Context."
60. John Skylitzes, *Synopsis historion*, in Thurn, *Joannae Scylitzae Synopsis historiarum*, 225.86–89, 226.26–227.62 (Wortley, *Synopsis*, 217, 219–20); for illustration in Matr. vitr. 26–2, fol.127v–128v, see Tsamakda, *Illustrated Chronicle*, figs 300, 302, 303, 304, 305.
61. John Skylitzes, *Synopsis historion*, in Thurn, *Joannae Scylitzae Synopsis historiarum*, 167.79–170.46 (Wortley, *Synopsis*, 162–62); for illustration in Matr. vitr.26–2, fols. 104v, 105r, 105v, see Tsamakda, *Illustrated Chronicle*, figs. 234, 235, 236, 237, 238.
62. John Skylitzes, *Synopsis historion*, in Thurn, *Joannae Scylitzae Synopsis historiarum*, 91 (Wortley, *Synopsis*, 91).

63. John Skylitzes, *Synopsis historion*, in Thurn, *Joannae Scylitzae Synopsis historiarum*, 179.80–180.92; Wortley, *Synopsis*, 173–74, for illustration in Matr. vitr. 26–2, fol. 110 top, see Tsamakda, *Illustrated Chronicle*, fig. 249.
64. On these texts, see, respectively, Kaldellis, *Argument*; Gouma-Peterson, *Anna Komnene*; Buckley, *Alexiad of Anna Komnene*; Simpson and Efthymiadis, *Niketas Choniates*.
65. Michael Psellos, *Chronographia*, 7.20–25, in Renauld, *Michel Psellos Chronographie*, 2:94–98 (trans. Sewter, *Fourteen Byzantine Rulers*, 286–90).
66. Niketas Choniates, *Chronike diegesis*, 104–105 (trans. Magoulias, *O City of Byzantium*, 60).
67. See Mullett, "Novelisation," 8–14.
68. Anna Komnene, *Alexiad*, 7.4.1, in Reinsch and Kambylis, *Annae Comnenae Alexias*, 215 (Sewter, *Alexiad of Anna Comnena*, 196).
69. Anna Komnene, *Alexiad*, 8.4.5, in Reinsch and Kambylis, *Annae Comnenae Alexias*, 244–45 (Sewter, *Alexiad of Anna Comnena*, 223).
70. Anna Komnene, *Alexiad*, 1.2.7–10, in Reinsch and Kambylis, *Annae Comnenae Alexias*, 327–29 (Sewter, *Alexiad of Anna Comnena*, 302–4).
71. Anna Komnene, *Alexiad*, 13.1.5–10, in Reinsch and Kambylis, *Annae Comnenae Alexias*, 385–87 (Sewter, *Alexiad of Anna Comnena*, 358–60).
72. Symeon Seth, *Stephanites kai Ichnelates*, 1.24, in Sjöberg, *Stephanites und Ichnilates*, 166 (Noble, "Cultural Interchange," 1:64); Patterson, "Friends in High Places," 137–38.
73. For the most comprehensive bibliography, see Beaton and Ricks, *Digenes Akrites*.
74. See Ricks, *Byzantine Heroic Poetry*, on the Escorial Digenes as a collection of five separate but related poems. For a warning against seeing the folk poems about Digenes collected since 1800 as sources for the written heroic poems, see Beaton, *Folk Poetry of Modern Greece*.
75. Lord, *Singer of Tales*, 17–29.
76. On this issue, see Mullett, "Monastic Culture."
77. Chadwick, "John Moschos." For a reading that argues for a specialist meaning of *diegesis*, narration, in Late Antiquity, see Rapp, "Storytelling as Spiritual Communication"; mine is less specialist and more integrated.
78. John Moschos, *Pratum spirituale*, Ed. PG 87:2851–3116 (trans. Wortley, *Spiritual Meadow*).
79. Paul of Evergetis, *Synagoge*, in Makarios of Corinth and Nikodemos Hagiorites, *Evergetinos etoi synagoge*.
80. Crostini, "*Katechetikon* of Paul."
81. For the dossier, see Mullett, Wilson, and Nicholson, *Forty Martyrs of Sebasteia*.
82. Paul of Evergetis, *Synagoge*, 1.12.6, in Makarios of Corinth and Nikodemos Hagiorites, *Evergetinos etoi synagoge* (7th ed.), 185–86.
83. Symeon Seth, *Stephanites kai Ichnilates*, 2.57, 60b, 61, 72, in Sjöberg, *Stephanites und Ichnilates*, 191–92, 194–95, 200 (Noble, "Cultural Interchange," 1:82–83, 84–85, 89–90).

84. On Anna Dalassene, see Anna Komnene, *Alexiad*, 3.6.1–2, in Reinsch and Kambylis, *Annae Comnenae Alexias*, 100 (Sewter, *Alexiad of Anna Comnena*, 91–92); on mothers, see Mullett, "Alexios I Komnenos."

85. *Diegesis merike*, in Meyer, *Die Haupturkunden*, 163–84 (ed. Uspenskij, *Istorija Afona*, 37–78); Mullett, "Diegesis epistolike."

86. *Diegesis merike*, in Meyer, *Die Haupturkunden*, 169.

87. Ibid., 173–74.

88. Ibid., 180.

89. Ibid., 173–74.

90. Nicholas Kataskepenos, *Bios kai politeia*, ch. 47.1; Mullett, *Death of the Holy Man*.

91. Nicholas Kataskepenos, *Bios kai politeia*, ch. 47.14, 235.

92. Ibid., ch. 34, 143–46.

93. Ibid., ch. 35, 146–53.

94. On the tellers, see Wilson, *Storytelling and Theatre*, 17–21; and for the medieval West (travelers, entertainers, the old, peasants, preachers, courtiers), see Ziolkowski, *Fairy Tales*, 5. For the relationship between storyteller and listener and the part played by memory in "the art of repeating stories," see Benjamin, "Storyteller." In our case, a shared rhetorical education in mythos and diegesis made both animal fables and stories in a recognizable historical setting equally attractive.

95. Scheub, *Story*, 15: "The essential component in story is emotion."

96. Advisory: see Benjamin, "Storyteller"; affirmative: see Bauman, *Verbal Art*, 37–45, on the power inherent in performance to transform social structures, see Zipes, *Creative Storytelling*, 224, on truth-telling, and Gottschall, *Storytelling Animal*, esp. 136–38, on story as a cohering force; for ludic, see Bauman, *Story, Performance, and Event*, 11–53, on tall tales and trickster narratives (cf. esp. Kekaumenos). Huizinga, *Homo Ludens*, does not draw the connection between play and storytelling (unlike poetry and play; 119–35), but his functions of display and contest (113–14) ring true in our context.

8

Error and the Abbasid Performer

The "Rare Slips" of the Fifth/Eleventh-Century Ghars al-Niʿma al-Ṣābiʾ

MAURICE A. POMERANTZ

A Rare Slip

While attending a gathering of scholars, the Abbasid littérateur (*adīb*) Ghars al-Niʿma Abū l-Ḥasan Muḥammad b. Hilāl al-Ṣābiʾ (d. 480/1086–87) once made a fateful slip of the tongue. As the group moved between topics, one scholar mentioned tales involving "the dimwits of the age who recklessly perpetrate errors" (*thuqalāʾ al-zamān al-mutaʿassifīn al-mutaʿāṭīn*).[1]

Hearing this delightful tale, Ghars was eager to share another. Relishing the opportunity, he swiftly volunteered an anecdote, saying, "so-and-so in that story reminds me of the way in which Ibn al-Qādisī oversteps truth and disregards it" (*innahu la-yushbihu ibn al-Qādisī fīmā yataʿāṭāhu mimmā yatajāwazu al-ṣawāb wa-yatakhāṭāhū*). Ghars's phrase even rhymed, demonstrating that he could play this courtly game with skill.

Ghars soon felt that something was amiss. Looking around the circle, he realized that sitting next to him was the same Ibn al-Qādisī he had just lampooned! Trying to cover his blunder, Ghars stated that the man he was speaking of was not Ibn al-Qādisī but his idiotic brother. He then tried to flatter Ibn al-Qādisī, telling him that while he was a great source of eloquence, his brother's feeble imitations of him were shameful. Fortunately for Ghars, Ibn al-Qādisī proved to be as dimwitted as his sibling, and Ghars escaped this awkward situation with only an interesting tale to tell.

Errors: Revealing the Texts and Contexts of Performance

Ghars's story about this verbal slip emphasizes that there was much at stake in erring in front of one's peers. Narrated in the first person, his account plays on the anxieties of an elite in which the insult of an esteemed person at a literary salon might have important repercussions. While the conversation seemed on first blush to be on a frivolous topic, Ghars's language reveals his fear over the shame that his mistake could have caused him, as genres shifted from lighthearted to serious in an instant. His tale dramatizes the embarrassment and loss of face that was a "nightmare scenario" for the leading scholarly figures of fifth/eleventh-century Baghdad.

Verbal performance in learned settings, such as that which Ghars describes, was rich with social meaning. Elites in Abbasid society lived in a face-to-face world in which personal reputation and honor took precedence. Roy Mottahedeh in his classic work on Buyid-era social relations, *Loyalty and Leadership in an Early Islamic Society*, describes the bonds of loyalty between men of similar groups as a fundamental feature of social and political life in Muslim society of the fourth–fifth/tenth–eleventh centuries. Mottahedeh points to the existence of formal and informal ties of "loyalty, obligation and leadership" between individuals that were vital to "sustaining a resilient and self-renewing social order" in Baghdad and other cities in Buyid Iraq and western Iran.[2] By performing at scholarly circles, the literati hoped to affirm ties with one another while solidifying their place among the leading notables and authorities of the city.

Given the ad hoc nature of most of these social arrangements, elites shared a common system of comportment and behavior that found its greatest source and expression in ornate literary language. Literary culture and cultivation, known as *adab*, offered a rich store of replicable verbal and behavioral scripts on which courtiers could rely in particular situations. As Jocelyn Sharlet has noted, the *udabā'* were professionals who had skills in rhetoric that they could deploy at court.[3] These literary intellectuals performed with the sense that their words and actions were themselves generic models that had value.

Ghars's speech in this learned circle was part of an established system of communication at court that linked style, genre, and emotion. The discussion in which he took part, even as it considered "the dimwits of the age who recklessly perpetrate errors," served as a theater for the control of expression. In telling a tale of this type, the performer encouraged a spirit of levity (*hazl*) that was surely familiar to the audience.[4] Such generic stories offered moments to divert the mind and dispel the tedium of learned discussions.[5] Even on the level of expression, scholars needed to regulate and control both their style and genre in ways that were pleasing to others. Ghars spoke using rhymed prose (*sajʿ*), and he was deemed the most eloquent by the men of his time; the cadence of his prose offered a measure of control in a potentially volatile setting.

Ghars's retelling of a courtly encounter was not unusual. Courtiers often wrote and spoke about court matters, being the preeminent subject of *adab*. Ghars's narration of his own embarrassment, however, casts his first telling of the tale into sharp relief. His recording of errors in performance reveals the social context of the courtly circle as a place where one's honor and social standing were at stake. And his retelling emphasizes the narrow distance between success and failure. Ghars intended his speech at the court to create levity in his audience, but instead it provoked astonishment. And while he had hoped that the story would have solidified his social honor, his performance brought him nothing but shame.

Ghars's recounting of his failure in performance raises further questions. What did he imagine this second-order reflection on the performance of the tale would create for his listeners? Were the listeners of Ghars's tale supposed to take pity on him for his ill fortune? Were they impressed with Ghars's capacity to extricate himself from this embarrassing situation? Did they feel relief at the end of the tale? Or did they feel chastened and resolved themselves to be more vigilant?

This chapter considers the different meanings that Ghars and his contemporaries attached to the act of performance and errors at court by reading accounts of mistakes that Ghars relates in his compendium, *Al-Hafawāt al-Nādira* (The rare slips). In particular, we will focus on these narratives of error as a way to understand the operative codes of courtly performance. Like Ghars and his contemporaries, we will consider the transformative power of performance by reading accounts of when things went wrong.

A Collection of Errors: *Al-Hafawāt al-Nādira*

Ghars's report of his predicament comes at the beginning of his *adab* compilation. The context of the work's authorship is unknown, other than what Ghars states about the circumstances of its composition. His description of the frame in which he wrote the work hardly seems to go beyond the conventional:

> كنت جاريتني من الهفوات الجارية على ألسنة المتحفّظين المتحرّزين والسقطات الآتية من الغارّين الغافلين وما أشبه ذلك من المقالات وطريف الاتفاقات طرفاً استطرفناه وحديثاً استغربناه واتفق أن لحقني منه ما صدّق العجب والاستطراف ونالني فيه من الخجل والحياء ما بلغ من الإفراط والإسراف

> You accompanied me in recalling the slips that had been transmitted by the tongues of those who were careful and cautious, the errors that had issued from the mouths of the heedless and mindless, and the wonderful occurrences that we found delightful, and the speech that we found strange. From all this, there came to me that which provoked wonder and the sense of the novel, while I was overcome with shame and embarrassment.[6]

Despite Ghars's customary address to the patron, his language in this passage is revealing. In it, he evokes two central notions of Arabic *adab*, namely, the provocation of wonder and the appreciation of rarity. Ghars states how recalling these stories led him to a secondary set of emotions including shame (*ḥayāʾ*) and embarrassment (*khajal*) for those who erred. Through reading these tales, the reader undergoes a double transformation: the first involves the pleasure of reading the tale; the second, an identification with the fate of its protagonist.

Ghars al-Niʿma entitles his book "The Rare Slips," drawing on the well-established notion of inadvertent error. Lexicographers understood the term *hafwa* as relating to other terms connoting "loss of footing" (*zalla*) or "falling" (*saqṭa*).[7] The term was perhaps most commonly associated with the widely known proverb "Every sharp sword glances off, every stallion stumbles, and every learned man will slip." (*li-kulli jawād*^{in} *kabwat*^{un} *wa-li-kulli ṣārim*^{in} *nabwat*^{un} *wa-li-kull ʿālim*^{in} *hafwat*^{un}).[8]

The notion of a *hafwa* as an unwitting error appears first in pre-Islamic poetry as the root meaning of movement or flight in the poet al-Akhṭal's verse (d. before 92/710), in which the term imparts a sense of the error that falling in love might pose. The term, however, does not consistently have this sense in other poets' works.[9] By the Abbasid period, *hafwa* connotes an inadvertent mistake. The poet Abū Tammām (d. 232/846) understands the term in the sense of an unintentional mistake toward the patron, while a generation later, Ibn al-Rūmī (d. 283/896) understands *hafwa* as a mistake in judgment.[10] Much like the term *sahw*, used for the wandering of the mind in which one can be "unmindful in prayer" (*sahā fī al-ṣalāt*), the term *hafwa* does not suggest a willful commission of a wrong.

Ghars al-Niʿma's compendium, however, does not simply record famed slips and errors. Rather, the adjective describing the noun in the title, *nādira*, means both "rare" and "choice." Thus, in his book, Ghars al-Niʿma collects examples of mistakes by people who rarely make them. At the same time, the title also signals that the work is part of the larger generic conception of *al-nawādir*, "rarities." *Nawādir* included works dealing with the rarities of language, such as those compiled by Abū Isḥāq al-Zajjāj (d. 311/923). Thus, *al-hafawāt al-nādira* are rare in the sense that they are rich in potential meaning and become moments that demonstrate the element of chance in performance. Rare slips are fear inducing for performers because they point to errors in performance and are engaging for readers because they signal the intrusion of chance in a literary system based on the predictability of established codes.

Ghars's work is the first of its kind to dwell on rare errors (*hafawāt*). His collection, however, owes much in its spirit and even structure to the two story collections of the previous century written by the littérateur al-Tanūkhī (d. 383–84/994), *Al-Faraj baʿd al-shidda* (Relief after hardship) and *Nishwār al-Muḥāḍarah* (The table talk of a Mesopotamian judge). In the stories of *Al-Faraj baʿd al-shidda*, often told in the first person, the narrator undergoes a particular hardship, and just as the events of the tale seem to be at their bleakest for the narrator, some form of relief (*faraj*) intervenes, and the story concludes.[11]

Ghars was familiar with al-Tanūkhī's collections of tales. In their structure, the tales of *Al-Hafawāt al-Nādira* are similar to those of al-Tanūkhī's *Faraj*. A majority of the stories in the *Al-Hafawāt al-Nādira*, like al-Tanūkhī's *Faraj*, are related in the first person. Emotionally, they consider an analogous set of issues, in which a chance occurrence might lead to the narrator's downfall. The resolution of the tales in the *Al-Hafawāt al-Nādira*, much like those in al-Tanūkhī's *Faraj*, is found often in the telling and retelling of the story. In both cases, narrative serves a redemptive function in the face of the vicissitudes of fate that periodically disrupt the lives of every human.

Like the collections of al-Tanūkhī, Ghars includes stories from the first five centuries of Islam. Unlike al-Tanūkhī's collection, Ghars's *Al-Hafawāt al-Nādira* does not group tales in any order. As C. E. Bosworth describes the *Al-Hafawāt al-Nādira*,

> It comprises, after a short exordium in rhymed prose, 405 anecdotes, all on the basic theme of errors and solecisms committed by intelligent, normally prudent persons, or the blunders of the negligent, heedless persons, most of whom are usually profoundly embarrassed when the realize the inappropriateness or inauspiciousness of their hasty words or actions. The stories vary in length from a few lines to four or five printed pages, and all are in a simple, straightforward prose style.[12]

Although there are stories included from the pre-Islamic period until the author's lifetime, the majority take place during the second/eighth century and mainly at the court of the Abbasid caliphs. Ghars collected these stories from reading sources including those of al-Jāḥiẓ (255/868–69), al-Ṣūlī (d. 335/947), and al-Tanūkhī, among others. He also derives much information from the works of his father, Hilāl.[13]

The paradigmatic notion of the *hafwa* found in the majority of the stories in the collection is one committed by a weaker person in the presence of a more powerful person, usually a ruler or patron. Thus the court was a common location for stories of this type. Yet the collection does not only focus on the court: there are tales that consider errors committed among a group of friends sitting together.[14] Errors, it seems, like manners could extend beyond the realm of the court affecting the ways in which men related to one another when they were distant from the patron's sight.

Ghars al-Niʿma was in a good position to compile this collection about courtly performance in the Abbasid period. Ghars was the last major author of the Ṣābi' clan that had served the Abbasid caliphs for eleven generations. The family included several important state officials, physicians, and historians, such as his grandfather, the famed chancellery writer and historian Abū Isḥāq Ibrāhīm b. Hilāl al-Ṣābi' (d. 384/994), who had been an intimate consort of some of the most important literary figures of the fourth/tenth century. Ghars's father, the well-known historian and littérateur Hilāl b. Muḥassin b. Ibrāhīm al-Ṣābi' (d. 448/1056), had served in the Buyid administration and had authored an important chronicle of the Buyid *amīrs*' reign, as well as a book devoted to their viziers. The most significant of his works, however, was a historical collection devoted to the courtly protocols of the Abbasid caliphs, *Rusūm dār al-khilāfa* (Customs of the caliphal court), which was among other things an attempt to preserve features of Abbasid court ceremonies after customs had languished and changed during this period of Buyid rule in Baghdad.[15]

Ghars may even have held the government post as the head of the chancery under the Abbasid caliph al-Qā'im (r. 421–465/1031–75).[16] Ghars's connection to the Abbasid state and the stories that he reported on the authority of his ancestors lent his work the sort of prestige that others would not have had. He compiled *Al-Hafawāt* by copying information from written sources, as well as by recording oral reports from leading members of the Baghdādī élite. Having inherited wealth from his father, Ghars appears to have lived much of his life among books. He founded a library in Baghdad as a public endowment (*waqf*). In addition to the *Al-Hafawāt al-Nādira*, Ghars wrote several other works, including a continuation of his father Hilāl's history and a work based on al-Tanūkhī's *Nishwār al-Muḥadara* (Table talk of a Mesopotamian judge), entitled *Kitāb al-Rabīʿ* (The book of springtime).

Ghars's *Al-Hafawāt al-Nādira* is surely an entertaining work of *adab* literature with much historical detail. But the collection is more than this. For the stories contain multiple layers of narrative complexity: they create suspense over the nature of a verbal slip, wonder at the complexity of such situations, and relief at their eventual resolution. The following sections consider various accounts of errors from Ghars's collection. By examining accounts of where performers' literary cultivation of *adab* was tested, these tales reveal nuances of *adab* as a courtly code of language and comportment.

Between the Oral and the Written

Although selections in *Al-Hafawāt al-Nādira* follow no particular order, stories in the collection fall into several general types. The most notable tales for the historian of performance are those that emphasize how performers unwittingly made errors in the course of performing a written text.

In one tale, Ghars al-Niʿma relates that in Basra there was a singing girl named Faḍla. Like many singing girls, she went by a moniker, *khayṭ al-barrāda*, "the string of the jug of the water cooler."[17] Ghars states that Faḍla was extremely beautiful (*mufriṭa fī l-jamāl*) and possessed a pleasing singing voice (*ṭayyib al-ghināʾ*). She customarily received five gold *dīnār*s for her services at court. The term Ghars uses for the payment (*jadhr*) was slang for the payment of a singing girl.[18] Faḍla often confused the letter *qāf* with the letter *kāf*. As the famed essayist al-Jāḥiẓ (d. 255/868–69) makes plain in his *Epistle on the Singing Girls*, professional singing girls (*qiyān*) such as Faḍla ought to have been well educated; he states that a skilled singer has a repertoire of "upwards of four thousand songs, each one containing two to four lines, making a total of ten thousand lines of poetry."[19] Yet Faḍla's inability to distinguish certain Arabic consonants properly proved a serious flaw.

Invited to the court of one of the *amīr*s of Baṣra, Faḍla attempted to sing the following lines of the Abbasid poet Ismāʿīl b. Jāmiʿ:

ومالي لا أبكي وأندُب ناقتي　　إذا صَدَرَ الرُّعيانُ وِردَ المناهِل
وكنتُ إذا ما اشتدّ شوقي ورَحَلتها　　فسارت بمحزون كثير البَلابِل

Why should I not cry and mourn my she-camel
when the shepherds left the watering places?
Were not my desire to increase and I mounted it,
it would have transported me to a place full of trials.[20]

While singing this verse, Faḍla mispronounced the *qāf* as a *kāf* and said, "Why should I not cry and lament my *coitus* (*andubu nākatī*)."

According to Ghars, the *amīr* hearing the mistake took it as a bad omen (*taṭayyara min qawlihā*).

The *amīr* then stated,

> قد وزنَّا لك خمس دنانير وأحضرناكِ لما يُحضر مِثلُك له فإذا كنت تبكين وتَنْدُبين ناكتك
> فما نريد مُقامَك عندنا

> We had weighed out five *dīnār*s for you, and we brought you here to do the same things that others have done. Yet if you are mourning and lamenting your *coitus*, we don't want you to stay here any longer.[21]

Then the *amīr* sent Faḍla away. The anecdote ends with Faḍla's first-person report, "I was ashamed, and most embarrassed."

This anecdote, much like the first involving Ghars, seems intended to provoke two responses. Faḍla's verbal error leads her from within the normal boundaries of polite speech to mention a sexual taboo. At a further remove, the story portrays an entertaining scene that demonstrates how an error in pronunciation might lead to real consequences, moving from certain reward to humiliating failure.

Such inability on the part of a servant to perform a written text reverses a common pattern in other tales of the clever servant capable of reading and manipulating language to gain an advantage over a patron. For instance, in the following tale, which incidentally also turns on the interpretation of a text of a song by Ibn Jāmiʿ, Abū l-Faraj al-Iṣfahānī (d. c. 363/972) in his *Kitāb al-Aghānī* (Books of songs) describes how al-Rabīʿ b. Yūnus (d. 169/785–86 or 170/786) came into the service of the Abbasid caliphs. He had been one of fifty slaves given to the Abbasid caliph al-Manṣūr (r. 136–58/754–75) and had served as an assistant to a certain Yāsir, who was in charge of aiding the caliph's ablutions at court.[22] Gaining the caliph's favor by his attentive service, the clever al-Rabīʿ stands by as the caliph sees the verses of Ibn Jāmiʿ written on a wall but does not understand the words written beneath them. Al-Rabīʿ with innate cleverness explains to the caliph that the marks below the verses (*āh āh*) are placed there to indicate the despair of the one recording the verses.

In contrast to al-Rabīʿ in the previous story, Faḍla proves a less adroit reader than her master. Her error overturns the power that she ought to have maintained over her patron. Rather than moving her patron to melancholy reflection by evincing a delicate understanding of a text—something implied in the story of al-Rabīʿ b. Yūnus and the caliph—Faḍla's "slip" creates a sense of discomfort and anger on the part of her patron. Rapture turns to rage, and the *amīr* desires only that she leave his presence.

While on one level the narrative offers a serious account of how one feels shame for the singer, one could also understand the story as a rare comedic event that provokes wonder at its occurrence. Faḍla's slip from *qāf* to *kāf* accidently exposes the latent erotic possibilities in her performance. Her mistake is not simply an error—it imparts a sexual undertone to the performance. By restaging this moment, the story prompts the reader to weigh the significance of her slip.

Slips between Affect and Reason

Performing well at court demanded that *udabāʾ* develop skills that necessitated not only linguistic mastery but also the management of emotions. The capacity to influence a patron through an emotional plea was a central skill of the rhetor or poet. But what about those moments when the poet's or performer's own emotions caused him to miss the mark?

One such tale describes how the Abbasid caliph Abū Jaʿfar al-Manṣur (r. 136–58/754–75) once summoned "a member of the Umayyad family to his presence and scolded him for the acts of his family."[23] Dramatically portraying a confrontation between the power of the new rulers over the former dynasty, the situation dramatizes the court as a location for the projection of state authority. Such court theatrics made an apposite frame for later readers to consider the emotions involved in court performance.

This tale told on the authority of al-Rabīʿ b. Yūnus (in this story, now the caliph's chamberlain) describes how the caliph then enumerated the many wrongs that members of the Umayyad family had committed. Listening to the caliph's performance, the Umayyad was certain that the "sword was coming soon" (*lam yashukk al-rajul anna al-sayf baʿduhu*), and he "turned pale in color and fear almost killed him" (*fa-ʾmtaqaʿ lawnuhu wa-kāda an yaqtulahu khawfuhu*). But after his show of anger, al-Manṣūr then pardoned the Umayyad, "turning away from that speech and moving toward pardon" (*rajaʿ ʿan dhalika ʾl-qawl ilā l-ṣafḥ ʿanhu wa īmānihi*).

The Umayyad falls silent, stunned by the events. Al-Rabīʿ prompts him to speak, saying, "The Commander of the Faithful has granted your life, so thank him and offer prayers to him!" (*qad wahabaka amīr al-muʾminīn damak fa-ushkurhu wa-adʿu lahu*). The Umayyad then recites the following verse:

فما بُقْيا عليَّ تركتُماني ولكن خِفْتُما صَرَدَ النِّبال

> It was not by mercy that you two spared me
> Rather, you feared the downpour of arrows![24]

Al-Rabīʿ states,

واتفق لسعادته أن لم يسمع المنصور قوله وورد عليّ ما حيّرني وأدهشني فأَما الرجل فلم يدرِ ما قاله لسانه لزوال عقله عنه ومفارقةِ لبِّهِ له

> It so happened for his good fortune that al-Manṣūr did not hear his speech. And that which I had heard had confused and astonished me. For the man [the Umayyad] did not know what his tongue was speaking because of the temporary loss of his mind and rationality.[25]

Since al-Manṣūr did not hear the Umayyad's words, he asked the chamberlain to repeat them. Al-Rabīʿ then substituted the following verses attributed to the famed pre-Islamic poet ʿAntara b. Shaddād:

العبدُ عبْدُكُمُ والأمرُ أمرُكُمُ فهَلْ عَذابُكَ عنِّي اليومَ مصْروفُ

> The servant belongs to you, and so too the command,
> Will you postpone your torment of me today?[26]

The caliph then tells al-Rabīʿ to dismiss the Umayyad, suggesting that he is perhaps deaf and did not hear what al-Manṣūr had said about granting his freedom. As the vignette concludes, al-Rabīʿ tells the Umayyad what he said at that fateful moment. When al-Rabīʿ relates his response, he has the following conversation with the man:

ثمّ حدَّثته من بعد بما كان منه فانذعر له وحلف أنه لا يدري ما قاله وقال: قد حقنتَ دمي بحسن تلطّفك بعد أن أراد أن يطيح بسوء الاتفاق ويكون لساني القاتل لي

Then I told him about what had happened to him. And he became alarmed for himself. He swore that he did not know what he had spoken. And then he said, "You have saved my life, by your kindness, after it was threatened because of a bad coincidence. And my tongue would have been my own killer."[27]

This story, like many in the *Al-Hafawāt al-Nādira*, features errors in poetic verse uttered unwittingly because of the extreme emotions of the speaker. Such moments suggest that verse—rather than prose—was often a vehicle for the performance of emotion at court. Yet what is even more striking is the suggestion in this tale that the Umayyad is unaware of the verses he is reciting because of his terror. The patron, oblivious to the real emotion contained in the verses that criticize him, hears only servile flattery.

The final frame of the story takes the reader outside the realm of courtly power, where along with al-Rabīʿ and the Umayyad, we marvel at the events. From a safe remove, what had once seemed a harrowing interlude morphs into a pleasant tale. The fear of imminent death has become an occasion to wonder at the workings of chance that almost caused a man to be "killed by his own tongue." While such an example is surely an extreme representation of the problems caused by emotions gaining the upper hand during situations of high pressure at court, it equally foregrounds real anxieties about "slips" of the tongue during live performances.

Ghars's collection explores another dimension to emotions and performance through the story of a singer at the court of the *amīr* Sharaf al-Dawla Muslim b. Quraysh, the ruler of Mosul from 453–78/1061–85. The singer tells of how in the course of one session at court, he invoked his former patron, the recently deceased Seljuk vizier Abū Nāṣir al-Kundurī (d. 455/1063), known for his generosity.

The singer describes how he was extolling Kundurī:

> I mentioned his [Kundurī's] excellences. How he customarily dealt with me and my comrades providing us with a great amount of stipends and gifts. I exaggerated and overstepped the mark in order to encourage Muslim to do the same. The song ended with my mention of [Kundurī], and my prayers upon him, and then I stopped and sang:
>
> قَوَاصِدَ كافورٍ تَوَارِكَ غيرِهِ   وَمَن قَصَدَ البَحرَ استَقَلَّ السوَاقيا
>
> Whoever goes to Kāfūr forgoes any other patron;
> for he who has sought his ocean of generosity will deem other streams slight.[28]

The singer's patron, Muslim b. Quraysh, hearing this line interjects, "God damn you! What sort of companionship [*muʿāshara*] is this?" The poet then states, "I awoke from my slumber, and swore that I didn't say what I said with any intent against him; it only represented what had occurred to me and occurred to my heart [*ittafaqa lī wa-ʿuriḍa ʿalā qalbī*]." The sequence ends with the singer stating, "I feared his anger would get the better of him, but God made up for it [*kafā Allāh*] and he restrained himself."[29] Performing before his patron, this singer sought to encourage his generosity. Yet he explains instead how he overspent (*asraftu*) in his description of his former patron al-Kundurī. His use of this economic metaphor to describe his speech here is telling: *isrāf* refers to extravagant or wasteful spending. The implication is that the poet's praise of the generous patron al-Kundurī was a verbal overexpenditure.

The singer hoped his lavish speech would encourage generosity. His exaltation of another, however, had the opposite effect: rather than fostering friendship with his patron, the singer's language revealed his blindness to the emotional needs of the patron who was before him.

The singer's quotation from al-Mutanabbī's praise of Kāfūr al-Ikhshīdī (d. 357/968) adds further layers of meaning to the episode. The verses he quotes are from al-Mutanabbī's long ode *Kafā bika dāʾan* (It is sickness enough). Al-Mutanabbī composed this ode for Kāfūr in 342/957 when he came to the court of Kāfūr in Egypt, after leaving his patron, Sayf al-Dawla. While his ode contained lines describing al-Mutanabbī's great initial passion for Kāfūr, these lines stand out for being uttered at the beginning of a patronage relationship that eventually fails.

As both Suzanne Stetkevych and Margaret Larkin note, al-Mutanabbī's poem implies strong disavowal of his former patron Sayf al-Dawla (r. 333–56/944–67) and generous praise of his new patron, Kāfūr. Both scholars read the verse cited by this singer as showering praise on Kāfūr while veiling criticism of Sayf al-Dawla, implying that his generosity was but a stream compared to the ocean of Kāfūr's largess.[30]

The singer's misreading of the social situation is then followed by his ill considered use of the verses of al-Mutanabbī. Caught up in his own reverie and feelings for his former patron, the singer makes an unfortunate mistake.

Ghars's tale of this ill-received performance operates on two levels. One reading follows the course of the intended aims of the singer and the failed outcome of the performance. Another encourages the reader to reflect on how the assessment of an emotional situation at court is vital to a successful performance.

Slips between the Imaginary and the Real

Many literary genres performed at court contrast, for instance, the audience's shared participation in the imaginative constructions of the performer as well as the real exchange between performer, audience, and patron. In poetic genres, such as the polythematic ode (*qaṣīda*) with its opening section (*nasīb*) describing a lost love, the performer often moved from depicting an actual courtly situation to an imaginary one.

Poets would describe the experience of a lost love to indicate their departure from one patron to another. Through the imaginative language of love, they signaled the possibility of real bonds of fealty and loyalty to their current patron. In the course of such a performance of fictive romance, the performer had the power to evoke hidden passions, like sparks from a flint.

Yet in recalling romances, performers often did not pass as easily between nuances of the real and imaginary as they would have liked. The figurative language of love poetry could and did act as a shield for subtle critiques. Singers were not immune to analogous problems of intention. Patrons were known to wonder if there were motives behind their singer's choice of song texts.

Ghars al-Niʿma relates a story, on the authority of his grandfather Abū Isḥāq al-Ṣābi’ (d. 384/994) of how the *amīr* ʿAḍud al-Dawlah (d. 373/983) invited two female singers to entertain at his court.[31] The narrator, Abū Isḥāq al-Ṣābi’, states that this gathering took place after ʿAḍud al-Dawlah had defeated and executed his cousin ʿIzz al-Dawlah Bakhtiyār (d. 367/997–98), who had rivaled him for leadership of the Buyid dynasty. The first singer, Mashgala al-Thaqiliyya, performed a poem that began with a lament over a lost beloved (*nasīb*):

أيا عمرو لم أصبِرْ ولي فيكَ حيلةٌ   ولكن دعاني اليأْسُ منكَ إلى الصبرِ
سَأصبرُ محزونًا وإني لمُوجَعٌ   كما صبر العطشانُ في البلد القَفر

ʿAmr! I won’t be patient as long as I can still find a way to you
But my despair forced me into patience!
I’ll be patient in sadness, while I’m in pain
Like the patience of a thirsty man in the desert.[32]

Abū Isḥāq reports that the ruler ʿAḍud al-Dawla responded with anger:

فظنّ أَنها عرَّضت بعزّ الدولة بختيار، فأَعرض عنها وغاظه ذلك منها، وأَقلَّ الحفلَ بغنائها، مع أَنها واحدةُ زمانها، وأخذتُ أُطريها فلا يرعيني سمعاً فيها

He believed that she was hinting at ʿIzz al-Dawlah Bakhtiyār, and so he became angry and shunned her. For this reason, she found difficulty finding other work, despite the fact that she was the preeminent singer of her time. I began to praise her, but he wouldn’t listen to me.[33]

Following Mashgala al-Thaqiliyya, the other singer, Ẓalūm al-Shahramiyya, sang a poem that was lighter:

سَيُسليكَ عمّا فاتَ دولةُ مقبلٍ   أوآئلُهُ محمودةٌ وأواخرُهْ
ثنى اللّٰهُ عِطفَيهِ وألّفَ شخصهُ   على جُود مُذ شُدَّت عليه مآزرُهْ

Good fortune will make you forget that which has passed;
that which has a blessed beginning ends well.
God will clothe and accustom him to generosity
since the time that He first supported him.[34]

Hearing this singer's performance, Abū Isḥāq reported that ʿAḍud al-Dawla reacted in the following manner:

فتهلَّل وجهُه وطربَ وشرب واستعاد الصوتَ وقال لي: يا أَبا إِسحق هذا الغناء! ولم يكن بين المرأَتين تقاربٌ

> His face lit up, and he rejoiced and drank. He wanted to hear the verse sung once more. He said to me, "Abū Isḥāq, this is singing!" even though she wasn't in the same league.[35]

Abū Isḥāq al-Ṣābiʾ then states his wonder at this occurrence:

فما أدري كيف اتفق ذلك على مشغلة وأن غنّت ظلوم بعدها ما غنّت فإن كان عن نيّة من ظلوم وعمد فما قصَّرت أو اتّفاق فقد وُفِّقَتْ

> I don't know how this occurred to Mashghala and that Ẓalūm sang after her what she sang. If it was an intentional act by Ẓalūm, she did not miss the mark, or if it was a coincidence, she found success.[36]

This story turns on the conventions of genre and performance. While Mashghala performs a serious ode meant to evoke the patron's melancholy reflection, the verse she sings elicits thoughts of real political events that the ruler does not wish to remember. There is no hint that Mashghala intended to do this. Moreover, there is no indication that anything in the verses is a veiled allusion or intimation (*taʿrīḍ*) of the death of ʿIzz al-Dawla. Rather, the sadness evoked by the genre of the *nasīb* appears to provoke the anger of ʿAḍud al-Dawla at a perceived sleight. In contrast, the poetic verses of Ẓalūm, the second singer, foster unrestrained joy in ʿAḍud al-Dawla, which leads him to exalt the performance.

Abū Isḥāq's reasoned assessment of the two singers' performances contrasts with ʿAḍud al-Dawla's passionate responses. During the first performance, the ruler, gripped by fear and paranoia about the seemingly subversive undertones of the verse, is unable to hear the beauty of the tune. He is then enraptured by the second performance and seemingly revels in the poem's summons to forget past woes.

ʿAḍud al-Dawla's inability to hear the musical artistry before him points to the discord that often came between the performer's intentions and the patron's perceptions. Patrons could understand poems in ways that greatly differed from performers. Mashgala erred in singing a mournful tune for a patron who wanted to celebrate.

At the end of the tale, Abū Isḥāq's wonder centers on whether the final performer succeeded because she intended to sing a verse that would better suit the patron. The first performance, though beautifully sung, did not address the patron's needs; the second appears to have captured the ruler's state of mind. Encouraging the act of forgetting, it hints none too subtly that the ruler was in need of putting the past behind him.

Slips between This World and the Hereafter

One common genre of tales in the collection considers the "predictive power" of poetic performance, in which a poet's or performer's choice of words appears to contain hidden knowledge or to influence events. Patrons were vigilant listeners at court performances, believing that one could derive a sign or augury (*taṭayyur*; *ṭīra*) of future troubles from these performers' words.[37]

Ghars provides an example of the kind of error that could result from this "predictive power" in his account of the poet Abū l-Walīd Arṭah b. Suhīyya al-Muzanī's performance for the Umayyad caliph ʿAbd al-Malik b. Marwān (r. 65–86/685–705).[38] The poet, who had been alive in the pre-Islamic age, was an old man when he recited the following verses:

رأيتُ المرء تأكله اللَّيالي   كأكْلِ الأرْضِ ساقطةَ الحديدِ
وما تَبْغي المنِيَّةُ حين تأْتي   على نفسِ ابن آدَمَ من مزيدِ
وأعلمُ أنَّهَا سَتَكُرُّ حَتّى   تُوَفّي نَذْرَها بأبي الوَليدِ

I know man to be a creature consumed by time,
Like the way the earth devours scraps of iron.
Death does not seek more than this
when it comes to the soul of a human.
Know that death will keep charging forward
until it fulfills its vow with Abū l-Walīd.[39]

When the caliph heard the al-Muzanī sing this final line, the caliph responded with fright, believing that the old poet had just foretold his imminent death, for Walīd was the name of the caliph's son. The poet hastened to explain that this was merely a coincidence, that the *kunya* (*agnomen*) Abū l-Walīd was a reference to his own son, not the caliph's, which the audience all affirmed to the caliph, attempting to calm his fright.

This tale does not simply highlight the error of the poet or the coincidence of the poet and the patron having children of the same name. Rather, it suggests the patron's anxiety because the poem's words appeared to foretell his imminent death. It bespeaks the ways in which courtly performance was understood as revealing possible truths that would have otherwise remained hidden.

Revealing Slips

In *The Psychopathology of Everyday Life*, first published in German in 1901 as *Zur Psychopathologie des Alltagslebens*, Sigmund Freud describes an error that he made while reciting a poem to his young daughter:

> Der Affe gar possierlich ist,
> Zumal wenner vom Apfel frisst.
> [The monkey is very funny, particularly when he's eating an apple.]

> Instead, I began to say: "Der Apfe . . ." This seems to be a contamination of *Affe* by Apfel (a compromise structure), or alternatively it may be seen as anticipation of the word *Apfel* which I was about to utter. The fact is, however, that I had already begun on the quotation once, and I made no mistake the first time. My slip of the tongue was made only when I repeated it, as I had to because my daughter's attention was elsewhere when I first quoted her the lines, and she was not listening. This repetition, and my impatience to get my quotation of the lines over and done with, must be included as part of the motivation for my slip of the tongue, which represents a case of compression.[40]

Freud, in this example highlighting his own mistake, believes that the error has significance and meaning for him because it relates to his psychic state at the time of uttering the verses. His impatience with his daughter led to his "added impatience," which was the immediate "motivation" behind his blunder.

Later in the chapter, after providing many similar examples of errors, he discusses his claim about speech disturbances with greater generality:

> I do not, therefore, think that those instances of obvious or subtler speech disturbances which can also be subsumed under "slips of the tongue" are mainly due to the influence of phonetic contacts; I believe that such slips derive from ideas outside what the speaker intends to say, which are sufficient to explain the slip. I do not mean to imply any doubt of the phonetic laws causing sounds to modify each other, but they do not seem to me strong enough to impair correct speech by their own influence alone. In those cases that I have studied closely and of which I can claim some understanding, they merely represent an existing mechanism that can easily be used by a more remote psychic motive without its binding itself to the sphere of influence of those connections. In a great many substitutions, a slip of the tongue occurs quite regardless of such laws of phonetics.[41]

In some cases, Freud saw mistakes in language as issuing from a disturbing factor, a result of striking against obscene words and meanings. In others, he saw the blunders in speech as examples of self-betrayal, as if the *lapsus linguae* was an example of what one does not wish to say. In order to describe the reality of these "lapses of the tongue," Freud further points to the ways that other speakers seize on a speech blunder when it occurs: "If a slip of the tongue that turns what the speaker intended to say into its opposite is made by one of the adversaries in a serious argument it immediately puts him at a disadvantage, and his opponent seldom wastes any time in exploiting the advantage for his own ends." For Freud, this becomes evidence of the fact that such blunders in speech are significant:

> It is clear, then, that in general people interpret slips of the tongue like other slips, just as I do in this book, even if they do not theoretically support my ideas and are not themselves inclined to reject the toleration of slips as a convenient attitude. But the mirth and derision occasioned by such slips of the tongue at important moments militate against what is

claimed to be the general consensus of opinion: That a slip of the tongue is merely a *lapsus linguae* with no psychological significance.[42]

Ghars al-Ni'ma's volume *Al-Hafawāt al-Nādira* also suggests a world in which such errors are meaningful. The case of the singer Faḍla's confusing *qāf* with *kāf* and her performance's slide from the solemn to the sexual fits well with Freud's comments on speech errors in *The Psychopathology of Everyday Life*. The ways in which the Umayyad poet expressed his concealed vengeance against the Abbasid ruler through lines he recited unaware of his own speech suggest that the Umayyad's verse may well have conveyed his repressed desire. Such moments surely point to the fact that an error in the Abbasid context often could take impetus from the psychology of the performer.

Yet the "slips" and errors recorded in the *Al-Hafawāt al-Nādira* go beyond a singular performer's psychology into the complex relationships among performer, patron, and audience at court. The stories in this collection locate tension not in the confrontation of the individual with his own psychological drives but rather in the particular constraints (real and implicit) placed on a poet or performer relating to a far more powerful patron. Emotions in this courtly context are much less about understanding one's interior state and far more about understanding one's relationship with the other. While anxiety surely does play a role in blunders in the *Al-Hafawāt*, the characters are portrayed in the main more often simply erring on account of misreading their patron's needs.

Such misreadings of the courtly context and the errors associated with them were inevitable. *Adab* could go only so far in providing a script for human activity. Given the limited nature of human perception, there was simply far too much chance at play to guarantee a performer certain success by following literary and behavioral codes. Recording these slips afforded moments to marvel at the ways that performance could reflect the powerful role of chance in human life.

NOTES

1. Ghars al-Ni'ma, *Al-Hafawāt*, 5. On the genre of *thuqalā'* in Arabic literature, see Joseph Sadan, *Al-Adab al-'arabī al-hāzil wa-nawādir al-thuqalā'*. All translations are mine, unless otherwise noted.
2. Mottahedeh, *Loyalty and Leadership*, 5–6.

3. Sharlet, *Patronage and Poetry*, 2–3.
4. Gelder, in "Mixtures of Jest and Earnest," 84, describes jest and earnest as "one of the many oppositional expressions in Arabic that combine true antonyms (like *ḥilm* and *jahl*) or complementaries (like pen and sword, *lafẓ* and *maʿnā* and *ʿaql* and *naql*)."
5. Ibid., 85.
6. Ghars al-Niʿma, *Al-Hafawāt*, 4. I read *al-maqālāt* for the editor's *al-qālāt*.
7. Ibn Manẓūr, *Lisān al-ʿArab*, 15:73.
8. Abū ʿUbayd al-Qāsim ibn Sallām, *Al-Amthāl*, 51.
9. R. Blachère, "al-Akhṭal," in *Encyclopaedia of Islam*, 2nd ed., ed. P. Bearman, Th. Bianquis, C. E. Bosworth, E. van Donzel, and W. P. Heinrichs (Brill Online, 2012). See al-Akhṭal, *Dīwān al-Akhṭal*, 39; by contrast, Dhū al-Rumma, in *Dīwān Dhū al-Rumma*, 255, glosses *hafwa* as a "shudder" (*khafqa*) of fear and does not seem to have the meaning of mistake or error.
10. Abū Tammām, *Dīwān Abī Tammām bi-sharḥ al-Khaṭīb al-Tibrīzī*, 2:117; Ibn al-Rūmī, *Dīwān*, 2:299.
11. The standard edition of "Relief after Hardship" is al-Tanūkhī, *Kitāb al-faraj baʿd al-shidda*. Weiner's "Die Farağ baʿd aš-Šidda-Literatur" is still a fundamental study of the genre. On the generic features of al-Tanūkhī's work, see Hakan Özkan, *Narrativität im Kitāb al-Farağ baʿda š-šidda*; Beaumont, "In the Second Degree"; Khalifa, *Hardship and Deliverance*; al-Tanūkhī, *Nishwār al-Muḥāḍara*.
12. Bosworth, "Ghars al-Niʿma [b.] Hilal al-Ṣābi''s Kitāb *al-Hafawāt al-Nādira*," 134.
13. Ibid.
14. E.g., Ghars, *Al-Hafawāt*, 15.
15. See Hilāl al-Ṣābi', *Rusūm dār al-khilāfa* (trans. Salem).
16. Bosworth, "Ghars al-Niʿma [b.] Hilal al-Ṣābi''s Kitāb *al-Hafawāt al-Nādira*," 134.
17. Ghars, *Al-Hafawāt*, 20. The reference is perhaps to her role in cooling the heat of men's desires?
18. The term *jadhr* sometimes implies a fee for sexual services; see al-Tawḥīdī, *Akhlāq al-Wazīrayn*, 375.
19. Colville, *Sobriety and Mirth*, 199; al-Jāḥiẓ, *Rasā'il al-Jāḥiẓ*, 2:177.
20. Al-Iṣfahānī, *Al-Aghānī* (2010), 6:325.
21. Ghars, *Al-Hafawāt*, 21.
22. Al-Iṣfahānī, *Al-Aghānī* (2010), 6:326.
23. Ghars, *Al-Hafawāt*, 25.
24. Ibid. The editor identifies this verse as belonging to the Umayyad poet al-Laʿīn al-Minqarī; see Ghars, *Al-Hafawāt*, 461. One wonders at the possible significance of the choice of verses.
25. Ghars, *Al-Hafawāt*, 25.
26. Ibid. These verses are attributed to al-ʿAntara b. Shaddād; see ibid., 454.
27. Ibid., 25–26.
28. Ibid., 8.
29. Ibid.

30. Larkin, *Al-Mutanabbi*, 59. Given the "reluctant" praise that al-Mutanabbī offers Kāfūr elsewhere in this poem and the poet's later famed angry satires against Kāfūr, the verse is difficult to read as straightforward praise of a patron. Cf. Stetkevych, *Poetics of Islamic Legitimacy*, 211.
31. Ghars, *Al-Hafawāt*, 14.
32. Ibid., 15.
33. Ibid.
34. Ibid.
35. Ibid.
36. Ibid.
37. On the use of the terms *taṭayyur* and *ṭīra*, see Fahd, *La divination arabe*, 104.
38. Ghars, *Al-Hafawāt*, 39. On this poet, see al-Iṣfahānī, *Al-Aghānī* (2010), 13:29–44.
39. Ghars, *Al-Hafawāt*, 39.
40. Freud, *Psychopathology of Everyday Life*, 60.
41. Ibid., 79.
42. Ibid., 89.

9

Cross-Gender "Acting" and Gender-Bending Rhetoric at a Princely Party

Performing Shadow Plays in Mamluk Cairo

LI GUO

Setting the Stage: The Shadow Play and Mamluk Courtly Entertainment

The uneven development of theatrical arts in the pre-modern Arab world experienced a few creative impulses.[1] The Arabic shadow play produced in Mamluk times (1250–1517) was perhaps one of them. As an art form, it had long been popular, insofar as its performances were described by a great number of literati, who lived throughout the Islamic empire, from Central Asia to Muslim Spain, between the eleventh and the sixteenth centuries.[2] The Arabic shadow play is usually thought of as a form of street entertainment, of low comedy. Paradoxically, perhaps because of the nature of our sources, we learn more about its performances at the royal courts and private gatherings of the elite instead. When a shadow play depicting the hanging of Ṭūmān Bāy (d. 1517), the last Mamluk sultan, was staged for the Ottoman sultan Salīm (d. 1520), he liked it so much that he asked to bring the show to Istanbul. It was not without controversy though. When the Ayyubid sultan Ṣalāḥ al-Dīn (d. 1193, known in the West as Saladin) had a shadow play performed, his vizier—a scholar and jurist—voiced misgivings. The Mamluk sultan Jaqmaq (d. 1453), who had earlier taken a liking to shadow plays, was so concerned with the "lascivious" reputation that their repertoire had gained that he banned their performance and ordered the puppets to be burned. This, of course, should not give us the impression that the shadow play had, until this incident, been thought of as a "court art." Still, there is no dispute that shadow plays were indeed performed at court, entertaining many a sultan and his entourage, while offending others at times.

This court connection may also be established, albeit by proxy, for the play we will examine in the following pages. Titled *Ṭayf al-khayāl*, "The Phantom," one of only three surviving theatrical texts from the pre-Ottoman Arab world, it was attributed to Ibn Dāniyāl (d. 1310), a Cairo-based eye doctor and poet, who at one point served the Mamluk sultan al-Ashraf Khalīl b. Qalāwūn (d. 1293) as a court panegyrist and jester.[3] A performance is described by the playwright in the opening monologue of the play as "a party [*majlis al-surūr*]."[4] The term *majlis*, literally "a sitting place," is rich in connotations; in classical usage, it denotes a "royal salon," as it was closely associated with high culture in Abbasid Baghdad. The term appears in Ibn Dāniyāl's three plays: aside from the aforementioned *majlis al-surūr*, literally "joy party," variants range from *majlis al-īnās* (or *al-uns*), "private gathering,"[5] to *majlis ṣadr min ṣudūr ahl al-zamān*, "a salon hosted by a notable of the age."[6] The performance of Ibn Dāniyāl's plays, then, was by and large a private event. Although there is no way of knowing whether "The Phantom" was ever performed at court, its potential was evidently in his mind when he was commissioned by a *rayyis*-maestro to write the script.

With respect to the contents, "The Phantom" also indirectly touches on the subject of court and power (or power lost) one way or the other. At the center is the protagonist, a retired prince (the Anglicized title "Emir," *amīr*, also means "commander" or "military governor"), whose trajectory resembles that of the Zangid emirs of Mosul, Ibn Dāniyāl's hometown.[7] Of course, it would be a stretch to read this play strictly as a cautionary tale for men in power to entertain and contemplate or as political satire aimed at those who fell out of it; yet the Emir's redemption was certainly a worthy yarn to spin.

Regarding the repertoire in general, sources suggest that the Arabic shadow play took all sorts of forms: epic-like romances, historical tales, fables, fantasies, and farces. The three plays that have come down to us, all by Ibn Dāniyāl, strike a more realistic chord, depicting life and people in Mamluk Cairo, and therefore demand perhaps more theatrical skill to pull off. One, titled "The Amazing Preacher and the Stranger," is a song-and-dance piece, featuring a carnival-like street parade. Another, "The Charmed and the Charmer," revolves around a love affair between two men. The third, "The Phantom," the subject of this study, tells the story of a retired emir's redemptive journey. The longest, most complex plot-wise, and most sophisticated in character portraits among the three, it has long received scholarly attention, mainly as a literary text. However, as a play, what did "The Phantom" sound, look, and feel like in a *majlis* setting? What was required of, or desired in, a performer? What do we know about his training and preparation? In the following pages, I attempt to visualize a performance of three episodes from "The Phantom," with special reference to cross-gender acting, arguably one of its crowd-pleasing traits, and gender-bending rhetoric, one of the most effective tools of characterization.[8] I conclude with a few words on the roles of the solo performer as suggested by the text.

Reading the Episodes: Woman's Speech, Men's Songs

The shadow play "The Phantom" is loosely built on a string of remotely related episodes. In performance, these episodes form "acts" or "scenes" that require changing sets, introducing new characters, and utilizing novel narrative devices. The following presents a synopsis of the main story line (in italics), along with a detailed summary of the three episodes selected for discussion.

The protagonist Amīr Wiṣāl, "Emir Mating," a retired soldier, tells his sidekick, Ṭayf al-Khayāl, the "Phantom," that he is tired of his playboy lifestyle and is ready to settle down. He summons his secretary and panegyrist to put his finances in order and his mind at peace. The matchmaker Umm Rashīd, "Mother Guidance," questions his sincerity by recounting some of his salacious activities that occurred not long ago.

Episode 1: The Matchmaker's Monologue (in Rhymed Prose and Verse)

The matchmaker begins by reminding the Phantom (and the Emir, who is supposedly in the background) of "the good old days," when the Emir "used to fancy boys." She proceeds to recount a tall tale about her "landlord" (*ṣāḥib baytī*, a pimp), a teacher (actually her husband), and a pupil. The story told by the matchmaker runs like this: the pimp invited the "lovely lad" to his house for a "party, with sweets, candles, and wine." But the teen said he could come only in the company of his teacher, who in turn protested that it was too early for "Happy Hour," that he must close his Qur'ān school first. The pimp sings a song encouraging him to come along. The song, in the strophic poetic form of *muwashshaḥ*, replete with puns, makes fun of an Animal House–like school scene: the teacher drinks, and the pupils learn too little; worse, they learn about things they are not supposed to. The teacher passes out, leaving the pimp to do "his thing with that lad."

The Emir reiterates his determination by renouncing (or recounting) all his past sins.[9]

Episode 2: The Emir's Song (in Verse)

In a languid song (eighty-five lines, one of the longest in the play) that parodies the theme of repentance, the Emir recounts, among many incidents, a secret rendezvous with a girlfriend arranged by a go-between. The young woman lives in a crowded quarter amid neighbors' watchful eyes, so the Emir, in his own words, resorts to "dressing myself like a woman, wearing a scarf / and hiding my beard under a veil." When he arrives at the door of the woman's house—for reasons unexplained—he makes a scene. Trying to cover it up, his girlfriend tells the folks gathering around, "This is the daughter of my neighbor, the butcher." A catfight between the two "women" erupts; but they end up sleeping together.

The matchmaker then produces a bride, who turns out to be a hideous-looking grandmother. Insulted, the Emir demands to punish the matchmaker and her husband 'Aflaq, "Big Pussy-Short Fatty," the schoolteacher. The husband informs that the matchmaker has just died at the hands of a quack named Yaqṭīnūs, "Dr. Squash," who confirms the sad news.[10]

Episode 3: The Doctor's Monologue and Song (in Rhymed Prose and Verse)

Dr. Squash retells the scene at the brothel where the matchmaker-cum-madam is dying. On her deathbed, the Madam performs her final rite and delivers one of the memorable monologues in the play. Dying, all she thinks of are good business practices and work ethics. Chaos ensues on the Madam's passing. Several former clients accuse the doctor of malpractice and demand their money back. The doctor resorts to lip service instead, singing a song eulogizing and memorializing the deceased Madam's life achievements through narration and occasionally mimicking her speech.

Time for the Emir to repent. Off he goes to Mecca.
The end.[11]

Performing the Episodes: One Voice for All

As we can see, there is much theatrical potential for impromptu acting. And all the acts—sounds and movements—were to be executed by one person, as made clear at the outset by the script. The show begins, as it dictates, "with a song, in the mode of Rāst."[12] And in this opening song, one finds further instructions:

> In the play, there is *one single voice*, in disguise,
> speaking on behalf of each character.

Evidently, Ibn Dāniyāl envisioned his plays as narrated and "acted" by one shadow master. However, an alert reader cannot help but note that these kinds of "stage directions," including the imperative verb (*ghanni*, "sing!"), does not seem to be part of the performer's monologue. Here we witness what Bridget Connelly terms the "two voices"—the *mu'allif*-compiler (speaking in the first person) and the *rāwī*-performer (who is usually referred to in the third person)—that mark the textual features of the written transmission process of orally performed materials.[13] I hypothesize that in the actual performance, Ibn Dāniyāl's introductory segment, in which the playwright addresses the *rayyis* (variant: *rā'is* = classical: *ra'īs*) in the second person, was not meant to be staged. Rather, the show begins with *the song*, sung by the *rayyis*, on behalf of the author *and* himself. So there is only one voice, through and through. In all likelihood, the *rayyis*-maestro would probably be accompanied by a small troupe that would play music while helping with the puppets.[14] Since throughout the play all the songs are assigned to male characters (the matchmaker has recitative lines in rhymed prose; she only mimics men's speech *and* songs within her narration), it would be reasonable to suppose that a male *rayyis* would be doing all the singing, in falsetto if necessary. At any rate, in essence, Ibn Dāniyāl's play was a one-man show.

The lengthy monologue in episode 1 is delivered by a male performer who mimics the female voice of Umm Rashīd, the matchmaker, who in turn imitates three voices of men of different ages—the pimp, a middle-aged person; the teacher, an elderly man; and the pupil, an adolescent. Then there is the pimp's song, a minidrama in its own right, in which all the characters act. This multilayered cross-gendered acting (speaking/singing) scheme—shadow play master > Umm Rashīd > male characters—certainly tests a performer's versatility. The pimp begins by challenging the teacher ("Take this tiny goblet, O teacher, and drink, you all!") and moves on to command him to turn his class into a madhouse ("Then call out: O children, go play. / And dance for me. Be Happy! Have fun!"). We find in the next line an outcry, apparently from the teacher ("O, dear Madame, I am fearful of [losing] my job"). The "Madame" refers to the matchmaker, the female narrator of this play-within-a-play. The teacher then goes on to imagine a situation in which one of his pupils sees him drunk in his study and lashes out ("Hey, kids, stop studying! / Our teacher is drunk. Get up and go play!") As it turns out, this whistleblower proves quite a handful. The audience is made aware of this because the narrative voice used for the song now switches back to that of the pimp ("I have got a gold-digger here, O teacher, a very smart lad"). He then encourages the teacher to "beat the hell out of him" and "teach him a lesson" but in a sexual way. The song ends with the pimp's speech to the "dear Madame"; the narrator cites this story as yet another proof that certain of men's habits do not change.

It should be noted here that in this episode all the characters, caricatures to be sure, perform their expected gender roles. This is, however, not the case in episode 2, in which gender bending appears to be the aim. The Emir, in describing his attempt at dressing like a woman to sneak into his girlfriend's house, recalls an embarrassing moment:

> They didn't buy it; so she came to me, in anger:
> "Don't sit [*lā taqʿudī*] on doorsteps!
> "I swear—by soot and smut—that you will

> come into [*tadkhulī*] my house, or enter [*wa-illā dakhaltī*] it by force!"
> "Don't be afraid [*lā takhāfī*]! You and I, both
> without a husband, will sleep under one sheet."

And sleep together they do. The verses were not punctuated, as was the norm in medieval Arabic manuscripts. So there remains a slight ambiguity as to who said what to whom. In my present translation, the three lines are interpreted as a dialogue between two "women," insofar as all the verbs are in second-person feminine, either imperative or subjunctive. The Emir, disguised as a woman, is addressed by his girlfriend as a woman, in the first two lines. The last line is perhaps to be taken as his response to her outburst, with a mischievous wink (if a puppet could manage that).

A man in a veil was thought to be funny. So was a woman in pants. This is alluded to in episode 3. At first glance, what the audience encounters repeats the same tactic seen before, when a female character, the matchmaker-cum-madam, imitates several male voices. In this episode, however, the role is reversed, in that we now have a male character, the doctor, emulating a female, the Madam. The high point arrives, as the dying Madam slips in and out of a trance. The narrator, Dr. Squash, describes the scene in a melodramatic fashion, in rhymed prose, as "the folks shouted loudly, so she opened her sleepy eyes, looked around tearfully" (again, imagine if a shadow figure could do that), "and dictated the following in a barely audible voice": to entrust the charge of the brothel to her partner, along with instructions to her "chaps and girls." For the manager/pimp, she advises, "Don't delay calls, and don't haggle over fees for shitting. Leave your doors wide open for johns, take gold and silver ores and craps in lieu of cash payment." As for the prostitutes, they "should fulfill the promised dates and strive to satisfy those artisans and craftsmen, even on the eve of a holiday. Relax at lovers' parties, sell fuck-for-pay, even if the guy is not your type." Her "voice" is mocked again later, in the quack's song, which further glorifies her many professional virtues: "She always wins hearts and minds, / does not differentiate a Muslim from a Jew." "She would come in with her girls, yelling: / Who is going to Upper Egypt?"[15] What kind of a "voice" were audiences expected to hear here?

Gendered Speech, Cross-Gender Acting

As the leading female character, Umm Rashīd the matchmaker is without doubt the linchpin that ties all three episodes together. It is through her narration that a pederast's scheme, with the help of a schoolteacher, is revealed in episode 1. It is at her urging, in episode 2, that the Emir, a symbol of the military and political establishment, confesses his past sins. Again it is her confident assurance, in episode 3, of the everlasting prosperity of her "business" that prompts the Emir to finally realize that leaving a hedonistic Cairo is the only way for him to attain salvation. While satirical critique of male sexual hypocrisy is an unmistakable running theme, Mother Guidance, who single-handedly manages to turn the male-dominated universe around her upside down, is by no means a moral compass. Like her male counterparts, she behaves badly, breaks rules, and worse, bends accepted gender roles. Hence the fun.

First, Dr. Squash describes the hideous appearance of this old woman, "whose gray hair was piled up, and whose outfits and makeup betrayed her tacky tastes," in sharp contrast to the beautiful girls surrounding her, "like the flowers in the garden: the thirsty water lilies and fresh radiant roses." Next, the doctor's eulogy parodies her movements and posture: not only does she "run as fast as an official courier [*jary al-barīd*],"[16] but it is also hinted that she resembles a horse:

> She has white locks of hair at her temples [*abyaḍ al-sawālif*],
> stiff and sleek, rock solid [*al-julmūd*].[17]

The line employs figures of speech that were staples for horses. The audience would recognize the mockery of the Arabic literary convention that designated gender symbolism via animals: women likened to gazelles, men to horses. So all along, Dr. Squash is mocking a mannish woman. But she is not a man, to be sure. Her hard-to-define mannerisms are only implied through words, slyly often her own.

Umm Rashīd is characterized by Mustafa Badawi as "a cross between Juliet's Nurse and Celestina, a bawd and a female Pandarus," and "a most complex creation which belongs to a different order of writing." One striking feature, according to Badawi, is her peculiar language: "when she appears she greets the company in a different manner from the other characters." Two examples are cited: "The very rhythm and diction she uses are feminine. For instance, her greeting whenever she appears is *mussītum bi-l-sa'āda* and not the masculine *al-salāmu 'alaykum*. Or listen to the way she informs the Prince (the Emir) of the woman she wants him to marry. . . . Note the use of the expression *bisalāmithā* (for *bisalāmatihā*), which no male would use in this context, and yet right and apt it is."[18] While the overtly gendered expression *mussītum bi-l-sa'āda* appears frequently (rendered variably as "howdy y'all" or "wasup") in the play, the feminine utterance for shock and exacerbation, *bi-salāmithā* ("Gosh! O good heavens!"), appears also in episode 1, with the slight variant *bi-salāmtak* (for *bi-salāmati-ka*), when the matchmaker informs the Phantom, "The master of my house, mind you [*bi-salāmtak*], was into passive boys, and he drove me nuts about this one lovely lad."

The matchmaker's language is sometimes gender specific (lexically, as just shown) but also at times gender blurring (in socio-linguistic terms). A bizarre hybrid of high and low, of masculine and feminine, is shown in the following dialogue, in rhymed prose, when she speaks to the Phantom: "O Virgin of Paradise [*yā ḥūrīya*]! Did you forget [*nasītī*] those ruins of yours? Have you come back [*'udtī*] to your palaces? Our neighborhood is small, and everybody knows everybody. Girl, how can you forget what happened to the master of my house?" The audience is quick to recognize that the man, the Phantom, was addressed not only as a woman but as a virgin at that. The dubious iconic imagery of a *houri* (in Arab lore, the term denotes an attractive woman with eyes like that of a wild cow) is further manifested through intimate rhetorical questions, all using verbs (note the colloquial suffix *-tī*, instead of the classical *-ti*) in the feminine. The thinly veiled parody of the classical *aṭlāl*-topos, namely, the poet's lamentation of the deserted ruins of his departed beloved, is dramatically enhanced by gender-bending teasing. The audience might also recall that earlier in the episode, the matchmaker greets her male counterpart, the Phantom, with "my girl!" The double take is obvious: by calling the mighty male character, the Phantom (and his friend the Emir by proxy), "my girl," the Madam is not only inferring his supposed effeminateness but also reducing him, a princely figure, to one on a par with her "girls," prostitutes. She sabotages peace and order not only by transgressing her own gender role but by destabilizing those of her male counterparts. (On a related note, her husband, whose name is ʿAflaq, "Big-Pussy," does not connote a particularly masculine image either.) By assaulting the masculinity of the leading men, her speech acts level the playing field between genders.

So we have here a bunch of "girlie men" as depicted through the eyes and words of a mannish woman. However, the characters in question, the Emir, the Phantom, and the matchmaker (arguably among the most memorable "female" characters produced in medieval Arabic literature), do not fit into the staples of male-female gender irregularities as found in earlier and contemporary texts.[19] The Emir, for one, is merely an occasional cross-dresser. His companion, the Phantom, is only a "virgin" in the matchmaker's teasing. There is no actual effeminateness to speak of. On the other hand, the matchmaker does not come off as a cross-dresser either: her mannishness is embedded in her persona. She does not "bend" gender roles by faking but rather acts the way she is. What the audience will eventually encounter, I suspect, is a much-simplified, and cartoon-like, gender-identity "crisis" aimed at quick laughter. We might hypothesize that Ibn Dāniyāl created this economic gender-bending situation with more focus on language itself, mindful of the practical limits (visual and vocal being the most prominent) of the sole performer in staging the show.

Mamluk sources suggest that a shadow play performance at a private party might resemble our image of a variety show, featuring puppetry and shadow plays, live theater, music, and dance. The poet al-Wajīh al-Munāwī, a contemporary of Ibn Dāniyāl, for one, was mesmerized by a sole female actor who would step out in front of a live audience, singing, dancing, and flirting, and then retreat behind the screen, pulling off even more tricks with shadow figures.[20] (That male and female performers acted "alone" seems to have been often the case in live theater as well.)[21] In this regard, Ibn Dāniyāl's *rayyis*-maestro and al-Wajīh al-Munāwī's female performer present themsevles as quintessential Arab *rāwī*-storytellers, working primarily within the confines of oral performance. As storytelling goes, the ability to mimic cross-gender speech would be crucial.[22] However, as he or she moved along from pure oral performance to rudimentary theatrical acting, something more must have been desirable: in light of Ibn Dāniyāl's script, we expect the actor to sing with a wide range and "act" with considerable virtuosity, mocking gender-specific speech patterns (rhythm, diction) and manipulating puppets' moves. A few good roles, like the wacky characters with gender irregularities and other bizarre traits discussed here, would have given the performer an edge to shine, to the delight of audiences at many a princely party in Mamluk Cairo.

NOTES

1. Cf. Moreh, *Live Theatre*.
2. For a history of the Arabic shadow play, see Guo, *Performing Arts*, 105–8 (with bibliography of earlier scholarship).
3. Guo, *Performing Arts*, 50–67.
4. Arabic text in Kahle, *Three Shadow Plays*, 1; translation in Guo, *Performing Arts*, 158.
5. Kahle, *Three Shadow Plays*, 55.
6. Ibid., 90.
7. The Zangid dynasty, of Badr al-Dīn Lu'lu' (1211–59) and his sons, was brought to an end by the invading Mongols. For the parallels between the disastrous fate of the princes and that which is depicted in the Emir's monologue in the play, see Guo, *Performing Arts*, 10–11.
8. By "cross-gender acting," I follow the common definition, "an actor or actress portraying a character of the opposite gender," whereas the term "gender bending" signifies "a person who actively transgresses, 'bends,' expected gender roles."
9. Arabic text in Kahle, *Three Shadow Plays*, 23–24; translation in Guo, *Performing Arts*, 185–87.
10. Arabic text in Kahle, *Three Shadow Plays*, 37–41; translation in Guo, *Performing Arts*, 199–203. Curiously, this episode is very similar, in content and language, to the famous poem by 'Umar ibn Abī Rabī'a (d. 721?), which Robert Irwin describes as "effectively a short story about a perilous assignation"; translated by Adel Suleiman Gamal, cited in Irwin, *Night, Horses and the Desert*, 50–54. The only differences are that 'Umar's assignation took place at a camp site, where, on his *way out after* the meeting, he disguises himself as a woman, with the help of the lover's two sisters.
11. Arabic text in Kahle, *Three Shadow Plays*, 52–53; translation in Guo, *Performing Arts*, 217–19.
12. *Rāst* is the premier of the twelve melodic modes (sing. *maqām*; not to be confused with *maqāma*, the narrative genre) in classical Arab music.
13. Bridget Connelly theorizes that "internal depictions of the singer-poet performing before the assembled cast of fictional characters occur in other epics, like *Beowulf* and the *Odyssey*, as well as in what many critics see as a self-reflecting device wherein the singer puts himself and his tale-bearing progenitors *into the song* as a kind of copyright or claim of authorship" (*Arab Folk Epic and Identity*, 243–44). Also noteworthy is Connelly's observation that although a similar device is used in the *maqāmāt* of Badī' al-Zamān and al-Ḥarīrī taken from the high-

written tradition of letters (*adab*), the *rāwī* in these works is a fictive persona used for ironic purposes (244, citing Monroe, *Art of Badīʿ az-Zamān al-Hamadhānī*). In contrast, the *rāwī* mentioned in the *sīra*-epics is a real person, an actual performer.

14. Of course this is an imagined scenario, which I do not have texts to prove. Moreh points out that the *rayyis* was more likely a "maestro of troops of actors" (shadow play and/or live theater), but this does not mean that he acted along with a "troupe" of actors, often known as *khayālīs*. As a matter of fact, of the live theater plays culled from sources, most seem only to have involved one actor. Moreh, *Live Theatre*, 118, 138.
15. "Upper Egypt" perhaps alludes to the fact that she also had businesses outside Cairo.
16. A variant in other manuscripts, *khayl al-barīd*, "a post horse," is also telling.
17. The word *sālifa* (pl. *sawālif*) means "sideburns" but also "side of the forepart of [a horse's] neck [*sālifat al-faras*]." For "rock solid," Imruʾ al-Qays's (d. 540) famous line describing a stallion comes to mind: "charging, fleet-fleeing, head-foremost, headlong, all together / the match of a rugged boulder hurled from on high by the torrent [*ka-julmūdi ṣakhrin ḥaṭṭahu l-saylu min ʿalin*]"; translated by Arberry, *Seven Odes*, 64.
18. Badawi, "Medieval Arabic Drama," in Kahle, *Three Shadow Plays*, 19.
19. One may also recall the effeminate buffoon-musician-actor (*mukhannath*), singing girls dressed up as boys (*ghulāmīyāt*), Amazonian women warriors in Arabic epics, and the famous cross-dressers in *The 1001 Nights*.
20. "She played various characters [*ashkhāṣ*] behind the screen, / In the same manner she toyed with men"; see Guo, *Performing Arts*, 95–96.
21. Moreh's study shows that of the twenty-one known cases, "actresses only appear in three . . . and only once together with men" (*Live Theatre*, 138).
22. We do not know what kind of characters al-Wajīh's female performer played, but it is reasonable to infer that they were of both sexes.

PART IV

Delight

10

The Court Cuisine of Medieval Cyprus

Food as Table Theater

WILLIAM WOYS WEAVER

The court cuisine of medieval Cyprus is mostly unknown to scholars of medieval culture, yet relics of this once-sophisticated international style of cookery are everywhere embedded in western European manuscripts from the period. Not surprisingly, Cypriot court cuisine was far more complex in situ than the material transmitted to the West, as I shall demonstrate later in this chapter. In terms of display of power and status, in terms of food as theater, and in terms of the use of cuisine for political and theological agendas, the Luisgnan court found few European parallels. Due to the island's role as an outpost of the West in the Muslim world, Cyprus created its own rules of survival and self-identity.

The goal of this chapter is to reveal the inner mechanisms of this self-created identity and how it operated via several avenues of expression. On the literary level, it was fortified by poetical narrative; on the material level, it was expressed through distributions of valuable and symbolic table implements; on the culinary level, it was defined by dishes that represented cultural and political agendas; and finally, on a philosophical level, it drew on a dimension of food as religious dietetics, a moral control mechanism over the devout Catholic nobility who moved in and out of ethical and religious constraints as opportunity occasioned.

Literary Evidence: Poetical Narratives

Courtly performance and the display of power in the medieval kingdom of Cyprus are doubtless best evidenced in the cycles of poetical narratives that include the *Gestes chyproise*, *La chanson d'Antioche*, *La chanson de Jérusalem*, and most famously Guillaume de Machaut's *La prise d'Alexandre*. These courtly tales reinforcing the heroic character of the Crusader ruling class were read aloud or accompanied by music as entertainments during royal banquets. Their popularity was both cultural and political, since the Cypriot court was sensitive to its role as protector of the East, a bulwark against Islam, and a colonial outpost of western European culture.

The Lusignan court, established in 1192 after the island was seized from a renegade Byzantine governor, divided itself into real and titular kingdoms representing feudal lands, the real representing what they owned on the island, the rest lost to Arab conquest. The French-speaking court, which represented a small minority of the total population, was keenly aware of its tenuous existence. Thus the symbolic meaning of the narratives just mentioned and their relationship to the food served during these performances assumed special importance: who served it, which kingdom it represented, and how it would perpetuate the idea that the Lusignans were the true lords of Jerusalem, the rightful princes of Antioch, kings of Armenia, and so forth. Since the Lusignans could not act out their former medieval privileges on the mainland, they re-created the titular court cuisines and symbolic foods in their palace at Nicosia.

Due to the status of medieval diarists, largely noble pilgrims en route to or from Jerusalem, they gained easy entry into the royal court. It was there that they witnessed the pomp and symbolism that defined the unusual fusionist culture that had evolved on the island. In essence, this courtly cuisine represented a voluptuous lifestyle unknown in Europe, derived from wealth acquired from sugar plantations, wine exports, and Silk Road trade. It embodied a blend of eastern Mediterranean customs enriched with heavy borrowings from the aristocratic cuisine of Byzantium. Regardless of local nuances that gave the food its unique color and character, we should picture these courtly meals that were sent to the royal table as being in the prevailing French style, with French rolls (manchet breads—called the "king's bread" in Cyprus), thus defining the difference between the court elites and the lesser gentry employed by them. These round bread rolls, made of the best emmer wheat flour from the royal mills at Kythrea, appear in several Cypriot icons paid for by wealthy Latins. While the icons are fascinating for their religious fusionism (Roman Catholic and Greek Orthodox), the bread depicted in them clearly defined the class and cultural orientation of the patrons.

The King's Spoons: Who Sat at the Royal Tables

Like the distribution of the king's bread during courtly banquets, other objects on the table also projected themes of power and performance due to their physical iconography and role in the meal. The use of ornamental spoons is an excellent example. A number of elaborate Cypriot silver spoons survive from the 1400s in connection with weddings. The royal couple distributed silver spoons to A-list attendees, a symbol of royal largess as much as a reinforcement of the idea that the king is the kingdom's father, and thus it is his obligation to pay homage to his flock. In reality, this silver represented dowry money from his new wife, so it also conveyed the message that he had married well for the common good—lavish wedding distributions of similar kind are still practiced in Cyprus today. Since the silver spoons were the equivalent of money, they could be melted down, thus offering a way to confirm noblesse oblige and, through this symbolic financial reward, to strengthen political loyalties.

The rare bronze "sorbet" spoon (figure 10.1) from circa 1200 gives material expression to the theme of table theater. Formerly gilded, it is derivative of a Byzantine prototype used by both Christian and Islamic courts in the eastern Mediterranean. Precious metals for table implements were forbidden by Islam but not by Maronite Christians: this would explain an Aramaic owner's stamp on the spoon. The arrangement of symbols, including the falcon near the top (an aristocratic symbol of the hunt), and the traces of gilding to give the appearance of gold anticipate the later medieval Cypriot wedding spoons in which the flower motif near the bowl is replaced with an image of the Cypriot king. The design of this bronze spoon suggests that the original owner was a high-placed Maronite courtier, definitely a man privy to royal hunts.

But let us take this analysis one step further. The twisted spoon handle is eight inches (twenty centimeters) long and awkward to hold and to eat from. It does not rest in the hand comfortably like smaller, common wooden or pewter spoons of the period. The ornamentation suggests that its purpose was largely symbolic or ceremonial or at least used only during special occasions. The eating of sorbet (snow flavored with rose syrup) would certainly be one of these occasions, since snow from the Cypriot Mount Olympus stored in ice cellars at the

Figure 10.1. Cypriot bronze sorbet spoon with a Maronite Christian ownership mark. Formerly gilded. Private collection. Photo by William Woys Weaver.

royal palace was a prerogative exclusive to the royal family: they owned the snow and the villagers whose feudal obligation it was to collect it.

Spice Powders for Status and Love

Likewise, the thirteenth-century alabaster spice cellar (figure 10.2) dug up in the nineteenth century at Aya Napa Monastery on the southeast

Figure 10.2. *Artima gliki* and *artima apsi* as served from a Byzantine-style alabaster spice cellar. The sweet spice powder is garnished with a marzipan comfit, while the piquant powder is garnished with a cubeb berry, one of its peppery ingredients. One manchet bread has been sliced according to proper table custom of the medieval Cypriot court. Private collection. Photo by William Woys Weaver.

coast of Cyprus was designed to hold two types of Byzantine spice mixtures: *poudre forte* (*artima apsi*) and *poudre douce* (*artima glyki*), as they were called in court Frankish and Byzantine Greek. These costly spice powders—one piquant and colored red with saunders, the other sweet—were added "a volent"—to the taste of the diner—at the table, a custom mentioned by Machaut in *La prise d'Alexandre*.[1]

A faded inscription in Latin (now illegible) marks this piece as one-time property of the Frankish elite, most likely a high church official since Latin was seldom used outside Catholic church circles—the lingua franca of the island being Greek or Aramaic. The significant point here is not just the alabaster (a costly stone not indigenous to Cyprus) but also the fact that it was intended to hold condiments used only by the nobility or highborn members of the Latin church: its presence on the table confirmed the power and status of those who used it. Since the *artima glyki* contains roughly thirty grams of sugar, and the sugar can be equated in medieval terms to thirty grams of gold (as expressed in Venetian ducats), the real market value of this spice powder was enough to buy basic food staples for several villages. In this manner, Cypriot court cuisine was openly ostentatious and exhibitionist, and it imposed stark lines of distinction between the court as rulers and the other folk who worked in the kitchens or simply labored in the fields. This exhibitionism is further enhanced by the phallic design of the spice cellar, which is meant to allude to the aphrodisiac properties of the condiments.

The recipes for these spice powders are intertwined with this type of bald financial display; in fact, they give it meaning. All the same, the problems with using recipes alone to illustrate power and performance are several by virtue of the subjectivity or lack of it that emerges when viewing old texts. Recipes are generally isolated from the context of the meal, and the meal is where inherent symbolisms assume form and substance. Furthermore, the visual games that each dish played to entertain the rich and powerful in Cyprus may be foreign and strange to our sensibilities; thus we are not often privy to the subtle "messages" that these dishes send when delivered to table. Yet, like the sugar in the spice powder, the ingredients themselves do reveal useful clues. Dragon's blood, a Silk Road import, provides a telltale example and launches this discussion into an area of Cypriot court cuisine hitherto unexplored and poorly understood, a subject that I shall take up shortly: red foods and white foods.

The Recipe as Cultural Agenda

In short, aside from the dynamics of context and delivery and the iconographic symbols of bread and table implements, court cuisine also adhered to religious dietetics that enhanced the complexity and sophistication of the dishes prepared. This further separated the food from commonplace and framed it in terms of the rich and powerful who consumed it. Like jousting, these dietetics represented a form of noble entertainment, not to mention backhanded lip service to the chaste Christian life that the Cypriot nobility was expected to exemplify.

Reality was quite the opposite, since activities like the hunt, which were commonly explained as beneficial to the health, were in practice realms of escape from accepted norms. Moral and dietary restraints were left in the palace courtyard, and even royal pages were not off-limits for sexual encounters. The phallic alabaster spice cellar in figure 10.1 should remind us that, far removed from the moral restraints of Europe, Cyprus is where foreign nobility came for escape and entertainment. We can only surmise that as a table centerpiece, the spice cellar played a role in some sort of courtly contest in which sex became the *prise du jour*. But let us return to the themes of color and outward display, since they too allowed for escape from social conventions and an obsession with visual power plays or, for convenience's sake, what we might dub "riddle food."

White Food, Red Food: The Riddle of Table Aesthetics

Two Cypriot blancmange recipes are preserved in the circa 1450 *Diversa Cibaria*; both specifically call for dragon's blood (a plant-derived coloring agent) to render the dishes as bloody red as any food can be made, and yet one is carnal (contains meat) and one is totally vegan.[2] Even the startling Frankish name *viande de sang dragonée* (a dish of dragon's blood) graphically suggests that the pudding was probably molded into a fantastical dragon shape for table display or decorated with images like that shown in figure 10.4. These dragon's blood puddings are culinary conceits in their total inversion of the dietary schema: food that appears to be one thing but is in fact something opposite, blood that is not blood. This visual riddle could be accentuated if the accompanying dinner rolls were shaped like the realistic serpent breads of Stroumbi, an old feudal village in the Paphos District of Cyprus (figure 10.3).

Perhaps most important is the local Cypriot context from which these puddings drew larger meaning. Dragon's blood invoked the mythical *sarandapechos* (forty-yard dragon; see figure 10.4), an indigenous monster in Cypriot folk tradition that was woven into the fabric of the Melusine legend, the half-woman, half-creature who was presumed to be the ancestress of the House of Lusignan. In short, dishes associated with dragons conveyed mythic symbolism and complex political meanings because they fortified Lusignan claims to the island. Let us not forget that this blood-red pudding was consumed with an ornamental spoon

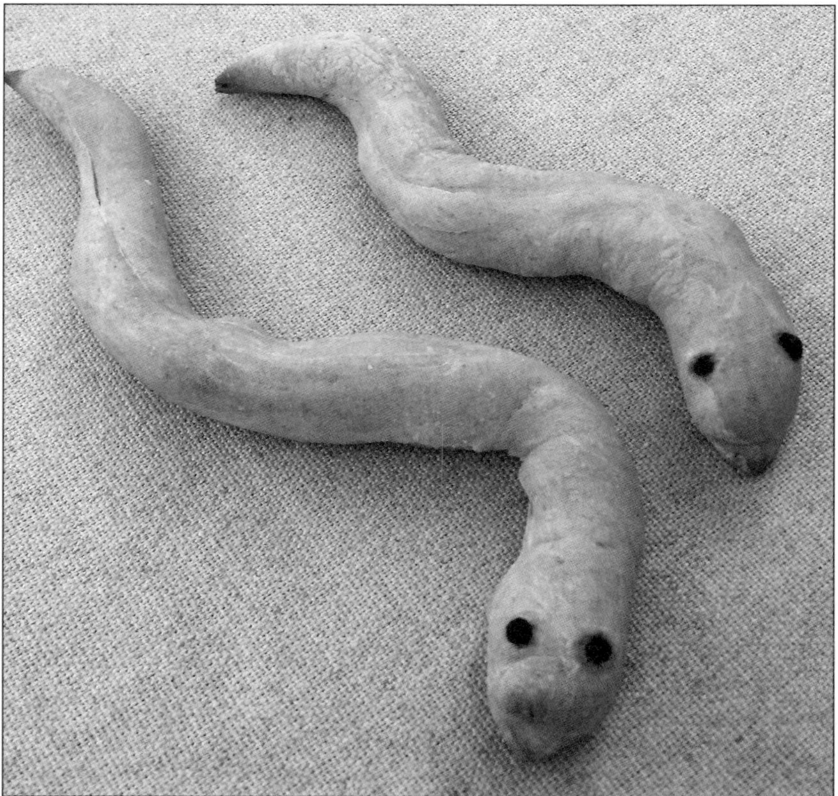

Figure 10.3. Snake "baguettes" from the feudal village of Stroumbi, Cyprus. This medieval bread tradition has not died out; these examples were made for the author by village bakers. Photo by William Woys Weaver.

like the one in figure 10.1. Spoons were not carried by guests (they brought their own knives and forks), so here is yet another opportunity for a noble distribution and a means for expressing status and rank at the high table.

In spite of the color of the dragon's blood dishes, both represented a type of blancmange styled as *lefkofagó* (white food) in Byzantine aristocratic cuisine. There were several types, often white in ways other than color since white consisted of more than one value: visual and moral. For clarification, the English word "blancmange" derives from Old French *blancmanger* (the same word used in Cyprio-Gallic) and like the Greek term literally means "white food." The dessert was once popular well

Figure 10.4. Carved marzipan mold depicting the *sarandapechos* (forty-yard dragon) of Cypriot folk mythology. Modern copy of a fifteenth-century original. Private collection. Photo by William Woys Weaver.

into the late Victorian era, by which time it had devolved into a sweet white pudding or jelly made with cornstarch.

Blancmange stiff and jelly-like was considered one of the iconic medieval standing dishes called *viande de Chypre*. Its medieval antecedents were far more complex than the Victorian counterpart and generally composed of white meat (veal or chicken), starch, ground almonds, and any number of spices. It was a popular display piece because, like the *viande* of dragon's blood, it could be colored or ornamented in any number of ways. This leads us into the arena of recipe as evidence of courtly performance, since the color white was a key to religious dietetics: white representing fasting food, red the opposite. Courtly display of penance and denial were part of the public persona of the Cypriot court, church as spectacle confirming the virtue of its Christian knights. King Peter I of Cyprus was assassinated in 1369 over a tiff about the lack of oil for his fasting-day salad of asparagus (white food in terms of religious ethics). The ugly dustup took place in front of the entire court, much to the mortification of all who witnessed it. In Cypriot court politics, these seemingly petty details sometimes led to high drama and, in King Peter's case, to a string of royal murders at the hands of his avenging wife.

Texts as Tracking Devices for Byzantine Diffusionism

Several culinary texts from the Lusignan period were transmitted to the West as early as 1250, among them the *Libellus de arte Coquinaria*, which internal evidence suggests was compiled at Famagusta in Cyprio-Gallic sometime between 1250 and 1285 and then later (about 1310) translated into Latin. King Peter I—or more likely his royal cook—during his 1364 peregrinations of Europe was responsible for disseminating the sophisticated court text from which the *Libellus* was derived. Guido da Bagnolo, his royal physician, passed another version of that same text to Venetian humanists in 1368. These two Cypriot cookbooks—one courtly, the other adapted to the tastes of the bourgeoisie—were mined for recipes and incorporated piecemeal into later western European culinary texts. The underlying theme was imitation: to live like the Cypriot nobility in their fabled luxury, a handbook was required.

Fortunately from the standpoint of culinary research, the French and Greek spoken in medieval Cyprus were idiosyncratic. Furthermore, Cypriot Greek is a language enriched with loanwords from Aramaic, French, Italian, and Catalan. Thus, by flagging certain culinary code words, it is possible to spot recipes of eastern Mediterranean origin in western European texts, recipes using vocabularies specific only to Cyprus or to its sister kingdom of Cilician Armenia. This methodology has led to a number of unanticipated discoveries, one of which is the existence of a dietary regimen that was conceived out of Orthodox Christian philosophies and that survives in relic form even in the eating habits of modern Cyprus. This is the text that defined Cypriot court cuisine according to seemingly unwritten codes of conduct; yet the codes were there, and they mitigated or accentuated the power plays of daily court banqueting.

The Rule of Red and White

This system codified foods by their physical color or moral quality and then correlated them to their role in religious fasting: a critical point in the court politics of the period, since the court led the kingdom in this important ritual. The significance for the subject of this book is that this dietary code represented a "top-down" schema, a courtly philosophy (not necessarily practiced by everyone) that created a map for dietetics as practiced by the elite and then mimicked by the urban well-to-do. Given is the fact that this schema is based on Christian philosophy, and its practitioners must be able to read and communicate in writing. This precludes the illiterate middle class and for certain the serfs but not monks or others in Cypriot society who used books in their daily lives. More important, food as symbol of power or as a delineation between the underclasses and the elite assumed potent meaning when viewed in hindsight against medieval sensibilities. In Cypriot terms, this became the table politics of the red and the white.

The foundation for this red-white schema was based on the theories of Galenic medicine and supported by indigenous philosophies peculiar to the Cypriot Orthodox church. For example, on the forbidden consumption of blood-based foods like black puddings (*aimatias*), to which the patriarch of Constantinople often turned a blind eye, the Cypriot church remained closer to its Judaic roots than other branches of Orthodox Christianity did. This necessity for greater dietary purity (stricter faithfulness to the nonconsumption of blood dishes) was justified on theological grounds by virtue of the fact that Saint Barnabas, founder of the Cypriot church, was a Levite Jew from Salamis (ancient center of a large Cypriot Jewish community) and a personal follower of Jesus who helped establish the earliest congregations of Christianity on the island. It also played into the tension between the Roman Catholic overlords and the local Greek church that claimed one-upsmanship over the Latins, who could not invoke Barnabas or other symbols of early Christian theological priority. This is where the red and the white assumed a quasi-religious/political dimension that could not have been attained anywhere else in Christian Europe.

Evidence of the Red and White Schema in Western Texts

While analyzing an Italian medieval cookbook by Martino of Como (an Italian court cook during the 1450s and 1460s), it became clear that something had been missed by his previous editors and translators or, in some cases, his mistranslators. While Martino's collection is eclectic, many of the recipes appear Eastern in character: all the cornelian cherry recipes, for example, use the medieval Cypriot Greek term *pitartema* (which is not coriander according to the University of California Press translation but specifically gingerbread or in this case gingerbread spice: *pitta* plus *artima*).[3] Martino's "Genoese" recipes, more specifically his spinach tart and onion tart using phyllo pastry, are Cypriot *spanakopitta* and *kromidopitta*, respectively, and Genoese only by way of Famagusta, which Genoa occupied from 1374 to 1463.[4] While the onion tart is "white" in its vegan simplicity as monastic fare (perhaps from the monastery of Saint Barnabas near Famagusta, which vied with other Greek monasteries for spiritual purity?), the red-and-white schema emerges more clearly in a preparation Martino styled a mustard, or *mostarda bianca*, in his original Italian but not in the University of California translation.[5]

Martino's term means "white pickle" because it is both white in color and white in its lack of animal-based ingredients. The recipe is itself of Cypriot origin and calls for the seeds of *lapsana* (Cypriot Greek for wild mustard or charlock), which are added to a batter of fermented barley flour, the same sourdough preparation in which Cypriots ferment cauliflower for Lent. This white cauliflower dish called *moungra* was borrowed directly from early Byzantine Maronite Christians, who called the fermented liquid *murri*. For this reason, Martino's white pickle can be traced to the most ancient roots of Christianity; thus in medieval Arabic texts, *murri* was a topic of interest as a fasting food.

The Nacci Book of Dietetics

A regimen invoked but not mentioned by name in Platina's famous *De Honesta Voluptate et Valetudine* is now known to be the same as a book taken to Italy in 1463 by Hypolito Nacci, a noble in the entourage of the exiled queen Charlotte of Cyprus. Nacci's regimen is one of the few known literary sources that evidently codified Franco-Cypriot dietetics and the unique division of foods into *kokkinofagá* and *lefkofagá*: "meats" that contain blood and "meats" that do not. In short, the regimen divided Christian diet into two spiritual spheres: carnivore and vegan. Platina plagiarized Nacci's book and recycled it into his own cookbook, which became one of the most popular culinary texts in Renaissance Italy.

Medieval dishes of this type were both food and performance. Like the dragon's blood puddings discussed earlier, blancmanges tinted various colors were brought to the king's table like another documented dish, standing pie of ostrich surrounded on a grand platter by cooked ostrich eggs—confirmed by surviving banquet plates decorated to imitate these foods served in them. For heightened effect, the pie was accompanied to table with music and an entourage of dancing ostriches; thus there was no distinct line between food and theater. Theatrics were possible because one of the culinary features of a *viande de Chypre*, as the Cypriot-style blancmange was often called in medieval texts, was its "standing" texture and three-dimensional form. This meant that like the dish of dragon's blood, it could be molded and sculpted, but similarities to modern puddings stop there.

Nacci's Greek regimen aside, this red-white schema has become evident in medieval Cypriot dietary patterns: the *kokkinofagá* are the "red foods," specifically dishes made with red meat and red wine, meat as defined by Byzantine statutes as pork, mutton, goat, and all sorts of game. These are fat dishes, foods that are eaten when there are no constraints on the diet, no fasting, and that correspond with the dishes known in Cypriot Greek as *millomena* or in Frankish (Cyprio-Gallic) as *charnage*. From a gastronomic standpoint, these are dishes that were also accompanied by or at least matched well with red wine, which in the case of Cypriot court cookery would be the noble wines of the Maratheftiko grape or wines made with a blend of Maratheftiko and other indigenous varietals that were grown on the royal allodia expropriated by the Lusignans from the last Byzantine governor of Cyprus.

Within the larger framework of *millomena*, we find a subset of recipes styled Syrian because they were of Arab-Christian origin or because they were artificially colored red. The usual coloring ingredient was most often saunders (a species of powdered sandalwood) or Syrian rue (*Peganum harmala*), which also had powerful hallucinogenic properties. Medieval Arabic texts suggest that this custom of coloring food red evolved in Persia. It was made known to the Cypriots via Syrian Christians, hence the literal connection of their name with that style of food presentation. The association was probably fortified by the fact that the Cypriot Maronites consumed *kibbah nayyah* (raw meatballs), which were naturally red or tinted to make them appear even redder.

Furthermore, among the Catholics of Cyprus, Syrian was a positive code word for Arab Christians as opposed to Sarasine, which implied a host of pejorative ideas. Thus Syrian dishes were morally acceptable because the Maronites of Cyprus recognized the authority of the pope, whereas true Sarasine cookery was infidel and therefore suspect. On the other hand, there were also other subtle complexities involved.

Symbolically, the red color may have been a visual signal intended to confirm that the dish contained fat ingredients (that is, a red-wine dish) or, conversely, that it was "fat" without being fat—in short, a fasting dish turned out as *faux charnage*. Such game playing and visual trickery were given high marks by medieval Cypriot cooks. The opposite of red foods were the *lefkofagá*, "white" foods, bloodless dishes associated with fasting (*nistissima*), as well as faux dishes that were white in color but contained meat, normally some kind of white meat such as poultry, as in the case of the blancmanges already mentioned. Furthermore, these were dishes made with or eaten with white wine (or sweet golden wine) as opposed to red. The reference to white conveyed the idea of purity and humility, and for the strictest adherents of fasting rules, plain white wine was interpreted as the "vinegar" that was offered to Christ on the cross. It was therefore an ascetic symbol of bodily suffering, the opposite of red wine, which symbolized joy and communion and the blood of Christ. Perhaps it is not at all coincidental that Cypriot Commandaria, which was called *nama* (sacred wine) in ancient times, is made by combining red and white grapes. Thus it represented a unification of two opposites, something more potent than its parts—and not surprisingly was considered a health wine, a promoter of longevity.

The issue of blood is perhaps best illustrated by *garos*, which is generally translated as "fish sauce." This preparation was used extensively in medieval Greek Cypriot cookery, at least by the Greek gentry and the urban well-to-do, since it was an imported item and thus subject to a 10 percent tax. The only *garos* allowed in Cypriot Greek cookery was imported specifically from Egypt, where it was made from Nile perch by Coptic Christians. The fermentation process was devoid of fish blood, hence its acceptability under Cypriot Orthodox canon. The salted perch were shipped in jars holding both the brine and whole fish. These items were then sold separately; it was the brown oxidized liquid that was marketed as *garos*.

According to Byzantine medical tradition, *garos* exhibited the humoral qualities of hot and dry; thus it was considered good for activating the appetite. Its role, then, was both culinary and medicinal, and that is why it was widely used in Cypriot dishes treated as appetizers or as a component in *bastonades* (basting sauces). According to the red-and-white schema, *garos* was red because it was derived from fish, yet because it was derived in a bloodless manner, it was acceptable to Cypriot religious custom. When recipes using *garos* migrated to the West, the fish sauce was invariably substituted with a similar salty ingredient, most notably anchovies. However, this substitution changed both the humoral character and the color since it became a white dish under Catholic canon and totally unsuitable to Cypriot Greeks since anchovies were processed with their own blood. While it may seem at first glance that certain culture wars separated Cypriot Greeks from their Frankish overlords, the long-term process was one of accommodation: both groups used food to define who they were with similar goals. For the old Cypriot Greek families, food expressed their ancient ties to the island; for the Latin nobility, the same food was employed to emphasize their legitimacy as Cypriots in a political sense.

Clumsy German Holds the Key to an Ancient Text

Unknown to the editor of *Das Buch von Guter Spise* (The book of good fare), Melitta Weiss Adamson, the 1380s German cookbook contains several "suites" of Cypriot recipes—that is, parts of chapters removed intact from an earlier Cyprio-Gallic text that was written in French but that incorporated Cypriot Greek dialect terms. I have designated that urtext as *Cuysinier A* in my forthcoming book since it can be traced to the 1364 peregrinations of King Peter I. The original recipe in question, called in German a *blamensir* (a contraction of *blancmange de Syrie*), heads a series of recipes all styled as Greek.[6]

The recipe's designation as Syrian warns us that this will not be a white dish in the strictest sense; indeed it may be unusually colored, and it is. In this case, the pudding is made with goat's milk (the standard milk of Cypriot cuisine), rice flour (an indication of expense), ground breast of chicken, sugar, and violets. Violets are meant to color the pudding to give it a high blush of bluish-purple and an unusual flavor or, more correctly, a distinct perfume: Cypriot cookery was noted for its perfumed character and relied heavily on ambrette (musk mallow) to add floral tones to food aromas.

Sweet violets (*Viola odorata*), common all over the island from November to February, were one of the constituents in Cypriot perfumes sold for export. In local culture, they were a symbol of virginity and as such were scattered on wedding beds. This symbolic association may itself suggest that the blancmange here was a dish featured on aristocratic wedding menus and thus consumed with the silver spoons mentioned earlier. Indeed all of the Cypriot dishes preserved in *Das Buch von Guter Spise* would make appropriate additions to a wedding feast, and that may be why they were saved and passed on to posterity.

Further, "dried violets" is one of the aromas used to describe wines with a light floral perfume, and this aroma is present in several types of Cypriot wine. By adding violets to the blancmange, the cook is essentially creating the sort of food-and-wine match that appealed to sophisticated medieval palates. While the recipe traveled West with its red character intact (by remaining a meat dish), two important contextual aspects were lost: its festive and symbolic role as a wedding dish and its inevitable pairing with one of the costly Cypriot white or golden wines with a characteristic violet nose.

And finally, as perhaps the ultimate challenge to Franco-Cypriot palates and medical sensibilities, the German recipe provided an addendum stating that the dish could be converted to fasting fare by substituting fish (pike, no less!) for the poultry, missing entirely the fact that the floral nature of the blancmange and the humoral character of violets (which are cooling) do not temper the cold, moist humoral nature of fish. In short, by shifting the dish into the realm of white cuisine, it becomes a medicinal and epicurean disaster.

Not much has been written about these complex red-and-white culinary dichotomies, which may hint of Persian dualism, yet Platina's culinary foray initially highlighted the fact that this division has survived from medieval Cyprus and persists in the form of such classic preparations as the brown and white fricassee: originally one was a fat dish (*charnage*) and the other lean (*maigre*).

Medieval Cypriot fricassees were called *kapamá* when prepared as a fat dish with meat and red wine (red fricassee of chukar or wood pigeon being typical of the hunt) and *yiachní* when prepared with white wine and vegetables. However, *yiachní* could be transformed into red by adding kid or lamb, as in the case of *arni yiachnisto me mussa* (lamb *yiachní* with bananas). Among the nobility, both preparations were sometimes cooked in the center of the table in a chafing pan called a *saltsarion*; the contents were eaten fondue style with forks long before table forks were introduced to Renaissance Italy. Cypriot forks were called *peronas* and like knives were brought by guests to the dinner table, along with a large linen napkin in which to carry food home. Gifting food to visitors was an important gauge both of one's hospitality and of one's economic standing in the community.

We are fortunate in that a large number of medieval table implements have been preserved in Cypriot collections, but the literary sources for the period need further mining for details on food and diet. As more material comes to light and brings greater order to this research, the goal is to publish both original annotated texts and recipes showing how the old dietary system worked. In the meantime, more ethnographic fieldwork is needed in Cyprus to ascertain what terms or culinary ideas may survive in the traditional cuisine and how they may or may not validate what has been emerging from a wide range of medieval texts.

All the same, the highly scripted and theatrical character of Cypriot court cuisine sets it apart from the cuisines of surrounding regions. Like the indigenous music of the island, it has no counterpart in western Europe, even though recipes did in fact migrate west. The curious and often paradoxical performability of Cypriot court cuisine, especially within the context of the red-and-white schema, may explain in part why the island became so deeply embedded in the mythology of the Middle Ages.

NOTES

1. Machaut, *La prise d'Alexandre*, 306.
2. Hieatt and Butler, *Curye on Inglysch*, 47, 49.
3. Martino of Como, *Art of Cooking*, 56.
4. Ibid., 123.
5. Ibid., 78.
6. M. Adamson, *Das Buch von guter Spise*, 57.

11

Mystical Poetics

Courtly Themes in Early Sufi Akhbār

BILAL ORFALI

It is common practice in modern times to read mystical poetry and apply it to our mundane lives and loves. Sufis in the early period did the opposite. Their mystical hymns often spun out of the courtly poetic *ghazal*, panegyric, and wine songs.

This chapter highlights the relation of the Arabic courtly poetic canon to early Sufism. Poetry appears to have been closely associated with the lives, thoughts, and legacy of the Sufi personalities of the eighth to tenth centuries, as is apparent in the primary anthologies of their *akhbār* and statements. These Sufis and Pietists used poetry to describe mystical experiences and thoughts that were better hidden in subtle intimations than expressed in statements of prose. Sufis often talk about *ʿibāra* (expression) and *ishāra* (allusion), and many Sufi states (*aḥwāl*) and thoughts are hard to express in plain prose and require the use of poetic language. Consider, for example, the following anecdote:

> Someone asked Samnūn about God's saying "So they plotted a plot: and We plotted a plot" (27:50). Is it permissible to ascribe plotting (*makr*) to the God? Samnūn replied:
>
> ويقبحُ مِنْ سواكَ الفعلُ عندي   فتفعلُه فيحسُنُ منكَ ذاكا
>
> The act, from someone other than you, is hateful to me,
> You carry it out—and I find it beautiful.
>
> The person said: I ask you to comment on a Qur'anic verse and you reply in poetry! Samnūn asked him: From which land are you? From the

> mountain, he replied. Samnūn then said: Oh you coarse one (*lujāfī*), God took an oath not to entrust His wisdom to a barbarian heart (*aʿjamiyy al-qalb*). I did not answer in poetry because I am incapable of clear expression; rather, I wanted to teach you that in the merest trifle of things lies the strongest indication to Him.[1]

This chapter focuses on the formative period of Sufism (tenth to twelfth centuries).[2] Many anecdotes, reports, and poems from this period survive in Sufi anthologies, handbooks, and treatises. These anthologies and treatises contain hundreds of lines of poetry, often with separate chapters dedicated to the performance of this poetry in the beatific auditions (*samāʿ*) and other chapters on the poetic verses chosen by Sufis to illustrate their mystical experiences.[3] Interestingly, in both cases, this poetry is often juxtaposed with prose, usually borrowed from the Arabic courtly poetic tradition.[4] By looking at reports and anecdotes surviving in early Sufi anthologies from the tenth to the twelfth centuries, this chapter examines how the themes or motifs of the pre-Islamic, Umayyad, and early Abbasid periods were used perfomatively to create a mystical poetics. Reframing these courtly poetic topoi, Sufis reperformed this poetry and reinterpreted it in a new context.

Remembering the Beloved: Poetry and Authorial Voices in Beatific Auditions

The term *samāʿ* (translated here as "beatific audition") can be applied to singing or any musical performance or sound that delights the ear. Poetry recitation, which can be seen as a type of singing, is included in this category. We find its application to the Sufi musical tradition in ritualized form.[5] The discussion of *samāʿ* is found in almost every handbook or anthology on Sufism and was a subject of controversy even among the Sufis themselves.[6]

The surviving literature demonstrates that the use of poetry in *samāʿ* was very common, and in fact, it was preferred to the Qurʾān.[7] Surprisingly, most of this poetry is court poetry from the *ghazal*, wine, or panegyric tradition, sometimes even taken from the *dīwāns* of well-known pre-Islamic, Umayyad, and Abbasid poets. So how did this poetry gain the dimensions that exerted such a strong influence on the Sufis?

The Sufi masters Junayd and Ruwaym, when asked about the cause of the rapture associated with *samāʿ*, explain that *samāʿ* is an act of recollection (*dhikr*); the souls reawaken at remembering the archetypal moment of divine awareness, the primordial covenant, *yawm al-mīthāq* or *yawm alastu* (Junayd: *ḥarrakahum dhikr dhālik*, Ruwaym: *fa-inzaʿajū*).[8] On this preexistential day described in the Qurʾān, human beings before their creation stood witness in the form of specks of light to God's Lordship. God asked them, "Am I not your lord?" (*alastu bi-rabbikum*), to which they affirmed, *balā*. The Sufis' aim is to reenact the witnessing on the day of the primordial covenant through constant recollection of God (*dhikr*). *Dhikr* means both "to mention" and "to remember." Thus, the role of poetry in *samāʿ* is to remind the Sufis of that moment.

The same line of poetry, however, can elicit different reactions at a *samāʿ* gathering. Abū ʿAbd al-Raḥmān al-Sulamī, in his treatise on *samāʿ*, declares that the object of listening is one and the same, but the difference lies in the listeners.[9] Similarly, Junayd states that *samāʿ* is fashioned by the listeners.[10] Sarrāj relates several statements that enumerate the different kinds of listeners (*ḍurūb al-mustamiʿīn*) or their hierarchy (*ṭabaqāt al-mustamiʿīn*).[11] Sulamī narrates a related anecdote:

> I heard ʿAbdallah b. Muḥammad say: "One night I was with Shiblī and a group of Sufis in a listening session [*samāʿ*]. When a singer sang something, Shiblī shrieked, while the group was silent.
>
> A sheikh asked him: Abū Bakr, aren't they listening like you? What's wrong with you?
>
> He rose in ecstasy and recited:
>
> لو يسمعون كما سمعتُ كلامها   خرّوا لعَزّة ركّعًا وسجودا
>
> If they heard her speech as I did,
They would prostrate themselves to ʿAzza in prayer
>
> He then recited:

لي سَكْرتان وللنُّدمان واحدةٌ   شيءٌ خُصِصْت به من بينهم وحدي

I have two intoxications, whereas my boon companions have just one
This is the thing that singles me out"[12]

In these texts, the assignment of authorship is not determined by the creation of new words but rather by the perception of a sincere expression of true feeling. Poetry thus is the product of a social network of textual producers. Everyone is to some degree a poet. Most often, the performer recites a line of court or religious poetry. The listeners give the line a new meaning through interpretation and remembrance. They are free to apply the lines to their own states and conditions.[13] Every performance is a collection of new texts that depend on the individual and collective state (*ḥāl*) of the listeners.[14] Another famous example is an anecdote related to Dhū l-Nūn's visit to Baghdād:

> When Dhū l-Nūn al-Miṣrī entered Baghdad, [local] Sufis gathered around him. Among them was a singer [*qawwāl*]. The Sufis asked Dhū l-Nūn's permission to have him [the singer] perform something for them. He gave them permission, and the singer began to recite:
>
> صغيرُ هواكَ عَذّبَني   فكيف به إذا احْتَنَكا
> وأنت جَمَعتَ من قَلبي   هَوًى قد كانَ مُشْتَرَكا
> أما ترثي لمكْتَئبٍ   إذا ضحك الخَليُّ بكى
>
> Even a little amount of [my] passion for you has caused me [great] pain
> What would happen, if it were to take full control over me?
> You have brought together in my heart a passion that used to be shared with others.
> Have you no sympathy for one who is broken by mourning,
> who weeps, while one who is free [from affliction] is laughing?!
>
> [On hearing this] Dhū l-Nūn stood up and fell on his face, blood streaming from his forehead onto the ground. Then, one of the Sufis also

> stood up and displayed ecstatic behavior. Dhū l-Nūn told him [quoting the Qurʾān]: "[The All-Compassionate] who sees you when you stand" (26:218), and the man sat down.[15]

The *ghazal* poetry recited by the singer is one of the organizing groups of songs offered by Abū l-Faraj al-Iṣfahānī (d. 356/967) in his great book of songs *K. al-Aghānī*. Iṣfahānī attributed the poetry to the Abbasid vizier poet Muḥammad b. ʿAbd al-Malik al-Zayyāt and the original song to Abū Ḥashīsha.[16] We do not know exactly how Dhū l-Nūn interpreted the three lines, but one possible Sufi interpretation ascribes the pronoun in the phrase "your love" (*hawāka*) to God; the "bringing together of the heart" (*jamaʿta fī qalbī*) could refer to the state of unification (*jamʿ*) in Sufism, in which the Sufi sees everything as one and directed to the one. The third line could refer to the state of separation (*farq*), in which the poet is returned to his human existence and sees the calamity of being at a distance from God.

The lines brought Dhū l-Nūn to a state of genuine ecstasy. The poetry to Dhū l-Nūn referred to God and to God's love and his own human existence in relation to the divine. In the same anecdote, another man attempted a similar interpretation and reaction that was denied by Dhū l-Nūn, who cited decisive evidence from the Qurʾān that the man could not deny or reject. We are not told why Dhū l-Nūn reacted this way. He may have sensed that the man was not sincere in his emotions or that in a state of ecstasy he could not control his reactions, but when he returned to his initial state of awareness, he was able to see his action through the behavior of the other man and then make a rational response to it by disapproving of it. The example shows how a *ghazal* poem recited in a Sufi context can bring listeners to a state of ecstasy through remembrance and interpretation.

Walking in the Steps of Poets: Poetic Examples and Illustrations in Sufi Akhbār

The use of the motifs of love and wine in Sufi poetry, in Arabic, Persian, Urdu, and Turkish, is common knowledge to any scholar of Sufism. In Arabic, a quick glance at the *dīwān*s of Ibn al-Fāriḍ and Ibn ʿArabī suffices to reveal the strong reliance on these motifs. But how did this come about in the early period?

Early Sufi anthologies dedicated chapters to the poetic verses chosen by Sufis to illustrate their mystical experiences and sometimes composed works for this purpose, such as *K. al-Amthāl wa-l-istishhādāt* (Book of examples and poetic illustrations) by Abū ʿAbd al-Raḥmān al-Sulamī[17] and *K. al-Shawāhid wa-l-amthāl* (Book of poetic illustrations and examples) by Abū Naṣr al-Qushayrī.[18] This section draws examples from these two works to demonstrate how Sufis were constantly looking over their shoulder to see how earlier poets had expressed certain motifs, themes, and emotional and psychological states in order to reference them, thus making the inherited poetic conventions a medium for the expression of their own experiences.

As the titles of the two works indicate, the authors try to collect "similes" (*amthāl*; literally, "likenesses") that give poetic expression to the Sufis' mystical experiences, along with "illustrations" (*istishhādāt*) found in a variety of Sufi writings. The authors may have understood these "illustrations" as the fruit of the Sufi experience of *mushāhada* ("witnessing" or "contemplation"), using them to give testimony in verse to the height of mystical experience.[19]

Sulamī's treatise has a somewhat unusual introduction, presenting an anonymous Sufi who, when asked about his own mystical experiences or doctrines, explained them by quoting poetic verses composed by others.[20] Thus Sulamī's *K. al-Amthāl wa-l-istishhādāt* can be seen as a compilation of such verses, often mentioned in relation to the circumstances under which they were recited. Sulamī is meticulous in introducing each quotation of poetic verses with a chain of narrators (*isnād*), thereby identifying his direct informants and their sources. In *K. al-Shawāhid wa-l-amthāl*, Abū Naṣr al-Qushayrī records Sufi teachings from his father and other Sufis (including himself), which are followed by lines of poetry that express the same motifs. Qushayrī quotes some poetry in Persian, while Sulamī provides only Arabic poems.

Huda Fakhreddine notes in her article on defining metapoesis in the Abbasid age that "meta-poetic compositions often voice the anxieties of a poet towards his/her role and place in a tradition."[21] Fakhreddine distinguishes thematic metapoetry (poetry about poetry) from "referential or contextual metapoesis" that reflects the conscious manner in which a poet engages poetic references in front of his alert audience.[22] Fakhreddine explains how the Abbasid poets strived to decipher the elegiac motifs, interpreting them and assigning to them new meanings and significances, how they participated in the poetic debates of their day, and how they reflected on the nature and function of their poetry.

Sufi *akhbār*, in their turn, evoke past poets and their poetic heritage. They tend to quote eminent poets whose poetry must have been widely circulated and memorized. Yet Sufi *akhbār* place this readily recognizable poetry in a new context that deliberately changes the past. Majnūn (d. ca. 68/688) becomes the Sufi who left reason aside; his beloved Laylā stands as a symbol of divinity. Abū Nuwās (d. ca. 200/814) becomes a toxic Sufi, and his wine a symbol for divine wisdom and knowledge. Ibn al-Rūmī (d. 283/896), Abū Tammām (d. 231/846), Buḥturī (d. 284/898), and Mutanabbī (d. 354/965) stand in the court of the quintessential generous patron, Allah, and seek his bounty. It is in some sense a process of a metaphorization in which the reality of the pre-Islamic, Umayyad, and Abbasid models now acts as a device or metaphor for the Sufi poetics. Sufis who recite the poem illustrate, explain, or justify their mystical experience or idea via the embedded motif or theme, but at the same time, Sufi performers evoke, link, and reinterpret the poetic heritage associated with the poem, thus placing themselves within a poetic tradition against which their own experience becomes more evident. Despite the evocation of the poetic heritage and in order to dehistoricize the poems, these texts rarely name the original composers.

The Ruined Abodes (*al-aṭlāl*)

Whether Bedouin or courtly, the pre-Islamic *qaṣīda* often begins with the ritualistic elegiac *nasīb*, which contains motifs that revolve around decay, loss, and nostalgia for times past.[23] Among them is the motif of the "ruined abodes" (*dhikr al-diyār* or *al-aṭlāl*), which reflects the Bedouin lifestyle.[24] In the Abbasid age, the conventions of the pre-Islamic *qaṣīda* needed to be explained, modified, and reinterpreted to fit the new urban setting.[25] As Suzanne Stetkevych observes, "the *badīʿ* poets . . . replaced the obsolete mnemonic rhetorical devices with ones whose primary function was now the expression for the first time of modern, abstract concepts."[26] Similarly, we find in *K. al-Amthāl wa-l-istishhādāt* and *K. al-Shawāhid wa-l-amthāl* an abstraction of the ruined abode in which the beloved once dwelled. Consider the following example:

> I heard Abū Bakr Muḥammad b. ʿAbdallāh b. Shādhān saying: A man said to Abū Muḥammad al-Jurayrī:
>
> "I was once standing on the plane of delight, and a path to openness became evident. But I slipped, and my former station became hidden from me. How can I reach it again? Please show me the way back to where I was."
>
> Abū Muḥammad al-Jurayrī cried and said, "Oh Brother, everyone is attempting to overcome this obstacle. But I will recite to you verses, which have an answer to your question."
>
> He recited:
>
> قِفْ بالدّيارِ فهذه آثارُهُمْ   تبكي الأحبَّة حَسْرةً وتشوُّقا
> كم قد وقفتُ بها أسائلُ مُخْبِرًا   عن أهلها أو صادقًا أو مُشفِقا
> فأجابني داعي الهَوى في رَسمِها   فارَقتَ من تهوى فَعَزَّ الملتقى
>
> Stand upon the abodes! These are their traces
> Mourning for the loved ones, in grief and yearning.
> How I have stood inquiring after its people, asking
> An informant, an honest man, or a sympathizer.
> What in these ruins awakens passion answered me
> You left your beloved. Oh how precious is reunion![27]

The ruins refer to the lost station in the Sufi path. The Sufi, like his pre-Islamic predecessors, stands abandoned, lost, and bewildered, seeking news, truth, or comfort. The traces remind the Sufi of a station of nearness (*qurb*) or gathering (*jamʿ*) that was followed by remoteness (*buʿd*) or dispersion (*farq*), and they tragically announce the hard truth: "Oh how precious is reunion." While the pre-Islamic poet suffers from the vicissitudes of time, the Sufi grieves his own slips. But if all pre-Islamic poets had to stand and reflect by the abode, so do all Sufis, as Jurayrī proclaims: "Everyone is attempting to overcome this obstacle."

Travel (*al-safar*) and the Journey (*al-raḥīl*)

In Arabic literature, motifs and themes relating to travel and the associated feelings of yearning, alienation, and estrangement can be traced back to the pre-Islamic period, manifested in the journey section of the *qaṣīda* or the scene of the departed caravan (*riḥlat al-ẓawāʿin*). These motifs and themes did not, however, form an independent genre until they were collected, starting from the third/ninth century in specialized and multithematic anthologies under the rubric of "longing for the homeland" (*al-ḥanīn ila l-awṭān*).[28]

Moreover, the Abbasid poets employed the *raḥīl* in their *qaṣīda*s. In this section of the classical *qaṣīda*, which follows the elegiac introduction, the poet usually describes his mounting animal and/or embarks on a journey through the desert.[29] The Abbasid poets and critics interpreted the *raḥīl* as an invitation for the compassionate concern of the patron, thus paving the way to the panegyrical section.[30] The destination of the *raḥīl* is the patron, and his reward is a compensation for family and possessions left behind and for the adversity the poet endures on the way.

The motifs and themes of *al-ḥanīn ila l-awṭān* are frequently visited in Sufi *akhbār*. In fact, Sufi anthologies often include a chapter on travel, its benefits and etiquette. The Sufi is a perpetual traveler, the journey is the Sufi path, and the homeland is a moment rather than a place—the pre-existential day of *yawm alastu* or *yawm al-mīthāq* described earlier. Sufis accepted the Abbasid interpretation of the *raḥīl* but replaced the earthly patron with the ultimate one. The outer journey is a flight from material possession, wealth, family, and reputation in search for certitude. The outer journey supports the inward journey. Here is an example from *K. al-Shawāhid wa-l-amthāl*:

> He [Abū l-Qāsim al-Qushayrī] said: through service one reaches the reward [*thawāb*], and by reverence one reaches the Real [*al-ḥaqq*]. There is a difference however between one arrival and the other. He chanted:
>
> فسرتُ إليكَ في طلبِ المعالي   وسار سواي في طلب المعاشِ
>
> I marched to you pursuing high stations
> Others marched in quest of earthly needs

He then chanted:

وما الفقرُ عن أرض العشيرة ساقنا   ولكنّنا جئنا بلقياكَ نسعدُ

We left the lands of our clan, not because of poverty
Rather, we sought happiness in encountering you.[31]

Love Poetry (*Ghazal*)

Sufi anthologies often dedicate a chapter to the topic of love (*maḥabba*) that elaborates on the nature and characteristics of divine love, from the human and the divine perspectives. God's love is infinite and manifests itself in mercy. From the human side, we encounter love as gratitude, as God's due, as an act or remembrance, as obedience, as a consequence of free well, and as annihilation.

In Arabic poetry, starting from the second part of the second/seventh century, the independent love poem, the *ghazal*, emerged, in two main categories: the Ḥijāzī *ghazal* and the ʿUdhrī *ghazal*. The Ḥijāzī poets used urban themes and stressed a lady's nobility and her lover's submissiveness. A favorite topic was the encounter of the lovers while on pilgrimage to the shrines of Mecca and Medina. The poetry of ʿUmar b. Abī Rabīʿa (d. 93/712 or 103/721) played a leading part in this pleasure-oriented urban society of Ḥijāz. ʿUmar's *ghazal* is lighthearted, frivolous, but never obscene. He usually assigns the lover's friends and the beloved's maids an active part in the relationship.

The ʿUdhrī *ghazal*, in contrast, stressed the lover's chastity. The beloved was simply irreplaceable, and the poet now found no solace with another lover, with his material wealth, or with his camel, as we find in pre-Islamic poetry. Poets like Jamīl (d. 82/701), Qays b. al-Mulawwaḥ al-Majnūn, and others sang about the fatal nature of love, to which the lover is not only victim but martyr. Love here is as powerful as fate. Love is often expressed in religious terms; the beloved is the object of the lover's total devotion, the shrine to which he makes his pilgrimage. The faithfulness of the loving poet is rewarded with sickness and madness, *junūn*. One offshoot of the ʿUdhrī *ghazal* is the so-called courtly *ghazal*, which shares many of the topoi with the ʿUdhrī narrative but denotes an "ideology of servile love," in which unrequited love is a sign of identification with a courtly group.[32] Both categories of love influenced the development of early Sufi poetry, and the symbolic worldview of the Sufis facilitated the proliferation of these topoi.[33] Umayyad and early Abbasid love poetry was frequently quoted in Sufi *akhbār*, as the following examples from *K. al-Amthāl wa-l-istishhādāt* demonstrate:

I heard Aḥmad b. ʿAlī b. Jaʿfar say: When Murtaʿish was asked about Sufism he said: "Sufism is ambiguity and disguise." He chanted:

سرِّي وسرُّك لا يعلمْ به أحدٌ   إلَّا الخليلُ ولا ينْطِقْ به ناطقُ

My secret and your secret, no one knows it
But the friend and no one else speaks of it

He then chanted:

إذا جئتَ فامنح طرف عينَيك غيرنا   لكي يحسبوا أنّ الهوى حيث تنظرُ

If you return, cast your eye on someone else
So that our tribe will think you love another[34]

Both lines tackle the topic of secrecy among the lovers to protect them from blame and envy, relatives and enemies. The second line is by the Ḥijāzī love poet ʿUmar b. Abī Rabīʿa, and in it the beloved takes an active role and asks for concealment and secrecy.[35]

We now turn attention to the ʿUdhrī *ghazal*. Consider the following anecdote from *K. al-Shawāhid wa-l-amthāl*:

I heard al-Ḥusayn b. Aḥmad al-Rāzī say: I heard al-Shiblī say: from your perspective, am I not a madman and you sound of mind? May God increase me in madness, and you in sanity. He suddenly proclaimed:

قالوا جُنِنتَ بمن تَهوى فقلتُ لهم   ما لذّةُ العشقِ إلّا للمجانينِ

They say, you have gone mad for the one you love
I replied, It is only the mad who know the pleasure of love

He also chanted:

بي جنونُ الهوى وما بي جنون   وجنون الهوى جنون الجنونِ

I have madness of passion, no madness
And madness of passion is the madness of madness![36]

The dominant theme in the last two lines is madness. In Sufism, we encounter the suffering of the lover and his wish for redemption in death, the *fanāʾ*. In this type of *ghazal*, the Sufi describes how love itself is his affliction. As in the ʿUdhrī *ghazal*, the focus is not the object of love but the suffering of the lover. The prototype here, Majnūn Laylā, had no need for the sensual reality of his beloved. The suffering shows that his love for God is unconditional. The faithful lover enjoys the affliction that God sends while remaining totally obedient to Him. Laylā often appears in this context as a symbol for the divinity. The following epigram from *K. al-Shawāhid wa-l-amthāl* serves as an example for the evocation of her symbolism in Sufism:

Many a person finds comfort in his heart and strength in his eyes when he sees his beloved. How many a woman confined to her home [*mukhaddara*], not used to embellishment [*tabarruj*], going out, and coming into view, when her little child [*waladuhā l-qalāsh*] gets lost, she goes after him. If someone tells her: You have changed your habit and came to this place! She would reply: My trial [*balāʾī*] is here! He chanted:

وقفتُ لليلى بالملا بعد هجعة   أراقبُها فانهلّت العينُ تدمعُ
وأتبعُ ليلى حيث سارت ووَدَّعت   وما الناسُ إلّا آلفٌ ومودِّ عُ
كأنّ زمامًا في الفؤاد مُعَلَّقًا   تقودُ به حيثُ استَمَرَّت وأتبعُ

I woke up to appear before Laylā in a crowd
Observing her, the eye burst into tears
I follow Laylā wherever she goes
People are of two kinds: a lover and another bidding farewell
As if I have put around my heart a leash
Laylā drags it and I follow[37]

Panegyric (*madīḥ*)

The panegyric is among the most enduring elements in Arabic literature. In the panegyric *qaṣīda*, we find the sociopolitical role of literature in Muslim culture. *Madīḥ*, in the words of Beatrice Gruendler, "fulfilled a twofold role as a ruler's commemorative portrayal and as an occasion for him to practice Patronage."[38] The panegyric *qasīda* often dwells on the complex relation between the poet and the patron. It acts as a pact and names the duties of both. The poet offers his devotion, loyalty, gratitude, service, and words in return for material tokens of generosity. In Sufism, the poet stands in the presence of the ultimate giver, the most perfect of patrons. In *K. al-Amthāl wa-l-istishhādāt*, we encounter, for example, these lines by Abū Tammām, originally in praise of the caliph al-Muʿtaṣim (r. 218/833–227/842); they emphasize the unusual generosity of the patron, a favorite motif in panegyric poetry from pre-Islamic times.[39]

I heard ʿAbdallāh b. Muḥammad of Damascus saying:

I once was attending the study circle of Shiblī in the mosque of Medina, when a beggar approached.

The beggar said, "Oh God, Oh most Generous!"

Shiblī groaned and then shouted, "How can I describe the Truth [viz. God] by generosity, when His creature says concerning His form:

تعوَّدَ بسطَ الكَفِّ حتّى لوَ انَّه   ثناها لقَبضٍ لم تُجِبهُ أناملُهْ
تَراهُ إذا ما جِئتَهُ مُتَهَلِّلًا   كأنَّك تعطيه الذي أنت سائلُهْ
ولو لم يكن في كفِّه غيرُ روحه   لجادَ به فليَتَّقِ اللّٰهَ آمِلُهْ
هو البحر من أيِّ النَّواحي أتيته   فَلُجَّتُهُ المعروف والجود ساحلُهْ

The opening of the hand was his custom
Were he to close it in a fist, his fingers would not obey.
When you visit him, he appears radiant
As if you had given him the very thing you desired.
Had there been something else in his hand besides his lifeblood
He would have generously given it. Let the one who hopes for his reward fear God!

For he is the ocean, from any side you approach.
His depths are goodness, while generosity is but its shore.[40]

The Wine Song (*khamriyya*)

Wine poetry is a legacy from pre-Islamic times. The wine song flourished in the Abbasid age in the poems of Abū Nuwās, the most important Arabic wine poet of all times. In his wine songs, we find the motifs of the journey toward the wine house or monastery, the rebuke for drinking, detailed descriptions of wine and its effects, the wine *majlis*, the cupbearer, and the boon companions. The consumption of wine is often likened to a wedding, and wine itself is the bride. In these poems, wine is associated with Christian monks, Jewish merchants, and the Zoroastrian community. As early as Abū Nuwās, we can see the idealization and sometimes the abstraction of wine. It is remarkable how often Abū Nuwās is quoted in the Sufi tradition. That which is most profane is transformed into that which is most sacred. Wine is linked to intoxication or drunkenness; it refers to spiritual love or divine knowledge. The cup is the Sufi's heart; the cupbearer is often God or the prophet, the source of knowledge. Two lines attributed to Ibn Shibl al-Baghdādī (d. 473/1080–81), Ibn Durayd (321/933), or Idrīs b. al-Yamān (d. 450/1058–59)[41] in *K. al-Shawāhid wa-l-amthāl* describe the lightness of wine and its transformative effect:

He was asked: Why is the dead body heavier than the live one?
He chanted:

ثقلت زجاجاتٌ أتتنا فُرّغًا   حتّى إذا مُلئتْ بصرفِ الرّاحِ
خفّتْ فكادت تستطيرُ بما حَوتْ   إنّ الجسومَ تخفّ بالأرواحِ

The empty bottles arrived heavy
When we filled them with the pure wine
They weighed less and almost flew with their content
Bodies become lighter when souls inhabit them.[42]

In Sufi poetics, all the devices of the classical model are still there, but they have been transformed into something very different, whether in the Sufi beatific audition (*samāʿ*) or in the Sufi *khabar*. As we have seen in the anecdote about Samnūn, there were those who disapproved of the use of poetry itself.[43] Moreover, not everyone accepted this metaphorical use of the motifs and topoi of classical poetry. Consider the following anecdote from *K. al-Shawāhid wa-l-amthāl*:

He said: one *faqīr* heard a singer chanting:

يقولون ليلى بالعراق مريضةٌ   فأقبلتُ من مصرٍ إليها أعودُها

They say Laylā is in Iraq and is sick
I came from Egypt to visit her

The *faqīr* stood and displayed ecstatic behavior. A common man asked: "Who is Laylā to him?" People told him: "There is no relation [*qarāba*] between them; this is a coining of a likeness [*ḍarb mathal*]." The man then insulted and beat him.[44]

Yet, to the Sufis, these earlier poets are the Sufis' predecessors, their prototypes. The courtly motifs and topoi refer to the human experience of the divine or to the memory of it. The same motifs are also a reminder of past poets who have stood in the same position. The poetic past gives meaning and justifies the present. This transformation reaches its zenith in Arabic in the poetry of Ibn ʿArabī, with whom we will conclude this chapter:

ونادِ بدعدٍ والرباب وزينبٍ   وهندٍ وسلمى ثمّ لبنى وزمزمِ[45]

Call out to Daʿd and Rabāb, Zaynab and Hind,
Salmā and Lubnā then listen[46]

أدينُ بدين الحبّ أنّى توجّهت   ركائبه فالحبُّ ديني وإيماني[47]
لنا أسوةٌ في بِشر هندٍ وأختها   وقيسٍ وليلى ثمّ ميٍّ وغيلانِ

I profess the religion of love.
Wherever its caravan turns along the way, that is the belief, the faith I keep.

Like Bishr of Hind and her sister, love-mad Qays and the lost
Laylā, Mayya and her lover Ghaylān.[48]

NOTES

1. Orfali and Saab, *Sufism*, 338.
2. For a detailed survey of this period, see Karamustafa, *Sufism*.
3. Such chapters can be found, for example, in *Kitāb l-Taʿarruf li-madhhab ahl al-taṣawwuf* (Introducing the way of the people of Sufism) by al-Kalabādhī (d. 380 or 384 / 990 or 994); *Al-Lumaʿ* (Book of flashes) by al-Sarrāj (d. 378/988); *Tahdhīb al-asrār* (Refining the secrets) by Khargūshī (d. 407/1016); the famous treatise on Sufism by Abū l-Qāsim al-Qushayrī (d. 465/1074); the recently published *Salwat al-ʿārifīn* (The comfort of the mystics) by Abū Khalaf al-Ṭabarī (d. ca. 470/1077); and of special importance because of its heavy use of poetry, *K. al-Bayāḍ wa-l-sawād* (Book of black and white) of Abū l-Ḥasan al-Sīrjānī (d. ca. 470/1077). There are at least two anthologies that were solely dedicated to the use of poetry as a *mathal* (example) or *shāhid* (illustration, witness) in early Sufism: (1) *K. al-Amthāl wa-l-istishhādāt* (Book of examples and poetic illustrations) by Abū ʿAbd al-Raḥmān al-Sulamī (d. 412/1021); and (2) *Kitāb al-Shawāhid wa-l-amthāl* (Book of poetic illustrations and examples) by Abū Naṣr al-Qushayrī (465/1072). For *Kitāb al-Shawāhid wa-l-amthāl*, see Chiabotti, "Spiritual and Physical Progeny"; and Shahsavari, "Abū Naṣr al-Qushayrī."
4. Prosimetrum is a widespread phenomenon in Arabic literature but one that is surprisingly little studied. For examples and some functions of poetry within prose narratives, see Heinrichs, "Prosimetrical Genres"; Heinrichs, "Function(s) of Poetry."
5. *Samāʿ* is relatively well studied in modern scholarship. Most of the studies are concerned with the permissibility and/or practice of *samāʿ*, its rituals, and the instruments employed in it. For example, see Klein, "Music, Rapture and Pragmatics"; Gribetz, "*Samāʿ* Controversy"; Michon, "Sacred Music and Dance"; Avery, *Psychology of Early Sufi Samāʿ Listening*; Lewisohn, "Sacred Music of Islam." See also the primary and secondary sources listed in these articles.
6. This is evident, for example, in Sulamī, *K. al-Samāʿ*; Pourjavady, "Dū athar-i kuhan dar samāʿ." Sarrāj offers a detailed treatment of the phenomenon in his chapter on *samāʿ* with a separate section on its permissibility (*bāb fī waṣf samāʿ al-ʿāmma wa-ibāḥat dhālika lahum*) and another on those who disapproved of it (*bāb fī man kariha l-samāʿ*); see Sarrāj, *K. al-Lumaʿ*, ed. R. A. Nicholson (Leiden: Brill, 1914), 267–314. Sīrjānī in his *Kitāb al-Bayāḍ wa-l-sawād* includes a chapter on listening to music, its permissibility, and its prohibitions (*bāb ithbāt al-samāʿ wa-l-radd ʿalā man yunkiruh*); see Orfali and Saab, *Sufism*, 340–42.
7. Sarrāj (followed by Qushayrī, Sīrjānī, and Ṭabarī) relates a story of Abū Ḥusayn al-Darrāj's (d. 320/932) meeting with Yūsuf b. al-Ḥusayn al-Rāzī (d.304/916–17). Yūsuf weeps at the recital of a verse of secular poetry after a whole morning's

recital of the Qur'an had failed to elicit any response from him; see Sarrāj, *K. al-Luma'*, 291. Sarrāj justifies this by stating that human passions ought not to be satisfied by melodic recitation of the Qur'an. Rather, these passions are better served by poetry, which, in its very nature, has an affinity to human sensitivities and is better able to arouse human passions. See Avery, *Psychology of Early Sufi Samā'*, 18–19; Sarrāj, *K. al-Luma'*, 283–85.

Later, Ghazālī in his detailed chapter on *samā'* in *Iḥyā' 'ulūm al-dīn* acknowledges the preference of poetry in *samā'* sessions over the Qur'ān and gives seven reasons for the effectiveness of sung poetry in producing rapture (*wajd*): (1) correspondence to listeners' states, (2) novelty, (3) meter, (4) musical modes and rendition, (5) percussion instruments in *ghinā'*, (6) author's intent, (7) the Qur'an as a divine attribute. See a detailed discussion of Ghazālī's argument in Klein, "Music, Rapture and Pragmatics," 234–37.

8. Orfali and Saab, *Sufism*, 348, Khargūshī, *Tahdhīb al-asrār*, 336; Abū Naṣr al-Qushayrī, *Al-Risāla al-Qushayriyya*, 509; Böwering and Orfali, *Comfort of the Mystics*, 281.
9. Sulamī, *K. al-Samā'*, 81. See also Orfali and Saab, *Sufism*, 342.
10. *Al-samā' min ḥaythu l-mustami'*. See Sulamī, *K. al-Samā'*, 81. See also Orfali and Saab, *Sufism*, 342.
11. Sarrāj, *K. al-Luma'*, 277–83. For Ghazālī's different states of listeners, see Klein, "Music, Rapture and Pragmatics," 226–28.
12. Sulamī, *Rasā'il ṣūfiyya*, 88.
13. Ghazālī writes, "Any verse can be applied to carry [any] meaning, and this according to the depth of the listener's knowledge and the pureness of his heart." See Ghazālī, *Iḥyā' 'ulūm al-dīn*, 359. The quotation and translation are from Klein, "Music, Rapture and Pragmatics," 228.
14. See Frishkompf, "Authorship in Sufi Poetry." Frishkompf speaks of an "inter-author" and an "inter-text" to describe the collaborative assignment of meaning in poetic practices in *samā'*.
15. Orfali and Saab, *Sufism*, 367; Böwering and Orfali, *Comfort of the Mystics*, 286; Sarrāj, *K. al-Luma'*, 186, 290; Abū Naṣr al-Qushayrī, *Al-Risāla al-Qushayriyya*, 513. Translation is adapted with changes from Knysh, *Al-Qushayri's Epistle*, 350–51.
16. Al-Iṣfahānī, *Kitāb al-Aghānī*, 23:45.
17. Sulamī's life and works have been examined in Böwering, "Qur'ān Commentary of al-Sulamī"; the editors' introduction to Sulamī, *Rasā'il ṣūfiyya*, 9–20; and Thibon, *L'œuvre d'Abū 'Abd al-Raḥmān al-Sulamī*.
18. For the career of Abū l-Qāsim al-Qushayrī's sons in general and the career of Abū Naṣr in particular, see Chiabotti, "Spiritual and Physical Progeny," 47–60; Shahsavari, "Abū Naṣr al-Qushayrī," 279–95. The text of *K. al-Shawāhid wa-l-amthāl* occupies folios 2a–137a of MS Ayasofya 4128; for the authorship of the text, see Chiabotti, "Spiritual and Physical Progeny," 57–60. It should be noted that there is a problem with the folio order in the manuscript. Fol. 93a does not follow fol. 92b;

fol. 96a does not follow 95b; fol. 105a does not follow fol. 104b; fol. 115a does not follow fol. 114b; fol. 125a does not follow fol. 124b; and fol. 137a does not follow fol. 136b.

19. See the editors' introduction to *Rasā'il ṣūfiyya*, 26. See also the various usages of the word *shāhid* in *tafsīr* and Sufi literature in Chiabotti, "Spiritual and Physical Progeny," 60–64, 69–70.
20. See Sulamī, *Rasā'il ṣūfiyya*, 87.
21. Fakhreddine, "Defining Metapoesis," 205. See also Wellek, *Discriminations*, 261–63.
22. Fakhreddine, "Defining Metapoesis," 206.
23. Renate Jacobi points to the transformation of the desert *qaṣīda* from a Bedouin poem to a court poem toward the end of the sixth century under the influence of panegyric. See Jacobi, "Camel-Section," 13. On the history of the *nasīb*, see Hamori, *Art of Medieval Arabic Literature*, 16–19.
24. For the *aṭlāl* motif and its relation to *nasīb* and *madīḥ*, see Sperl, *Mannerism in Arabic Poetry*, 9–27.
25. See the discussion on this change in the nature of the *qaṣīda* in Fakhreddine, "Defining Metapoesis," 211–18.
26. Stetkevych, *Abū Tammām*, 34.
27. Sulamī, *Rasā'il ṣūfiyya*, 96.
28. For a detailed treatment of the subject of *al-ḥanīn ila l-awṭān* in pre-modern Arabic literature, see al-Qāḍī, "Dislocation and Nostalgia"; Müller, "*Al-Ḥanīn ilā l-awṭān*"; Arazi, "*Al-ḥanīn ilā al-awṭān*"; see also the editors' introduction to Thaʿālibī, *Zād safar al-mulūk*.
29. It is worth noting that the Abbasid *qaṣīda* significantly reduced the *raḥīl* section; see Jacobi, "Camel-Section," 14–19.
30. See Sperl, *Mannerism*, 9–10; for the opinions of pre-modern critics on the coherence of the *qaṣīda* and the relation of its parts, see Gelder, *Beyond the Line*, 23–67, and especially relevant is the opinion of Ibn Qutayba, 42–46.
31. Abū Naṣr al-Qushayrī, *K. al-Shawāhid wa-l-amthāl*, MS Ayasofya 4128, f. 22r. The first line is by al-Mutanabbī; see Thaʿālibī, *Yatīmat al-dahr fī maḥāsin ahl al-ʿaṣr*, 1:155.
32. See Bauer, *Liebe und Liebesdichtung*, 59.
33. See Kuntze, "Love and God."
34. Sulamī, *Rasā'il ṣūfiyya*, 100.
35. ʿUmar b. Abī Rabīʿa, *Dīwān ʿUmar b. Abī Rabīʿa*, 189.
36. Sulamī, *Rasā'il ṣūfiyya*, 104–5. Both lines are attributed to Ibn al-Muʿtazz; see Ibn al-Muʿtazz, *Dīwān ashʿār al-amīr Abī l-ʿAbbās ʿAbdillāh Ibn Muḥammad al-Muʿtazz*, 428; and Ibn Ḥabīb al-Naysābūrī, *ʿUqalāʾ al-majānīn*, 27.
37. Abū Naṣr al-Qushayrī, *K. al-Shawāhid wa-l-amthāl*, f. 24r. See Qays b. al-Mulawwaḥ, *Dīwān Majnūn Laylā*, 146–47.
38. Gruendler, *Medieval Arabic Praise Poetry*, 229.
39. Muḥammad b. Yaḥyā al-Ṣūlī, *Sharḥ al-Ṣūlī li-Dīwān Abī Tammām*, 203.
40. Sulamī, *Rasā'il ṣūfiyya*, 98–99.

41. The two lines are attributed to Idrīs b. al-Yamān in Ibn Diḥya al-Kalbī, *Al-Muṭrib min ash'ār ahl al-Maghrib*, 197; to Ibn Durayd in al-Irbilī, *Risālat al-ṭayf*, 17; and to Ibn Shibl al-Baghdādī in al-Ḥamawī, *Mu'jam al-udabā'*, 3:1084.
42. Abū Naṣr al-Qushayrī, *K. al-Shawāhid wa-l-amthāl*, f. 5r.
43. See also Böwering and Orfali, *Comfort of the Mystics*, 279.
44. Abū Naṣr al-Qushayrī, *K. al-Shawāhid wa-l-amthāl*, f. 63v.
45. Ibn 'Arabī, *Turjumān al-ashwāq*, 23.
46. Translation is taken from Sells, *Stations of Desire*, 56–57.
47. Ibn 'Arabī, *Turjumān al-ashwāq*, 44.
48. Sells, *Stations of Desire*, 73 (with modification).

12

Chaste Lovers, Umayyad Rulers, and Abbasid Writers

JOCELYN SHARLET

Stories of Umayyad-era chaste love affairs, which appear in conjunction with poetry about chaste love, play an important role in Abbasid-era literature. These stories of chaste love are a performance of individual identity in the context of family, tribal, and court authority. In addition, they contribute to the development of Abbasid-era poetry and prose literature on unrequited love, fulfillment in love, courtly love, love theory, and mysticism, which in turn influence these kinds of literature in other languages of the Middle East, the Mediterranean region, and later in South Asia. Abbasid writers record chaste love stories that become canonical as well as a range of other chaste love stories that display noncanonical features. The canonical chaste love stories are viewed as a performance of individual identity that revolves around chaste, obsessive love and resistance to family, tribal, and court authority. Chaste love stories that display noncanonical features, which are the focus of this chapter, are a performance of individual identity through chaste, obsessive love and diverse trajectories of power and desire, as well as different literary modes and registers. Writers display the diversity of these other stories in part through comparisons to the canonical chaste love stories. I discuss these noncanonical chaste love stories using the examples of the stories of Kuthayyir, Laylā al-Akhyaliyya, Waḍḍāḥ al-Yaman, Qays b. Dharīḥ, Sallāma, and Sulaymān b. ʿAbd al-Malik.

Chaste love is known as "ʿUdhrī love" in Arabic, after the ʿUdhra tribe of eastern Arabia, which became famous for chaste love in the first centuries of Islam under the Umayyads (661–750), who were based mainly in Damascus, by way of literature written under the Abbasids (750–1258), who were based mainly in Baghdad.[1] Although not recorded until Abbasid times, it is clear that there was a core of poetry from Umayyad times from which this literature about Umayyad lovers developed.[2]

Most scholars agree that the emergence of Islam in Arabia, the impact of its values on pre-Islamic tribal ways, the Islamic conquests of the Middle East, and the shift in the political center of gravity from Arabia to Damascus with the establishment of the Umayyad Empire entailed major social dislocations in work and family patterns in Arabia. Most identify a contrast between the poetry and stories of urban poets and the poetry and stories of the ʿUdhrī poets, but some also observe the overlap between the two and show that social dislocations cannot explain everything about this love literature or at least not directly.[3]

The stories of Umayyad-era chaste lovers that were recorded by Abbasid-era writers serve as commentary on poetry attributed to Umayyad-era chaste lovers, and they also offer perspectives on the dynamic of individual, social, and political life. In the dominant paradigm in these stories as it appears in research on this topic, ʿUdhrī love is chaste love between a man and a woman that develops in childhood or youth in a pastoral setting and overwhelms the self so that there is no space for anything else. This love is neither frivolous nor physical, and the lovers are totally committed only to each other so that they live and die for love.[4] The version of the chaste love story that has received the most attention features a male center of gravity and lovers who are free people who remain separated except for brief meetings. These canonical stories unfold in a pastoral setting beyond the court and are characterized by a melancholy and even morbid mood. In this canonical chaste love story, the family and tribe attempt to exert control over the lovers' choice of a mate. The story unfolds far from the court, but the ruler observes the situation and attempts to back up the family and tribe in their resistance to the lovers' choice of a mate. Together, the family, tribe, community, and court succeed in keeping the lovers apart, while the lovers' chaste obsession with each other, and their anxiety about it, also plays a role in the separation.

Research often focuses on chaste love stories that fit this dominant paradigm. Umayyad love poetry portrays conflicting ideas that follow from social dislocations and articulates anxiety about new ways of thinking about individuality and social life.[5] The canonical chaste love stories that develop out of Umayyad love poetry are viewed as a performance of individual identity that consists of both lovers' chaste, obsessive love and their resistance to attempts by family, tribe, and rulers to end it.

In these stories, individual identity follows a trajectory from love that is initiated by the lovers rather than their kin and kept secret to love that is a public performance, which is scandalous in the eyes of family, tribe, community, and from afar, the court. This public spectacle of inner life unfolds in scenes in which a lover encounters members of the family, the tribe, the community, or the court and resists their efforts to end the chaste yet scandalous love affair.

Some of the best-known Umayyad-era chaste love stories fit this pattern fairly neatly, such as the stories of Jamīl, ʿUrwa, and Majnūn. However, others do not, such as those of Laylā al-Akhyaliyya, Kuthayyir, and Qays b. Dharīḥ. Still other Umayyad love stories combine typical chaste love themes with other themes and feature lovers who are rulers, such as the stories of Waḍḍāḥ al-Yaman, Dhalfāʾ, and Sallāma, or who receive support from alternatives to the main political authority, such as those of Qays b. Dharīḥ. This chapter explores the dynamics of these chaste love stories that do not fit neatly into the dominant paradigm of the chaste love story. Features in these stories that do not fit into the paradigm include sex between the lovers or allusions to it, infidelity or allusions to it, marriage, divorce, characters with forms of masculinity or femininity that are not typical in the canonical chaste love stories, emotions other than sadness (such as humor or rage), lovers who are rulers or slaves, and lovers who display priorities other than the beloved or who work more closely with family or figures of authority than is typical in the canonical chaste love stories. Further research may reveal that the paradigmatic stories, however central they have become in the heritage, are in the minority; the pre-modern and modern reception of these stories may be about asserting conventions of political power, individual identity, and social life as much as they are about analyzing these genres of literature.

This broader range of chaste love stories provides a new perspective on our understanding of how the chaste love story depicts individual identity in the context of social and political life. The canonical chaste love stories are often viewed as a somewhat romantic performance of individual identity that consists of a chaste, obsessive love affair that is established without approval from kin and resistance to any members of the family, tribe, and court who attempt to undermine it. On the basis of the evidence in the stories that do not fit the dominant paradigm,

I argue that these other stories offer a performance of individual identity through diverse networks of authority and trajectories of power and desire. The less canonical chaste love stories are more involved in real life because they have less emphasis on pastoral settings and a larger role for the court and other forms of authority, urban settings, and mercantile priorities.

This more nuanced understanding of the implications of Umayyad-era chaste love stories will contribute to more nuanced approaches to genres of Arabic literature that the chaste love stories influenced, including the poetic modes of *nasīb* and *ghazal* and literature on courtly love, love theory, and mystical literature.[6] These kinds of Arabic literature on courtly love also contributed to the development of these kinds of literature in Persian, Ottoman Turkish, Urdu, and other literatures of the Muslim world, as well as literature in Hebrew and Spanish of the medieval Iberian Peninsula and other European literatures.

The stories discussed in this chapter have features that do not fit the dominant paradigm of Umayyad chaste love in different ways. Kuthayyir and Laylā al-Akhyaliyya each compose political poetry, and their patronage relations differ from typical patronage relations in important ways. Qays b. Dharīḥ and Waḍḍāḥ al-Yaman live with their lovers for part of the story, and each story involves alternatives to the mainstream political authority of rulers. Dhalfā' (with Sulaymān b. 'Abd al-Malik) and Sallāma are slaves, and each story features a form of performance that is not related to the chaste love genre. Abbasid writers who record Umayyad-era chaste love stories use the dominant paradigm of chaste love to explore variations on it and to develop diverse approaches to the performance of individual identity in the context of social and political life.

Chaste Lovers as Court Poets: Kuthayyir and Laylā al-Akhyaliyya

Chaste love is not necessarily an all-encompassing love that develops in a pastoral setting and that the lovers live and die for, as in the canonical chaste love stories. In the stories of Kuthayyir and Laylā al-Akhyaliyya, each poet-lover is also busy at work as a court poet. Unlike the focus on the male point of view in canonical chaste love stories, the stories of Kuthayyir and Laylā al-Akhyaliyya feature particularly assertive female characters. While the dominant paradigm of chaste love emphasizes the melancholy suffering of separated lovers, the story of Kuthayyir (d. 723) alludes to infidelity, insincerity, and comedy and features ʿAzza's playful and frank demeanor. Abbasid writers set the story of Kuthayyir in counterpoint to the canonical stories of Majnūn and Jamīl.

In the most elaborate version of Kuthayyir's story in *The Book of Songs* by al-Iṣfahānī (d. 356/966), the story is sometimes set in counterpoint to the stories of Jamīl or Majnūn, which have more in common with the dominant paradigm of chaste love.[7] Kuthayyir has a dual role as a political poet and a lover and is depicted as a leading political poet of Arabia and a supporter of the Shiʿa opposition to the Umayyads, whom he also praised.[8] The ʿUdhrī lover Jamīl leads in love poetry, but Kuthayyir, who is right behind him in love poetry, also has skills in political poetry. Kuthayyir is said to have been a transmitter of Jamīl's poetry. The earliest versions of Kuthayyir's story refer to ʿAzza but focus on his politics, while later reuses of his story sometimes focus on his role as a chaste lover.[9]

This role for the leading political poet of Arabia in an Umayyad chaste love story demonstrates the extent to which the love story shapes the Umayyad cultural sphere as it is imagined by Abbasid writers. Kuthayyir's lack of success in the literary marketplace for poetry north of Arabia is important for his function in Umayyad love stories as told by Abbasid writers. In the Abbasid writers' imagination, chaste love stories should focus on a time and place that are distinct from their own urban Iraqi scene. Kuthayyir's involvement in politics includes his support for the family of the prophet.[10] The love story does not dominate his biography as it does in the case of chaste lovers like Jamīl, ʿUrwa, and Majnūn.

It is said that Kuthayyir's first poetry was about a camel, thus placing him in a pastoral context, and this beginning leads to his second use of poetry about ʿAzza.[11] His affair with ʿAzza begins with meetings in a pastoral setting, but the mercantile motif in the story contrasts with the dominant paradigm of chaste love. Kuthayyir passes by some women as he takes some camels and sheep for trade, and the women summon him and offer to sell a ram on his behalf. ʿAzza, a young girl, is the one who takes the ram from him. When he returns from his destination, another woman offers him the money from the sale, but he refuses to accept it from anyone but ʿAzza and says, "Every debtor has paid his creditor, but ʿAzza wears her creditor out, making him wait."[12] ʿAzza is interrogated by the wife of al-Walīd b. ʿAbd al-Malik, Umm al-Banīn bint ʿAbd al-ʿAzīz b. Marwān (or ʿĀtika bint Yazīd), about Kuthayyir's verse.[13] ʿAzza offers a figurative meaning of the debt: she says that she owes Kuthayyir a kiss that she had promised to him. Umm al-Banīn is charmed and tells her to give him the kiss and says that she herself will take the legal/moral responsibility for it. The interview at court reveals the erotic and playful aspect of the affair in the context of mercantile exchange. (Umm al-Banīn's role as the court interviewer of an outspoken lover complements Umm al-Banīn's own role as a controlling court lover in her affair with Waḍḍāḥ al-Yaman, which is discussed later in the chapter.) The verse and the interrogation call attention to the intersection of secrecy and publicity in the story. ʿAzza's debt and her interpretation of the verse offer a counterpoint to Kuthayyir's career as a professional poet.[14] ʿAzza mostly appears in groups of women who sometimes make fun of Kuthayyir for his loyalty to ʿAzza. These scenes show that she does not have the lofty status of the beloved in the dominant paradigm of chaste love—the women even try to steal him from her.

When ʿAbd al-Malik b. Marwān (r. 685–705, d. 705) asks ʿAzza what Kuthayyir liked about her, her answer points back to the role of playfulness that is sometimes erotic in her story: she says, "Everything!" She also says that he likes her for the same reasons that the Muslims made ʿAbd al-Malik caliph, which causes him to laugh so hard that a black tooth he usually hides is revealed.[15] ʿAzza's answers in court interviews show how the love story can function as a world turned upside down in the court. This function of the love story fits into the broader context of a time out for disorder in the court in Abbasid literature—the ruler laughing so hard that his black tooth shows is a common motif. The temporary disorder highlights the parameters of order in the court. Court hegemony means absorbing forms of disorder and showing them to be as irrelevant as they are irreverent.

This love story also playfully alludes to the boundaries of chastity in a number of ways. ʿAzza confronts Kuthayyir about obscene verses, but Kuthayyir denies them and offers chaste verses as evidence instead.[16] Kuthayyir encounters ʿAzza without recognizing her, since she is veiled, and tries to pick her up. When she reveals herself, he rushes off in embarrassment.[17] ʿAzza tests Kuthayyir's loyalty by setting him up with Jamīl's beloved, Buthayna, while ʿAzza watches secretly. He passes the test, and they share a laugh.[18] The misrecognition of the beloved as the other woman and the beloved's arrangement of a meeting between her lover and another woman create an upside down, carnivalesque parody of the canonical chaste love story. In spite of Kuthayyir's commitment to ʿAzza, he starts another affair with a woman whom he seeks in marriage, so as to avoid the scandal that occurred with ʿAzza. The woman tells him to come back when he has more money and in the meantime is married to someone else. This scene echoes the more serious theme of the lover raising money to win his cousin's hand in marriage from her father in the canonical love story of ʿUrwa; assigning this patriarchal role to the woman herself makes it comic.[19] This love story sets up exclusive intimacy in the relationship between Kuthayyir and ʿAzza only to break it down. Male lovers suffer in their commitment to the beloved in the dominant paradigm of chaste love, but Kuthayyir's story features allegations that his love was false, in contrast with Jamīl's, which was known to be true.[20] This accusation probably occurs as a result of Kuthayyir's role as a panegyric poet, since the question of the validity of praise poetry relates to the use of poetry for patronage.

Court interviews of Kuthayyir refer to the love story of Majnūn, which, like the story of Jamīl, displays more of the dominant paradigm of chaste love than the story of Kuthayyir does. When ʿAbd al-Malik b. Marwān asks Kuthayyir about his most amazing story with ʿAzza, he tells of encountering her while camping at the pilgrimage.[21] Her husband had sent her to get butter, and she came to Kuthayyir's tent without recognizing him. As he stared at her pouring the butter, he was sharpening arrows, and before he knew it, he had cut his hand. She recognized him and cleaned his blood on her robe. When she returned home, her husband, seeing the stains, questioned her and beat her when he found out what had occurred. The anecdote echoes a similar one about Majnūn, which in turn seems to have grown out of the scene of women who cut their hands while staring at the prophet Yūsuf (Joseph) recorded in the Qurʾān and reused in Islamic literatures. In Majnūn's story, this anecdote has a lofty tone, but in Kuthayyir's story, the mistreatment of ʿAzza gives the anecdote a low tone.

Kuthayyir's response to ʿAbd al-Malik when he asks if he ever saw anyone more in love than he is evokes the role of Majnūn. Kuthayyir tells ʿAbd al-Malik that he encountered a man in the wilderness on a gazelle hunt and learned that his family was waiting at home starving.[22] Kuthayyir arranged to hunt with him and eat the animal if they succeeded. However, the man kept catching gazelles in his snare and then letting them go because they reminded him of his beloved, just as Majnūn rescued gazelles from hunters. In Majnūn's story, this anecdote has a lofty tone. In Kuthayyir's story, the starving family in the background, set in counterpoint to the lover's emotional intensity, gives it a contradictory tone. Kuthayyir's stories for the caliph are about chaste love, but they are also stories about hunger and food and wife beating and deadbeat dads.

The comparison of the poetry by Kuthayyir and Jamīl displays the difference between them, but one anecdote argues for the equivalence of Jamīl and Kuthayyir as lovers. They each help the other person to arrange a secret meeting with the beloved by way of figurative language in code: Buthayna, while in her family's house, complains about a dog that barks from behind a certain hill at night, so that Kuthayyir reports to Jamīl that he is to meet her behind that hill. ʿAzza speaks of collecting dates while washing clothes, so that Jamīl reports to Kuthayyir that she can be found near the date palm.[23] This mutual help contrasts with the antagonism between the two poets that occurs when ʿAzza sets up Kuthayyir with Buthayna to test him or when Kuthayyir becomes jealous when he catches ʿAzza looking at Jamīl. The playful references to the canonical chaste love stories of Jamīl, Majnūn, and ʿUrwa display the parody of the canon in Kuthayyir's story.

The features of the story of Kuthayyir and ʿAzza that do not fit into the dominant paradigm of the chaste love story are central to understanding this story. Kuthayyir's attention is divided between chaste love and political commitment and between his commitment to the current rulers and his commitment to the opposition. In several anecdotes of the story, the tone is divided between the loftiness of chaste love and low themes of the body. The story is divided between a parody of paradigmatic chaste lovers and cooperation with them. Kuthayyir's story is a performance of individual identity through chaste love, as well as the authority of the community and rulers, and through diverse literary registers.

* * *

The story of Laylā al-Akhyaliyya (d. ca. 700) and Tawba differs in important ways from the dominant paradigm of chaste love. The center of gravity of the story is the female lover rather than the male lover, and Laylā is a court poet. A verse by Tawba is used to accuse Laylā of infidelity, and Laylā is accused of lying about Tawba's excellent qualities. Finally, Tawba is killed in a Jāhilī-style conflict, while the canonical love stories typically feature a male lover who dies of lovesickness. This is a chaste love story in which challenges to Laylā's chastity are a major theme that Laylā and her audience of rulers and governors discuss.[24]

Elaborate versions of Laylā's story appear in *The Book of Songs* by al-Iṣfahānī and in *Poetry by Women* by al-Marzubānī (d. 384/994).[25] Research has addressed women's speech framed by men's speech as a context for understanding gender identity and dynamics.[26] Medieval and modern scholars have sometimes neglected Laylā's political poetry and focused on her role as a lover instead.[27]

In Laylā's day job, she gains a reputation for her skillful invective in an exchange with a male poet, a genre marked by obscenity in which gender matters, and panegyric, a genre in which she demonstrates her affinity with the court that becomes the audience for her love affair.[28] Laylā's life as a professional poet intersects with her life as a lover. Her work in invective includes defending her reputation when members of the court question it. Her work in panegyric both generates her audience for the love affair and includes her praise and boasting about Tawba. Laylā's relationship is staged mainly as a series of such court interviews. In a similar way, Kuthayyir's work as a professional poet for pay intersects with the mercantile motif in his love story with ʿAzza.

Scenes of misrecognition, like the comic scenes in the story of Kuthayyir and ʿAzza, are an important part of chaste love stories, which revolve around a combination of secrecy and publicity. Misrecognition also occurs in stories of patronage relationships when a professional poet enters the court and becomes known to a ruler. Laylā's love story features both kinds of misrecognition. ʿAbdallāh b. Marwān went to see a female family member and found a Bedouin woman who turns out to be Laylā.[29] The Bedouin motif reflects the pastoral setting in many Umayyad love stories, which leads to the reputation of Bedouin for expertise in love in Abbasid literature. In another case of a secret that gives way to a spectacle, the governor al-Ḥajjāj b. Yusuf interrogates Laylā about a verse that Tawba had composed about her after he tried to visit her: "When I came to visit Laylā, she was veiled, and I was left with doubt on the day that she unveiled."[30] Laylā explains that her family had staked him out, so she appeared unveiled to warn Tawba not to approach. She also explains that he did say something questionable once, but nothing happened.[31] This scene complements the way that Laylā becomes unveiled in composing poetry, especially praise and invective, and in her back talk to rulers. Like Kuthayyir's problematic verse about ʿAzza, this verse calls attention to secrecy that bursts into a spectacle of scandalous publicity.

Criticism of professional poetry for pay frequently touched on the subject of poetry as lies, and the professional poets Kuthayyir and Laylā were accused of embellishing their love stories. Kuthayyir was accused of lying about being in love with ʿAzza, and Laylā was accused of exaggerating the qualities of Tawba. The Umayyad Muʿāwiya b. Abī Sufyān challenged her, asking if Tawba was really as good as she says, a female Umayyad claimed that she misrepresented him, and one transmitter criticized Tawba, saying that he was wicked and often went on raids and visited women.[32] These doubts about Tawba complement the doubt about Laylā's reputation in the court interrogation of her about Tawba's verse. In her defense of Tawba to the court, Laylā combined the love story with her work as a professional poet.

In the course of interviewing Laylā about Tawba, the discussion of what she liked about him leads ʿAbd al-Malik b. Marwān to ask, "What did he see in you?" Here again, the answer displays the intersection of the love affair and Laylā's professional life at court. According to Laylā, Tawba saw in her exactly what the people saw in ʿAbd al-Malik (r. 685–705, d. 705) when they made him caliph—the same answer attributed to ʿAzza in her interview with ʿAbd al-Malik.[33] Thus the Muslims choose the caliph the way a woman chooses a man or a man chooses a woman. The revelation about the nature of political authority in the context of the love story occurs along with a more concrete revelation, as ʿAbd al-Malik laughs so hard he reveals a rotten tooth that he usually tries to hide. This theme occurs in Abbasid literature when the back talk of a ruler's interlocutor gets cheeky enough to matter—so that it *must not matter* and does not matter as the ruler dissolves into laughter. The ruler and his subject meet on a plane of informal intimacy only to return to their places in the hierarchy—everything is just as it was, but it is never quite the same. In conjunction with this hierarchy and intimacy, Laylā receives an inheritance "like that of one of the daughters" from her

Umayyad family, which is also her employer.[34] Unlike the canonical love stories, her story does not include real family members, but her relationship with the Umayyads at court resembles a family relationship.

The coercive implications of the interrogation by al-Ḥajjāj about Tawba's doubt in Laylā parallels the coercive force of another interaction. Al-Ḥajjāj says of Laylā, "Cut off her tongue," a figurative expression meaning "reward her well." The fleeting concealment of meaning gives way to a burst of publicity as Laylā clarifies the expression for the assistant who is about to follow the literal meaning of the instruction. After the confusion is cleared up, she remains indignant and says, "This idiot was about to cut off my tongue!" In both cases, gender matters. The love story intersects with Laylā's life at court: she is unveiled when she should be veiled, and she composes poetry when she should not, according to typical patterns of femininity, which do not always define the case of Laylā or of ʿAzza.[35] In the verse about doubt, Tawba escapes the coercive authority of Laylā's family, and she escapes the coercive authority of al-Ḥajjāj by explaining the verse. In the order to cut off her tongue, Laylā escapes the coercive authority of al-Ḥajjāj and gains his reward in their patronage relationship.

Like the story of Kuthayyir, the story of Laylā is set in counterpoint to that of the canonical chaste love story of Jamīl. After Tawba's brush with death when he tries to meet Laylā, he experiences another brush with death in conjunction with the love story. According to Laylā's poetry, she thinks that every free woman would like to carry Tawba's child, and apparently Jamīl's beloved Buthayna is no exception. Jamīl becomes jealous when Buthayna looks at Tawba, and he challenges Tawba to a three-stage duel.[36] The three-stage duel is figurative violence, like the coercive implication of al-Ḥajjāj's interrogation about doubt in Laylā or his order to cut off her tongue. These forms of figurative violence are set in contrast with the real violence over camel raiding in which Tawba is killed. Although his death occurs outside the sphere of the love story, the story absorbs it in the series of elegies for Tawba. Laylā's love story also absorbs the anecdote about Laylā's death, which is only indirectly related to the love affair: she forces her husband to let her visit Tawba's tomb and dies in an accident there.

The story of Laylā and Tawba differs from the pattern of canonical love stories because Laylā is the main protagonist, not Tawba; because

Laylā works closely with the court as a political poet and she is accused of infidelity and dishonesty about her beloved's excellent qualities; and because Tawba dies for reasons not related to his chaste love affair. This story is a performance of individual identity through chaste love as well as of Laylā's navigation of court authority and threats to her reputation and of Tawba's commitments that are unrelated to the chaste love affair.

Chaste Lovers Who Live Together: Qays b. Dharīḥ and Waḍḍāḥ al-Yemen

The stories of Qays b. Dharīḥ and Waḍḍāḥ al-Yaman differ from stories of chaste love that develop in a pastoral setting in which the lovers live, suffer, and die only for love while separated. In both cases, the lover and beloved live together for part of the story. Each story also features an alternative form of political authority that differs from mainstream political authority.

Qays b. Dharīḥ (d. 688) succeeds in marrying Lubnā. While family and tribe, with the help of rulers, work successfully to keep lovers apart in the dominant paradigm of chaste love, in the version of Qays's story in *The Book of Songs* by al-Iṣfahānī, he is able to marry because of the help of Ḥusayn b. ʿAlī b. Abī Ṭālib from the family of the Prophet Muhammad, who was nursed by Qays's mother, so that the two men are related as nursing siblings.[37] The Prophet's family represents an alternative source of authority that parallels the court, especially Ḥusayn, who led the family and its allies in the battle of Karbala after he refused to recognize the Umayyad caliph Yazīd b. Muʿāwiya.[38] In contrast, in a shorter and earlier version in *Poetry and Poets* by Ibn Qutayba (d. 276/885), Qays is identified as one of the lovers of the Arabs who is married to Lubnā and divorces her, only to pine for her, with no reference to the powerful intercessor and the parents' role in obeying Ḥusayn and then divorcing the couple.[39]

After Qays has recourse to Ḥusayn b. ʿAlī, Qays's father and Lubnā's father are quickly persuaded, and the lovers marry. However, immediately after the marriage occurs, Qays's mother seeks his attention. She insists that the couple produce an heir for Dharīḥ's ample wealth, and when no heir appears, she argues for a divorce. Qays resists but eventually gives in out of respect for his father. Lubnā's family has recourse to the caliph to arrange a restraining order when Qays remains obsessed with Lubnā after the divorce, at least until he gives in to his family once more and remarries.[40] The end of the story looks more like the dominant paradigm of chaste love. It is chaste love reined in by a restraining order, but it is directed toward an ex-wife.[41]

While lovers are committed only to the beloved in the dominant paradigm of chaste love, Qays b. Dharīḥ has other commitments: first, to his mother and father and his powerful intercessor; second, to the mercantile priorities that his mother uses as an excuse to argue for divorce and regain some of his attention; and later, to a second wife. The parents of both lovers do not fit into the chaste love conventions either, since they are at first more interested in the status of the Prophet's family than they are in the patriarchal prerogative of preventing marriage. The story of Qays b. Dharīḥ is a performance of individual identity that is patched together from his own desire for Lubnā as well as the priorities of his family and the family of the Prophet Muhammad, who serve as a form of authority that is an alternative to the Umayyad court.

* * *

The story of Waḍḍāḥ al-Yaman (d. ca. 708) is partly a chaste love story of separated lovers in a pastoral setting, with Rawḍa, and partly a story of lovers who live together, with Umm al-Banīn bint ʿAbd al-ʿAziz b. Marwān, wife of the caliph al-Walīd b. ʿAbd al-Malik (r. 705–15, d. 715). Members of court often interview chaste lovers or place restraining orders on male lovers to prevent them from disturbing the female lover's family. In contrast, this story features a member of court as a lover and a theme of actual violence. The most elaborate version of Waḍḍāḥ's story, in *The Book of Songs* by al-Iṣfahānī, charts a path from chaste love in Yemen with a local girl to a dangerous affair with the caliph's wife in Damascus, because of which the caliph kills him.[42] This elaborate story of Waḍḍāḥ with Rawḍa and then Umm al-Banīn coexists with a very different account in the *Book of Genealogy* by al-Balādhurī (d. 279/892), which says he got in trouble with al-Walīd for composing panegyric for Umm al-Banīn.[43] Praise of women dovetails with *nasīb*, which is often an introduction about unrequited or lost love in panegyric. However, patrons definitely do not appreciate praise of the women in their family.

Waḍḍāḥ's early life in Yemen is not a pastoral paradise as in the canonical chaste love story but a site of serious politics. He is said to have been a son of one of the Persian soldiers brought in to help the Yemenis in their war against the Ethiopians. This political strife takes shape in family politics and discussions about whether he is Persian or Yemeni, since his father dies and his mother remarries, only to have her husband claim the child for himself.[44] A judge rules in favor of his father's family and gives him his new name, Waḍḍāḥ ("very handsome").[45] In this family conflict, he is assigned a nonhegemonic masculinity that goes beyond that of the dominant paradigm of chaste love, since his lineage is unclear. His nonhegemonic masculinity also appears in his role as an object of desire, because of the beauty that the judge notices while ruling on the custody battle. For example, he and two friends veil themselves while on an outing to protect themselves from the evil eye and women.[46]

In this version of the story, Waḍḍāḥ begins his career as a chaste lover in Yemen with Rawḍa, also described as a child of a Persian soldier or a Yemeni, like Waḍḍāḥ himself. He wants her and she wants him, but her family marries Rawḍa to someone else. She also becomes ill and is sent to a leper colony, so that Waḍḍāḥ does not end up following a married local woman who has been denied to him, as in the dominant paradigm of chaste love.[47] This story with Rawḍa veers off in another direction to the affair with the caliph's wife, Umm al-Banīn, which begins in Mecca and continues in the Umayyad palace in Damascus. Umm al-Banīn contravenes al-Walīd's specific instructions to her and to the poets of Arabia to avoid any poetry about her, and she summons Kuthayyir and Waḍḍāḥ to compose love introductions to panegyric about her.[48] Kuthayyir, the panegyrist who doubles as a chaste lover, already has ʿAzza, and as a panegyrist, he is too clever to use Umm al-Banīn's real name and substitutes her servant's name instead. Waḍḍāḥ, portrayed as single in the wake of Rawḍa's marriage and illness, is not so savvy and uses Umm al-Banīn's name. They become a couple. In taking up with Umm al-Banīn as a kind of kept man, Waḍḍāḥ again shows his capacity for extreme forms of nonhegemonic masculinity.

In a shorter version of Waḍḍāḥ's story in *True Stories about Women* by Pseudo-Ibn Qayyim al-Jawziyya (d. 751/1359), Waḍḍāḥ's beloved in Yemen is none other than the girl who would become Umm al-Banīn in Yemen.[49] She is a local who is taken off to be married to al-Walīd.

Waḍḍāḥ prays to be reunited with her in Mecca and circumambulates the Umayyad palace in Damascus where she lives until this chaste, childhood affair is revived. In the more elaborate version of the story, Waḍḍāḥ's chaste love with Rawḍa in Yemen gives way to his relationship with the caliph's wife, Umm al-Banīn. In this version, his chaste love with Umm al-Banīn *becomes* love and a secret life together at court. This version makes Umm al-Banīn's betrayal of him all the more dramatic because of the jarring juxtaposition of chaste love and betrayal.

Waḍḍāḥ is like a husband to his Umayyad patron, who allows him to hide in her palace rooms.[50] In the box in which he is kept in Umm al-Banīn's residence, Waḍḍāḥ is like a possession, a kept man. This is a more literal elaboration of the male lover's figurative possession by the beloved that defines the dominant paradigm of chaste love. He is a possession like the jewels given to Umm al-Banīn by her husband, the caliph. Had she shared one with the nosy servant who had discovered Waḍḍāḥ, she could have kept everything quiet and continued to keep Waḍḍāḥ.[51] He both invades the caliph's residence and is absorbed into it as a subordinate figure.[52] The caliph's son warns him against making a scandal.[53] The veil, the box, and the tomb help to articulate the central issue of love stories in general, of the fleeting secret that bursts into a spectacle of publicity that elevates and disgraces the lovers. The affair suggests the limits of the caliph's power in a more dramatic way than in the conventional chaste love story.

The story concludes with another intersection of chaste love and courtly life: Waḍḍāḥ bore witness to the beauty and talent of Ḥabāba in Arabia before she was purchased by the caliph Yazīd b. ʿAbd al-Malik. The parallel between Waḍḍāḥ the poet who becomes a kept man and Ḥabāba the singing slave girl is distinct from yet connected to his chaste love in Yemen.[54]

The noncanonical features of the story of Waḍḍāḥ are central to understanding its implications. The juxtaposition of chaste love with Rawḍa or with Umm al-Banīn early in Waḍḍāḥ's life with the later relationship between Umm al-Banīn and Waḍḍāḥ emphasizes the contrast between typical chaste love and the later relationship, in which the lovers secretly live together. The ties of Waḍḍāḥ and Rawḍa to the Persian court serve as an alternative source of authority in the story. Umm al-Banīn is a member of the court, but she also opposes the caliph. This story is a performance of individual identity that incorporates diverse trajectories of desire and relations to political power.

Slaves and Chaste Lovers: Sallāmat al-Qass and the Story of Sulaymān b. ʿAbd al-Malik

The stories of Sallāma, often known as Sallāmat al-Qass, and of Sulaymān and his beloved, who is called Dhalfāʾ in some versions of the story, combine themes of chaste love with the stories of these two female slaves who were sought and obtained by caliphs. Like the stories of Laylā and Kuthayyir, the story of Waḍḍāḥ with Umm al-Banīn and the story of Qays b. Dharīḥ with Ḥusayn b. ʿAlī b. Abī Ṭālib, these stories display a larger role for the court than is typical of the chaste love story. Each woman's status as a slave complicates the possibility of canonical chaste love, in which each lover lives, suffers, and dies for love. After all, what kind of performance of individual identity can occur for a lover who is a slave? As these stories show, an individual identity that revolves around the navigation of different relationships can occur within the confining context of slavery. While most chaste love stories are based on poetry by the lovers or on the topic of chaste love, these two stories revolve around different forms of cultural production. Sallāma's story is based mainly on performances of Qurʾān reading and also incorporates a range of poets, including an effeminate poet, and Dhalfāʾ's story with Sulaymān b. ʿAbd al-Malik is based on performances by singers, including a male effeminate singer.

Although stories and poetry about same-sex relationships are common in Abbasid literature, the genre of Umayyad-era chaste love stories entails a relationship between a male and female lover. However, the effeminate men included in these stories complicate this convention and also point to the broader texture of the full range of gender and relationships in Abbasid culture. Thus the role of effeminate men serves to integrate the Umayyad-era chaste love story, in this less canonical form, into the diversity of the Abbasid cultural sphere.

Sallāma's encounters with men occur in cities, not in a pastoral setting. The singing female slave Sallāmat al-Qass, who was trained in Medina, was loved by a Qurʾān reader (or jurist) of Mecca, ʿAbd al-Raḥmān b. Abī ʿAmmār, called al-Qass ("the priest") because of his piety. She is also pursued by the Umayyad caliph Yazīd b. ʿAbd al-Malik in the most elaborate version of her story in *The Book of Songs* by al-Iṣfahānī.[55] In this chaste love affair, al-Qass accidentally overhears Sallāma sing and falls in love with her. Her master repeatedly offers her to al-Qass, but he refuses. Later, Sallāma directly expresses her eagerness to be with him, but he still refuses. "She says to him one day, 'By God, I love you.' He replies, 'And by God I love you too.' Then she says, 'I would love to kiss you on the mouth.' He answers, 'By God I would love that.' Sallāma replies, 'So what's stopping you! We're all alone.'" The Qur'ān reader responds that he heard God say, "Companions on that day are enemies of each other except for the pious" (al-Zukhruf: 67).[56] The views on this verse in the story deal with licit and illicit kinds of companionship.[57] The conversation with al-Qass and the verse that he cites serve as an intersection of secrecy and a spectacle of chaste love. In spite of his restraint in the two versions of this exchange, al-Qass remains devoted to Sallāma. Like other chaste lovers, he composes poetry for her and even asks her to sing some of his poetry in her praise.[58]

In the most elaborate version of Sallāma's story, Yazīd b. ʿAbd al-Malik (r. 720–24) came to Mecca and sought to purchase her.[59] Waḍḍāḥ's chaste love with Rawḍa gave him qualifications as a chaste lover and poet that led the caliph's wife, Umm al-Banīn, to seek him out and demand praise and then take him back to the palace. In a similar way, Sallāma's chaste love with al-Qass leads Yazīd to seek her out. She displays her talent by singing a verse that al-Qass composed about her. Yazīd asks about it, and Sallāma tells her chaste love story; pleased, Yazīd purchases her to work in the palace. Different versions of Sallāma's story emphasize different men and different values.[60]

Sallāma's connection to the political sphere appears again in an encounter between her and the Umayyad governor of Medina, who has been sent to root out corruption in the city. She amazes the governor with her Qur'ān reading and then her singing; the sequence parallels the sequence of her chaste love with al-Qass and work as a singing slave girl for Yazīd.[61]

Sallāma also has connections to the political sphere through her association with the entertainment sector in her relationships with the leading poet of Medina, al-Aḥwaṣ, and the effeminate male singer al-Gharīḍ. She connects al-Gharīḍ with the caliph Yazīd b. ʿAbd al-Malik with the help of al-Aḥwaṣ, who in turn uses al-Gharīḍ to meet with Sallāma.

Yet another version of Sallāma's story features a parallel set of men with the same first name and different last names: al-Aḥwaṣ competes with ʿAbd al-Raḥmān b. Ḥassān (same first name as al-Qass) for Sallāma, since she sings poetry composed by each of them and chooses al-Aḥwaṣ. Meanwhile, al-Aḥwaṣ praises Yazīd b. Muʿāwiya (same first name as Yazīd b. ʿAbd al-Malik) and recommends that he purchase Sallāma to spite ʿAbd al-Raḥmān b. Ḥassān. This Yazīd purchases her, ʿAbd al-Raḥmān pines for her, and al-Aḥwaṣ praises Yazīd. Meanwhile, Sallāma arranges for a servant to sneak al-Aḥwaṣ in to see her. Yazīd spies on them and interrogates them, but because they are in love, he gives her to al-Aḥwaṣ.[62]

Sallāma's identity as a slave is the main difference between this story and the canonical chaste love stories. In addition, the pursuit of Sallāma by a range of men, including rulers, and her pursuit of lovers distinguish this story from the typical chaste love story. It is a very crowded love story that seems to be chaste in the first stage but not later on, as in the story of Waḍḍāḥ. Finally, Qur'ān reading provides an interesting context for chaste love in this story, given that chaste love developed in part because of the changes that the expansion of Islam brought to the region. Sallāma's experience is a performance of individual identity through a complex network of connections to men from different sectors of society.

* * *

The story of the Umayyad Sulaymān b. ʿAbd al-Malik (r. 715–17) is barely a love story in some sources, while it appears as a very elaborate one in others. Sulaymān had a female slave whose name is not mentioned in the brief version of the story in *The Book of Songs* by al-Iṣfahānī. The story appears in the article on Dalāl, who was one of the leading *mukhannath* (effeminate) male singers of Medina. This chaste love story differs from the canonical chaste love stories because the female lover is a slave, she is tempted by a male singer, Sulaymān is a member of the court, and the setting of the story is urban country outings and palace gardens, not pastoral.

The article focuses on the reason for Sulaymān b. ʿAbd al-Malik's command for effeminate men to be castrated and mentions his infamous jealousy in two explanations. The first explanation is an obscene story about Dalāl working as a go-between to make a match between a man and a woman and recommending (and providing) illicit sex for the prospective bride and groom.[63] Sulaymān's story with the female slave, who is distracted by a male singer, offers a second possible explanation for the castration of effeminate male singers. Sulaymān tells the slave girl to pour water for his ablutions for prayer, but she is distracted by singing coming from the army base. He seeks out the offending singer, learns his name (Sumayr), and finds out that he was trained by the effeminate male singers of Medina. After musing on the desire of females for males, Sulaymān has Sumayr castrated and also orders the castration of other male singers. The comment about desire in response to the male singer, which recurs in most versions of the story with the slave girl, serves as a focal point for the intersection of secret desire and a public spectacle.

Alternatively, Sulaymān is in bed with his beloved slave girl, who is decked out in fine clothes and jewels, but he cannot stop thinking about the fact that she is distracted by Sumayr, a soldier in his army who is a singer. He is overwhelmed with jealousy and compares male animals attracting female animals with their sounds to men attracting women by singing. He accuses the slave girl of loving the singer and threatens to kill her; but she says that she is just a slave girl in a strange land, so he relents. He also spares the singing soldier's life but castrates him and orders the castration of the effeminate male singers of Medina who taught him how to sing.[64]

The love story of Sulaymān the caliph and his slave Dhalfā' appears in the longer version in *The Unique Necklace* by Ibn 'Abd Rabbih (d. 328/940), which also appears in *True Stories of Women* by Pseudo-Ibn Qayyim al-Jawziyya. It features the jealous Sulaymān, his female slave Dhalfā', and the male singer Sinān (or Yasār), who is both Sulaymān's favorite singer and an object of desire for Dhalfā'. Unlike the canonical chaste love stories, this story is mediated by a narrator and features actual violence.

The narrator, spotting the slave girl outside Sulaymān's brother's house without knowing her identity, gives Sulaymān the opportunity to identify her to the narrator, in a dramatic and introspective recognition scene that takes place in a palace garden, in which Sulaymān repeatedly lowers his head in a gesture of emotional intensity.[65] Before the lovers get together, the discussion between the narrator and Sulaymān, both drawn to Dhalfā', implies intimacy. This intense intimacy solicits the emotions of the audience. The lavish description of the palace garden and Dhalfā' herself complements the slow-paced, introspective quality of this long first scene of the love story. Family or tribe and sometimes a royal restraining order serve as barriers to love in the dominant paradigm of chaste love. In this story, it is Sulaymān's own brother, Sa'īd, the current owner of Dhalfā', and a very high price that serve as the barrier that prevents the union of the lover and beloved.[66] Desire for Dhalfā' circulates around her, linking Sulaymān, his brother, the narrator, and her former owner, who died of love after she went to Sulaymān's brother. Sulaymān has a sense of impending doom, which he likens to the last day, as he waits for a chance to be with Dhalfā'.

When Sulaymān's brother dies and Sulaymān inherits Dhalfā', the story proceeds to an outing at a country pavilion (or monastery) that includes Sulaymān's favorite male singer, Sinān/Yasār.[67] Nature and palace meet in this story but on urban terms, in the palace garden and at the provincial outing, a favorite place for urban elites to gather for parties.

Prohibitions define the love relationship: Dhalfā' is a slave, and Sinān/Yasār is not allowed to sing for anyone but Sulaymān. However, in the marginal space of the provincial outing, Sulaymān cannot have the same degree of control over his slave or his singer. A group of people on an outing stop at the residence of Sinān/Yasār and will not be content with food and drink but also demand music. When Sinān/Yasār gives in, Dhalfā' hears him while she is out getting some air and is tempted by him. Sulaymān muses on the desire of women for men and of female animals for male animals, as if to attribute his loss of political control to natural causes. He is furious.

The version in *The Unique Necklace* by Ibn 'Abd Rabbih mentions jealousy, which echoes the importance of this theme in the dominant paradigm of chaste love, in which jealousy defines the boundaries of the intimate relationship. In the case of the ruler-lovers Umm al-Banīn and Sulaymān b. 'Abd al-Malik, possessiveness about the beloved is linked to the coercion of political authority. The later version in *True Stories of Women* by Pseudo-Ibn Qayyim al-Jawziyya (d. 751/1359) demonstrates Sulaymān's jealousy in a chapter on that topic. At the end of Ibn Qayyim's story about jealousy, Sulaymān gives orders for Yasār to be castrated and also sends word to the governor of Medina to castrate other male singers, thus explaining why the monastery is called the monastery of eunuchs.[68] The problem that effeminate men caused was apparently their reputation as go-betweens arranging meetings between men and women.[69] The outing becomes the context for the mutually disruptive intersection of the love story and political authority as prohibitions break down. The later version of the love story that incorporates castration inscribes jealousy on Yasār's body. The failed prohibitions expose the limits of political power and reveal the disturbing affinity between the exclusive obsession of lovers, coercion, and violence. Philology leads the castration story in *The Book of Songs* and the later combined love and castration story in *True Stories of Women* in two directions: there was a misunderstanding, and Sulaymān did not say "castrate them" but rather "count them," a much less invasive form of political control.

The story of Sulaymān and his slave, called Dhalfa' in some versions of the story, is defined by themes of chaste love. However, he is a member of the court, she is a slave, and the story is mediated by singing and the role of the effeminate male singers. In contrast with the pastoral setting of the canonical chaste love story, this story takes place in palace gardens and urban country outings. Unlike the threat of violence in the canonical chaste love story, versions of this story conclude with actual violence. Sulaymān's story is a performance of individual identity in a network of trajectories of desire and power that incorporates the court.

* * *

Linguistic, poetic, or other literary confusion marks the intersection of secret desire and scandal in many of these noncanonical chaste love stories. ʿAzza's debt to Kuthayyir is identified as a kiss, and a verse by Tawba refers to doubt. Waḍḍāḥ refers to Umm al-Banīn in a *nasīb*, which is normally about an anonymous or legendary woman, so that the story implies confusion between the modes of *nasīb* and *ghazal*. The story of Qays b. Dharīḥ does not focus on linguistic confusion, but the family of the Prophet replaces the role of the Umayyad court in this story. Sallāma's story and the concept of chaste love is defined by a verse from the Qur'ān. Sulaymān's story features a misunderstanding between the words for "count" and "castrate" in his jealousy of the male singer who distracts his beloved. Paradigmatic chaste love stories make it possible to interpret the implications of noncanonical chaste love stories. These linguistic, poetic, and literary episodes are key to understanding the intersection of secret desire and scandal or between the lofty sentiment of chaste love and real-life needs, priorities, and interests.

Each of these noncanonical chaste love stories incorporates a less pastoral setting, a closer interaction with the court, and more mercantile priorities than are found in the canonical chaste love stories. The court and the love affair intersect in elaborate ways in these stories so that they entail a performance of individual identity in conjunction with the court and other real-life priorities.

These lovers are not romantic rebels against authority. They are embroiled in negotiations and tactics as they pursue their desires. They are safely ensconced in the realist narrative context of chains of transmission and the style of eyewitness reports, as well as the empirical practice of juxtaposing available accounts within the same text or in multiple texts. These realist features make the stories seem like they adhere to standards of rational observation in scholarship and just evaluation in law, even though the only rules that they obey are the rules of the code of love. The code of love that takes shape in these stories is one in which everyone is entitled to his or her opinion when the opinion is a matter of the heart, and the desires that spring from inner life are valued more than their fulfillment. This leads not to free love or to romantic rebels but rather to a complex network of competing interests that includes the court. The stories join the lofty sentiments of chaste love with the desire of the body and the competing mercantile, political, tribal, and family interests in society. In Abbasid literature on a variety of themes including love, this kind of navigation of competing interests lies at the heart of individual identity. Individual inner life is performed through real life.

Abbasid writers who recorded stories of Umayyad-era chaste lovers, which serve as a form of commentary on poetry about chaste love, defined canonical love stories that facilitated interpretation of stories with noncanonical features. Canonical chaste love stories are often viewed by medieval writers and modern scholars as a performance of individual identity that consists of obsessive chaste love in opposition to the coercion of the family, tribe, and court. The interpretation of these stories is important for understanding Abbasid-era *nasīb* and *ghazal* modes of poetry as well as literature of courtly love, love theory, and mysticism in

Arabic, Hebrew, Spanish, Persian, and other literatures. Equally important are the interpretation of the less canonical chaste love stories such as the stories of Kuthayyir, Laylā al-Akhyaliyya, Waḍḍāḥ al-Yaman, Qays b. Dharīḥ , Sallāmat al-Qass, and Sulaymān b. ʿAbd al-Malik. These stories are performances of individual identity that consist of obsessive chaste love and a network of trajectories of desire and power as well as diverse literary modes. In this way, the less canonical chaste love stories display a rich complexity in the development of *nasīb*, *ghazal*, courtly love, love theory, and mysticism in Arabic and other literatures.

NOTES

1. Discussions of ʿUdhrī love can be found in a number of sources, such as Ḍayf, *Al-Ḥubb al-ʿUdhrī ʿinda al-ʿArab*; al-Jawārī, *Al-Ḥubb al-ʿUdhrī*; Hamori, "Love Poetry"; Leder, "ʿUdhrī Narrative"; Jacobi, "ʿUdhra"; Jayyusi, "Umayyad Poetry," 419–22; Bauer, *Liebe und Liebesdichtung*, 39–47; Enderwitz, *Liebe als Beruf*, 9–25; Vadet, *L'esprit courtois*, 361–78; Djedidi, *La poesie amoureuse*.
2. Hamori, "Love Poetry," 205.
3. Jayyusi, "Umayyad Poetry," 419–22; Bauer, *Liebe und Liebesdichtung*, 39–47; Enderwitz, *Liebe als Beruf*, 15–24. Jayyusi refers to a Bedouin poet who writes obscene poetry, a pious poet who is urban, and a pious poet whose poetry shows no sign of his religious values. Enderwitz observes that the leading ʿUdhrī chaste love poet and the leading urban love poet interacted, and Bauer discusses two urban poets who sometimes used ʿUdhrī-style chaste portrayals of love.
4. Jawārī, *Al-Ḥubb al-ʿUdhrī*, 49.
5. Jayyusi, "Umayyad Poetry," 420; Bauer, *Liebe und Liebesdichtung*, 45–47.
6. Aside from the importance of ʿUdhrī love literature for the history of Umayyad culture in Arabic literature, it played a major role in the development of ideas about courtly love, orthodox Islamic and Sufi love theory, and their impact on Islamic and the other cultures of Asia, Africa, and Europe. See Jawārī, *Al-Ḥubb al-ʿUdhrī*; Bell, *Love Theory*; Giffen, *Theory of Profane Love*; Vadet, *L'esprit courtois*; and Algazi and Drory, "L'amour à la cour des abbassides." Chaste (ʿUdhrī) love does not require celibacy, so it is different from Platonic or courtly love; marriage is fine and even desirable, though often not possible for the ʿUdhrī lover (Jacobi, "ʿUdhra," 140). While in European courtly love, love leads to virtue, the virtue of love is the sensibility itself in Arabic courtly love (Hamori, "Love Poetry," 209).
7. "Kuthayyir ʿAzza," in al-Iṣfahānī, *Kitāb al-Aghānī* (2002/1422), 9:5–50 (subsequent citations refer to this edition). This twenty-seven-volume work is at the heart of Abbasid literature about chaste Umayyad lovers (and other kinds of Umayyad and Abbasid characters), elaborating on early accounts of characters and offering a framework from which later accounts use characters to articulate points of view about social values. Subsequent citations refer to this edition. On the dynamics of

this work, see the detailed study by Hilary Kilpatrick, *Making the Great Book of Songs*.

8. Al-Iṣfahānī, *Kitāb al-Aghānī*, 9:6–9. See Rabīʿī, *Kuthayyir ʿAzza*, 101–28, 155–85. Rabīʿī believes that the praise of the Umayyads was *taqiyya*, or the concealing of Shiʿa beliefs to avoid persecution or discrimination (120).
9. Al-Jumaḥī, *Ṭabaqāt Fuḥūl al-Shuʿarāʾ*, 2:545. The shorter version Kuthayyir's story in *The Categories of Great Poets* by al-Jumaḥī (d. 231/845), one of the earliest books of biographies of poets, focuses on Kuthayyir's life as a political poet and refers to his talent in the love prelude to panegyric but does not delve into the relationship with ʿAzza. Al-Jumaḥī, *Ṭabaqāt Fuḥūl al-Shuʿarāʾ*, 2:540–48. Another shorter version of Kuthayyir's story, in *Poetry and Poets* by Ibn Qutayba (d. 276/885), combines themes of Kuthayyir's life as a political poet and his role as a famous Arab lover with ʿAzza. Ibn Qutayba, *Al-Shiʿr wa-l-Shuʿarāʾ*, 1:503–17. In some cases, Kuthayyir is reused as an ideal chaste lover without any of the references to the themes of politics, comedy, or infidelity that occur in the most elaborate version of his story. For example, a verse about ʿAzza by Kuthayyir appears in *The Malady of Hearts* by al-Kharāʾiṭī (327/938), in which the verse is the key to a brief story about an anonymous chaste lover. al-Kharāʾiṭī, *Iʿtilāl al-Qulūb*, 1:190.
10. Al-Iṣfahānī, *Kitāb al-Aghānī*, 9:19, 23–24.
11. Ibid., 9:31, 33–34.
12. Ibn Qutayba, *Al-Shiʿr wa-l-Shuʿarāʾ*, 1:510.
13. Ibid.
14. Ruqayya Khan has argued that the secret as a theme in a range of genres of literary and religious texts is a crucial way of articulating a sense of the self. Khan, *Self and Secrecy*.
15. Al-Iṣfahānī, *Kitāb al-Aghānī*, 9:35.
16. Ibn Qutayba, *Al-Shiʿr wa-l-Shuʿarāʾ*, 1:511.
17. Al-Iṣfahānī, *Kitāb al-Aghānī*, 9:41.
18. Ibid., 9:46.
19. Ibid., 9:43.
20. Al-Jumaḥī, *Ṭabaqāt Fuḥūl al-Shuʿarāʾ*, 2:545.
21. Al-Iṣfahānī, *Kitāb al-Aghānī*, 9:37.
22. Ibn Qutayba, *Al-Shiʿr wa-l-Shuʿarāʾ*, 1:509–10.
23. Ibid., 1:434–44 (in the entry on Jamīl).
24. See Mubayyaḍīn, *Al-Wāliha al-Ḥarī*. In spite of the accusations, Laylā was always chaste. Ibid., 44.
25. Al-Iṣfahānī (d. 356/966), *Kitāb al-Aghānī*, 11:210–51; al-Marzubānī, *Ashʿār al-Nisāʾ*, 25–59. In the shorter version in *Poets and Poetry* by Ibn Qutayba (d. 276/885), Tawba's entry opens with his role as the lover of Laylā and concludes with the tribal conflict that led to his death. Laylā's entry opens with her invective exchange with another major poet and then continues with court interviews on her relationship with Tawba. Ibn Qutayba, *Al-Shiʿr wa-l-shuʿarāʾ*, 1:448–51, 1:445–47.

26. See Hammond, *Beyond Elegy*; Meisami, "Writing Medieval Women"; and Myrne, *Narrative, Gender and Authority.*
27. Renate Jacobi says that 50 percent of Laylā's poetry and story is about political life, not ʿUdhrī love, but scholars, medieval and modern, have focused on love. However, these medieval and modern sources have also focused on her political life. Jacobi, "Laylā al-Akhyaliyya." On the other hand, the reuse of Laylā's story in *The Battlefields of Lovers* by al-Sarrāj (d. 500/1106) focuses on the court interview with al-Ḥajjāj about Tawba; her relationship with al-Ḥajjāj is the main issue, and the topic of Tawba is just a way to articulate that relationship. Al-Sarrāj, *Maṣāriʿ al-ʿUshshāq*, 1:283–87. On this close relationship, see Mubayyaḍīn, *Al-Wāliha al-Ḥarī*, 80.
28. The invective contest with the male poet al-Nābigha al-Jaʿdī is the first section of Laylā's story in al-Marzubānī, though the relationship with Tawba opens her story in al-Iṣfahānī. On Laylā's use of the male-dominated genre of the *qasida*, see Sajdi," Trespassing the Male Domain"; and Jacobi, "Laylā al-Akhyaliyya."
29. Al-Iṣfahānī, *Kitāb al-Aghānī*, 11:247.
30. Ibid., 11:211.
31. Ibid., 11:213; Al-Marzubānī, *Ashʿār al-Nisāʾ*, 54.
32. Al-Iṣfahānī, *Kitāb al-Aghānī*, 11:238.
33. Ibid., 11:231.
34. Al-Marzubānī, *Ashʿār al-Nisāʾ*, 46.
35. Al-Iṣfahānī, *Kitāb al-Aghānī*, 11:242.
36. Ibn Qutayba, *Al-Shiʿr wa-l-shuʿarāʾ*, 1:446.
37. "Qays b. Dharīḥ," in Al-Iṣfahānī, *Al-Aghānī*, 9:210–60, 212.
38. The Ḥusayn b. ʿAlī role in a love story is not an isolated case for the Prophet's family; Sukayna bint al-Ḥusayn b. ʿAlī b. Abī Ṭālib features prominently in the narrative of ʿUmar b. Abī al-Rabīʿa, the leading figure of urban, promiscuous, unchaste love, and in other sources on love and on poetry.
39. Ibn Qutayba, *Al-Shiʿr wa-l-shuʿarāʾ*, 2:628–29.
40. Al-Iṣfahānī, *Kitāb al-Aghānī*, 9:229–30.
41. Ibid., 9:213.
42. "Waḍḍāḥ al-Yemen," ibid., 6:222–55.
43. Arazi, "Waḍḍāḥ al-Yemen."
44. Bāsim ʿAbbūd al-Yāsirī says that Waḍḍāḥ al-Yaman had an Arab father and a Persian mother. al-Yāsirī, *Waḍḍāḥ al-Yaman*, 38.
45. Al-Iṣfahānī, *Kitāb al-Aghānī*, 6:222–23.
46. Ibid., 6:224.
47. Ibid., 6:224–26.
48. Ibid., 6:231–34.
49. Pseudo-Ibn Qayyim al-Jawziyya, *Akhbār al-Nisāʾ*, 111–113. Another version in *The Battlefields of Lovers* by al-Sarrāj (d. 500/1106) dispenses with chaste love altogether and opens when al-Walīd has a servant give Umm al-Banīn the jewel, and the servant finds Waḍḍāḥ in her room. Al-Sarrāj, *Maṣāriʿ al-ʿUshshāq*, 1:192.

Many reuses of these stories of chaste lovers that originally had political angles dispense with the political aspect and focus on the chaste love; in contrast, this one dispenses with chaste love and focuses on the political angle.

50. Al-Iṣfahānī, *Kitāb al-Aghānī*, 6:237–238.
51. Pseudo-Ibn Qayyim al-Jawziyya, *Akhbār al-Nisā'*, 111–13.
52. His beauty, his desiring lover, her betrayal, and his foreign origin as a Persian and/ or Yemeni link him to the role of Yūsuf with Zulaykhā.
53. Al-Iṣfahānī, *Kitāb al-Aghānī*, 6:239.
54. Ibid., 6:243.
55. "Dhikr Sallāmat al-Qass wa-khabarihā," in Al-Iṣfahānī, *Kitāb al-Aghānī*, 8:347–65.
56. Ibid., 8:349, and a more obscene version at the end of the article, 8:364.
57. Hammond, "Morphing of a Folktale."
58. Al-Iṣfahānī, *Kitāb al-Aghānī*, 8:353.
59. Ibid.
60. Yazīd enjoys the company of Sallāma and the female slave singer Ḥabāba (and the leading poet of Medina, al-Aḥwaṣ) together; and this is the only part of the story that appears in the short, early version of her story in *Poetry and Poets* by Ibn Qutayba (d.276/885), which is about Yazīd's brother warning him to stop neglecting his duties for the sake of pleasure. Ibn Qutayba, *Al-Shi'r wa-l-Shu'arā'*, 1:520. In contrast, the encounter with al-Qass is the only part of Sallāma's story that appears in another version, in *The Unique Necklace* by Ibn 'Abd Rabbih (d. 328/940). Ibn 'Abd Rabbih, *Al-'Iqd al-Farīd* (2001), 6:18–19. In *Elegance and Elegant People*, al-Washshā' (d. 325/937) focuses on the encounter with al-Qass but also says that she ended up with Yazīd b. 'Abd al-Malik. al-Washshā', *Al-Ẓarf wa-l-Ẓurafā'*, 114–15.
61. Al-Iṣfahānī, *Kitāb al-Aghānī*, 8:255–56. See Hammond, "Morphing of a Folktale," 118. Hammond considers the encounter with al-Qass and the encounter with the governor "anecdotes A and B." It may be more useful to consider her encounters with men as a series of interlocking and in some cases mixed-up stories: al-Qass, Yazīd, the governor, and also al-Aḥwaṣ.
62. Al-Iṣfahānī, *Kitāb al-Aghānī*, 9:155–59 (in "Nasab 'Amr b. Sa'īd b. Zayd").
63. Ibid., 4:267–72. Dalāl used to meet men arriving at Medina and offer to find a wife for them among the women of the city. He would describe one woman after another to the man and describe one man after another to the woman, until the match was made. The real mischief started after the match was made. He would tell the woman, "Now you are about to consummate the marriage, but you are so lustful that he will find you disgusting." Dalāl's solution is for the woman to fornicate with an African man first, but she will not do that; so he offers himself to relieve some of her lust, and she agrees. He tells the groom that women in the city like to have sex slowly for a long time, so he will not have the stamina. He suggests that he fornicate with an African woman a few times first to prepare himself, but he will not do that; so Dalāl offers himself, and he agrees.
64. Ibid., 4:272. An even shorter version of the story in the encyclopedic compilation *The Unique Necklace* by Ibn 'Abd Rabbih (d. 328/940) has no female slave; it

features only Sulaymān's jealous fear when he hears the male singer in the army, his claim that it will inspire women to engage in illicit erotic relationships just as male animals attract females with the sounds they make, his command for castration of male singers, and the execution of the command. Ibn ʿAbd Rabbih, *Al-ʿIqd al-Farīd*, 6:25, 6:53.

65. Pseudo-Ibn Qayyim al-Jawziyya, *Akhbār al-Nisā'*, 74–75; Ibn ʿAbd Rabbih, *Al-ʿIqd al-Farīd*, 6:68–69.
66. Pseudo-Ibn Qayyim al-Jawziyya, *Akhbār al-Nisā'*, 76; Ibn ʿAbd Rabbih, *Al-ʿIqd al-Farīd*, 6:70.
67. Pseudo-Ibn Qayyim al-Jawziyya, *Akhbār al-Nisā'*, 76; Ibn ʿAbd Rabbih, *Al-ʿIqd al-Farīd*, 6:70.
68. Pseudo-Ibn Qayyim al-Jawziyya, *Akhbār al-Nisā'*, 78. Ibn ʿAbd Rabbih already used the motif of male animals attracting female animals in his short notices about Sulaymān ordering the castration of singers and in his love story about Sulaymān, Dhalfa', and Sinān. Pseudo-Ibn Qayyim al-Jawziyya builds on this combination of stories and makes the castration command the conclusion of Sulaymān's love story about Dhalfa' and Yasār.
69. Rowson, "Effeminates of Early Medina."

Epilogue

EVELYN BIRGE VITZ AND MAURICE A. POMERANTZ

This volume approaches the issues of power, performance, and courts in a variety of ways. Yet as readers may have noted, a majority of contributors to this volume approach these issues through textual evidence. Although many scholars from many other fields such as musicology, theater studies, and art history are used to thinking about performance, the importance and concepts of performance are still rather unfamiliar to many literary scholars.[1]

As this volume has, we hope, begun to show, texts can provide a valuable guide to court performance. Works of verbal eloquence were in the medieval and pre-modern period performed aloud, often in strongly dramatic ways. And this in turn illuminates literary works that often contain many signs and indicators of their performability, indeed often of their performance. It is the goal of this volume to demonstrate how important performance was in this period—and how thinking in these terms can open up the meaning of literary works of the past.

Geographically, the volume attempts to demonstrate commonality and diversity across the pre-modern landscapes of the Middle East. Centered on the court, it focuses attention on several main cities: Baghdad, Isfahan, Cairo, Constantinople, and Jerusalem. The volume also considers a broad range of performers: orators, boon companions, singers, storytellers, shadow puppeteers, and others—including rulers themselves. It looks at different kinds of courts. Here, too, there is commonality and diversity: many of the chapters focus on highly centralized courts with fixed locations (see Constantinou, Marlow, El Cheikh, Hämeen-Anttila, Pomerantz, and others). But Mullett also examines more centrifugal aspects of the court: at times, the imperial family, in its travels, resided in tents rather than in their palaces; moreover, much early Byzantine storytelling bears on heroes of the frontier, rather than figures in Constantinople. Vitz also shows Charlemagne's (admittedly imaginary) court on the move: the king/emperor travels with all his great "barons," no tents mentioned (by contrast, King Hugo's court is fixed—and presented as dwelling in a glorious palace). Hämeen-Anttila also focuses at various points on the power and importance ascribed to tribal groups whose power lay outside the court. Thus we see, on the one hand, centripetality (the court as a fixed place, focused on the ruler) but also sometimes centrifugality (the court on the move, traveling, and perhaps staying in tents). We also see absolute rulers versus sometimes more diffuse kinds of power, as embodied by princes and tribal figures.

With regard, then, to many aspects of court structures, we see diversity and some interesting dichotomies. But some central themes emerge from these essays when taken as a whole; a number of strong and ongoing themes are highlighted clearly—often even quite dramatically. Here we focus on three of them, which we see as perhaps the most striking and significant. The first issue is that of performativity: performance in court is almost always in some important way perform*ative*: that is, performers do not just offer delights to their rulers but typically attempt to make something happen, to effect some sort of change—perhaps to give advice or counsel that will be followed, perhaps only to increase their own prestige; their performances are in that sense generally intended to be persuasive. Second, an element of danger, often indeed of trepidation, is almost always obvious in performances in court settings—especially those that take place in the presence of a powerful ruler: we see over and over that performers are at grave risk of failure, disgrace, and a loss of status, even of death. Third comes the element of what is commonly today called "transgressivity": performers in court settings, in the pleasures they provide, often play (mostly very prudently!) with what is forbidden; they may invite laughter where laughter is normally forbidden; they may test boundaries of the sovereign's or patron's power.

First, then, we note that several chapters particularly exemplify the important issue of perform*ativity* within the larger framework of performance. Marlow shows how performed discourses—many of them essentially "mirrors for princes"—are characterized by an "advice-centered morality," filled with "edifying narratives." Orators wove advice and admonitions into their speeches; their goal is to influence the ruler—being careful not to offend him.

Performance in courtly settings necessarily involved the ruler's power, which was on display in various ways and is evident in many of the pieces in this volume. Vitz points out how threatening powerful rulers can be: first, King Charles threatens his wife with death for having openly insulted him by suggesting that another king wore his crown better; later, Charles and his men are in danger of death from the Byzantine ruler, King Hugo, for having insulted him by their bragging and hostile boasts (overheard by the shocked spy). It was dangerous to offend a powerful ruler! Constantinou emphasizes the theme of the blood-thirstiness of Byzantine emperors and their pleasure in torturing and killing martyrs—holy men and women. Rahimi shows how the Safavid public square is fundamentally a display of imperial power: spectators and participators are always in the presence of power. But these are just the most obvious—the least subtle—examples of the dangers presented by rulers and by performance at court. El Cheikh discusses the complex etiquette and appropriate comportment that were necessary when one performed before an absolute ruler, whether as an adviser or as a boon companion. The question always was "What could please the caliph?" (And it was very dangerous to displease him.) One had to be extremely careful in "his words, his gestures, his immobility, the language he ch[ose] and his *adab*, even his breathing." All this was necessary for survival—literal survival—and this "precariousness linked to the ruler's whims clearly fostered an ethics of dissimulation." It was not easy to escape from "the noose of ruin and the snare of death" by one's "good wits, genial pleas, smooth answers, and pleasant excuses." Pomerantz focuses on the unintentional "slips" made by Abbasid performers; to make a mistake in a speech or song might turn out all right, but it might not. Slipups could cost performers their livelihood, their reputation, or their lives. Many chapters emphasize at various points the caution and prudence necessary for someone performing before a great ruler—performing in the presence of power.

Performers and storytellers also had their own power, and this allowed them often to venture into areas that would otherwise be off-limits. Several pieces in the volume engage, explicitly or implicitly, directly or indirectly, the issue of transgressivity, which perhaps paradoxically coexists with the theme of danger. In Guo's chapter, we see how sexually immoral plays were appreciated by the Mamluk courts of Egypt in the form of the shadow play (the very "shadow-y," low, and unrealistic nature of the plays may all have contributed to their being tolerated by the people in power). In Weaver's chapter, we see how, in the performed realm of food, the courts of Cyprus wittily played with and manipulated the strict Christian regulations on fasting and feasting, with their manipulation of white and red foods. (When this complex tradition of cuisine migrated West, the subtly transgressive religious and cultural wit was misunderstood—and lost.) Another kind of potential transgressivity—at once religious and courtly—is clear in Orfali's discussion: he shows how Sufi poets consistently drew, sometimes shockingly so, on courtly themes and metaphors in their religious mystical discourses. Such transgressive analogies between divine and earthly love served to distance one from the other. Sharlet focuses on stories of chaste love, which are often in their own ways transgressive, pitting the desires of lovers against political and courtly pressures.

It is our hope that the chapters in this volume will make a significant contribution to the knowledge and understanding of how performance—performers and performances of many kinds—functioned in the courts of the pre-modern Middle East.

NOTE

1. This despite some recent work highlighting performance of literary works, such as Öztürkmen and Vitz, *Medieval and Early Modern Performance*.

BIBLIOGRAPHY

ʿAbdalqādir al-Baghdādī. *Khizānat al-adab*. Edited by ʿAbdassalām Muḥammad Hārūn. 11 vols. Cairo: al-Hayʾa al-Miṣriyya al-ʿ Āmma li-l-Kitāb, 1979–83.

Ābī, al-. *Nathr al-durr*. Edited by ʿAlī Muḥammad al-Bajāwī et al. 7 vols. Cairo: al-Hayʾa al-Miṣriyya al-ʿ Āmma li-l-Kitāb, 1981–91.

Abisaab, Rula Jurdi. *Converting Persia: Religion and Power in the Safavid Empire*. London: I. B. Tauris, 2004.

Abū l-ʿAtāhiya. *Abū l-ʿAtāhiya: Ashʿāruhu wa-akhbāruhu: Ṭabʿa muḥaqqaqa ʿalā makhṭūṭatayn wa-nuṣūṣ lam tunshar min qabl*. Edited by Shukrī Fayṣal. Damascus: Maṭbaʿat Jāmiʿat Dimashq, 1965.

Abū Naṣr al-Qushayrī. *Al-Risāla al-Qushayriyya*. Edited by ʿAbd al-Ḥalīm Maḥmūd and Maḥmūd b. al-Sharīf. Cairo: Dār al-Kutub al-Ḥadītha, 1966.

Abū Nuwās. *Dīwān*. Edited by Ewald Wagner and Gregor Schoeler. 5 vols. Beirut: Bibliotheca Islamica, 1378–1424/1958–2003.

Abū Ṭāhir al-Baghdādī. *Qānūn al-balāgha fī naqd al-nathr wa-l-shiʿr*. Edited by Muḥsin Ghayyāḍ ʿAjīl. Beirut: Muʾassasat al-Risāla, 1409/1989.

Abū Tammām. *Dīwān = Sharḥ Dīwān Abī Tammām*. Edited by Shāhīn ʿAṭiyya. Beirut: Dār al-Kutub al-ʿIlmiyya, 1407/1987.

———. *Dīwān Abī Tammām bi-sharḥ al-Khaṭīb al-Tibrīzī*. Edited by M. ʿAzzām. Cairo: Dār al-Maʿārif, n.d.

Abū ʿUbayd al-Qāsim ibn Sallām. *Al-Amthāl*. Damascus: Dār al-Maʾmūn lil-Turāth, 1980.

———. *Kitāb al-Nasab*. Edited by Maryam Muḥammad Khayr al-Dirʿ. Cairo: Dār al-Fikr, 1410/1989.

Achaya, K. T. *Indian Food: A Historical Companion*. Delhi: Oxford University Press, 1994.

Adamson, John. "The Making of the Ancien-Regime Court: 1500–1700." In *The Princely Courts of Europe: Ritual, Politics and Culture under the Ancien Regime 1500–1750*, edited by John Adamson, 7–41. London: Weidenfeld and Nicolson, 1999.

Adamson, Melitta Weiss, ed. *Das Buch von guter Spise* (The book of good fare). Krems, Austria: Sonderband IX, Medium Aevum Quotidianum, 2000.

Aḥmad, Fuʾād ʿAbd al-Munʿim, ed. *Naṣīḥat al-mulūk al-mansūb ilā Abī l-Ḥasan al-Māwardī*. Alexandria, Egypt: Muʾassasat Shabāb al-Jāmiʿa, 1988.

Akhfash al-Aṣghar, al-. *Kitāb al-Ikhtiyārayn*. Edited by Fakhraddīn Qabāwa. Beirut: Muʾassasat al-Risāla, 1394/1974.

Akhṭal, al-. *Dīwān al-Akhṭal*. Edited by M. Nāṣir al-Dīn. Beirut: Dār al-Kutub al-ʿIlmiyya, 1994.

Alexander, Paul J. "Religion Persecution and Resistance in the Byzantine Empire of the 8th and 9th Centuries: Methods and Justifications." *Speculum* 52, no. 2 (1977): 238–64.

Algazi, Gadi, and Rina Drory. "L'amour à la cour des abbassides: Un code de compétence sociale." *Annales* 6 (November–December 2000): 1255–82.

Ali, Samer M. *Arabic Literary Salons in the Islamic Middle Ages: Poetry, Public Performance, and the Presentation of the Past*. Notre Dame: University of Notre Dame Press, 2010.

ʿAllām, ʿIzz al-Dīn al-. *Al-Sulṭa wa-l-siyāsa fī al-adab al-sulṭānī*. Casablanca: Ifrīqiyya al-Sharq, 1991.

Allen, Roger. *The Arabic Literary Heritage*. New York: Cambridge University Press, 1998.

Almagor, Ella. "The Pious Man and the Ruler: A Literary Form in the Service of Government." *JSAI* 33 (2007): 179–92.

Anagnostakis, Illias, ed. *Flavours and Delights: Tastes and Pleasures of Ancient and Byzantine Cuisine*. Athens: Armos, 2013.

Anderson, Jeffrey C., and Michael J. Jeffreys. "The Decoration of the Sebastokratorissa's Tent." *Byzantion* 64 (1994): 8–18.

Anna Komnene. *Alexiad*. In *Annae Comnenae Alexias*, edited by Dieter Roderich Reinsch and Athanasios Kambylis, 2 vols. Berlin: Corpus fontium historiae byzantinae, 2001. Translated by Elizabeth R. A. Sewter as *The Alexiad of Anna Comnena*. Harmondsworth, UK: Penguin, 1969.

Arazi, Albert. "*Al-ḥanīn ilā al-awṭān* entre la Ǧāhiliyya et l'Islam: Le Bédouin et le citadin réconciliés." *Zeitschrift der deutschen morgenländischen Gesellschaft* 143 (1993): 287–327.

———. "Waḍḍāḥ al-Yaman." In *Encyclopaedia of Islam*, 2nd ed., edited by P. Bearman, Th. Bianquis, C. E. Bosworth, E. van Donzel, and W. P. Heinrichs. Brill Online, 2012. www.brillonline.nl.

Arbel, Benjamin. "Cypriot Population under Venetian Rule (1473–1571)." *Μελεται και Ψπομνιματα* 1 (1984): 183–215.

Arberry, Arthur J. *The Koran Interpreted*. Oxford: Oxford University Press, 1983.

———. *The Seven Odes: The First Chapter in Arabic Literature*. London: Allen and Unwin, 1957.

Arjomand, Said. *The Shadow of God and the Hidden Imam: Religion, Political Order, and Societal Change in Shiʿite Iran from the Beginning to 1890*. Chicago: University of Chicago Press, 1984.

ʿAskarī Abū Hilāl, al-. *Dīwān al-maʿānī*. 2 vols. Beirut: Dār al-Jīl, n.d. Edited by Aḥmad Salīm Ghānim. 2 vols. Beirut: Dār al-Gharb al-Islāmī, 1424/2003.

———. *Kitāb al-Ṣināʿatayn*. Edited by ʿAlī Muḥammad al-Bajāwī and Muḥammad Abū l-Faḍl Ibrāhīm. Cairo: ʿĪsā al-Bābī al-Ḥalabī wa-Shurakāʾuhu, 1371/1952.

Austin, J. L. *How to Do Things with Words*. 2nd ed. Edited by J. O. Urmson and Marina Sbisà. Cambridge, MA: Harvard University Press, 1975.

Avery, Kenneth. *A Psychology of Early Sufi Samāʿ Listening and Altered States*. London: RoutledgeCurzon, 2004.

Azdī, al-. *Ḥikāyat Abī l-Qāsim* = A. Mez, *Abulḳasim, ein bağdāder Sittenbild*. Heidelberg: Carl Winter's Universitätsbuchhandlung, 1920. Reprint, Baghdād: Maktabat al-Muthannā, n.d.

Azmeh, Aziz al-. *Muslim Kingship: Power and the Sacred in Muslim, Christian and Pagan Polities*. London: I. B. Tauris, 1997.

Babaie, Sussan. *Isfahan and Its Palaces: Statecraft, Shiʿism and the Architecture of Conviviality in Early Modern Iran*. Edinburgh: Edinburgh University Press, 2008.

———. "Sacred Sites of Kingship: The Maydan and Mapping the Spatial-Spiritual Vision of the Empire in Safavid Iran." In *Persian Kingship and Architecture: Strategies of Power in Iran from the Achaemenids to the Pahlavis*, edited by Sussan Babaie and Talinn Grigor, 175–218. London: I. B. Tauris, 2015.

Babaie, Sussan, Kathryn Babayan, Ina Baghdiantz-McCabe, and Massumeh Farhad. *Slaves of the Shah: New Elites of Safavid Iran*. London: I. B. Tauris, 2004.

Babayan, Kathryn. *Mystics, Monarchs, and Messiahs: Cultural Landscapes of Early Modern Iran*. Harvard Middle Eastern Monographs 35. Cambridge, MA: Harvard University Press, 2003.

Badawi, Mustafa. "Medieval Arabic Drama: Ibn Dāniyāl." *Journal of Arabic Literature* 13 (1982): 83–107. Reprinted in Paul Kahle, ed., *Three Shadow Plays by Muḥammad Ibn Dāniyāl*, prepared for publication by Derek Hopwood and Mustafa Badawi, 6–28. Cambridge, UK: E. J. W. Gibb Memorial, 1992.

Baghdādī, al-Khaṭīb al-. *Taʾrīkh Baghdād*. Beirut: Dār al-Kitāb al-ʿArabī, 1966.

Bagley, F. R. C., trans. *Ghazālī's Book of Counsel for Kings* (*Naṣīḥat al-mulūk*). London: Oxford University Press, 1964.

Bakrī, al-. *Simṭ al-laʾālī fī sharḥ al-Qālī*. Edited by ʿAbd al-ʿAzīz al-Maymanī. 3 vols. N.p., 1936. Reprint, Dār al-Kutub al-ʿIlmiyya, n.d.

Balādhurī, al-. *Ansāb al-ashrāf*. Edited by ʿAbd al-ʿAzīz al-Dūrī. Vol. 3. Wiesbaden, Germany: Bibliotheca Islamica, 1978.

———. *Ansāb al-ashrāf*. Edited by Ramzī Baʿlbakkī. Vol. 7, sec. 1. Beirut: Bibliotheca Islamica, 1997.

———. *Ansāb al-ashrāf*. Edited by Maḥmūd al-Firdaws al-ʿAẓm. 24 vols. Dimashq: Dār al-Yaqaẓa al-ʿarabiyya, 1997–2003.

Bashshār ibn Burd. *Dīwān*. Edited by Ṣalāḥaddīn al-Hawwārī. 4 vols. Beirut: Dār wa-Maktabat al-Hilāl, 1998.

Bauden, Frederic, and Antonella Ghersetti. "L'art de servir son monarque: À propos d' un traité pseudo-platonique inedit." *Quaderni di studi arabi* 20–21(2002–3): 245–50.

———. "L'art de servir son monarque: Le *Kitāb waṣāya Aflāṭūn al-Ḥakīm fī khidmat al-mulūk*. Edition critique et traduction precedée d'une introduction." *Arabica* 54 (2007): 295–313.

Bauer, Thomas. *Liebe und Liebesdichtung in der arabischen Welt des 9. und 10. Jahrhunderts*. Wiesbaden, Germany: Harrassowitz Verlag, 1998.

Bauman, Richard. "American Folklore Studies and Social Transformation: A Performance-Centered Perspective." *Text and Performance Quarterly* 9 (1989): 175–84.

———. *Story, Performance, and Event: Contextual Studies of Oral Narrative*. Cambridge Studies in Oral and Literate Culture 10. Cambridge: Cambridge University Press, 1986.

———. *Verbal Art as Performance*. Rowley, MA: Newbury House, 1978. Reprint, Long Grove, IL: Waveland, 1984.

Bauman, Richard, and Charles L. Briggs. "Poetics and Performance as Critical Perspectives on Language and Social Life." *Annual Review of Anthropology* 19 (1990): 59–98.

Bayhaqī, al-. *Al-Maḥāsin wa-l-masāwī*. Beirut: Dār Ṣādir, n.d.

Beaton, Roderick. "Byzantine Historiography and Modern Greek Oral Poetry: The Case of Rhapsomatis." *Byzantine and Modern Greek Studies* 10 (1986): 41–50.

———. "Cappadocians at Court: Digenes and Timarion." In *Alexios I Komnenos*, vol. 1, *Papers*, Belfast Byzantine Texts and Translations 4.1, edited by Margaret Mullett and Dion Smythe, 329–38. Belfast: Belfast Byzantine Enterprises, 1996.

———. *Folk Poetry of Modern Greece*. Cambridge: Cambridge University Press, 1980.

———. *The Medieval Greek Romance*. 2nd ed. Cambridge: Cambridge University Press, 1989.

Beaton, Roderick, and David Ricks, eds. *Digenes Akrites: New Approaches to Byzantine Heroic Poetry*. Aldershot, UK: Variorum, 1993.

Beaumont, Daniel. "In the Second Degree: Fictional Technique in al-Tanūkhī's *al-Faraj ba'd al-Shidda*." *Arabic and Middle Eastern Literatures* 1, no. 2 (1998): 125–39.

Behzadi, Lale. "The Art of Entertainment: Forty Nights with Abu Ḥayyān al-Tawḥīdī." In *The Weaving of Words: Approaches to Classical Arabic Prose*, edited by Lale Behzadi and Vahid Behmardi, 165–79. Beirut: Orient-Institut, 2009.

Beihammer, Alexander, Stavroula Constantinou, and Maria Parani, eds. *Court Ceremonies and Rituals of Power in Byzantium and the Medieval Mediterranean: Comparative Perspectives*. Leiden: Brill, 2013.

Bell, Joseph Norment. *Love Theory in Later Hanbalite Islam*. Albany: SUNY Press, 1979.

Benjamin, Walter. "The Storyteller: Reflections on the Works of Nikolai Leskov." In *Illuminations: Essays and Reflections*, translated by Hannah Arendt and edited by Harry Zohn, 83–109. New York: Harcourt Brace Jovanovich, 1973.

Benporat, Claudio. *Cucina italiana del Quattrocento*. Florence: Leo S. Olschki, 1996.

Bernhardt, Paul C., James J. Dabbs, Jr., Julie A. Fielden, and Candice D. Lutter. "Testosterone Changes during Vicarious Experiences of Winning and Losing among Fans at Sporting Events." *Physiology and Behavior* 65 (1998): 59–62.

Beta, Simone. *Vino e Poesia: Centocinquanti epigrammi greci sul vino*. Milan: La vita felice, 2006.

Blachère, Régis. *Histoire de la littérature arabe des origines à la fin du XVe siècle de J.-C.* 3. vols. Paris: Jean Maisonneuve successeur, 1952–66.

Blake, Stephen P. *Half of the World: The Social Architecture of Safavid Isfahan, 1590–1722*. Costa Mesa, CA: Mazda, 1999.

Bosworth, C. E. *The ʿAbbāsid Caliphate in Equilibrium = The History of al-Ṭabarī*. Vol. 30. Albany: SUNY Press, 1989.

———. "Ghars al-Niʿma [b.] Hilal al-Ṣābiʾ's Kitāb *al-Hafawāt al-Nādira* and Buyid History." In *Arabicus Felix: Luminosus Britannicus: Essays in Honour of A. F. L. Beeston on His Eightieth Birthday*, edited by A. Jones, 129–41. Oxford, UK: Ithaca, 1991.

Böwering, Gerhard. "The Qurʾān Commentary of al-Sulamī." In *Islamic Studies Presented to Charles J. Adams*, edited by W. B. Hallaq and D. P. Little, 41–56. Leiden: Brill, 1991.

Böwering, Gerhard, and Bilal Orfali. *The Comfort of the Mystics: A Manual and Anthology of Sufism*. Leiden: Brill, 2013.

Brinner, William M. *Prophets and Patriarchs*. Vol. 2 of *The History of al-Ṭabarī*. Bibliotheca Persica. Albany: SUNY Press, 1987.

Brockelmann, Carl. *Geschichte der arabischen Litteratur*. 2 vols. *Supplementbände*. 3 vols. Leiden: Brill, 1936–44.

Brookshaw, Dominic P. "Palaces, Pavilions and Pleasure-Gardens: The Context and Setting of the Medieval Majlis." *Middle Eastern Literatures* 6 (2003): 199–223.

Brubaker, Leslie, and John Haldon. *Byzantium in the Iconoclast Era, c. 680–850: A History*. Cambridge: Cambridge University Press, 2011.

Bryer, Anthony. "The Historian's *Digenes Akritas*." In *Digenes Akrites: New Approaches to Byzantine Heroic Poetry*, edited by Roderick Beaton and David Ricks, 93–102. Aldershot, UK: Variorum, 1993.

Buckley, Penelope. *The Alexiad of Anna Komnene: Artistic Strategy in the Making of a Myth*. Cambridge: Cambridge University Press, 2014.

Burgess, Glyn S., ed. and trans. *The Pilgrimage of Charlemagne / Le Pèlerinage de Charlemagne*. Published with *Aucassin and Nicolette / Aucassin et Nicolette*, edited by Anne Elizabeth Cobby. Vol. 47: Series A. New York: Garland, 1988.

Burgwinkle, Bill, and Cary Howie. *Sanctity and Pornography in Medieval Culture: On the Verge*. Manchester: Manchester University Press, 2010.

Burton, Joan B. "Byzantine Readers." In *The Cambridge Companion to the Greek and Roman Novel*, edited by Tim Whitmarsh, 272–81. Cambridge: Cambridge University Press, 2008.

———. "A Reemergence of Theocritean Poetry in the Byzantine Novel." *Classical Philology* 98 (2003): 251–73.

Calmard, Jean. "Shiʿi Rituals and Power II: The Consolidation of Safavid Shiʿism: Folklore and Popular Religion." In *Safavid Persia: The History and Politics of an Islamic Society*, edited by C. Melville, 139–90. London: I. B. Tauris, 1996.

Canby, Sheila R. *The Golden Age of Persian Art: 1501–1722*. London: British Museum, 1999.

Chadwick, Henry. "John Moschos and His Friend Sophronios the Sophist." *Journal of Theological Studies*, n.s. 25 (1974): 41–74.

Chareyon, Nicole. *Les pèlerins de Jérusalem au Moyen Age*. Paris: Imago, 2000.

Chehabi, H. E., and Allen Guttmann. "From Iran to All of Asia: The Origin and Diffusion of Polo." *International Journal of the History of Sport* 19, nos. 2–3 (2002): 384–400.

Chejne, Anwar. "The Boon-Companion in Early 'Abbāsid Times." *Journal of the American Oriental Society* 85 (1965): 327–35.

Chiabotti, Francesco. "The Spiritual and Physical Progeny of 'Abd al-Karīm al-Qushayrī: A Preliminary Study in Abū Naṣr al-Qushayrī's (d. 514/1120) *Kitāb al-Shawāhid wa-l-Amthāl*." *Journal of Sufi Studies* 2, no. 1 (2013): 46–77.

Chiesa, Paolo, ed. *Le versioni latine della Passio Sanctae Febroniae: Storia, metodo, modelli di due traduzioni agiographichae altomedievali*. Spoleto: Centro Italiano di Studi sull' Alto Medioevo, 1990.

Colville, Jim. *Sobriety and Mirth*. London: Routledge, 2002.

Conca, Fabrizio, ed. *Il romanzo bizantino del XII secolo*. Turin: Unione tipigrafico-editrice torinese, 1994.

Condylis-Bassoukos, Hélène. *Stephanites kai Ichnelates, traduction grecque (XIe siècle) du livre Kalila wa-Dimna d'Ibn al-Muqaffa' (VIIIe siècle)*. Étude lexicologique et littéraire. Leuven, Belgium: Peeters, 1995.

Connelly, Bridget. *Arab Folk Epic and Identity*. Berkeley: University of California Press, 1986.

Constantinou, Stavroula. *Female Corporeal Performances: Reading the Body in Byzantine Passions and Lives of Holy Women*. Studia Byzantina Upsaliensia 9. Uppsala: Acta Universitatis Upsaliensis, 2005.

———. "Rewriting Beauty and Youth in Female Martyr Legends." In *"Pour une poétique à Byzance": Hommage à Vassilis Katsaros*, Dossiers Byzantins 16, edited by Stephanos Efthymiadis, Charis Messis, Paolo Odorico, and Ioannis Polemis, 99–112. Paris: Centre d'études byzantines, néo-helléniques et sud-est européennes, École des Hautes Études en Sciences Sociales, 2015.

———. "Satirical Elements in Hagiographical Narratives." In *A Companion to Byzantine Satire*, edited by Ingela Nilsson and Przemyslav Marciniak. Leiden: Brill, in press.

Coon, Lynda L. *Sacred Fictions: Holy Women and Hagiography in Late Antiquity*. Philadelphia: University of Pennsylvania Press, 1997.

Cooperson, Michael. *Classical Arabic Biography: The Heirs of the Prophets in the Age of al-Ma'mūn*. Cambridge: Cambridge University Press, 2000.

Crostini, Barbara. "The *Katechetikon* of Paul, Founder of the Monastery of the Theotokos Evergetis, in Relation to the Foundational Documents." *Orientalia Christiana Periodica* 64 (1998): 123–41.

Cunningham, Mary B., ed. and trans. *The Life of Michael the Synkellos: Text, Translation and Commentary*. Belfast Byzantine Texts and Translations 1. Belfast: Universities Press, 1991.

Dähne, Stephan. *Reden der Araber: Die politische ḫuṭba in der klassischen arabischen Literatur*. Frankfurt: Peter Lang, 2001.

Damīrī, al-.*Ḥayāt al-ḥayawān al-kubrā*. 5th ed. 2 vols. Cairo: Maktabat wa-maṭba'at Muṣṭafā al-Bābī al-Ḥalabī, 1398/1978.

Darke, Hubert. *The Book of Government or Rules for Kings*. London: Routledge and Kegan Paul, 1978.

Darrouzès, Jean. "Les conférances de 1112." *Revue des études byzantines* 23 (1965): 51–59.

Ḍayf, Shawqī. *Al-Ḥubb al-ʿudhrī ʿinda al-ʿarab*. Cairo: Dār al-Miṣriyya al-Lubnāniyya, 1999.

de Blois, François. *Burzōy's Voyage to India and the Origin of the Book of Kalīlah Wa Dimnah*. Prize Publication Fund 23. London: Royal Asiatic Society, 1990.

De Cerimoniis. Translated and edited by Albert Vogt as Constantin VII Porphyrogénète, *Le livre de cérémonies*, 4 vols. Paris: Les Belles Lettres, 1935–39. Translated by Ann Moffatt and Maxeme Tall as *The Book of Ceremonies: With the Greek Edition of the Corpus scriptorum historiae Byzantinae (Bonn, 1829)*, Byzantina Australensia 18, 2 vols. Canberra: Australian Association for Byzantine Studies, 2012.

Dembinska, Maria. *Food and Drink in Medieval Poland*. Edited by William Woys Weaver. Philadelphia: University of Pennsylvania Press, 1999.

Dhu l-Rumma. *Dīwān Dhū l-Rumma*. Edited by C. Macartney. Cambridge: Cambridge University Press, 1919.

Diegesis merike. In *Die Haupturkunden für die Geschichte des Athosklöster*, edited by Philipp Meyer, 163–84. Leipzig: Hinrich, 1894. Edited and translated by Fedor Ivanovich Uspenskij as *Istorija Afona*, vol. 2.1, 37–78. Kiev: V. L. Frontskevicha, 1877.

Dillon, Janette. *The Language of Space in Court Performance, 1400–1625*. Cambridge: Cambridge University Press, 2010.

Djedidi, Tahar Labib. *La poesie amoureuse des Arabes: Le cas des ʿUdhrites contribution a une sociologie de la littérature Arabe*. Algiers: Etudes et documents, n.d.

Dodge, Bayard, trans. *The Fihrist of al-Nadīm: A Tenth-Century Survey of Muslim Culture*. 2 vols. New York: Columbia University Press, 1970.

Duindam, Jeroen. *A Global History of Power, 1300–1800*. Cambridge: Cambridge University Press, 2016.

Durak, Koray. "Performance and Ideology in the Exchange of Prisoners between the Byzantines and the Islamic Near Easterners in the Early Middle Ages." In *Medieval and Early Modern Performance in the Eastern Mediterranean*, edited by Arzu Öztürkmen and Evelyn Birge Vitz, 167–80. Turnhout, Belgium: Brepols, 2014.

El Cheikh, Nadia Maria. "The Court of al-Muqtadir: Its Space and Its Occupants." In *ʿAbbāsid Studies II: Occasional Paper of the School of ʿAbbāsid Studies, Leuven 28 June–1 July, 2004*, edited by John Nawas, 319–36. Leuven, Belgium: Peeters, 2010.

Elias, Norbert. *The Court Society*. Translated by Edmund Jephcott. Oxford, UK: Blackwell, 1983.

Elliott, Alison Goddard. *Roads to Paradise: Reading the Lives of Early Saints*. Hanover, NH: Brown University Press, 1987.

Enderwitz, Susanne. *Liebe als Beruf: al-ʿAbbās b. al-Aḥnaf und das Ġazal*. Beirut: In Kommission bei Franz Steiner Verlag Stuttgart, 1995.

Erasmus. *The Education of a Christian Prince*. Translated by Neil M. Cheshire and Michael J. Heath, with the *Panegyric for Archduke Philip of Austria*, translated by Lisa Jardine. Edited by Lisa Jardine. Cambridge: Cambridge University Press, 1997.

Fahd, Toufic. *La divination arabe: Études religieuses, sociologiques et folkloriques sur le milieu natif de l'Islam*. Leiden: Brill Archive, 1966.

Fakhreddine, Huda. "Defining Metapoesis in the ʿAbbāsid Age." *Journal of Arabic Literature* 42 (2011): 205–35.

Featherstone, Jeffrey-Michael, ed. "The Praise of Theodore Graptos by Theophanes of Caesarea." *Analecta Bollandiana* 98 (1980): 93–150.

Foucault, Michel. *Discipline and Punish: The Birth of the Prison*. Translated by Alan Sheridan. 1977. Reprint, London: Penguin, 1991.

Frankfurter, David. "Martyrology and the Prurient Gaze." *Journal of Early Christian Studies* 17, no. 2 (2009): 215–45.

Freud, Sigmund. *The Psychopathology of Everyday Life*. London: Penguin, 2003.

Frishkompf, Michael. "Authorship in Sufi Poetry." *Alif: Journal of Comparative Poetics* 23 (2003): 78–108.

Fuess, Albrecht, and Jan-Peter Hartung, eds. *Court Cultures in the Muslim World: Seventh to Nineteenth Centuries*. New York: Routledge, 2011.

Galdieri, Eugenio. "Two Building Phases of the time of Shah ʿAbbas I in the Maydan-i Shah of Isfahan—Preliminary Note." *East and West* 20 (1970): 60–69.

Garnaud, Jean-Philipp, ed. *Achille Tatius d'Alexandrie, Le Roman de Leucippe et Clitophon*. Paris: Les Belles Lettres, 1991.

Gelder, Geert Jan van. *Beyond the Line: Classical Arabic Literary Critics on the Coherence and Unity of the Poem*. Leiden: Brill, 1982.

———. "Mixtures of Jest and Earnest in Classical Arabic Literature: Part I." *Journal of Arabic Literature* 23 (1992): 83–108.

———. "Ṣāliḥ ibn ʿAbd al-Quddūs (d. c.167/783)." In *Encyclopedia of Arabic Literature*, edited by J. S. Meisami and P. Starkey, 2:680. New York: Routledge, 1998.

Geries, Ibrahim. *Un genre littéraire arabe: al-Maḥāsin wa-l-masāwī*. Paris: Publications du Département d'islamologie de l'Université de Paris-Sorbonne (Paris IV), 1977.

Ghars al-Niʿma. *Al-Hafawāt al-nādira*. Edited by Ṣ. al-Ashtar. Beirut: Dār al-Awzāʿī, 1987.

Ghazālī, Abū Ḥāmid al-. *Iḥyāʾ ʿulūm al-dīn*. Beirut: Dār Ṣādir, 2000.

———. *Naṣīḥat al-mulūk*. Edited by J. Humāʾī. Tehran: Anjuman-i Āthār-i Millī, 1972.

Giffen, Lois Anita. *Theory of Profane Love among the Arabs: The Development of the Genre*. New York: NYU Press, 1971.

Glassen, Erika. *Der mittlere Weg: Studien zur Religionspolitik und Religiosität der späteren Abbasiden-Zeit*. Wiesbaden, Germany: Franz Steiner Verlag, 1981.

Goffman, Erving. "Social Life as Drama." In *The Goffman Reader*, edited by Charles Lemert and Ann Branaman, 95–107. Malden, MA: Blackwell, 1997.

Gottschall, Jonathan. *The Storytelling Animal: How Stories Make Us Human*. Boston: Houghton Mifflin Harcourt, 2012.

Gouma-Peterson, Thalia, ed. *Anna Komnene and Her Times*. New York: Garland, 2000.

Gravdal, Kathryn. *Ravishing Maidens: Writing Rape in Medieval French Literature and Law*. Philadelphia: University of Pennsylvania Press, 1991.

Greenblatt, Stephen. *Renaissance Self-Fashioning: From More to Shakespeare*. Chicago: University of Chicago Press, 2005.

Grewe, Rudolf, and Constance Hieatt, eds. *Libellus de arte Coquinaria: An Early Northern Cookery Book*. Tempe: Arizona Center for Medieval and Renaissance Studies, 2001.

Gribetz, Arthur. "The *Samā'* Controversy: Sufi vs. Legalist." *Studia Islamica* 74 (1991): 43–62.

Grodecki, Roman. *Kongress Krakowski w Roku 1364*. Kraków: Uniwersytet Jagielonski, 1995.

Gruendler, Beatrice. *Medieval Arabic Praise Poetry: Ibn al-Rūmī and the Patron's Redemption*. London: RoutledgeCurzon, 2003.

———. "Meeting the Patron: An Akhbār Type and Its Implications for Muḥdath Poetry." In *Ideas, Images and Methods of Portrayal: Insights into Classical Arabic Literature and Islam*, edited by Sebastian Günther, 59–88. Leiden: Brill, 2005.

———. "*Qaṣīda*: Its Reconstruction in Performance." In *Classical Arabic Humanities in Their Own Terms: Festschrift for Wolfhart Heinrichs on His 65th Birthday Presented by His Students and Colleagues*, edited by Beatrice Gruendler with the assistance of Michael Cooperson, 325–89. Leiden: Brill, 2008.

Grünbart, Michael, and Katrin Beyer, eds. "Urbanitas und ἀστειότης. Kulturelle Ausdrucksformen von Status im 10.–13. Jahrhundert." *Frühmittelalterliche Studien* 45 (2011): 169–389.

Grunebaum, G. E. von. "Aspects of Arabic Urban Literature Mostly in the Ninth and Tenth Centuries." *Islamic Studies* 8 (1969): 281–300.

Gunn, Steve, and Antheum Janse. Introduction to *The Court as a Stage: England and the Low Countries in the Later Middle Ages*, edited by Steve Gunn and Antheum Janse, 1–12. Woodbridge, UK: Boydell, 2006.

Günther, Sebastian. "Praise to the Book! Al-Jāḥiẓ and Ibn Qutayba on the Excellence of the Written Word in Medieval Islam." *JSAI* 32 (2006): 125–43.

Guo, Li. *The Performing Arts in Medieval Islam: Shadow Play and Popular Poetry in Ibn Dāniyāl's Mamluk Cairo*. Leiden: Brill, 2012.

Gutas, Dimitri. *Greek Thought, Arabic Culture: The Graeco-Arabic Translation Movement in Baghdād and Early 'Abbāsid Society (2nd–4th/8th–10th Centuries)*. New York: Routledge, 1998.

Haberland, Detlef. *Engelbert Kaempfer, 1651–1716: A Biography*. Translated by Peter Hogg. London: British Library, 1996.

Haddawy, Husain, trans. *The Arabian Nights*. New York: Norton, 1990.

Ḥamawī, Yāqūt al-. *Mu'jam al-udabā'*. Edited by Iḥsān 'Abbās. Beirut: Dār al-Gharb al-Islāmī, 1993.

Hämeen-Anttila, Jaakko. "Al-Kāmil al-Khwārizmī and His Kitāb ar-Riḥal as a Maqāma Collection." *Anaquel de Estudios Árabes* 8 (1997): 141–62.

———. "Al-Kisrawī and the Transmission of the Book of Kings Tradition." *Studia Orientalia* 114 (2013): 65–92.

———. "Dukayn: One Poet or Two?" *Zeitschrift der Deutschen Morgenländischen Gesellschaft* 163 (2013): 365–82.

———. "Khālid ibn Ṣafwān—The Man and the Legend." *Studia Orientalia* 73 (1994): 69–166.

———. "Short Stories in Classical Arabic Literature: The Case of Khālid ibn Ṣafwān and Umm Salama." In *The Weaving of Words: Approaches to Classical Arabic Prose*, Beiruter Texte und Studien 112, edited by Lale Behzadi and Vahid Behmardi, 35–54. Beirut: Ergon Verlag, 2009.

———. "Unity and Variation in a Mediaeval Anecdote." In *The Middle East: Unity and Diversity: Papers from the Second Nordic Conference on Middle Eastern Studies, Copenhagen 22–25 October 1992*, Nordic Proceedings in Asian Studies 5, edited by H. Palva and Kn. S. Vikør, 153–64. Copenhagen: NIAS Books, 1993.

Hammond, Marlé. *Beyond Elegy: Classical Arab Women's Poetry in Context*. Oxford: Oxford University Press for the British Academy, 2010.

———. "The Morphing of a Folktale: Sallāma and the Priest." *Middle Eastern Literatures* 15, no. 2 (2012): 113–36.

Hamori, Andras. *The Art of Medieval Arabic Literature*. Princeton, NJ: Princeton University Press, 1974.

———. "Ascetic Poetry (zuhdiyyāt)." In *The Cambridge History of Arabic Literature, 'Abbasid Belles-Lettres*, edited by Julia Ashtiany, T. M. Johnstone, J. D. Latham, R. B. Serjeant, and G. Rex Smith, 265–74. Cambridge: Cambridge University Press, 1990.

———. "Love Poetry (ghazal)." In *The Cambridge History of Arabic Literature: 'Abbasid Belles-Lettres*, edited by Julia Ashtiany, T. M. Johnstone, J. D. Latham, R. B. Sergeant, and G. Rex Smith, 202–18. Cambridge: Cambridge University Press, 1990.

———. "Prudence, Virtue, and Self-Respect in Ibn al-Muqaffaʿ." In *Reflections on Reflections: Near Eastern Writers Reading Literature*, edited by Angelika Neuwirth and Andreas Christian Islebe, 161–79. Wiesbaden, Germany: Reichert Verlag, 2006.

———. "Shameful and Injurious: An Idea of Ibn al-Muqaffaʿ's in *Kalīla wa-Dimna* and *al-Adab al-kabīr*." *JSAI* 32 (2006): 189–212.

Haneda, Masashi. "The Character of the Urbanization of Isfahan in the Later Safavid Period." In *Safavid Persia: The History and Politics of an Islamic Society*, edited by Charles Melville, 369–88. London: I. B. Tauris, 1996.

Hanning, Robert W. "Castiglione's Verbal Portrait: Structures and Strategies." In *Castiglione: The Ideal and the Real in Renaissance Culture*, edited by Robert W. Hanning and David Rosand, 131–41. New Haven, CT: Yale University Press, 1983.

Harmsen, Nils. *Die Wasiya als literarisches Genre bis ins 14. Jahrhundert. Magisterarbeit an der Universität Hamburg, Fachbereich Orientalistik, Oktober 1997 Angabe*. Hamburg: Diplomarbeiten Agentur, 1999.

Hathaway, Stephanie, and David Wikim, eds. *Intercultural Transmission in the Mediterranean*. London: Bloomsbury, 2012.

Hatlie, Peter. *The Monks and Monasteries of Constantinople, ca. 350–850*. Cambridge: Cambridge University Press, 2007.

Haynes, Katharine. *Fashioning the Feminine in the Greek Novel*. New York: Routledge, 2003.

Heinrichs, Wolfhart. "The Function(s) of Poetry in the Arabian Nights: Some Observations." In *O Ye Gentlemen: Arabic Studies on Science and Literary Culture in Honour of Remke Kruk*, edited by Arnoud Vrolijk and Jan P. Hogendijk, 353–62. Leiden: Brill, 2007.

———. "Prosimetrical Genres in Classical Arabic Literature." In *Prosimetrum: Cross-Cultural Perspectives on Narrative in Prose and Verse*, edited by Joseph Harris and Karl Reichl, 249–75. Woodbridge, UK: Brewer, 1997.

Heitty, Abdul-Kareem al-. *The Role of the Poetess at the Abbasid Court (132–247 AH / 750–861)*. Beirut: al-Rayyān, 2005.

Herbert, Thomas. *Some Yeares of Travels into Divers Parts of Asia and Afrique*. London: Jacob Blane and Richard Bishop, 1638.

Herrin, Judith. "Women and the Faith in Icons in Early Christianity." In *Culture, Ideology and Politics: Essays for Eric Hobsbawm*, edited by Raphael Samuel and Gareth Stedman Jones, 56–83. London: Routledge, 1983.

Hibri, Tayeb El-. *Reinterpreting Islamic Historiography: Hārūn al-Rashīd and the Narrative of the ʿAbbāsid Caliphate*. Cambridge: Cambridge University Press, 1999.

Hieatt, Constance, and Sharon Butler, eds. *Curye on Inglysch: English Culinary Manuscripts of the Fourteenth Century*. Oxford, UK: Early English Text Society, 1985.

Hillenbrand, Robert. "Safavid Architecture." In *The Cambridge History of Iran*, vol. 6, edited by Peter J. Jackson and Laurence Lockhart, 759–842. Cambridge: Cambridge University Press, 1986.

Holmes, Catherine. *Basil II and the Governance of Empire (976–1025)*. Oxford: Oxford University Press, 2005.

Hook, David. "Digenes Akrites and the Old Spanish Epics." In *Digenes Akrites: New Approaches to Byzantine Heroic Poetry*, edited by Roderick Beaton and David Ricks, 73–85. Aldershot, UK: Variorum, 1993.

Hours, Bernard. *Louis XV et sa cour: Le roi, l'étiquette et le courtesan. Essai historique*. Paris: Presses universitaires de France, 2002.

Huizinga, Johan. *Homo Ludens*. Boston: Roy, 1950.

Ḥuṣrī, Ibrāhīm b. ʿAlī al-. *Zahr al-ādāb wa-thamar al-albāb*. Cairo: Dār Iḥyāʾ al-Kutub al-ʿArabiyya, 1953.

———. *Zahr al-ādāb wa-thamar al-albāb*. 4th ed. Edited by Zakī Mubārak and Muḥammad Muḥyīddīn ʿAbdalḥamīd. Beirut: Dār al-Jīl, 1972.

Ibn ʿAbdalḥakam. *Al-Khalīfa al-ʿādil ʿUmar ibn ʿAbdalʿazīz (riwāyat ibnihi)*. Edited by Aḥmad ʿUbayd. Cairo: Dār al-Faḍīla, n.d.

Ibn ʿAbd Rabbih, Abū ʿUmar Aḥmad b. Muḥammad. *Al-ʿIqd al-Farīd*. 7 vols. Edited by Muḥammad al-Tūnjī. Beirut: Dār Ṣādir, 2001.

———. *Al-ʿIqd al-Farīd*. Edited by Aḥmad Amīn et al. Cairo: Maṭbaʿat Lajnat al-Taʾlīf wa-l-Tarjama wa-l-Nashr, 1940–49. Translated by Issa J. Boullata as *The Unique Necklace*, vol. 2. Reading, PA: Garnet, 2009.

———. *Al-ʿIqd al-Farīd*. 3rd ed. Edited by Aḥmad Amīn et al. 8 vols. Cairo: Maṭbaʿat Lajnat al-Taʾlīf wa-l-Tarjama wa-l-Nashr, 1384/1965.

Ibn Abī l-Ḥadīd. *Sharḥ Nahj al-balāgha*. Edited by Ḥasan Tamīm. 5 vols. Beirut: Dār Maktabat al-Ḥayāt, 1979.

Ibn Abī Ṭāhir Ṭayfūr, Abū al-Faḍl Aḥmad al-Khurāsānī. *Balāghāt al-Nisā'*. Edited by ʿAbd al-Ḥamīd Hindawī. Cairo: Dār al-Fāḍila, n.d.

Ibn al-Athīr. *Al-Kāmil fī l-ta'rīkh*. Beirut: Dār Ṣādir, 2008. Reprint of *Ibn-el-Athiri Chronicon quod perfectissimum inscribitur*, edited by C. J. Tornberg. Leiden: Brill, 1871.

Ibn al-Faqīh, *Mukhataṣar K. al-Buldān = Ibn al-Fakīh al-Hamadhānī, Compendium libri Kitāb al-Boldān*, Bibliotheca Geographorum Arabicorum 5, edited by M. J. de Goeje. New York: Brill, 1885. Reprint, Beirut: Dār Ṣādir, 1967.

Ibn al-Jawzī. *Al-Miṣbāḥ al-muḍī' fī khilāfat al-Mustaḍī'*. Edited by Nājiya ʿAbdallāh Ibrāhīm. Baghdad: Madrasa Musāʿida—Jāmiʿat Baghdād, 1976. Reprint, Beirut: Sharikat al-Maṭbūʿāt lil-Tawzīʿ wa-l-Nashr, 2000.

Ibn al-Kalbī. *Jamharat al-nasab*. Edited by Werner Caskel (*Ğamharat an-nasab. Das genealogische Werk des Hišām ibn Muḥammad al-Kalbī*). 2 vols. Leiden: Brill, 1966.

Ibn al-Murtaḍā, *Bāb dhikr al-Muʿtazila* = T. W. Arnold, *Al Muʿtazilah: Being an Extract from the Kitābu-l Milal wa-n niḥal by . . . B. al Murtadā*. Part 1: Arabic Text. Leipzig: Harrassowitz, 1902. Reprint, Beirut: Dār Ṣādir, n.d.

Ibn al-Muʿtazz. *Dīwān ashʿār al-amīr Abī l-ʿAbbās ʿAbdullāh ibn Muḥammad al-Muʿtazz*. Cairo: Dār al-Maʿārif, 1977.

Ibn al-Nadīm, *Kitāb al-Fihrist = Kitâb al-Fihrist*. Edited by Gustav Flügel. 2 vols. Leipzig: Vogel, 1871–72. Edited by Riḍā Tajaddud. Intishārāt-i Asāṭīr 348. Tehran: Intishārāt, 1381 A.Sh. Edited by Ayman Fu'ād Sayyid. 2 vols. London: Al-Furqan Islamic Heritage Foundation, 1430/2009.

Ibn al-Rūmī. *Dīwān*. Beirut: Dār al-Kutub al-ʿIlmiyya, 2002.

Ibn al-Sarrāj, *Jawāhir al-adab wa-dhakhā'ir al-shuʿarā' wa-l-kuttāb*. Edited by Muḥammad Ḥasan Qazqazān. 2 vols. Damascus: Wizārat al-Thaqāfa, 2008.

Ibn al-Shajarī, *Amālī*. Edited by Maḥmūd and Muḥammad al-Ṭanājī. 3 vols. Cairo: Maktabat al-Khānjī, 1413/1992.

Ibn ʿArabī. *Turjumān al-ashwāq*. Beirut: Dār Ṣādir, 2003.

Ibn Bassām, *Al-Dhakhīra fī maḥāsin ahl al-Jazīra*. Edited by Iḥsān ʿAbbās. 4 vols. Libya and Tunis: al-Dār al-ʿArabiyya li-l-Kitāb, 1398–99/1978–79.

Ibn Diḥya al-Kalbī, *Al-Muṭrib min ashʿār ahl al-Maghrib*. Edited by Ibrāhīm al-Abyārī. Beirut: Dār al-ʿIlm, 1955.

Ibn Ḥabīb al-Naysābūrī. *ʿUqalā' al-majānīn*. Edited by Muḥammad al-Saʿīd b. Basyūnī Zaghlūl. Beirut: Dār al-Kutub al-ʿIlmiyya, 1985.

Ibn Ḥamdūn, *Tadhkira*. Edited by Iḥsān ʿAbbās and Bakr ʿAbbās. 10 vols. Beirut: Dār Ṣādir, 1996.

Ibn Jinnī, *Al-Fasr: Sharḥ Ibn Jinnī al-kabīr ʿalā Dīwān al-Mutanabbī*. Edited by Riḍā Rajab. 5 vols. Damascus: Dār al-Yanābīʿ, 2004.

Ibn Khallikān, *Wafayāt al-aʿyān*. Edited by Iḥsān ʿAbbās. 4 vols. Beirut, n.d.

Ibn Manẓūr. *Lisān al-ʿArab*. Beirut: Dār Ṣādir, 2004.

———. *Muhktaṣar Ta'rīkh Dimashq li-Ibn 'Asākir*. Edited by various editors. 29 vols. Damascus: Dār al-Fikr, 1404–8/1984–88.

Ibn Qutayba, Muḥammad. *Al-Ma'ārif*. 2nd ed. Edited by Tharwat 'Ukāsha. Dhakhā'ir al-'arab 44. Cairo: Dār al-Ma'ārif bi-Miṣr, 1969.

———. *Al-Shi'r wa-l-Shu'arā'*. Edited by Aḥmad Muḥammad Shākir. 2 vols. Cairo: Dār al-Ḥadīth, 2001/1421.

———. *'Uyūn al-akhbār*. Edited by Yūsuf 'Alī Ṭawīl. 4 vols. Beirut: Dār al-Kutub al-'Ilmiyya, 1406/1986.

Ibn Rashīq al-Qayrawānī. *Al-'Umda*. Edited by Muḥyīddīn 'Abdalḥamīd. Cairo: Maṭba'at Ḥijāzī, 1934.

Ibn Rustah, *Kitāb A'lāq al-nafīsa*. Edited by M. J. de Goeje. Bibliotheca Geographorum Arabicorum 7. New York, 1892. Reprint, Beirut: Dār Ṣādir, 1967.

Ibn Shuhayd, *Rasā'il = Dīwān Ibn Shuhayd wa-rasā'iluhu*. Edited by Muḥyīddīn Dīb. Ṣaydā and Beirut: al-Maktaba al-'Aṣriyya, n.d.

Ibn Wahb al-Kātib, Isḥāq b. Ibrāhīm b. Sulaymān. *Al-Burhān fī wujūh al-bayān*. Edited by Aḥmad Maṭlūb and Khadīja al-Ḥadīthī. Baghdad: Maṭba'at al-'Ānī, 1967.

Ibshīhī, al-. *Al-Mustaṭraf fī kull fann mustaẓraf*. 2 vols. Beirut, n.d.

Irbilī, Bahā' al-Dīn al-. *Risālat al-ṭayf*. Edited by 'Alī al-Jubūrī. Baghdad: Wizārat al-Thaqāfa, 1968.

Irwin, Robert. *Night, Horses and the Desert: An Anthology of Classical Arabic Literature*. New York: Anchor Books, 2001.

Iṣfahānī, Abū al-Faraj al-. *Kitāb al-Aghānī*. Cairo: al-Hay'a al-Miṣriyya al-'Āmma lil-Kitāb, 1994.

———. *Kitāb al-Aghānī*. Cairo: al-Hay'a al-Miṣriyya al-'Āmma lil-Kitāb, 2010.

———. *Kitāb al-Aghānī*. Edited by 'Abd 'Alī Muhannā and Sāmir Jābir. 27 vols. Beirut: Dār al-Kutub al-'Ilmiyya, 2002/1422.

Iskāfī, Mukhtaṣar al-. *Kitāb al-'Ayn*. Edited by Hāwī Ḥasan Ḥammūdī. 3 vols. Oman: Wizārat al-Turāth wa-l-Thaqāfa, 1419/1998.

Istorikon Syntipa tou philosophou oraiotaton panue. Edited by Alfred Eberhard as *Fabulae romanenses graece conscriptae*, vol. 1, *De Syntipa et de Aesopo narrationes fabulosae partim ineditae*. Leipzig: Teubner, 1872.

Itlīdī, al-. *I'lām an-nās bi-mā waqa'a li-l-Barāmika ma'a banī al-'Abbās*. N.p.: n.d.

Jacobi, Renate. "Al-'Abbās b. al-Aḥnaf (d. 188/803, or after 193/808)." In *Encyclopedia of Arabic Literature*, edited by J. S. Meisami and P. Starkey, 1:2–3. New York: Routledge, 1998.

———. "The Camel-Section of the Panegyrical Ode." *Journal of Arabic Literature* 13 (1982): 1–22.

———. "Laylā al-Akhyaliyya—an Umayyad Feminist?" In *Poetry's Voice—Society's Norms: Forms of Interaction between Middle Eastern Writers and Their Societies*, edited by Andreas Pflitsch and Barbara Winckler, 189–200. Wiesbaden, Germany: Reichert Verlag, 2006.

———. "The 'Udhra: Love and Death in the Umayyad Period." In *Martyrdom in Literature: Visions of Death and Meaningful Suffering in Europe and the Middle East from*

Antiquity, edited by Friederike Pannewick, 137–48. Wiesbaden, Germany: Reichert Verlag, 2004.

Jacoby, David. "The Rise of a New Emporium in the Eastern Mediterranean: Famagusta in the Late Thirteenth Century." *Μελεται και Ψπομνιματα* 1 (1984): 145–79.

Ja'fariyān, Rasūl [Jafarian, Rasul]. "Pishīni-yi tashayyu' dar Iṣfāhān (The Background of Shi'ism in Isfahan)." In *Maqālat-i tārīkhī*, vol. 2. Qum: Anṣārīyān, 1376/1997.

Jāḥiẓ, al-. *Al-Bayān wa-l-tabyīn*. Edited by 'Abdassalām Muḥammad Hārūn. 4 vols. Beirut: Dār al-Jīl, n.d.

———. *Kitāb al-Ḥayawān*. 2nd ed. Edited by 'Abdallāh Muḥammad Hārūn. 8 vols. Cairo: 'Īsā al-Bābī al-Ḥalabī wa-Awlādihi, 1384–87/1965–69.

———. *Kitāb al-Qawl fī l-bighāl*. Edited by Charles Pellat. Reprint, Beirut: Dār al-Jīl, 1416/1995. As *Kitāb al-Bighāl*, in *Rasā'il al-Jāḥiẓ*, edited by 'Abdassalām Muḥammad Hārūn, vol. 2, 211–378. Cairo: Maktabat al-Khānjī, n.d.

———. *Kitāb Faṣl mā bayna l-'adāwa wa-l-ḥasad*. In *Rasā'il al-Jāḥiẓ*, edited by 'Abdassalām Muḥammad Hārūn, vol. 1, 333–73. Cairo: Maktabat al-Khānjī, n.d.

———. *Rasā'il al-Jāḥiẓ*. Edited by 'Abdassalām al-Hārūn. 2 vols. Beirut: Dār al-Jīl, 1991.

Jawārī, Aḥmad 'Abd al-Sattār al-. *Al-Ḥubb al-'Udhrī: Nash'atuhu wa-Taṭawwaruhu*. Beirut: al-Mu'assasa al-'Arabiyya li-l-Dirāsa wa-l-Nashr, 2006.

Jayyusi, Salma K. "Umayyad Poetry." In *Arabic Literature to the End of the Umayyad Period*, edited by A. F. L. Beeston, T. M. Johnstone, R. B. Sergeant, and G. R. Smith, 387–426. Cambridge: Cambridge University Press, 1983.

Jeffreys, Elizabeth. *Digenis Akritis*. Cambridge Medieval Classics 7. Cambridge: Cambridge University Press, 1998

———, trans. *Four Byzantine Novels*. Translated Texts for Byzantinists 1. Liverpool: Liverpool University Press, 2012.

———. "The Grottaferrata Version of Digenes Akrites: A Reassessment." In *Digenes Akrites: New Approaches to Byzantine Heroic Poetry*, edited by Roderick Beaton and David Ricks, 26–37. Aldershot, UK: Variorum, 1993..

Jeffreys, Elizabeth M., and Michael J. Jeffreys. "Who Was Eirene the Sevastokratorissa?" *Byzantion* 64 (1994): 40–68.

Jeffreys, Michael. "Manuel Komnenos' Macedonian Military Camps: A Glamorous Alternative Court?" In *Byzantine Macedonia: Identity, Image and History*, Byzantina Australensia 13, edited by John Burke and Roger Scott, 184–91. Melbourne: Australian Association for Byzantine Studies, Australian Catholic University, 2000.

Jirābaddawla, Aḥmad b. Muḥammad. *Min Kitāb Tarwīḥ al-arwāḥ wa-miftāḥ al-surūr wa-l-afrāḥ*. Edited by Ibrāhīm al-Sāmarrā'ī. Amman: Dār al-Karmil, 1997.

John Mauropous. *Ioannis Mauropodis Euchaitorum metropolitae epistulae*. Edited by Apostolos Karpozilos. Corpus fontium historiae byzantinae 34. Thessalonike: Association for Byzantine Research, 1990.

John Moschos. *Pratum spirituale, Patrologia Graeca* 87:2851–3116. Translated by John Wortley as *The Spiritual Meadow*. Cistercian Studies 139. Collegeville, MN: Cistercian, 1992.

John Skylitzes. *Synopsis historion.* In *Joannae Scylitzae Synopsis historiarum*, edited by Ioannes Thurn, Corpus fontium historiae byzantinae 5, 104.55–68. Berlin: de Gruyter, 1973. Translated by John Wortley as *A Synopsis of Byzantine History, 811–1057.* Cambridge: Cambridge University Press, 2010.

Jouanno, Corinne. "A Byzantine Novelist Staging the Ancient Greek World: Presence, Form and Functions of Antiquity in Macrembolites' Hysmine and Hysminias." In *He proslepse tes archaiotetas sto byzantine kai neoelleniko mythistorema*, edited by Stefanos Kaklamanis and Michael Paschalis, 15–29. Athens: Stigmi, 2005.

Journeys of Pietro della Valle the Pilgrim, The. Translated by George Bull. London: Folio Society, 1989.

Jumaḥī, Muḥammad b. Salām al-. *Ṭabaqāt fuḥūl al-shuʿarāʾ.* Edited by Maḥmūd Muḥammad Shākir. 2 vols. Jeddah: Dār al-Madanī bi-Jidda, n.d.

Junābadī, Mirzā Ḥasan. *Rawẓat al- Ṣafaviyya.* British Museum. MS. Or. 3388.

Kahle, Paul, ed. *Three Shadow Plays by Muḥammad Ibn Dāniyāl.* Prepared for publication by Derek Hopwood and Mustafa Badawi. Cambridge, UK: E. J. W. Gibb Memorial, 1992.

Kaldellis, Anthony. *The Argument of Psellos' Chronographia.* Leiden: Brill, 1999.

Karamustafa, Ahmet T. *Sufism: The Formative Period.* Berkeley: University of California Press, 2007.

Kazhdan, Alexander P., and Giles Constable. *People and Power in Byzantium: An Introduction to Modern Byzantine Studies.* Washington, DC: Dumbarton Oaks, 1982.

Kazhdan, Alexander P., and Annabel Wharton Epstein. *Change in Byzantine Culture in the Eleventh and Twelfth Centuries.* The Transformation of the Classical Heritage 7. Berkeley: University of California University Press, 1985.

Kazhdan, Alexander P., and Michael McCormick. "The Social World of the Byzantine Court." In *Byzantine Court Culture from 829 to 1204*, edited by Henry Maguire. Washington, DC: Dumbarton Oaks, 1997.

Kazhdan, Alexander P., and Alice-Mary Talbot. "Women and Iconoclasm." *Byzantinische Zeitschrift* 84–85, no. 2 (1992): 391–408.

Kennedy, Hugh. *Al-Manṣūr and al-Mahdī = The History of al-Ṭabarī.* Vol. 29. Albany: SUNY Press, 1990.

Kennedy, Philip F. "Abū al-ʿAtāhiya (131–211/748–826)." In *Encyclopedia of Arabic Literature*, edited by J. S. Meisami and P. Starkey, 1:27–28. New York: Routledge, 1998.

———. *The Wine Song in Classical Arabic Poetry: Abū Nuwās and the Literary Tradition.* Oxford, UK: Clarendon, 1997.

———. "Zuhdiyya." In *Encyclopedia of Arabic Literature*, edited by J. S. Meisami and P. Starkey, 2:828–29. New York: Routledge, 1998.

Khafājī, al-. *Sirr al-faṣāḥa.* Edited by Dāʾūd Ghaṭāsha al-Shawābika. Amman: Dār al-Fikr, 1427/2006.

Khalifa, Nouha. *Hardship and Deliverance in the Islamic Tradition: Theology and Spirituality in the Works of al-Tanūkhī.* London: I. B. Tauris, 2010.

Khalīl ibn Aḥmad, al-. *Kitāb al-ʿAyn.* Edited by Mahdī al-Makhzūmī and Ibrāhīm al-Sāmarrāʾī. 8 vols. Qom: Dār al-Hijra, 1405/1984.

Khan, Ruqayya Yasmine. *Self and Secrecy in Early Islam*. Columbia: University of South Carolina Press, 2008.

Kharā'iṭī, Muḥammad b. Ja'far b. Muḥammad b. Sahl b. Shākir al-Sāmirī al-. *I'tilāl al-Qulūb*. Edited by Ḥamdī al-Dimirdāsh. 2 vols. Mecca: Maktabat Nizār Muṣṭafā al-Bāz, 1421/2000.

Khargūshī. *Tahdhīb al-asrār*. Edited by Bassām Muḥammad Bārūd. Abu Dhabi: al-Mujamma' al-Thaqāfī.

Khismatulin, A. "To Forge a Book in the Medieval Ages: Nezām al-Molk's *Siyar al-molūk (Siyāsat-nāma)*." *Journal of Persianate Studies* 1 (2008): 30–66.

Khwārizmī, al-. *Rasā'il*. Edited by Muḥammad Mahdī Pūrgul. Silsila-ye intishārāt-e anjuman-e āthār u-mafākhir-e farhangī 338. Tehran: Anjuman-e āthār u-mafākhir-e farhangī, 1384 AHSh.

Kilpatrick, Hilary. *Making the Great Book of Songs: Compilation and the Author's Craft in Abū l-Faraj al-Iṣbahānī's "Kitāb al-Aghānī."* London: RoutledgeCurzon, 2003.

Kirschenblatt-Gimblett, Barbara. "Playing to the Senses: Food as a Performance Medium." *Performance Research* 4, no. 1 (1999): 1–30.

"Kitāb waṣāya Aflāṭūn al-ḥakīm fī khidmat al-mulūk." Edited and translated by Frederic Bauden and Antonella Ghersetti. *Arabica* 55 (2008): 52–77.

Klein, Yaron. "Music, Rapture and Pragmatics: Ghazālī on *Samā'* and *Wajd*." In *No Tapping around Philology*, edited by Alireza Korangy and Daniel J. Sheffield, 215–42. Wiesbaden, Germany: Harrassowitz Verlag, 2014.

Knysh, Alexander. *Al-Qushayri's Epistle on Sufism*. Reading, UK: Garnet, 2007.

Kuntze, Simon. "Love and God: The Influence of Ghazal on Mystic Poetry." In *Ghazal as World Literature*, vol. 1, *Transformations of a Literary Genre*, edited by Thomas Bauer and Angelika Neuwirth, 157–79. Beirut: Ergon Verlag, 2005.

Kushājim. *Adab al-nadīm*. Edited by Nabīl al-'Aṭiyya. Baghdād: Dār al-Shu'ūn al-Thaqāfiyya al-'Āmma, 1990.

Larkin, Margaret. *Al-Mutanabbi: Voice of the 'Abbasid Poetic Ideal*. Oxford, UK: Oneworld, 2008.

Lauxtermann, Marc. "Ninth-Century Classicism and the Erotic Muse." In *Desire and Denial in Byzantium*, Publication of the Society for the Promotion of Byzantine Studies 6, edited by Liz James, 161–70. Aldershot, UK: Variorum, 1999.

Lecker, Michael. "Tribes in Pre- and Early Islamic Arabia." In *People, Tribes and Society in Arabia around the Time of Muḥammad*, 1–106. Variorum Collected Studies 812. Aldershot, UK: Ashgate, 2005.

Leder, Stefan. "Aspekte arabischer und persischer Fürstenspiegel: Legitimation, Fürstenethik, politsche Vernunft." In *Specula principum*, edited by Angela de Benedictis, 21–50. Frankfurt: Vittorio Klostermann, 1999.

———. "Authorship and Transmission in Unauthored Literature." *Oriens* 31 (1988): 67–81.

———. "The Literary Use of the *Khabar*: A Basic Form of Historical Writing." In *The Byzantine and Early Islamic Near East*, vol. 1, *Problems in the Literary Source*

Material, edited by Averil Cameron and Lawrence I. Conrad, 277–315. Princeton, NJ: Darwin, 1992.

———. "Royal Dishes: On the Historical and Literary Anthropology of the Near and Middle East." In *Court Cultures in the Muslim World: Seventh to Nineteenth Centuries*, edited by Albrecht Fuess and Jan-Peter Hartung, 359–69. New York: Routledge, 2011.

———. "The ʿUdhrī Narrative in Arabic Literature." In *Martyrdom in Literature: Visions of Death and Meaningful Suffering in Europe and the Middle East from Antiquity to Modernity*, edited by Friederike Pannewick, 163–87. Wiesbaden, Germany: Reichert Verlag, 2004.

Lemerle, Paul. *Prolégomènes à une edition critique et commentée des "Conseils et Récits" de Kekauménos*. Brussels: Académie royale de Belgique. 1960.

Lewisohn, Leonard. "The Sacred Music of Islam: *Samāʿ* in the Persian Sufi Tradition." *British Journal of Ethnomusicology* 6 (1997): 1–33.

Lord, Alfred B. *The Singer of Tales*. Harvard Studies in Comparative Literature 24. Cambridge, MA: Harvard University Press, 1960.

Machaut, Guillaume. *La prise d'Alexandre*. New York: Routledge, 2002.

Magdalino, Paul. "In Search of the Byzantine Courtier: Leo Choirosphaktes and Constantine Manasses." In *Byzantine Court Culture from 829 to 1204*, edited by Henry Maguire, 141–65. Washington, DC: Dumbarton Oaks, 1997.

Maguire, Henry, ed. *Byzantine Court Culture from 829 to 1204*. Washington, DC: Dumbarton Oaks, 1997.

Maqqarī, al-. *Al-Mukhtār min nawādir al-akhbār*. Edited by Anwar Abū Suwaylim. Min ʿuyūn al-turāth al-ʿarabī. Beirut and Amman: Muʾassasat al-Risāla and Dār ʿAmmār, 1409/1989.

Marlow, Louise. "Advice and Advice Literature." In *Encyclopaedia of Islam*, vol. 3. Leiden: Brill Online, 2012.

———."A Samanid Work of Counsel and Commentary: The *Naṣīḥat al-mulūk* of Pseudo-Māwardī." *Iran* 44 (2007): 181–92.

———. "The Way of Viziers and the Lamp of Commanders (*Minhāj al-wuzarāʾ wa-sirāj al-umarāʾ*) of Aḥmad al-Iṣfahbadhī and the Literary and Political Culture of Early Fourteenth-Century Iran." In *Writers and Rulers: Perspectives on Their Relationship from Abbasid to Safavid Times*, edited by Beatrice Gruendler and Louise Marlow, 169–93. Wiesbaden, Germany: Reichert Verlag, 2004.

Martin, John. "Inventing Sincerity, Refashioning Prudence: The Discovery of the Individual in Renaissance Europe." *American Historical Review* 102 (1997): 1309–42.

Martino of Como. *The Art of Cooking*. Edited by Luigi Ballerini. Berkeley: University of California Press, 2005.

Marzubānī, Abū ʿUbayd Allāh Muḥammad b. ʿUmrān al-. *Ashʿār al-Nisāʾ*. Edited by Sāmī Makkī al-ʿĀnī and Hilāl Nājī. Beirut: ʿĀlam al-Kutub, 1995/1410.

Marzubānī, al-. *Kitāb Nūr al-qabas al-Mukhtaṣar min al-Muqtabas*. Edited by R. Sellheim. Vol. 1 (text). Wiesbaden, Germany: Bibliotheca Islamica, 1964.

———. *Muʿjam al-shuʿarāʾ (and Tatimmat Muʿjam al-shuʿarāʾ)*. Edited by ʿAbbās Hānī al-Charākh. 2 vols. Beirut: Dār al-Kutub al-ʿIlmiyya, 2010.

Masʿūdī, al-. *Murūj al-dhahab*. Edited by Barbier de Meynard and Pavet de Courteille. Revised by Charles Pellat. 8 vols. Beirut: Publications de l'Université Libanaise, 1966–79.

———. *Murūj al-dhahab wa-maʿādin al-jawhar*. Beirut: Dār al-Andalus, 1983.

Matthee, Rudolph P. *The Politics of Trade in Safavid Iran: Silk for Silver, 1600–1730*. Cambridge: Cambridge University Press, 1999.

———. *The Pursuit of Pleasure: Drugs and Stimulants in Iranian History, 1500–1900*. Princeton, NJ: Princeton University Press, 2005.

McChesney, Robert. "Four Sources on Shah ʿAbbas's Building of Isfahan." *Muqarnas* 5 (1988): 103–34.

———. "Postscript to 'Four Sources on Shah ʿAbbas's Building of Isfahan.'" *Muqarnas* 8 (1991): 137–38.

McGonigal, Jane. *Reality Is Broken: Why Games Make Us Better and How They Can Change the World*. New York: Penguin, 2011,

McKinley, James C. "It Isn't Just a Game: Clues to Avid Rooting." *New York Times*, August 11, 2000.

Meisami, Julie Scott. *Medieval Persian Court Poetry*. Princeton, NJ: Princeton University Press, 1987.

———. "Writing Medieval Women: Representations and Misrepresentations." In *Writing and Representation in Medieval Islam*, edited by Julia Bray, 47–88. Abingdon, UK: Routledge, 2006.

Membrè, Michele. *Mission to the Lord Sophy of Persia (1539–1542)*. Translated by A. H. Morton. London: School of Oriental and African Studies, 1993.

Michael Psellos. *Chronographia*. In *Michel Psellos Chronographie*, translated and edited by Émile Renauld, vol. 2. Paris: Les belles lettres, 1926. (Translated by Elizabeth R. A. Sewter as *Fourteen Byzantine Rulers: The Chronographia of Michael Psellus*. Harmondsworth, UK: Penguin Books, 1966.)

Michon, Jean-Louis. "Sacred Music and Dance in Islam." In *Sufism: Love & Wisdom*, edited by Jean-Louis Michon and Roger Gaetani, 153–77. Bloomington, IN: World Wisdom, 2006.

Milham, Mary Ella, ed. and trans. *Platina: On Right Pleasure and Good Health*. Tempe, AZ: Medieval and Renaissance Texts and Studies, 1998.

Mitylenaios, Christopher. "On a Tent." In *Poiemata*, edited by Eduard Kurtz, 45. Leipzig: Neumann, 1903.

Monroe, James. *The Art of Badīʿ az-Zamān al-Hamadhānī as Picaresque Narrative*. Beirut: American University of Beirut Press, 1984.

Munshī, Iskandar. *The History of Shah ʿAbbās the Great*. Translated by Roger M. Savory. 3 vols. Boulder, CO: Westview, 1978–86.

———. *Tārīkh-i ʿalam ārā-yi ʿAbbās*. Edited by Īraj Afshar. 2 vols. Tehran: Amīr Kabīr, 1350 [1970].

Morales, Helen. "Gender and Identity in Musaeus' *Hero and Leander*." In *Constructing Identities in Late Antiquity*, edited by Richard Miles, 41–70. New York: Routledge, 1999.

———. *Vision and Narrative in Achilles Tatius' "Leucippe and Clitophon."* Cambridge: Cambridge University Press, 2004.

Moreh, Shmuel. *Live Theatre and Dramatic Literature in the Medieval Arabic World*. New York: NYU Press, 1992.

Morris, Rosemary. *Monks and Laymen in Byzantium, 843–1118*. Cambridge: Cambridge University Press, 1995.

Mottahedeh, Roy P. *Loyalty and Leadership in an Early Islamic Society*. Princeton, NJ: Princeton University Press, 1980.

Mubayyaḍīn, Mahā. *Al-Wāliha al-Ḥarī: Laylā al-Akhyaliyya Shāʿirat al-ʿAṣr al-Umawī*. Amman: al-Ahliyya li-l-Nashr wa-l-Tawzīʿ, 2011.

Muḥammad b. Yaḥyā al-Ṣūlī. *Sharḥ al-Ṣūlī li-Dīwān Abī Tammām*. Edited by Khalaf Rashīd Nuʿmān. Baghdad: Wizārat al-Thaqāfa wa-l-Funūn, 1978.

Müller, Kathrin. "*Al-Ḥanīn ilā l-awṭān* in Early *Adab* Literature." In *Myths, Historical Archetypes and Symbolic Figures in Arabic Literature*, edited by Angelika Neuwirth, Birgit Embaló, Sebastian Günther, and Maher Jarrar, 33–58. Beirut: Franz Steiner Verlag Stuttgart, 1999.

Mullett, Margaret. "Alexios I Komnenos and Imperial Renewal." In *New Constantines: The Rhythm of Imperial Renewal in Byzantium, 4th–13th Centuries*, Society for the Promotion of Byzantine Studies Publications 2, edited by Paul Magdalino, 259–67. Aldershot, UK: Variorum, 1994.

———. *Death of the Holy Man, Death of a Genre*. Leiden: Brill, forthcoming.

———. "Did Byzantium Have a Court Literature?" In *The Byzantine Court: Source of Power and Culture: Papers from the Second International Sevgi Gönül Byzantine Studies, Symposium*, edited by Ayla Ödekan, Nevra Necipoğlu, and Engin Akyürek, 173–82. Istanbul: Koç University Press, 2013.

———. "Diegesis epistolike: Narration et communication à Byzance au XIIe siècle." In *Séminaires byzantins*. Paris: Les belles lettres, forthcoming.

———. "Experiencing the Byzantine Text, Experiencing the Byzantine Tent." In *Publications of the Society for the Promotion of Byzantine Studies*, vol. 18, edited by Mark Jackson and Claire Nesbitt, 269–91. Farnham, UK: Variorum, 2013.

———. "Monastic Culture in the Middle Byzantine Empire." In *Byzantine Culture*, edited by Dean Sakel, 343–56. Istanbul: Türk Tarih Kuruma, 2014.

———. "Novelisation in Byzantium: Narrative after the Revival of Fiction." In *Byzantine Narrative: Papers in Honour of Roger Scott*, Byzantina Australensia 16, edited by John Burke Ursula Betka, Penelope Buckley, Kathleen Hay, Roger Scott, and Andrew Stephenson, 1–28. Melbourne: Australian Association for Byzantine Studies, 2006.

———. "Reading the Tent: Four Komnenian Tent Poems." In *Reading Byzantium*, edited by Teresa Shawcross, Ida Toth, and Niels Gaul. Cambridge: Cambridge University Press, forthcoming.

———. "Tented Ceremony: Ephemeral Performances under the Komnenoi." In *Court Ceremonies and Rituals of Power in the Medieval Mediterranean*, edited by Alexander Beihammer, Stavroula Constantinou, and Maria Parani, 487–513. Leiden: Brill, 2013.

———. "Writing in Early Mediaeval Byzantium." In *The Uses of Literacy in Early Mediaeval Europe*, edited by Rosamund McKitterick, 156–85. Cambridge: Cambridge University Press, 1990.

Mullett, Margaret, and Dion Smythe, eds. *Alexios I Komnenos*. Vol. 1, *Papers*. Belfast Byzantine Text and Translations 4.1. Belfast: Belfast Byzantine Enterprises, 1996.

Mullett, Margaret, Anna Wilson, and Oliver P. Nicholson, eds. *The Forty Martyrs of Sebasteia*. Vol. 2, *Translations*. Belfast Byzantine Texts and Translations 4.2. Belfast: Belfast Byzantine Enterprises, forthcoming.

Munajjim, Mullā Muḥammad Jalāl al-Dīn Yazdī, al-. *Tārīkh-i ʿAbbāsī ya ruznāma-yi Mullā Jalāl*. Edited by Sayf-Allāh Vahīdnīyā. Tehran: Intishārāt-i Vahīd, 1366/1987.

Myrne, Pernilla. *Narrative, Gender and Authority in ʿAbbāsid Literature on Women*. Gothenburg: University of Gothenburg, Orientalia et Africana Gothoburgensia, 2010.

Naṣīr al-Dīn Ṭūsī. *Akhlāq-i Nāṣirī*. Edited by Mujtabā Mīnūvī and ʿAlīrizā Ḥaydarī. Tehran: Intishārāt-i Khavārazmī, 1982.

Nicholas Kataskepenos. *Bios kai politeia kai merike thaumaton diegesis tou osious patros emon Kyrillou tou Phileotou syngrapheis para tou osiou Nikolaou tou Kataskepenou*, chap. 47.1. In *La vie de saint Cyrille le Philéote, moine byzantine (1110)*, Subsidia Hagiographica 39, edited by Étienne Sargologos, F.S.C.. Brussels: Société des Bollandistes, 1964.

Nicholson, Jeremy. "Science Shows Dominant Behavior and Posture Increase Testosterone." Posted by Mike Cernovich. *Danger & Play* (blog), July 30, 2014. www.dangerandplay.com.

Nicol, Donald. "The Greeks and the Union of the Churches: The Report of Ogerius, Protonotarius of Michael VIII Paleologos, in 1280." *Proceedings of the Royal Irish Academy* 63 (1962–64): 1–16.

Niketas Choniates. *Chronike diegesis*. Edited by Jan Louis van Dieten. 2 vols. Corpus fontium historiae byzantinae 11. Berlin: de Gruyter, 1975. Translated by Harry Magoulias as *O City of Byzantium, Annals of Niketas Choniates*, Byzantine Texts in Translation. Detroit: Wayne State University Press, 1984.

Niketas Eugeneianos. *Drosilla and Charikles*. Translated by Joan Burton as *A Byzantine Novel: Drosilla and Charikles, a Bilingual Edition*. Wauconda, IL: Bolchazy-Carducci, 2004.

Niẓām al-Mulk. *Book of Government or Rules for Kings: The Siyāsatnāma or Siyar al-Mulūk*. Translated by Hubert Darke. London: Routledge, 1960.

———. *Siyar al-mulūk (Siyāsatnāmeh)*. Edited by Hubert Darke. Tehran: Bungāh-i Tarjameh va-Nashr-i Kitāb, 1962.

Noble, Alison. "Cultural Interchange in the Medieval Mediterranean: Prolegomena to a Text of the Eugenian Recension of Stephanites kai Ichnelates." 2 vols. PhD diss., Queen's University Belfast, 2004.

Nuwayrī, al-. *Nihāyat al-arab*. 31 vols. Cairo: Wizārat al-Thaqāfa, n.d.
Ödekan, Ayla, Nevra Necipoğlu, and Engin Akyürek, eds. *The Byzantine Court: Source of Power and Culture; Papers from the Second International Sevgi Gönül Byzantine Studies Symposium, Istanbul 21–23 June 2010*. Istanbul: Koç University Press, 2013.
Odorico, Paolo. "La cultura della συλλογή. 1) Il cosiddetto enciclopedismo bizantino. 2) Le tavole dei sapere di Giovanni Damasceno." *Byzantinische Zeitschrift* 83 (1990): 1–23.
Oikonomides, Nicolas. "L'épopée de Digénis et la frontière orientale de Byzance au Xe et XIe siècles." *Travaux et mémoires* 7 (1981): 375–97.
———. *Les listes de préséance byzantines des IXe et Xe siècles*. Le monde byzantin. Paris: Éditions du CNRS, 1972.
Omidsalar, Mahmoud. "Storytellers in Classical Persian Texts." *Journal of American Folklore* 97 (1984): 204–12.
Orfali, Bilal. "The Art of Anthology: Al-Thaʿālibī and His Yatīmat al-Dahr." PhD diss., Yale University, 2009.
Orfali, Bilal, and Nada Saab, eds. *Sufism, Black and White: A Critical Edition of "Kitāb al-Bayāḍ wa-l-Sawād" by Abū l-Ḥasan al-Sīrjānī (d. ca. 470/1077)*. Leiden: Brill, 2012.
Osa dei ginesthai tou megalou kai ypsilou basileos ton Romaion mellontos phossateusai (Text C). In *Constantine Porphyrogenitus: Three Treatises on Imperial Military Expeditions*, Corpus fontium historiae byzantinae 28, edited and translated by John F. Haldon, 275–80. Vienna: Österreichischen Akademie der Wissenschaften, 1990.
Ostafin, Barbara. "Abū al-Ibar al-Hāshīmī: Unknown Poet, Writer and Nadīm at Caliphs' Court." *Studia Arabistyezne i Islamistyezne* 10 (2002): 51–57.
Otto, Bernhard. *Dreihundertjähriges deutsches Kloster-Kochbuch*. Leipzig: R. Henningsche Buchhandlung, 1856.
Özkan, Hakan. *Narrativität im Kitāb al-Farağ baʿda š-šidda des Abū ʿAlī al-Muḥassin at-Tanūḫī*. Berlin: Klaus Schwarz Verlag, 2008.
Öztürkmen, Arzu, and Evelyn Birge Vitz, eds. *Medieval and Early Modern Performance in the Eastern Mediterranean*. Turnhout, Belgium: Brepols, 2014.
Pacha, Ahmed Zeki, ed. *Kitāb al-Tāj fī akhlāq al-mulūk lil-Jāḥiẓ = Le livre de la couronne*. Cairo: al-Maṭbaʿa al-Amīriyya, 1914.
Patterson, Jeremy. "Friends in High Places: The Creation of the Court of the Roman Emperor." In *The Court and Court Society in Ancient Monarchies*, edited by A. J. Spawforth, 121–56. Cambridge: Cambridge University Press, 2007.
Paul of Evergetis. *Synagoge*. In *Evergetinos etoi synagoge ton theophthongon rematon kai didaskalion ton theophoron kai agion pateron*, edited by Makarios of Corinth and Nikodemos Hagiorites. Venice: Para Antonio tō Vortoli, 1783. 7th ed. 4 vols. Athens: Ekdotikos Oikos Monēs Metamorphōseōs tou Sōtēros Kronizēs Kouvara Attikēs, 1983.
Pellat, Charles. *Le milieu Baṣrien et la formation de Ǧāḥiẓ*. Paris: Librairie d'Amérique et d'Orient Adrien-Maisonneuve, 1953.
Piamenta, Moshe. *Dictionary of Post-Classical Yemeni Arabic*. 2 vols. Leiden: Brill, 1990–91.

Picherit, Jean-Louis G., ed. and trans. *The Journey of Charlemagne to Jerusalem and Constantinople [Le voyage de Charlemagne à Jerusalem et à Constantinople]*. Birmingham, AL: Summa, 1988.

Pourjavady, N., "Dū athar-i kuhan dar samāʿ: Az ʿAbd al-Raḥmān-i Sulamī va-Abū Manṣūr-i Iṣfahānī." *Maʿārif* 15 (1367/1989): 291–318.

Prawler, Joshua. *The Crusader Kingdom: European Colonialism in the Middle Ages*. New York: Praeger, 1972.

Pseudo-Ibn Qayyim al-Jawziyya. *Akhbār al-Nisāʾ*. Edited by ʿAbd al-Majīd Ṭaʿma al-Ḥalabī. Beirut: Dār al-Maʿrifa, 1997/1417.

Pseudo-Jāḥiẓ. *Maḥāsin* = Gerlof van Vloten, *Le livre des beautés et des antithèses attribué à al-Djahiz*. 1898. Reprint, Amsterdam: Oriental Press, n.d.

Pseudo-Kodinos. Translated and edited by Ruth Macrides with Joseph Munitiz, S.J., and Dimiter Angelov as *Pseudo-Kodinos and the Constantinopolitan Court: Offices and Ceremonies*, Birmingham Byzantine and Ottoman Monographs 15. Farnham, UK: Variorum, 2013.

Qāḍī, Wadād al-. "Dislocation and Nostalgia: *Al-ḥanīn ilā l-awṭān*: Expressions of Alienation in Early Arabic Literature." In *Myths, Historical Archetypes and Symbolic Figures in Arabic Literature*, edited by Angelika Neuwirth, Birgit Embaló, Sebastian Günther, and Maher Jarrar, 3–31. Beirut: Franz Steiner, 1999.

Qālī, al-. *Kitāb al-Amālī*. 2 vols. N.p: n.d.

Qays b. al-Mulawwaḥ. *Dīwān Majnūn Laylā*. Edited by ʿAbd al-Sattār Aḥmad Farrāj. Cairo: Maktabat Miṣr, 1979.

Rabīʿī, Aḥmad. *Kuthayyir ʿAzza: Ḥayātuhu wa-Shiʿruhu 23–105*. Cairo: Dār al-Maʿārif bi-Miṣr, n.d.

Raddatz, H. P. "Sufyān al-Thawrī." *EI2* 9 (1997): 770–72.

Rāghib al-Iṣbahānī, al-. *Muḥāḍarāt al-udabāʾ*. 4 vols. Beirut: Dār Maktabat al-Ḥayāt, 1961.

———. *Muḥāḍarāt al-udabāʾ wa-muḥāwarāt al-shuʿarāʾ wa-l-bulaghāʾ*. Cairo: Maktabat al-Thaqāfa al-Dīniyya, 2009.

Rahimi, Babak. "The Rebound Theater State: The Politics of the Safavid Camel Sacrifice, 1598–1695 C.E." *International Journal of Iranian Studies* 37, no. 3 (2004): 451–78.

———. *Theater State and the Formation of Early Modern Public Sphere in Iran: Studies on Safavid Muharram Rituals, 1590–1641 C.E.* Leiden: Brill, 2012.

Rapp, Claudia. "Storytelling as Spiritual Communication in Early Greek Hagiography: the Use of Diegesis." *Journal of Early Christian Studies* 6, no. 3 (1998): 431–48.

Raqīq al-Qayrawānī, al-. *Quṭb al-surūr*. Edited by Sāra al-Barbūshī. Baghdad and Beirut: Manshūrāt al-Jamal, 1997.

Revel, Jacques. "The Court." In *Realms of Memory: The Construction of the French Past*, vol. 2, *Traditions*, edited by Pierre Nora, 70–122. New York: Columbia University Press, 1997.

Ricks, David. *Byzantine Heroic Poetry*. Bristol, UK: Aristide Caratzas, 1990.

Robertson, Duncan. *The Medieval Saints' Lives: Spiritual Renewal and Old French Literature*. Edward C. Armstrong Monographs on Medieval Literature 8. Lexington, KY: French Forum, 1995.

Robinson, Cynthia. *The Making of Courtly Culture in al-Andalus and Provence, 1005–1134 A.D.* Leiden: Brill, 2002.

Rodinson, Maxine, A. J. Arberry, and Charles Perry, eds. *Medieval Arab Cookery.* Totnes, UK: Prospect Books, 2001.

Roilos, Panagiotis. *Amphoteroglossia: A Poetics of the Twelfth-Century Medieval Greek Novel.* Hellenic Studies 10. Cambridge, MA: Harvard University Press, 2005.

Rosenthal, Franz, trans. *Ibn Khaldûn: The Muqaddimah: An Introduction to History.* New York: Pantheon Books, 1958.

Roueché, Charlotte. "Defining the Foreign in Kekaumenos." In *Strangers to Themselves: The Byzantine Outsider*, Publications of the Society for the Promotion of Byzantine Studies 8, edited by Dion C. Smythe, 203–14. Aldershot, UK: Variorum, 2000.

———. "The Literary Background of Kekaumenos." In *Literacy, Education and Manuscript Transmission in Byzantium and Beyond*, edited by Catherine Holmes and Judith Waring, 111–38. Leiden: Brill, 2002.

———. "The Place of Kekaumenos in the Admonitory Tradition." In *"L'éducation au gouvernement et à la vie": La tradition des "Règles de vie" de l'antiquité au moyen-âge. Actes du colloque international, Pise, 18 et 19 mars 2000*, Autour de Byzance 1, edited by Paolo Odorico, 129–44. Paris: Centre d'études byzantines, néo-helléniques et sud-est européennes, École des hautes études en science sociales, 2009.

———. "The Rhetoric of Kekaumenos." In *Rhetoric in Byzantium*, Publications of the Society for the Promotion of Byzantine Studies 11, edited by Elizabeth Jeffreys, 23–37. London: Variorum, 2003.

Rowson, Everett. "The Effeminates of Early Medina." *Journal of the American Oriental Society* 111, no. 4 (1991): 671–93.

Rudt de Collenberg, W. H. "Les Lusignan de Chypre." *ΕΠΕΤΗΡΙΣ* 10 (1979–80): 85–319.

Ṣābi', Ghars al-Ni'ma al-. *Al-Hafawāt al-nādira.* Edited by Ṣāliḥ al-Ashtar. Damascus: Majma' al-Lugha al-'Arabiyya bi-Dimashq, 1387/1967.

Ṣābi', Hilāl al-. *Rusūm dār al-khilāfa.* Edited by Mikhā'il 'Awwād. Baghdād: Maṭba'at al-'Ānī, 1964. Translated by Elie Salem as *Rusūm dār al-khilāfa: The Rules and Regulations of the 'Abbāsid Court.* Beirut: American University of Beirut, 1977.

Sadan, Joseph. *Al-Adab al-'arabī al-hāzil wa-nawādir al-thuqalā': Al-'āhāt wa-l-masāwi' al-insāniyya wa-makānatuhā fī l-adab al-rāqī.* Cologne: Manshūrāt al-Jamal, 2007.

———. "The Division of the Day and Programme of the Work of the Caliph al-Manṣūr." In *Studia Orientalia memoriae D. H. Baneth dedicata*, 255–73. Jerusalem: Hotsa'at sefarim 'al shem Y. L. Magnes ha-Universiṭah ha-'Ivrit, 739 (1979).

Ṣafadī, al-. *Al-Wāfī bi-l-wafayāt.* Vol. 22. Edited by Ramzi Baalbaki. Wiesbaden, Germany: Bibliotheca Islamica, 1983.

Sajdi, Dana. "Trespassing the Male Domain: The 'Qaṣīdah' of Laylā al-Akhyaliyyah." *Journal of Arabic Literature* 31, no. 2 (2000): 121–46.

Salawī ('Abdalqādir ibn 'Abdarraḥmān), al-. *Al-Kawkab al-thāqib fī akhbār al-shu'arā' wa-ghayrihim min dhawī l-manāqib.* Edited by 'Abdallāh al-Yāsimī. 3 vols. Manshūrāt Wizārat al-Awqāf wa-l-Shu'ūn al-Islāmiyya. Rabat: Dār Abī Raqrāq, 1427/2006.

Sarrāj, Abū Muḥammad Jaʿfar b. Aḥmad b. al-Ḥusayn al-Qāriʾ al-. *Maṣāriʿ al-ʿUshshāq*. 2 vols. Beirut: Dār Ṣādir, 1958/1378.

Sarrāj, Abū Nāṣr al-. *K. al-Lumaʿ*. Edited by R. A. Nicholson. Leiden: Brill, 1914.

Sawa, George Dimitri. *Music Performance Practice in the Early Abbasid Era, 132–320/750–932*. Toronto: Institute of Mediaeval Music, 1989.

Schechner, Richard. *Performance Studies: An Introduction*. New York: Routledge, 2003.

Scheub, Harold. *Story*. Madison: University of Wisconsin Press, 1998.

Schoeler, Gregor. "Abū Nuwās (c. 140–c. 198 / c. 755–c. 813)." Translated by A. Giese. In *Encyclopedia of Arabic Literature*, edited by J. S. Meisami and P. Starkey, 1:41–43. New York: Routledge, 1998.

———. "Bashshār b. Burd, Abū 'l-ʿAtāhiyah and Abū Nuwās." In *The Cambridge History of Arabic Literature, ʿAbbasid Belles-Lettres*, edited by Julia Ashtiany, T. M. Johnstone, J. D. Latham, R. B. Serjeant, and G. Rex Smith, 275–99. Cambridge: Cambridge University Press, 1990.

———. "Die Einteilung der Dichtung bei den Arabern." *ZDMG* 123 (1973): 9–55.

———. *The Oral and the Written in Early Islam*. Translated by Uwe Vagelpohl. Edited by James E. Montgomery. Routledge Studies in Middle Eastern Literatures. Abingdon, UK: Routledge, 2006.

———. "Verfasser und Titel des dem Ǧāḥiẓ zugeschriebenen sog. Kitāb at-Tāǧ." *ZDMG* 130 (1980): 217–25.

Scott, Roger. "Byzantine Chronicles." In *The Medieval Chronicle*, edited by Erik Kooper, vol. 6, 31–57. Leiden: Brill, 2009.

———. "Narrating Justinian: From Malalas to Manasses." In *Byzantine Narrative*, edited by John Burke, 29–46. Melbourne: Australian Association for Byzantine Studies, 2006.

———. "Text and Context in Byzantine Historiography." In *A Companion to Byzantium*, edited by Liz James, 256–59. Oxford, UK: Blackwell, 2010.

Sells, Michael A. *Stations of Desire*. Jerusalem: Ibis Editions, 2000.

Selwi, Ibrahim al-. *Jemenitische Wörter in den Werken von al-Hamdānī und Našwān und ihre Parallelen in den semitischen Sprachen*. Marburger Studien zur Afrika- und Asienkunde, Serie B: Asien 10. Berlin: Dietrich Reimer, 1987.

Ševčenko, Nancy. *Illustrated Manuscripts of the Metaphrastian Menologion*. Chicago: University of Chicago Press, 1990.

Shahsavari, Mojtaba. "Abū Naṣr al-Qushayrī and His *Kitāb al-Shawāhid wa-l-amthāl*." *Ishraq* 3 (2012): 279–300.

Sharīf al-Murtaḍā, al-. *Amālī = Ghurar al-fawāʾid wa-durar al-qalāʾid*. Edited by Muḥammad Abū l-Faḍl Ibrāhīm. 2 vols. Cairo: Dār al-Fikr al-ʿArabī, 1998.

Sharīshī, al-. *Sharḥ maqāmāt al-Ḥarīrī*. 4 vols. Beirut: Dār Maktabat al-Thaqāfiyya, n.d.

Sharlet, Jocelyn. *Patronage and Poetry in the Islamic World: Social Mobility and Status in the Medieval Middle East and Central Asia*. London: I. B. Tauris, 2011.

Shaw, Brent D. "Body/Power/Identity: Passions of the Martyrs." *Journal of Early Christian Studies* 4, no. 3 (1996): 269–312.

Shurūḥ Saqṭ al-zand. Edited by Muṣṭafā al-Saqqā, ʿAbdarraḥīm Maḥmūd, ʿAbdassalām Hārūn, Ibrāhīm al-Abyārī, and Ḥāmid ʿAbdalmajīd. 5 vols. Cairo: al-Hayʾa al-Miṣriyya li-l-Kitāb, 1408/1987.

Simard, Andrée Griselle. "The Manuscript Torino J.11.9: A Late Medieval Perspective on Musical Life and Culture at the Court of the Lusignan Kings at Nicosia." Master's thesis, University of Akron, 2005.

Simpson, Alicia, and Stephanos Efthymiadis, eds. *Niketas Choniates: A Historian and a Writer*. Geneva: Le Pomme d'or, 2009.

Sonderband IX, Medium Aevum Quotidianum, 2000. Reprint, 2004.

Spengel, Leonhard von, ed. *Rhetores Graeci*. 3 vols. Leipzig: Teubner, 1853–56. Translated by George A. Kennedy as *Progymnasmata: Greek Textbooks of Prose Composition and Rhetoric*, Writings from the Greco-Roman World 10. Atlanta: Society for Biblical Literature, 2003.

Sperl, Stefan. *Mannerism in Arabic Poetry: A Structural Analysis of Selected Texts (3rd Century AH / 9th Century AD–5th Century AH / 11th Century AD)*. Cambridge: Cambridge University Press, 1989.

Stetkevych, Suzanne. *Abū Tammām and the Poetics of the ʿAbbāsid Age*. Leiden: Brill, 1991.

———. *The Poetics of Islamic Legitimacy: Myth, Gender and Ceremony in the Classical Arabic Ode*. Bloomington: Indiana University Press, 2002.

Stierlin, Henri. *Isfahan: Spiegel des Paradieses*. Zürich: Atlantis, 1976.

Stone, Andrew. "Aurality in the Panegyrics of Eustathios of Thessaloniki." In *Theatron: rhetorische Kultur in Spätantike und Mittelalter*, Millennium Studies 13, edited by Michael Grünbart, 419–28. Berlin: de Gruyter, 2007.

Sulamī, Abū ʿAbd al-Raḥmān al-. *K. al-Samāʿ*. Edited by ʿAlī ʿAqalih ʿArsān. *Al-Turāth al-ʿArabī* 5 (1985): 80–94.

———. *Rasāʾil ṣūfiyya li-Abī ʿAbd al-Raḥmān al-Sulamī*. Edited by Gerhard Böwering and Bilal Orfali. Beirut: Dar el-Machreq, 2009.

Ṣūlī, al-. *Akhbār al-Buḥturī*. Edited by Ṣāliḥ al-Ashtar. Damascus: al-Majmaʿ al-ʿIlmī al-ʿArabī bi-Dimashq, 1378/1958.

Symeon Seth. *Stephanites kai Ichnilates*. In *Stephanites und Ichnilates: Überlieferungsgeschichte und Text*, edited by Lars Olof Sjöberg. Studia Graeca Upsaliensis 2. Stockholm: Almqvist and Wiksell, 1962.

Ṭabarī, Abū Jaʿfar al-. *Taʾrīkh al-rusul wa-l-mulūk = Annales quod scripsit . . . al-Ṭabarî*, edited by Michael Jan de Goeje et al. 15 vols. Leiden: Brill, 1879–1901.

———. *Taʾrīkh al-Ṭabarī = Taʾrīkh al-rusul wa-l-mulūk*. Edited by Muhammad Abū l-Faḍl Ibrāhīm. Cairo: Dār al-Maʿārif, 1966.

Tanūkhī, al-Muḥassin b. ʿAlī al-. *Kitāb al-faraj baʿd al-shidda*. Edited by ʿA. al-Shaljī. Beirut: Dār Ṣādir, 1978.

———. *Nishwār al-Muḥāḍara*. Edited by ʿA. al-Shaljī. Beirut: Dār Ṣādir, 1973.

Tawḥīdī, Abū Ḥayyān, al-. *Akhlāq al-Wazīrayn*. Edited by M. al-Ṭanjī. Damascus: Majmaʿ al-ʿIlmī al-ʿArabī, 1991.

———. *Al-Baṣā'ir wa-l-dhakhā'ir*. 9 vols. Edited by Wadād al-Qāḍī. Beirut: Dār Ṣādir, 1408/1988.

———. *Risālat al-Ṣadāqa wa-l-ṣadīq*. 2nd ed. Edited by Ibrāhīm al-Kīlānī. Damascus and Beirut: Dār al-Fikr and Dār al-Fikr al-Mu'āṣir, 1416/1996.

Tha'ālibī, Abū Manṣūr al-. *Adab al-mulūk*. Edited by Jalīl al-'Aṭiyya. Beirut: Dār al-Gharb al-Islāmī, 1990.

———. *Al-Kināya wa-l-ta'rīḍ*. In *Rasā'il al-Tha'ālibī*, by 'Alī al-Khāqānī. Baghdād and Beirut: Maktabat Dār al-Bayān and Dār Ṣa'b, n.d.

———. *Ghurar* = Hermann Zotenberg, *Histoire des rois des Perses*. Paris, 1900. Reprint, Amsterdam: Oriental Press, n.d.

———. *Thimār al-qulūb fī l-muḍāf wa-l-mansūb*. Edited by Muḥammad Abū l-Faḍl Ibrāhīm. Dhakhā'ir al-'arab 57. Cairo: Dār al-Ma'rifa, n.d.

———. *Yatīmat al-dahr fī maḥāsin ahl al-'aṣr*. Edited by Muḥammad Muḥyī l-Dīn 'Abd al-Ḥamīd. Cairo: Maṭba'at al-Sa'āda, 1956.

———. *Zād safar al-mulūk*. Edited by Ramzi Baalbaki and Bilal Orfali. Beirut: Orient-Institut, Bibliotheca Islamica, 2011.

Tha'labī, Muḥammad b. al-Ḥārith al-. *Akhlāq al-mulūk*. Edited by Jalīl al-'Aṭiyya. Beirut: Dār al-Ṭalī'a, 2003.

Theophylact of Ochrid. *Théophylacte d'Achrida: Discours, traités, poesies*, Corpus fontium historiae byzantinae 16.1, edited by Paul Gautier, 366–67. Thessalonike: Associatio de recherches byzantines, 1980.

Thibon, Jean-Jacques. *L'œuvre d'Abū 'Abd al-Raḥmān al-Sulamī (325/937–412/1021) et la formation du soufisme*. Damascus: Institut français du Proche-Orient, 2009.

Three Brothers, The; or, the Travels of Sir Anthony, Sir Robert, and Sir Thomas Sherely in Persian, Russia, Turkey, Spain, etc. with Portraits. London: Hurst, Robison, 1825.

Toth, Ida. "Authorship and Authority in the Life of Syntipas." In *The Author in Middle Byzantine Literature: Modes, Functions and Identities*, Byzantinisches Archiv 28, edited by Aglae Pizzone, 87–104. Berlin: de Gruyter, 2014.

Tsamakda, Vassiliki. *The Illustrated Chronicle of Ioannes Skylitzes in Madrid*. Leiden: Alexandros, 2002.

Ṭurṭūshī, Abū Bakr al-. *Sirāj al-mulūk*. Edited by Muḥammad Fatḥī Abū Bakr. Cairo: al-Dār al-Miṣriyya al-Lubnāniyya, 1994.

Typikon of the Great Church. Translated and edited by S. J. Juan Mateos as *Le Typicon de la Grande Église: Ms. Sainte-Croix no. 40, Xe siècle: Introduction, texte critique, traduction et notes. Orientalia christiana analecta*. Rome, 1962–63.

'Umar b. Abī Rabī'a. *Dīwān 'Umar b. Abī Rabī'a*. Edited by Muḥammad al-'Inānī. Cairo: Maṭba'at al-Sa'āda, 1911.

Vadet, Jean-Claude. *L'esprit courtois en orient dans les cinq premiers siècles de l'Hégire*. Paris: Éditions G.-P. Maisonneuve et Larose, 1968.

Vale, Malcolm. *The Princely Court: Medieval Courts and Culture in North-Western Europe, 1270–1380*. Oxford: Oxford University Press, 2001.

van Ess, Josef. "'Amr b. 'Obayd." *EIr* 1 (1985): 991–92.

———. *Theologie und Gesellschaft im 2. und 3. Jahrhundert Hidschra. Eine Geschichte des religiösen Denkens im frühen Islam.* 6 vols. Berlin and New York: Walter de Gruyter, 1991–97.

———. "Thumāma b. Ashras." *EI2* 10 (2000): 449–50.

Vitz, Evelyn Birge. "Type et individu dans l'autobiographie médiévale." *Poétique*, no. 24 (1975): 426–45.

Wagner, Ewald. *Die arabische Rangstreitdichtung und ihre Einordnung in die allgemeine Literaturgeschichte.* Abhandlungen der geistes- und sozialwissenschaftlichen Klasse 8. Mainz, Germany: Akademie der Wissenschaften und der Literatur, 1962.

Washshā', Abū al-Ṭayyib Muḥammad b. Aḥmad al-. *Al-Ẓarf wa-l-Ẓurafā'*. Edited by Fahmī Sa'd. N.p.: 'Ālam al-Kutub, 1986/1407.

———. *Kitāb al-Fāḍil fī ṣifat al-adab al-kāmil.* Edited by Yaḥyā Wahīb al-Jabbūrī. Beirut: Dār al-Gharb al-Islāmī, 1411/1991.

Wassiliewsky, B., and V. Jernstedt, eds. *Cecaumeni Strategicon et incerti scriptoris de officiis libellus.* Saint Petersburg, Russia: Typis Academiae Caesareae Scientiarum, 1896.

Waṭwāṭ, al-. *Ghurar al-khaṣā'iṣ al-wāḍiḥa wa-'urar al-naqā'iṣ al-fāḍiḥa.* Edited by Ibrāhīm Shamsaddīn. Beirut: Dār al-Kutub al-'Ilmiyya, 1429/2008.

Wazīr Abū l-Qāsim al-Ḥusayn b. 'Alī al-Maghribī, al-. *Kitāb fī l-Siyāsa.* Edited by Sāmī al-Dahhān. Damascus: al-Ma'had al-Firansī bi-Dimashq lil-Dirāsāt al-'Arabiyya, 1948.

Weaver, William Woys. "Food and Drink in Medieval Cyprus: The French Court, the Greek Gentry, the Common Man." Unpublished ms.

Webb, Ruth. "The Progymnasmata as Practice." In *Education in Greek and Roman Antiquity*, edited by Yun Lee Too, 289–316. Leiden: Brill, 2001.

Weiner, Alfred. "Die Farağ ba'd aš-Šidda-Literatur. Von Madā'inī († 225 H) bis Tanūḫī († 384 H). Ein Beitrag zur arabischen Literaturgeschichte." *Der Islam* 4 (1913): 270–98, 387–420.

Wellek, Rene. *Discriminations: Further Concepts of Criticism.* New Haven, CT: Yale University Press, 1971.

Werkmeister, Walter. *Quellenuntersuchungen zum Kitāb al-'Iqd al-farīd des Andalusiers Ibn 'Abdrabbih (246/860–328/940). Ein Beitrag zur arabischen Literaturgeschichte.* Islamkundliche Untersuchungen 70. Berlin: Klaus Schwarz, 1983.

Whitmarsh, Tim, trans. *Achilles Tatius, Leucippe and Clitophon.* Oxford: Oxford University Press, 2001.

Wickens, G. M., trans. *The Nasirean Ethics by Naṣīr ad-Dīn Ṭūsī.* London: George Allen and Unwin, 1964.

Wild, Stefan. *Das Kitāb al-'Ain und die arabische Lexikographie.* Wiesbaden, Germany: Harrassowitz, 1965.

Wilson, Michael. *Storytelling and Theatre.* Basingstoke, UK: Palgrave Macmillan, 2006.

Wirth, Albrecht, ed. *Danae in christlichen Legenden.* Vienna: F. Tempsky, 1892.

Yāqūt, *Irshād al-arīb ilā ma'rifat al-adīb.* 6 vols. Edited by Aḥmad Shamsaddīn, 7 vols. Beirut: Dār al-Kutub al-'Ilmiyya, 1411/1991. 2nd ed., edited by D. S. Margoliouth,

E. J. W. Gibb Memorial Series 6, 7 vols. London and Leiden: Luzac and Brill, 1923–31.

———. *Muʿjam al-buldān*. 7 vols. Beirut: Dār Ṣādir, 1995. Edited by F. Wüstenfeld, 6 vols. Leipzig, 1866–1870. Reprint, N.p: n.d.

Yāsirī, Bāsim ʿAbbūd al-. *Waḍḍāḥ al-Yaman: Dirāsa fī mawrūthihi al-shiʿrī*. Doha: Wizārat al-Thaqāfa wa-l-Funūn wa-l-Turāth, 2010.

Zakeri, Mohsen. "Ṣāliḥ b. ʿAbd al-Ḳuddūs." *EI2* 8 (1995): 984–85.

Zamakhsharī, al-. *Rabīʿ al-abrār wa-nuṣūṣ al-akhbār*. Edited by Salīm al-Nuʿaymī. 4 vols. N.p.: n.d.

Ziolkowski, Jan M. *Fairy Tales from before Fairy Tales: The Medieval Latin Past of Wonderful Lies*. Ann Arbor: University of Michigan Press, 2007.

Zipes, Jack. *Creative Storytelling: Building Community, Changing Lives*. New York: Routledge, 1995.

Zubayr ibn Bakkār, al-. *Al-Akhbār al-muwaffaqiyyāt*. 2nd ed. Edited by Sāmī Makkī al-ʿĀnī. Beirut: ʿĀlam al-Kutub, 1416/1996.

LIST OF CONTRIBUTORS

Stavroula Constantinou is Associate Professor of Byzantine Studies at the University of Cyprus (Department of Byzantine & Modern Greek Studies). Her research interests include Byzantine hagiography, literary genres, poetics, performance, gender, the body in Byzantine literature and culture, and literary theory. She has published many articles on these topics and a book on female holiness and the body. She has also coedited a volume on rituals and ceremonies in the medieval Mediterranean. Currently, she is coediting two other volumes: one on rewriting hagiographical texts and legends in Byzantium and one on gendered emotions in Byzantine art and literature. She is also writing a monograph on Byzantine miracle story collections.

Nadia Maria El Cheikh is Professor of History at the American University of Beirut (AUB). She has served as Director of the Center for Arab and Middle Eastern Studies and as Chair of the Department of History and Archaeology. She received the New York University Global Affairs International Visitors Program Grant in 2004 and in 2007 was the Shawwaf Visiting Professor of Arabic and Islamic Studies at the Department of Near Eastern Languages and Civilizations at Harvard University. Her book *Byzantium Viewed by the Arabs* was published in 2004 and translated into Turkish and Greek. She has coauthored a book titled *Crisis and Continuity at the Abbasid Court: Formal and Informal Politics in the Caliphate of al-Muqtadir (295–320/908–932)*. Her most recent book, *Women, Islam, and Abbasid Identity* was published in 2015. In 2016, she was appointed Dean of the Faculty of Arts and Sciences at the American University of Beirut.

Li Guo is Professor of Arabic at the University of Notre Dame. His *The Performing Arts in Medieval Islam: Shadow Play and Popular Poetry in Ibn Daniyal's Mamluk Cairo* won the IIM Prize for Research, Institut

International de la Marionnette, France, 2015. He is a coeditor of Brill's series Studies on Performing Arts and Literature in the Islamicate World.

Jaakko Hämeen-Anttila held the Chair of Arabic and Islamic Studies at the University of Helsinki from 2000 to 2016, and from 2016, he has been the Iraq Professor of Arabic and Islamic Studies at the University of Edinburgh. His main publications include *MAQAMA: A History of a Genre* (2002) and *The Last Pagans of Iraq: Ibn Waḥshiyya and His Nabatean Agriculture* (2006).

Louise Marlow, who teaches at Wellesley College, studies the intersections of history and literature in the medieval Islamic period. She is the author of *Hierarchy and Egalitarianism in Islamic Thought* (1997) and *Counsel for Kings: Wisdom and Politics in Tenth-Century Iran: The "Naṣīḥat al-mulūk" of Pseudo-Māwardī* (2016); editor of *Dreaming across Boundaries: The Interpretation of Dreams in Islamic Lands* (2008) and *The Rhetoric of Biography: Narrating Lives in Persianate Societies* (2011); and coeditor with Beatrice Gruendler of *Writers and Rulers: Perspectives on Their Relationships from Abbasid to Safavid Times* (2004).

Margaret Mullett is Professor Emerita of Byzantine Studies at Queen's University Belfast and Director Emerita of Byzantine Studies at Dumbarton Oaks in Washington, DC. She is currently Professor of Byzantine Social History at the University of Vienna. She is working on emotion and lament, on the performance of the Byzantine tragedy *Christos Paschon*, and on tents.

Bilal Orfali is Associate Professor of Arabic Studies at the American University of Beirut. He is the author of *The Anthologist's Art: Abū Manṣur al-Thaʿālibī and His Yātimat al-dahr* (2016) and the editor of *In the Shadow of Arabic* (2011); *Sufism, Black and White*, with Nada Saab (2012); *The Comfort of the Mystics*, with Gerhard Böwering (2013); and *The Book of Noble Character*, with Ramzi Baalbaki (2015).

Maurice A. Pomerantz is Assistant Professor of Literature at NYU Abu Dhabi. He is a scholar of Arabic literature of the pre-modern period, and his interests include Arabic belles lettres, poetry, and prose. He is the author of *Licit Magic: The Life and Letters of al- Ṣāḥib b. ʿAbbād* (2017). He also contributes numerous articles on a variety of topics to leading journals in the fields of Arabic and Middle Eastern studies. He is Associate Editor of the Library of Arabic Literature, published by NYU Press.

Babak Rahimi is Associate Professor of Communication, Culture, and Religion in the Department of Literature, University of California–San Diego. His research focuses on the history of public spheres and the relationship between culture, space, and state power. His book *Theater-State and Formation of the Early Modern Public Sphere in Iran: Studies on Safavid Muharram Rituals, 1590–1641 C.E.* (2011) studies the relationship between ritual, resistance, and power in early-modern Iranian history. Rahimi has been a visiting scholar at the Internet Institute, Oxford University, Berlin Graduate School Muslim Cultures and Societies, Freie Universität Berlin, Meiji University, and the Annenberg School for Communication at the University of Pennsylvania. He has also been the recipient of fellowships from the National Endowment for the Humanities and Jean Monnet Fellowship at the European University Institute.

Jocelyn Sharlet is Associate Professor of Comparative Literature with a specialization in classical Arabic and Persian literature at the University of California–Davis. She is the author of *Patronage and Poetry in the Islamic World: Social Mobility and Status in the Medieval Middle East and Central Asia* (2011); articles in *Middle Eastern Literatures*, the *Journal of Arabic Literature*, the *Journal of Arabic and Islamic Studies*, and the *Journal of Persianate Studies*; and several chapters in edited volumes.

Evelyn Birge Vitz is Professor of French at New York University and Affiliated Professor of Comparative Literature, Medieval & Renaissance Studies, and Religious Studies. In recent years, she has worked extensively on performance. Relevant book titles are *Medieval and Early Modern Performance in the Eastern Mediterranean* (coedited with Arzu Öztürkmen, 2014); *Performing Medieval Narrative* (coedited with Nancy Freeman Regalado and Marilyn Lawrence, 2005); and *Orality and Performance in Early French Romance* (1999). A few relevant articles are "'The Seven Sleepers of Ephesus': Can We Reawaken Performance of This Hagiographical Folktale?," in *Medieval and Early Modern Performance in the Eastern Mediterranean*; "*Le Roman de la Rose*, Performed in Court," in *Shaping Courtliness in Medieval France*; "Tales with Guts: A 'Rasic' Esthetic in French Medieval Storytelling," in *TDR* [*The Drama Review*]; and "Erotic Reading in the Middle Ages: Performance and Re-performance of Romance," in *Performing Medieval Narrative*. She codirects several performance websites for medieval narrative, including Medieval Tales in Performance and Performing Medieval Narrative Today: A Video Showcase.

William Woys Weaver has been described as the "Merlin of American regional cookery." He is an internationally known food historian and the author of seventeen books. Weaver is a rare four-time winner of the prestigious IACP/Julia Child Cookbook Awards, his most recent gold medal going to *Culinary Ephemera*, a beautifully illustrated survey of old food-advertising materials. His 1993 award-winning cookbook *Pennsylvania Dutch Country Cooking* had been included in the anthology *100 Great American Cookbooks of the 20th Century*. Weaver's most recent book, *Dutch Treats: Heirloom Recipes from Farmhouse Kitchens*, was in 2016. Weaver received his PhD in food ethnography from University College, Dublin (Ireland)—the first degree of its kind to be awarded by that university—and is also the founder and director of the Keystone Center for the Study of Regional Foods, a 501c3 nonprofit promoting Pennsylvania's regional foods and foodways. He maintains the Roughwood Seed Collection of heirloom food plants at the historic Lamb Tavern in Devon, Pennsylvania. Called "the Walden Pond of heirloom seeds," the Roughwood Seed Collection provides rare limited edition seeds online and from the Hudson Valley Seed Library in Accord, New York. He is presently working on a two-volume study of the medieval foods of Cyprus.

INDEX

Page numbers in *italics* refer to illustrations.